Transpersonal Psychology
in
Psychoanalytic Perspective

SUNY Series in the Philosophy of Psychology
Michael Washburn, editor

Transpersonal Psychology
in
Psychoanalytic Perspective

Michael Washburn

STATE UNIVERSITY OF NEW YORK PRESS

BF
204.7
W375
1994

Published by
State University of New York Press, Albany

© 1994 State University of New York

For information, address State University of New York Press,
State University Plaza, Albany, N.Y., 12246

Production by Marilyn P. Semerad
Marketing by Nancy Farrell

Library of Congress Cataloging-in-Publication Data

Washburn, Michael, 1943-
     Transpersonal psychology in psychoanalytic perspective / Michael
Washburn.
        p.   cm.—(SUNY series in the philosophy of psychology)
     Includes bibliographical references and index.
     ISBN 0-7914-1953-3 (alk. paper).—ISBN 0-7914-1954-1 (pbk. :
alk. paper)
     1. Transpersonal psychology.   2. Ego (Psychology)
3. Psychoanalysis.   4. Jung, C. G. (Carl Gustav), 1875–1961.
I. Title.   II. Series.
BF204.7W375   1994
150.19′8—dc20   93-38025
                                                                                      CIP

10 9 8 7 6 5 4 3 2 1

This book is dedicated to
PAMELA WARREN WASHBURN
dear friend, love of my life.

Contents

Preface

Transpersonal Psychology in Psychoanalytic Perspective builds upon the transpersonal theory of human development that I presented in initial formulation in *The Ego and the Dynamic Ground* ([1988] 2d ed. in press). The focus of *The Ego and the Dynamic Ground* was phenomenology. In that book, my primary objective was to elucidate the concrete lived experience that corresponds to stages of development leading to and beyond the transcendence of the ego. Although the phenomenology articulated in *The Ego and the Dynamic Ground* was set within a definite theoretical framework, it was not my intention in that book to pursue theory for theory's sake. Accordingly, in that book, I did not attempt any extensive integration of the multidisciplinary and cross-cultural literatures that bear upon transpersonal themes.

In particular, although *The Ego and the Dynamic Ground* drew upon classical psychoanalytic drive and structural theory, psychoanalytic ego psychology, and Jungian depth psychology, it did not venture into the vast body of literature in psychoanalytic object relations theory or the growing body of literature in psychoanalytic self psychology. Nor did it take advantage of many of the findings of cognitive-developmental psychology. Nor was it grounded in the recent literature in psychoanalytic and Jungian feminist theory. Also, although *The Ego and the Dynamic Ground* was guided by a few basic motifs of Western spirituality, it did not present in-depth consideration of any specific representatives or texts of the Western spiritual tradition. The focus was more on Eastern spiritual systems—especially classical yoga and Tantrism—insofar as they can be understood from a psychodynamic, depth-psychological standpoint. Only with the writing of *Transpersonal Psychology in Psychoanalytic Perspective* have I been able to bring the transpersonal perspective set forth in *The Ego and the Dynamic Ground* into fruitful communication with these and other important psychological and spiritual literatures.

In drawing upon this wider range of sources, *Transpersonal Psychology in Psychoanalytic Perspective* goes beyond *The Ego and the Dynamic Ground* in four principal ways: (1) it focuses not only on the inner (intrapsychic, depth-psychological) side but also on the outer (interpersonal, object-relational) side of the developmental process; (2) it explains how ego development is tied to dualism, understood both as an intrapsychic (ego-unconscious, control-spontaneity, thought-feeling, mind-body) and an interpersonal (self-other, private-public) dualism; (3) it considers the issue of gender differences, especially as these differences emerge in the process of ego formation and then are expressed later in life in the process of ego transcendence; and (4) it discusses all of the major stages of life recognized in psychoanalysis and analytically oriented transpersonal psychology: the neonatal stage, preoedipal childhood, the oedipal period, latency, adolescence, early adulthood, midlife transition, and the stages of transcendence leading to integration. My aim in this book has been to provide as comprehensive a foundation as possible for transpersonal psychology from a broadly psychoanalytic perspective.

Two primary paradigms currently guide transpersonal inquiry. One is a paradigm rooted in the psychoanalytic, Jungian, depth-psychological tradition. This paradigm sees human development as following a *spiral course* of departure and higher return to origins. According to this paradigm, the ego emerges initially from the deep sources of the psyche; the ego then separates itself from these sources during the first half of life, which is a time not only of ego development but also ego dominance; and the ego finally returns to the deep sources of the psyche in the second half of life to become integrated with them on a higher, transegoic, level. C. G. Jung was the first psychologist to use this spiral paradigm as a basis for a transpersonal theory of human development. More recently, Stanislav Grof (1975,

1985, 1988) and David M. Levin (1985, 1988, 1989) have employed the spiral paradigm in presenting important accounts of the sources and expressions of transpersonal experience. Also, the transpersonal perspective set forth in *The Ego and the Dynamic Ground* and further elaborated in this book follows the spiral paradigm.

The other major transpersonal paradigm is rooted in structurally oriented psychology (especially cognitive-developmental psychology) and sees development during this lifetime as following a course of straight ascent from preegoic levels to egoic levels to, finally, transegoic levels of development. This paradigm can be called a *ladder* paradigm because it conceives the path of development as a level-by-level ascent up a hierarchy of psychic structures (e.g., cognitive structures, moral structures, self structures). According to this view, the structures of a psychic level are merely potential until development reaches the level to which they belong, at which point they come actively into play, subsuming and reorganizing preceding or lower structures and thereby asserting themselves as the new governing structures of the psyche. This level-by-level process continues until development reaches an ultimate structural level that is all-inclusive, a level that integrates the full range of human experience within a universal unity in which consciousness and reality completely coincide. This ladder paradigm was formulated in a series of influential books by Ken Wilber (1977, 1980a, 1981) and is presently advocated by many transpersonal theorists.

The spiral and the ladder paradigms may reflect different cultural perspectives. I suggested in an earlier publication (1990) that the spiral paradigm has special affinities with motifs of Western spirituality and that the ladder paradigm has special affinities with the theoretical systems of Eastern (especially Indian) spirituality. Jung, for example, in originally formulating the spiral paradigm in psychological terms, based his formulation not only on analytically oriented depth psychology but also on Western spirituality (especially Christianity, Gnosticism, and Western alchemy). And Wilber, in formulating the ladder paradigm, based his formulation not only on structurally oriented psychology but also on Eastern spirituality (especially Buddhism and Vedanta). Proponents of the spiral and ladder paradigms intend for these paradigms to serve as bases for a unifying transpersonal theory, a theory that can reach beyond cultural differences and reveal universal dimensions of spiritually realized personhood. In setting their aim on this unifying goal, however, proponents of the spiral and ladder paradigms need to acknowledge that these paradigms may have distinctive cultural emphases. Alan Roland (1988) has argued that Western and Eastern conceptions of the self differ in important ways. The spiral and ladder paradigms may reflect these differences. This does not preclude the possibility that a truly cross-cultural, unifying transpersonal theory will some day be built upon either the spiral or the ladder paradigm. It does, however, serve as a caution against believing that this has already been accomplished.

Acknowledgments

I am grateful to Steven Rosen for his close reading of the initial version of the first six chapters of this book. I followed many of his helpful suggestions in an early revision of the manuscript. Sincere appreciation is extended to the following people for their comments on selected chapters: Keith Egan, Gerald Gudorf, Avak Howsepian, David M. Levin, James McGrath, Robin Robertson, Philip St. Romain, and Pamela Washburn. Appreciation is extended as well to my colleagues Richard Allen, Lawrence Clipper, Joanne Detlef, and John Lewis. They gave me expert advice on many matters of substance and style.

I am grateful to my school, Indiana University South Bend, for supporting me in this project by granting me a sabbatical leave for the 1990-91 academic year and by allowing me release time from teaching in the fall semester 1992.

The Journal of the American Academy of Psychoanalysis generously allowed me to borrow material from my "Reflections on a Psychoanalytic Theory of Gender Difference" (Vol. 22, no. 1, 1994). Sections of this paper are used in chapters 2 and 3. Also, ICS Publications kindly granted permission to quote passages from *The Col-*

lected Works of St. John of the Cross, translated by Kieran Kavanaugh and Otilio Rodriguez (c) 1979, 1991 by Washington Province of Discalced Carmelites: ICS Publications, 2131 Lincoln Road, N.E., Washington D.C.

Introduction

Transpersonal psychology explores stages of human development lying beyond the level of the fully developed ego. In investigating these stages, transpersonal psychology has understandably focused on the second half of life. This focus has been evident ever since Jung's break with Freud. As is well known, Jungian analytical psychology looks in a direction opposite to that of Freudian psychoanalysis. Whereas psychoanalysis looks back to the earliest stages of life to see how they lay the groundwork for ego development, analytical psychology looks forward to possible future stages of life to see how they represent possibilities for ego transcendence. In looking to the future in this way, Jung was led to a theory of the unconscious that is radically at odds with Freud's. Whereas Freud saw the unconscious (i.e., the deep inherited unconscious) as a lower instinctual realm that the ego surmounts in the process of ego development, Jung saw the unconscious as a higher spiritual realm to which the ego reopens itself in the process of ego transcendence. That is, whereas Freud saw the unconscious as a *pre*egoic id, Jung saw the unconscious as a *trans*egoic collective unconscious.[1] Jung's adoption of this transpersonal conception of the unconscious led him to turn psychoanalysis around 180 degrees and, in doing so, to throw into

1

question much of the original psychoanalytic project. Jung's about-face first became evident with the publication of the *Metamorphoses and Symbols of Libido* in two parts in 1911 and 1912, and this act of "apostasy" soon led to Jung's resignation from the International Psychoanalytic Association and his break with Freud.

Jung's break with Freud led to a period of strident conflict between psychoanalysis, which considered itself the guardian of scientific values, and analytical psychology, which considered itself the guardian of spiritual values. Fortunately, this period of conflict is now history. Overt hostilities ceased long ago, and psychoanalysis and analytical psychology began simply to pursue separate courses. At this time, psychoanalysis and analytical psychology remain on separate courses. Nevertheless, developments in the last twenty-five years have led to converging interests in some areas. For instance, the emergence of object relations theory in psychoanalysis and the application of Jungian ideas to early childhood by analytical psychologists such as Erich Neumann and Michael Fordham have led to shared interests in the role of the infant-caregiver relationship in the formation of psychic structure and the eliciting of developmental potentialities. Also, the focus on the self by psychoanalytic thinkers such as Heinz Kohut and Daniel Stern has moved psychoanalysis toward notions that have long been central to analytical psychology. Many psychoanalysts are now exploring notions of a "superordinate" self or self sense present at the outset of development and of a regulating self-principle that organizes development. These notions are parallel in certain respects to the Jungian notions of an archetypal self and transcendent function. And as psychoanalysts are exploring these notions of self and self-development, many analytical psychologists are drawing extensively on the work of individual psychoanalysts, especially Melanie Klein, D. W. Winnicott, Margaret Mahler, and Heinz Kohut. These developments indicate that psychoanalysis and analytical psychology now have significant interests in common.

If psychoanalysis and analytical psychology now have significant shared interests, they remain at odds in many ways. The current emphasis in psychoanalysis on relational and intersubjective factors is at the same time a downplaying of intrapsychic and depth-psychological factors, factors that are still of primary importance to analytical psychology. Also, if psychoanalysis and analytical psychology now both focus on the preoedipal infant-caregiver relationship, they do so for different reasons. Psychoanalysis focuses on this relationship primarily to understand the earliest foundations of ego or self development; analytical psychology in contrast focuses on this relationship primarily to understand the earliest precursors of ego transcendence. And if psychoanalysis and analytical psychology now both focus on issues of self psychology, they do so again for different reasons. Psychoanalysis focuses on these issues primarily to understand how a healthy or pathological self structure is formed in early childhood; analytical psychology in contrast focuses on these issues primarily to understand how a higher transpersonal self is realized in later life. Accordingly, although psychoanalysis and analytical psychology now have significant interests in common, they remain fundamentally divergent inquiries.

A major consequence of this continuing divergence of perspectives is, I believe, that analytical psychology, and transpersonal psychology more generally, is without an adequate theory of ego development. Psychoanalysis is to be credited for having formulated the theory of ego development. Psychoanalytic drive theory has investigated ego development in relation to instinctual and somatic life. Psychoanalytic structural theory has investigated ego development in relation to the competing demands of the id and the superego. Psychoanalytic ego psychology has investigated ego development in relation to the ego's autonomous processes and "apparatuses." And psychoanalytic object relations theory has investigated ego development in relation to the object world, the world of primary others and their internalized representations. Psychoanalysis has followed the course of the ego's development from birth to maturity, studying the ego's progress as it departs from its neonatal beginnings, as it negotiates the conflicts of the preoedipal and oedipal periods, as it grows rapidly during the calm of latency, as it meets the instinctual, interpersonal, and existential challenges of adolescence, and, finally, as it achieves mature relationships and a mature identity in adulthood. Analytical psychology, focusing on ego transcendence and divorced from psychoanalysis, has not given sufficient attention to any of these phases or aspects of ego development. Consequently, analytical psychology, and transpersonal psychology more generally, is without an adequate understanding of the ego's bases in being and therefore without an adequate understanding of the underpinnings of ego transcendence as well.

The purpose of this book is to explain how the Jungian-transpersonal theory of ego transcendence might be grounded in the psychoanalytic theory of ego development. In bringing together psychoanalysis and Jungian psychology in this way, the perspective of the book, it should be noted, is, strictly speaking, neither psychoanalytic nor Jungian. It is not psychoanalytic because the primary focus is on ego transcendence, which is a possibility that psychoanalysis does not acknowledge. And the perspective is not Jungian because the way in which I propose to ground the Jungian theory of ego transcendence in the psychoanalytic theory of ego development requires significant revisions to key Jungian ideas, revisions that are sufficiently extensive, I would think, to be unwelcome to most Jungians. Accordingly, the perspective of the book can best be described as transpersonal in a general analytic (i.e., depth-psychological, psychodynamic, ego-psychological, object-relational, self-psychological) sense. I have tried to convey this perspective in the title of the book by choosing *Transpersonal Psychology in Psychoanalytic Perspective* rather than *Jungian Psychology in Psychoanalytic Perspective* or *Psychoanalysis in Transpersonal Perspective.*

The chief difficulty standing in the way of the project of this book is the opposition, mentioned earlier, between the psychoanalytic and Jungian conceptions of the unconscious. To repeat, whereas Freud saw the deep unconscious as a preegoic id that the ego surmounts in the process of ego development, Jung saw the deep unconscious as a transegoic collective unconscious to which the ego opens itself in the process of ego transcendence. The contradiction between these conceptions of the unconscious must be resolved if the Jungian-transpersonal theory of ego transcendence is to be grounded in the psychoanalytic theory of ego development. The psychoanalytic theory of ego development cannot be separated from the psychoanalytic conception of the unconscious as preegoic id. If, then, Jungian-oriented transpersonal psychology is to build upon the psychoanalytic theory of ego development, it must find a way to accept the id. In accepting the id, however, Jungian transpersonal theory cannot abandon its own conception of the unconscious as a transegoic source or ground, because that would be to abandon the transpersonal perspective itself. Jungian transpersonal theory must therefore find a way of reformulating the psychoanalytic and Jungian conceptions of the unconscious that at once retains the opposition and eliminates the contradiction between these conceptions, a way of reformulating these conceptions, therefore, that allows *both* conceptions to be accepted.

The importance of this particular issue dictates that it be dealt with at the beginning of the book. Accordingly, chapter 1 introduces the notion of the nonegoic core of the psyche as a mediating concept. This notion is defined in general terms as the seat of the psychic depth potentials that *both* psychoanalysis and analytical psychology assign to the unconscious (i.e., the id or objective-collective psyche). These potentials include energy or dynamism, instinctual drives and predispositions, affect and emotion, the imaginal or autosymbolic process, and collective memories, complexes, or archetypes. Defined as the seat of these general types of potentials, the notion of the nonegoic core is neutral as far as the disagreement between the psychoanalytic and Jungian conceptions of the unconscious is concerned. It defines psychic depth potentials neither as lower preegoic potentials nor as higher transegoic potentials. In its neutrality, the notion of the nonegoic core explicates what is common to both the psychoanalytic and Jungian conceptions of the unconscious and can therefore, I suggest, serve as a basis for a reconciliation of these conceptions. Pursuing this approach, I propose in chapter 1 that the psychoanalytic and Jungian conceptions of the unconscious can be reconceived in a noncontradictory way if, rather than being interpreted as conceptions of the inherent nature of the unconscious, they are interpreted instead as conceptions of differing developmental expressions of the nonegoic core of the psyche.

More specifically, I propose that the psychoanalytic conception of the unconscious as preegoic id can be interpreted as the way the nonegoic core expresses itself during the first half of life—or at least from the onset of latency to midlife—when the developing ego is repressively protected from the powerful influences of the nonegoic core. Under these conditions, the nonegoic core is experienced as something antithetical to and lower than the ego, as a dark and dangerous realm from which the ego must be safely insulated. In turn, I propose that the Jungian conception of the unconscious as transegoic source or ground can be interpreted as the way the nonegoic core expresses itself after the transcendence of the ego, when the mature ego is finally reunited with the nonegoic core. Under these conditions, the nonegoic core is experienced as something supportive of and superior to the ego, as a deeper and higher "self."

A qualification is needed here. Describing the Jungian conception of the unconscious as a transegoic source or ground is not entirely accurate. Jung describes the collective unconscious as a realm of possible experience that is at once light *and* dark, redemptive *and* regressive, and therefore transegoic *and* preegoic. In chapter 1 I argue that this two-sidedness of Jung's account of the collective unconscious better describes the way the ego experiences the nonegoic core *during* the stages of transcendence than it does the way the ego experiences the nonegoic core *after* the stages of transcendence are complete. Jung's account of the collective unconscious, I suggest, reflects the ambivalence of the ego that is in the process of reopening itself to the nonegoic core, which, during this transitional process, is no longer merely the id nor yet a transegoic source or ground. That is, Jung's account of the collective unconscious accurately reflects how the nonegoic core is experienced during the process of individuation (i.e., psychospiritual transformation). This point acknowledged, it is useful—and need not be misleading—to speak of the Jungian conception of the unconscious as a transpersonal conception. Jung *does* describe the collective unconscious as a transegoic source or ground, even if as a transegoic source or ground that is not wholly transegoic but that, in certain respects, is preegoic as well. Accordingly, having alerted the reader to this complication—which is fully addressed in chapter 1—I shall continue in this introduction to speak of the Jungian conception of the unconscious as a transpersonal conception, as a conception of a higher source or ground.

If the psychoanalytic and Jungian conceptions of the unconscious are reinterpreted in the developmental manner suggested, the way is opened for integrating many otherwise inaccessible psychoanalytic ideas within the transpersonal perspective. The major point of contradiction between the psychoanalytic and Jungian perspectives is resolved in a way that allows a rethinking of the Jungian-transpersonal theory of ego transcendence in terms of the psychoanalytic theory of ego development. In such a rethinking, four concepts are most centrally involved and need especially to be addressed: ego, dualism, gender, and transcendence. In the rest of this introduction I present an overview of how I shall be working with these concepts in the pages that follow. I briefly indicate how these concepts can be rethought in a way that connects their Jungian-transpersonal meanings with their psychoanalytic meanings.

EGO

The ego, like the unconscious, plays a primary role in both psychoanalysis and analytical psychology, and it is the primary subject (double entendre intended) of this book. The ego, rather than the self (or Self), is chosen as the primary subject because, in the view I shall be presenting, the ego is the subject in relation to which forms of selfhood evolve in the course of development. According to main lines of psychoanalytic thought, the ego introjects a parentally based self-representation in infancy and early childhood; it awakens reflectively to the question of selfhood in adolescence; and it forges an independent and mature self, or ego identity, in early adulthood. And according to classical Jungian thought, the ego, in the second half of life, suffers from a sense of being an alienated and inauthentic self (the persona); it then experiences a deanimation or "death" of this "inauthentic" self; and it finally is "reborn" to a higher spiritual form of selfhood (ego-Self integration). Psychoanalysis and analytical psychology, it might be said, together chronicle a life history of the ego in search of self. The ego is the subject of this history, and of this book as well.

The contradiction between the psychoanalytic and Jungian conceptions of the unconscious is responsible for a corresponding contradiction between the psychoanalytic and Jungian conceptions of the ego. Given its conception of the unconscious as a lower preegoic id, psychoanalysis looks upon the ego as the highest achievement of both phylogeny and ontogeny. Psychoanalysis, as a theory of ego development during the first half of life, follows the course of the ego as it differentiates itself from its inner and outer sources during infancy, as it consolidates ego structure and develops ego functions during childhood, as it awakens to sexuality, intimacy, and reflective awareness during adolescence, and as it exercises ego functions and establishes an identity in the world during early adulthood. This course of development is conceived as a steady ascent, as a climb from fusion, fantasy, instinct, and drive-object dominance to individuation, reality, reason, and independent selfhood. Analytical psychology, in contrast, given its conception of the unconscious as a transegoic source or ground, has a much less generous assessment of the ego. Although Jung, unlike many other transpersonal theorists, recognized the indispensable importance of the ego within the psychic economy, he nonetheless saw the ego as something that is not only inferior to the source or ground from which it derives but also ignorant of this source or ground and therefore committed to a false stance of independence. The ego, for Jungian depth psychology, is therefore something that needs to be disabused of its sense of independence and brought into proper relation with the superior bases of its being. Jungian psychology follows the ego on a course not of ascent and independence but rather of descent (the night sea journey) and reunion with its transegoic source or ground.

The developmental interpretation of the unconscious proposed earlier allows Jungian transpersonal theory to accept not only the psychoanalytic notion of the id but also the theory of ego development based on that notion. For if the unconscious can be said to be first a preegoic id and later a transegoic source or ground, then there is no contradiction in saying that the ego should first surmount the unconscious and later return to it. It is entirely consistent that, in the first half of life, the ego should separate itself from the nonegoic core and establish itself in the world and then, in the second half of life, withdraw from the world and return to the nonegoic core. According to the developmental interpretation of the unconscious, the nonegoic core from which the ego separates itself in the first half of life *is* a dangerous preegoic id, a nucleus of nonegoic potentials from which the developing ego must protect itself. And the nonegoic core to which the ego returns in the second half of life *is* a higher transegoic source or ground, a nucleus of nonegoic potentials in which the ego can be rooted, regenerated, and "redeemed." To be sure, when the mature ego first reopens itself to the nonegoic core, the core more typically manifests itself as a threatening abyss than as a higher source or ground. Nevertheless, once the ego has endured the abyss and has been rooted in the nonegoic core, the core, I suggest, does begin to reveal itself in its transegoic aspects.

As the primary "subject" of this book, the ego figures centrally in every chapter. Chapter 1 examines the intrapsychic and interpersonal sources from which the ego emerges. Chapter 2 discusses the itinerary of ego development during the preoedipal and oedipal periods. Chapter 3 considers gender differences in early ego development. Chapters 4, 5, and 6 trace the course of ego development through latency, adolescence, and early adulthood, respectively. Chapter 7 describes some of the difficulties that can afflict the ego at midlife. Chapters 8 and 9 follow the ego through the principal stages of transcendence. Chapter 10 returns to the issue of gender and suggests that, owing to differences in original ego development, women and men experience ego transcendence in significantly different ways. Finally, chapter 11 discusses the goal of transcendence: the full integration of the ego with both the nonegoic core (intrapsychic wholeness) and others (I-Thou intimacy).

DUALISM

Dualism is the separation of the ego from the bases of its being. It manifests itself in two chief ways: (1) as an intrapsychic dualism separating the ego from the nonegoic core (mind from body, thought from feeling, will from dynamism, control from spontaneity), and (2) as an object-directed or interpersonal dualism separating consciousnesses from each other as circumscribed, privatized spheres (self-other, private-public dualism). Psychoanalysis and Jungian psychology agree that dualism, so described, is a reality of psychic life. They disagree, however, on whether dualism plays a positive or negative role in human development.

Psychoanalysis sees dualism as something positive, namely, as independence, for psychoanalysis sees life as proceeding from a starting point of ego fusion or symbiosis to a goal of ego independence. At the beginning of life, according to psychoanalysis, the ego is not yet differentiated from the inner and outer sources of its being, the id (primary matrix, nonegoic core) and the primary caregiver as original "object." The ego is at first immersed in the id and enveloped by the caregiver and only gradually, during the preoedipal and oedipal periods, separates itself from these sources. With the resolution of the Oedipus complex, the ego achieves a significant degree of independence, which it enjoys throughout the period of latency. The dualistic bases of the ego's independence during latency are limited, however, and they eventually prove inadequate when, during adolescence, the ego begins to be importuned by strong sexual feelings and related interpersonal longings. Adolescence is a period of transition during which the dualistic bases of the ego's independence are challenged and restructured so that the ego can achieve a more integrated form of independence, a form that includes sexuality and sexually based intimacy. The ego typically achieves this new form of dualistic independence at the beginning of adulthood or in the early years of adulthood, and this new form of independence serves as the basis for the completion of ego development during the first half of adult life.

Analytical psychology looks at the independence of the mature ego and sees its negative ramification: loss of connection with deeper sources of life. Analytical psychology, of course, is entirely in favor of a strong ego, but not in favor of an ego the strength of which is predicated on disconnection from the deep psyche (and others). The whole thrust of the Jungian theory of individuation is that the ego needs to open itself to the unconscious and thereby regain contact with psychic depths. Accordingly, whereas psychoanalysis lauds the ego's independence and encourages the ego to maintain secure boundaries, analytical psychology sees the stance of independence as an impediment to transpersonal development. Looking at the second half of human life, Jungian psychology sees the ego's dualistic bases as defensive-limiting structures rather than protective-supporting structures. For this reason analytical psychology advocates that the (mature) ego begin dismantling these structures, that it begin to "undo" and "let go" and thereby open itself in faith to what these structures have excluded from experience. In letting go of its "false" dualistic infrastructure in this way, analytical psychology maintains, the ego is brought back into connection with the "true" transegoic bases of its being.

This disagreement between psychoanalysis and analytical psychology over the nature of dualism, like the closely related disagreement over the ego, derives from the more fundamental disagreement over the nature of the unconscious. Psychoanalysis sees dualistic separation as independence because, for psychoanalysis, such separation is interpreted as freedom from a preegoic id (and corresponding object influences). Analytical psychology on the other hand sees dualistic separation as loss of connection because, for analytical psychology, such separation is interpreted as estrangement from a transegoic source or ground (and corresponding object possibilities). The opposite conceptions of the unconscious produce opposite evaluations of dualism. Accordingly, if, as I have suggested, the opposite conceptions of the unconscious can be rendered compatible by means of a developmental interpretation, then so too can the opposite evaluations of dualism. If the unconscious can at first be a preegoic id and later a transegoic source or ground, then dualism can at first be a positive separation properly conceived as independence and later a negative separation properly conceived as loss of connection. The developmental interpretation of the unconscious implies that a transvaluation occurs sometime around midlife, that is, sometime after the ego has reached full maturity. At this point, the developmental interpretation implies, the ego begins to undergo a vague but pervasive reversal in its sense of its standing in being. At this point the ego's self-possession begins to feel like self-loss and its autonomy like alienation. The ego's developmental achievements begin to lose their value and the ego begins to suffer from a sense of lack and isolation. It ceases enjoying dualistic independence and begins to suffer from dualistic loss of connection.

Chapters 2 through 10, in following the stages of ego development and ego transcendence, also follow the stages of the emergence, transvaluation, and dissolution of dualism. Chapter 2 sets the groundwork by discussing the origins of dualism in infancy and early childhood. I propose that the two chief challenges of these periods, the rapprochement crisis of the separation-individuation process and the Oedipus complex, have the double effect of causing the ego to sever decisively any remaining symbiotic ties to the primary caregiver and to disjoin itself repressively from the nonegoic core of the psyche.

This severing and disjoining, I argue, are two sides of the same primal "act." The inner or psychodynamic side of this "act" I, following Freud, call *primal repression*, and the outer or object-directed side I call *primal alienation*. Primal repression and primal alienation make up the infrastructure of dualism, which is initially laid down during the rapprochement subphase of the separation-individuation process and then consolidated with the resolution of the Oedipus complex. The immediate consequences of the consolidation of primal repression and primal alienation are, respectively, dormancy or latency (the quieting of nonegoic potentials by primal repression) and object constancy (stable interpersonal relations made possible by primal alienation). These consequences are the hallmarks of the period of latency, which is the first period of dualism.

Chapter 3 discusses gender differences in ego development and considers how women and men differ in their commitments to the dualistic bases of ego development. Chapters 4, 5, and 6 explain the distinctive ways in which dualism is organized during latency, adolescence, and early adulthood, in each case focusing on both the intrapsychic and interpersonal dimensions of dualism, on both primal repression and primal alienation. These three chapters track the changes in dualism from latency, during which dualism is stable but limited, through adolescence, during which dualism is destabilized by awakening sexual and intimacy needs, to early adulthood, during which sexuality and sexually based intimacy are integrated by the ego on a restructured dualistic basis.

Chapter 7, which discusses difficulties that can afflict the ego at midlife, traces these difficulties to, among other factors, the transvaluation of dualism, which here changes from an infrastructure that protects the ego from preegoic dangers and thereby supports ego development to a barrier that disconnects the ego from transegoic possibilities and thereby obstructs ego transcendence. Chapter 8 gives an account of the specific steps of the transvaluation of dualism conceived as a preliminary stage of ego transcendence: withdrawal from the world. Chapter 9 explores the stages of transcendence that correspond to the progressive dissolution of dualism. Chapter 10 discusses gender differences in ego transcendence and considers how women and men differ in the ways they experience the breakdown of dualism and the return to earlier, but now-transvalued, transegoic possibilities of life. Finally, chapter 11 discusses the postdualistic or integrated psyche, the psyche that is no longer divided against itself or others. In explaining transvaluation and the overcoming of dualism, chapters 7 through 11 stress that these processes are fundamentally bidirectional at every step of the way, involving a deconstruction of both primal repression and primal alienation and a corresponding reconnection of the ego with both the nonegoic core of the psyche and other conscious beings.

GENDER

Gender has always been an issue of importance to both psychoanalysis and analytical psychology, and in the last twenty years it has become an issue of primary concern. Freud left a strong patriarchal imprint on psychoanalysis. For Freud, human development is based on commitment to the oedipal father and submission to his authority and example. The young child makes a decisive shift from the mother to the father that is at the same time a shift from modes of experiencing associated with the mother (the pleasure principle, erotogenic ecstasy, feeling, relationship) to ways of functioning represented by the father (the reality principle, ego functions, reason, exercise of will). Analytical psychology, in contrast, sees human development as aiming ultimately at possibilities that traditionally have been associated with women. Jung saw the deep unconscious not only as a source of transegoic possibilities but also as a sphere that is primarily "feminine" in its content and general complexion. According to Jung, the deep unconscious is originally the realm of the Great Mother; it is symbolized by the anima archetype; and it is the seat of such "feminine" potentials as feeling, creative imagination, and intuition. Whereas Freud's basic focus was on "masculine" faculties and functions, Jung's was on "feminine" potentials and capacities.

The patriarchal assumptions of psychoanalytic theory have by now been thoroughly exposed and criticized, and psychoanalysis has made significant progress in understanding the role of women and the importance of gender in human development. The emergence of psychoanalytic object relations theory with its focus on the preoedipal infant-caregiver interaction opened the way for an understanding within psychoanalysis of the significance of the female basis of human development. Object relations theorists such as Melanie Klein, D. W. Winnicott, Edith Jacobson, Margaret Mahler, and Otto Kernberg have shown that the preoedipal period, with its crucial task of moving from symbiosis to separation from the mother, is in many respects the most important period of human development, the period during which the most basic of psychic structures are laid down. More recently, feminist object relations theorists such as Dorothy

Dinnerstein (1976) and Nancy Chodorow (1978) have shown that the fact that the principle "object" of the preoedipal period, the mother, has been female has had significantly different consequences for boys and girls, exaggerating separation for boys and burdening it with ambivalence for girls. Finally, Miriam Johnson (1988) has shown that analyses like Dinnerstein's and Chodorow's can be applied to the oedipal period to reveal that, owing to differences in gender relationships, the interaction with the oedipal father has significantly different consequences for boys and girls, "masculinizing" boys, who are challenged to emulate the father, and "feminizing" girls, who are forced to relate to the father in a gender-opposite way.

While many feminists are returning to psychoanalysis, other feminists are criticizing the original Jungian formulation of basic ideas of analytical psychology. Feminist critics have shown that Jung, despite his valorization of the "feminine," was strongly androcentric and misogynist in his thinking about women. Criticism has focused primarily on Jung's theory of the anima and animus, which has been shown to have implications strongly biased against women. According to this criticism, Jung's formulation of the notions of the anima and animus implies both that men are superior women (because men's anima or potential Eros is superior to women's actual Eros) and that women are inferior men (because women's animus or potential Logos is inferior to men's actual Logos). Women lose both ways. The "feminine" is indeed valorized, but only as men's potential Eros. Women, on the other hand, are devalued, both as having an inferior Eros (suited primarily for mothering) and an inferior potential Logos (prone to opinionatedness and stubbornness). Responding to this bias, some feminists (e.g., Naomi Goldenberg) have abandoned analytical psychology, whereas others (e.g., Polly Young-Eisendrath, Demaris Wehr) have remained within the Jungian intellectual community but have recommended thorough revisions of Jung's ideas dealing with gender, especially the ideas of the anima and animus. They have recommended ways in which Jung's valorization of the "feminine" can be understood also to be a valorization of women.

Despite the new developments and critical responses just noted, the original association of psychoanalysis with "masculine" values (ego functions, independence) and analytical psychology with "feminine" values (nonegoic potentials, relationship) remains strong. These enduring associations are entirely understandable. For psychoanalysis, as a theory of ego development, follows the ego's path early in life as it separates itself from the preoedipal mother and commits itself to the world represented by the oedipal father; and analytical psychology, as a theory of ego transcendence, follows the ego's path later in life when, after midlife transvaluation, it withdraws from the world of the father to reunite itself on a higher level with the realm originally represented by the mother. Simply stated, ego development as studied by psychoanalysis follows an anti-female–pro-male path, and ego transcendence as studied by analytical psychology—Jung's androcentrism notwithstanding—follows an anti-male–pro-female path. (Integration, I suggest, is neither anti-female nor anti-male).

The one-sided gender associations of psychoanalysis and analytical psychology reflect historical reality: in our society, social practices give a strong "masculine" emphasis to ego development and a strong "feminine" emphasis to ego transcendence. If our division of labor for child care were different, assigning the same parenting functions and responsibilities to women and men, and if our organization of social life were different, allowing women and men the same opportunities for ego expression, ego development and ego transcendence might not follow a path from the mother to the father and then, in a symbolic sense, back to the mother again. But the fact is that we live in a patriarchal world that continues to assign child care primarily to women and reserve ego expression primarily for men, a world in which, therefore, ego development is still conceived in "masculine" terms and ego transcendence in "feminine" terms.

In seeking to ground the Jungian-transpersonal theory of ego transcendence in the psychoanalytic theory of ego development, I accept the psychoanalytic view that ego development involves a separation from the mother and a commitment to the father. That is, I accept the view that ego development proceeds away from a de facto female realm of experience to a de facto male world. I assume that the dualistic bases of ego development, primal repression and primal alienation, are laden with anti-female–pro-male implicit meaning. In accepting these aspects of psychoanalytic theory, however, I accept them *from a transpersonal perspective* and therefore see them as describing only the first half of life (under conditions of patriarchy) and as being liable to transvaluation and reversal in the second half of life. As the preegoic id is transvalued and gives way to a transegoic source or ground and, correspondingly, as dualistic independence is transvalued and gives way to dualistic loss of connection, so, too, I suggest, "masculine" values are transvalued and give way to "feminine" values.

The fact that ego development and ego transcendence have distinctive gender biases raises the question of how women and men differ in the ways they express and are affected by these biases. Chapter 3 raises this question with respect to ego development. Drawing on the work of Dinnerstein, Chodorow, and Johnson, I argue that although both boys and girls develop their egos by separating from the mother and submitting to the father, that is, by committing themselves to dualism, they do so in significantly different ways. Boys, given their gender opposition to the preoedipal mother and gender identity with the oedipal father commit themselves to dualism in a one-sided and exaggerated way. Girls in contrast, given their gender identity with the preoedipal mother and gender opposition to the oedipal father, commit themselves to dualism in a much more ambivalent and qualified way. Girls, I argue, *do* commit themselves to dualism; like boys, their independence as egos is based on primal repression and primal alienation. However, girls' commitment to dualism is beset with inhibitions, constraints, and countervailing tendencies and identifications. Women's ego development occurs in "man's" world, but under much more difficult conditions than apply to men. Men, therefore, have a significant advantage in ego development, women a serious disadvantage.

The opposite is true, I propose, when it comes to ego transcendence. For transvaluation turns men's advantages in ego development into disadvantages in ego transcendence and women's disadvantages in ego development into advantages in ego transcendence. These reversals are discussed in chapter 10, where I argue that men's greater dissociation from the mother and more one-sided commitment to the father and dualism increase their difficulties in ego transcendence and that women's deeper residual ties to the mother and more qualified commitment to the father and dualism decrease their difficulties in ego transcendence. Although women sometimes have to begin ego transcendence before they have had a chance to give full expression to their egos, or have to postpone ego transcendence until after they have had such a chance, they nonetheless, I suggest, begin ego transcendence from a point that is closer to the goal and in a manner that engenders fewer difficulties. Men, given their exaggerated commitment to dualism, have a longer and more treacherous path to follow. Men have difficulties with ego transcendence not only because it requires them to confront what they have repressed and alienated but also because it goes against their sense of themselves as men.

TRANSCENDENCE

Psychoanalysis denies the possibility of ego transcendence. The possibility of the ego returning to the nonegoic core is interpreted as the risk of the ego being regressively reclaimed by the preegoic id. Ego transcendence, according to psychoanalysis, is a naive illusion the underlying reality of which is regression. Psychoanalysis has focused exclusively on this risk of regression. Jung, in affirming the possibility of ego transcendence, also acknowledged this risk. Not all Jungians, however, have heeded Jung's warnings, and transpersonalists more generally have tended to assume, incautiously, that anything that opens the ego to the "beyond" is good.[2] If psychoanalysis in its skeptical denial of transcendence has turned its back on the possibility of transcendence, transpersonal psychology in its enthusiasm for transcendence has closed its eyes to the possibility of regression. Accordingly, a grounding of the theory of ego transcendence in the psychoanalytic theory of ego development requires that renewed attention be given to the risks of regression.

The intersection of transcendence and regression can, I propose, be conceived in terms of the notion of *regression in the service of transcendence*.[3] According to this notion, ego transcendence involves a genuinely regressive process that is not however a merely regressive process, but rather is a process of regressive restoration of deeper sources of life. If ego development is based on dualistic separation from the nonegoic core (and others), ego transcendence requires a deconstruction of the bases of dualism and a return of the ego to the nonegoic core (and others). This return is a *regressus ad originem*. It is a dangerous passage that involves both the return of the repressed and a regression of the repressor. The ego has no guarantee that it will survive this "night sea journey"; regression in the service of transcendence can abort and collapse into regression pure and simple. For the ego that is "seaworthy," however, this regression to origins does not lead to ego disintegration but rather to a reconnection of the ego with the bases of its being and thereby, ultimately, to psychospiritual integration.

As I shall be explaining it, ego transcendence involves a regressive "night sea journey" because it moves in a direction opposite to ego development. Ego development proceeds by way of (1) differentiation, (2) primal repression–primal alienation, and (3) dualistic independence in the world. Ego transcendence, following upon transvaluation, reverses these steps, proceeding by way of (1) a sense of dualistic loss of connection and ensuing withdrawal from the world (the dark night of the senses, "dying to the world"); (2) derepression-dealienation and consequent regressive reopening of the ego to the nonegoic core and to others (regression in the service of transcendence, the dark night of spirit, "descent into the underworld"); and (3) reunion, regeneration, and higher integration of the ego with the intrapsychic and interpersonal bases of its being (wholeness, unity of opposites, the "spiritual wedding," the "mystical body"). In reversing the path of ego development, the path of ego transcendence coincides with the path of regression. However, in reversing the path of ego development *to achieve a higher form of integration*, the path of ego transcendence departs from the path of regression. The path of transcendence is a *spiral* rather than, to use Ken Wilber's (1982) term, a U-turn path. It is a path that bends back upon itself on the way to a higher stage of development rather than a path that merely returns to its point of departure and thus falls back to a lower stage of development.

The three stages of transcendence are dealt with in chapters 8 and 9. Chapter 8 focuses on the ego's withdrawal from the world. Drawing on John of the Cross's *Dark Night*, I discuss the steps of withdrawal in terms of John's account of the night of the senses, the period of aridity, weakening of will, and sobering encounter with self that leads to deep spiritual opening. Chapter 9 focuses on the spiral return to origins, dividing this process into an initial phase of regression in the service of transcendence and a later phase of regeneration in spirit. In discussing regression in the service of transcendence, I draw on John of the Cross's account of the dark night of spirit and address the issue of how redemptive and merely pathological regression can be distinguished. Finally, chapter 11 describes the ultimate goal to which transcendence points: the intrapsychically and interpersonally integrated psyche.

1

The Sources of
Experience in Infancy

As explained in the introduction, the project of this book presupposes that the contradiction between the psychoanalytic and Jungian conceptions of the unconscious can be eliminated. The psychoanalytic notion of the id and the Jungian notion of the collective unconscious must be rendered consistent if the Jungian-transpersonal theory of ego transcendence is to be grounded in the psychoanalytic theory of ego development. Given the importance of this matter to the book as a whole, I am placing it at the top of the agenda and addressing it here in the first chapter.

Finding a way of reconciling the psychoanalytic and Jungian conceptions of the unconscious is important not only to the book as a whole but also to the specific topic of this chapter, which treats the sources of experience in infancy. Both classical psychoanalysis and analytical psychology agree that the unconscious is a primary source of experience during infancy. They agree that the ego emerges from and is intimately open to the unconscious during infancy. If, then, we are to be able in this chapter to shed any light on how the unconscious functions as a source of the infant's experience, we must first address the issue of the nature of the unconscious itself. Accordingly, in the next section I shall present a brief sketch of the conception of the unconscious that will serve as the basis for the perspective of this book. This sketch, it must be stressed, is only a sketch. It is a preliminary formulation of a view that finds its full working out only in the book as a whole.

THE NONEGOIC CORE OF THE PSYCHE

Classical psychoanalysis and analytical psychology agree that the deep unconscious—that is, the id or collective unconscious—is a realm of possible experience that lies beyond (or beneath) the egoic system.[1] It is a nonegoic realm that is the source of the dynamic depth potentials of the psyche. In the terms I shall be using, psychoanalysis and analytical psychology agree that the deep unconscious is a *nonegoic core* of the psyche from which derive the following *nonegoic potentials:*

1. Energy, dynamism
2. Instinctual drives and predispositions
3. Affect, emotion
4. The imaginal, autosymbolic, process
5. Collective memories, complexes, or archetypes

Although psychoanalysis and analytical psychology both posit a nonegoic core of the psyche as just described, they of course interpret the nature of this core in radically divergent ways. Psychoanalysis interprets the nonegoic core and its potentials exclusively in a preegoic (i.e., biological, infantile, prerational) and negative (i.e., ego-alien, regressive) manner. Analytical psychology in contrast interprets the nonegoic core and its potentials in a much more complex manner, dividing nonegoic potentials into preegoic and transegoic (i.e., transcendent or spiritual), negative and positive (i.e., ego-transforming, redemptive), types.

For example, classical psychoanalysis interprets the nonegoic potentials listed above in the following way:

1. Libido, aggressive energy
2. Sexual and aggressive drives
3. Modulated and sublimated instinctual drives
4. The primary process
5. Phylogenetic memories and infantile complexes

This list, which is an inventory of the id, clearly reflects Freud's one-sidedly preegoic (henceforth, *pre²*) and negative interpretation of nonegoic potentials. (1) Energy is interpreted exclusively as bioinstinctual energy, specifically as libido and aggressive energy. (2) Instinctual drives and predispositions are reduced to the sexual and aggressive drives, which are considered the basic moving forces of the psyche. (3) Affect and emotions are interpreted reductively as discharges, modulations, or sublimations of the instinctual drives. (4) The imaginal, autosymbolic, process is interpreted as the prerational primary process, a cognitive process that is immensely creative (e.g., the creativity of dreams) but that also suffers from serious shortcomings (e.g., illogical condensations and displacements of meaning). And (5) collective species experiences are interpreted as either phylogenetic memories (e.g., the killing of the primal father) or infantile complexes (e.g., the Oedipus complex). In sum, Freud interpreted nonegoic potentials as forces or processes that are lower than the ego in evolutionary and developmental status and that are basically negative, ego-dystonic, in character. To be sure, the ego, for Freud, is a servant of the nonegoic id, which is the sovereign power of the psyche. Nevertheless, the ego is considered superior to the "bestial" master it serves.

Jung's understanding of nonegoic potentials is much more complex and ambivalent than Freud's. For whereas Freud interpreted all nonegoic potentials in a one-sidedly pre and negative manner, Jung tended to interpret nonegoic potentials in both pre and trans, both negative and positive, ways. This fact is evident in the following interpretations. (1) Energy is conceived as neutral psychic energy, as energy that empowers all psychic systems, processes, and experiences, whether lower or higher, merely biological or spiritual, pre or trans. (2) Instinctuality is interpreted very broadly to include not only biological instincts such as those of survival and procreation (pre) but also inherited developmental and spiritual predispositions such as those governing the individuation process (trans). (3) Feelings are interpreted in an equally broad manner to include not only primitive instinctual feelings and infantile and malevolent feelings deriving from the shadow (pre) but also sublimely numinous and beatific feelings issuing from inner spiritual resources (trans). (4) The imaginal, autosymbolic, process is considered the source of all dreams, spontaneous fantasies, symbols, and myths, whether primitive or spiritual, archaic or prophetic, pre or trans. And (5) collective species experiences are interpreted as the archetypes of the collective unconscious, which include both pre archetypes reflecting the prior evolution of the species and trans archetypes pointing toward future or higher developmental possibilities.

In Jung's account, as just stated, nonegoic potentials are either both pre and trans (e.g., instinctuality, feelings, archetypes) or neither pre nor trans but capable of serving both pre and trans ends (e.g., psychic energy and the imaginal or autosymbolic process). In either case the two-sidedness of Jung's perspective is clearly visible. Unlike Freud, whose conception of the nonegoic core of the psyche is exclusively negative, Jung's conception seems to go in opposite directions at once and to include both negative and positive aspects. Accordingly, whereas Freud unambivalently recommended that the ego protect itself from the depth potentials of the nonegoic core, Jung recommended that the ego be both wary and respectful, both cautious and inviting, in its relation to these potentials. For Jung, the nonegoic realm of the deep unconscious contains forces that, on the one hand, can engulf, regress, and even destroy the ego and that, on the other hand, can lead the ego toward higher wholeness and fully realized selfhood. For Jung, the nonegoic core of the psyche is the focus of both our deepest fear and our highest hope.

The conception of the nonegoic core that I shall recommend is Jungian in the general sense that it sees the nonegoic core as a source not only of lower, pre, but also higher, trans, influences. The major way, however, in which the conception I shall propose differs from Jung's is that it understands these influences exclusively in a developmental sense. That is, it understands *pre* and *trans* as referring to *stage-specific manifestations* of nonegoic potentials and not, as typically is the case with Jung, to opposing *sides* or *types* of nonegoic potentials. Jung, I believe, is correct in emphasizing our ambivalence toward nonegoic potentials, because these potentials can affect us in radically different, indeed opposite, ways. Jung, however, I suggest, is mistaken in assuming—as I believe he does, tacitly—that our ambivalence toward nonegoic potentials implies that nonegoic potentials are themselves inherently two-sided or of two contrary sorts. For the assumed implication, if stated as an inference, is clearly invalid. To infer opposing nonegoic potentials from our opposing reactions to nonegoic potentials is to infer a conclusion that is stronger than the premise allows. Moreover, the conclusion, I believe, is false. Although we have sharply divided reactions to nonegoic potentials, these reactions are due not to the divided nature of nonegoic potentials themselves but rather, I suggest, to developmental factors deriving from the unfolding interaction between the ego and the nonegoic core of the psyche.

Disentangling pre from trans expressions of the nonegoic core is an extremely difficult task to which I shall be returning repeatedly during the course of this book.[3] For the present it suffices to sketch a framework that includes a place for both Freud's one-sidedly pre and Jung's ambivalent pre-and-trans accounts of nonegoic potentials by reinterpreting these accounts in developmental terms. This framework, which is here sketched only in the broadest outline, is elaborated in this chapter and the chapters that follow.

Early Preoedipal Symbiosis

During the early preoedipal period, the nonegoic core expresses itself in a freely spontaneous but almost completely undeveloped (i.e., egoically unregulated and culturally unformed) manner. Moreover, because the nascent ego as yet knows no distinction between inner and outer, it experiences nonegoic potentials primarily as they are bound up with the experience of the primary caregiver, who is the emerging ego's initial "object" or "other." For the emerging ego, the nonegoic core is predifferentiatedly fused with the primary caregiver, who therefore is perceived not only as a being possessing basic personal qualities but also a being possessing magical endowments and archetypal dimensions, a being, that is, amplified and embellished by the nonegoic potentials that the caregiver's ministrations elicit from within the infant. For the preoedipal child, the nonegoic core and the caregiver coalesce as a single multidimensional being: the Great Mother. During the early preoedipal period, then, the nonegoic core expresses itself in a manner that is freely spontaneous but also undeveloped and not yet differentiated from the preoedipal child's principal outer "object" or "other."

Late Preoedipal and Oedipal Periods

At approximately eighteen months, as Margaret Mahler (Mahler, Pine, and Bergman 1975[4]) has explained, the young child begins to experience a rapprochement crisis in its relationship with the primary caregiver. The young child begins to experience intense ambivalence toward the caregiver, and this ambivalence splits the child's world in two. The caregiver is split into a "good object" and a "bad object"—or in the more Jungian terminology that I shall be using, the (inner-outer) Great Mother is split into a Good Mother and a Terrible Mother. Correspondingly, the child's sense of self is split into disconnected "good" and "bad" self-representations. This splitting marks a serious impasse, for the young child cannot continue to develop so long as its world and self are so seriously fissured. Continued development requires that the child reunify its experience. The child, I shall propose, accomplishes this reunification only by means of creating yet another division, namely, a division between itself and the sources of its ambivalence. That is, the child reunifies its experience by severing its remaining symbiotic ties to the Great Mother. Now because the Great Mother is not just the primary caregiver but the primary caregiver *as empowered and projectively elaborated by nonegoic potentials*, this severing of ties to the Great Mother is not only an interpersonal alienation of the primary caregiver but also an intrapsychic repression of the nonegoic core of the psyche. The outer dimension of this momentous act, the alienation of the caregiver, I shall call *primal alienation;* the inner dimension, the repression of the nonegoic core, I shall, following Freud, call *primal repression.* Primal repression is the first and ultimate layer of repression separating the ego from the nonegoic core of the psyche, which now becomes the deep dynamic unconscious organized as the id. Primal repression, originating during later preoedipal development, is consolidated with the resolution of the Oedipus complex when the child finalizes its divorce from the Great Mother by making a decisive commitment to the father and to the ego functions the father represents.

Latency through Ego Maturity: The Period of Dualism

The consolidation of primal repression quiets or deactivates nonegoic potentials, thereby ushering in the period of latency. With the exception of adolescence, during which nonegoic potentials are stirred by the awakening of sexuality, nonegoic potentials typically remain weak or dormant throughout childhood and early adulthood. Moreover, in suffering repression, nonegoic potentials are not only muted or silenced in their expression; they are also arrested in their development and subjected to a negative interpretation. They are arrested at a primitive-infantile level and interpreted as dangerous or evil. Negatively organized in these ways, nonegoic potentials are precisely the elements of the id as described by Freud. This organization of nonegoic potentials prevails throughout childhood and early adulthood, during which ego functions are developed without significant interference from nonegoic influences. The id, brought into being by primal repression, is only one developmental form assumed by the nonegoic core of the psyche. It is, however, an enduring form. It is understandable that Freud believed it to be the inherent or constitutional form of the nonegoic core.

Midlife Transvaluation

The full maturity of the ego—which is achieved, typically, after completion of the identity and relationship tasks of early adulthood—marks the turn of midlife. No age exactly corresponds to this transition, and the transition is by no means developmentally mandatory. Nevertheless, the ego is susceptible at midlife, or later, to experiencing a fundamental change in perspective. Having forged an identity, having worked at a primary relationship or relationships, and having otherwise established itself in the world, the ego is here prone to turn its attention inward toward a possible rapprochement with the nonegoic core of the psyche. Having completed the tasks of early adulthood, the ego has completed the agenda of its own development and is therefore ready to turn to a deeper developmental agenda, that of whole-psyche (egoic-nonegoic) integration. Accordingly, there is a developmental tendency at or after midlife for primal regression to loosen or begin to give way and for the ego to reopen itself to the nonegoic core. This tendency is frequently expressed in a loss of interest in worldly goals and compensations (existential alienation, "dying to the world," the dark night of the senses) combined with or followed by a strongly ambivalent fascination with nonegoic possibilities. The ego is drawn away from the outer world and drawn toward as yet unrevealed inner depths, toward a "within" that is "beyond": the nonegoic core. The nonegoic core at this juncture is still the submerged and feared id, but it is now also an impelling unknown, a *mysterium tremendum et fascinans.*

Initial Reopening to the Nonegoic Core

When primal repression finally gives way, the ego ceases being protected from the nonegoic core and comes under the direct influence of nonegoic potentials. These potentials spring to life in dramatic and diverse ways. Initially, the ego tends to be intoxicated and awed by resurging nonegoic potentials, intoxicated by liberated energy and awed by numinous feelings, images, and insights. This initial sense of ecstatic breakthrough (the "illuminative way," "pseudonirvana"), however, very soon gives way to disturbing prospects. For the ego's openness to the nonegoic core is not only a receptivity but also a vulnerability. It is an openness that renders the ego subject not only to infusive-intoxicating upwellings from the nonegoic core but also to the gravitational-abyssal suction of the nonegoic core. It is an openness that renders the ego subject not only to wondrous feelings, images, and insights but also to an ominous sense that it has suffered a wound deep within, a wound that exposes the ego to a terrifying "black hole" at the seat of the soul. The ego's initial reopening to the nonegoic core therefore has a double, "breakthrough-breakdown," character. This sharply divided experience intensifies the ego's ambivalence toward nonegoic potentials, which the ego is here disposed to perceive as if they were inherently divided into positive and negative, trans and pre, types. This divided experience is in certain respects an intrapsychic replay in reverse of the preoedipal rapprochement crisis. Nonegoic potentials are split into seemingly all-good (upwelling, bright, enrapturing) and all-bad (abyssal, dark, and frightening) forces. The realm of the deep unconscious is experienced as both a rejuvenating wellspring and an abyss-maw, as both a fount of spiritual life and a pit of seething energies. This splitting of the ego's experience places the ego in a precarious position, rendering the ego susceptible to borderline difficulties and even to episodes of psychotic regression. The ego's initial reopening to the nonegoic core thus divides the ego's experience into powerfully opposed possibilities and exposes the ego to very real psychological dangers. These difficulties attending the ego's reopening to the nonegoic core help explain why Jung thought that nonegoic potentials are inherently or constitutionally divided into higher and lower, redemptive and regressive, types. They do so because they were part of Jung's own reopening to the nonegoic core. Jung's conception of the collective unconscious was originally worked out while Jung was himself undergoing an acutely painful reopening process.

Regression in the Service of Transcendence

After the initial reopening of the ego to the nonegoic core, the ego enters a difficult period during which it suffers the fury of the "return of the repressed" and struggles to preserve its independence against the resurgence of nonegoic life. The ego is drawn into the unconscious and besieged by forces of the "underworld." This descent into the deep is a redemptive regression that I ([1988] 2d ed. in press) have called *regression in the service of transcendence*. It is what Jung (1912), following Leo Frobenius (1904), called the *night sea journey*, what St. John of the Cross (1991a) called the *dark night of spirit*, and what now, following Joseph Campbell (1949), is popularly known as the *hero's journey*.[5] During this phase of psychospiritual development, the ego's ambivalence toward nonegoic potentials is weighted heavily in the negative direction, and nonegoic potentials, reflecting this weighting, present themselves to the ego primarily in negative guises. The ego therefore is prone to suffer disturbing experiences, for example, menacing instinctual impulsions, tempting or terrifying imaginal formations, disconcerting feelings such as dread and strangeness, and frightening or morbid states of mind such as flooding, involuntary trance, and engulfment. Regression in the service of transcendence is rarely if ever an exclusively negative experience. The ego enjoys periods of relief and even periods during which positive expressions of the nonegoic core come to the fore. These periods, however, are exceptions to the rule during regression in the service of transcendence, which is for the most part a harrowing transformative process.

Regeneration in Spirit

If and when the ego weathers the regression to origins and finds that it can withstand the potent-numinous energy arising from the nonegoic core, the ego gradually loses its fear of nonegoic potentials and begins experiencing these potentials in increasingly positive ways. Accordingly, the ego's ambivalence and consequent splitting of nonegoic life begin to change from a predominantly negative to a predominantly positive weighting. This reversal marks the transition from regression in the service of transcendence to what in traditional religious terminology has been called *regeneration in spirit*. Regeneration in spirit is a period during which the negative experiences distinctive of regression in the service of transcendence gradually give way to positive correlates. For example, menacing instinctual impulsions give way to a sense of general somatic awakening; tempting or terrifying imaginal formations give way to "visions" that guide, inspire, and comfort; feelings such as dread and strangeness give way to feelings such as euphoria and enchantment; and states of mind such as flooding, trance, and engulfment give way to states of mind such as rapture, transport, and ecstasy. If regression in the service of transcendence is not an exclusively negative affair, neither is regeneration in spirit an exclusively positive one. During regeneration in spirit, the ego suffers occasional regressive relapses and at times falls under the grip of ominous feelings and fantasies. Nevertheless, as regression in the service of transcendence gives way to regeneration in spirit, a pervasive change from dark to light occurs: the ego's experience of nonegoic potentials becomes decreasingly negative and increasingly positive.

The Ideal of Postdualistic Integration

As the ego takes root in the nonegoic core and is progressively regenerated by nonegoic potentials, regressive relapses and ecstatic eruptions gradually disappear and the ego's experience begins to stabilize on a superior plane. The experiences distinctive of regeneration in spirit cease being eruptive "breakthrough" or "peak" experiences and become experiences that are more evenly integrated within the fabric of transegoic life. Accordingly, somatic awakening stabilizes as polymorphously sensual embodied life; spontaneous "visions" stabilize as disciplined symbolic creativity; feelings of euphoria and enchantment stabilize as feelings of bliss and hallowed resplendence; and states of mind such as rapture, transport, and ecstasy stabilize as states of mature contemplative attunement or absorption. The transition from regeneration in spirit to postdualistic integration joins nonegoic potentials and ego functions in harmonious and effective complementarity, in a *coincidentia oppositorum*. The ultimate goal toward which this transition moves is an ideal that may never be reached. To the degree the ideal is approximated, however, the ego reexperiences on a higher (i.e., developmentally mature) level the radical spontaneity, creativity, and sense of seamless wholeness that were first experienced in a primitive way during the early phases of preoedipal life. Full integration is an ideal higher harmony of the ego and the nonegoic core of the psyche: it is a transegoic rather than preegoic harmony.

This sketch of the main developmental expressions of the nonegoic core implies that the nonegoic core is not just a primitive-negative id or a split, lower-higher, collective unconscious. According to our sketch, these two conceptions of the nonegoic core of the psyche accurately describe specific developmental expressions of the nonegoic core but are incomplete as descriptions of the intrinsic character or constitution of the nonegoic core. Freud, oblivious for the most part to the preoedipal period of development and focusing almost exclusively on the psychic organization that obtains during the first half of life, understandably interpreted the nonegoic core as the id. And Jung, unconcerned for the most part with the first half of life and focusing almost exclusively on the ego's ambivalent reopening to the nonegoic core during the second half of life, understandably interpreted the nonegoic core as the collective unconscious. Each of these conceptions captures a distinctive mode of expression of the nonegoic core. The two conceptions, however, have to be placed in a larger developmental framework if they are to complement rather than contradict each other.

To avoid misrepresenting the larger project of this book, I should stress that the preceding sketch, in describing the developmental interaction between the ego and the nonegoic core, focuses only on the intrapsychic side of an inherently two-sided, intrapsychic-interpersonal, depth-psychological–object-relational process. The dialectical interplay between the ego and the nonegoic core is at the same time a dialectical interplay between the ego and the "object" world, that is, between the ego and primary others as experienced through evolving object representations. This unity of the inner and the outer is evident in all of the stages of development covered in the sketch just finished. For instance, the primitive ego–Great Mother symbiosis of the early preoedipal period is, albeit by default (i.e., by *lack* of differentiation), at once an inner (egoic-nonegoic) and an outer (infant-caregiver) symbiosis. The dissolution of this preoedipal symbiosis, the disconnection of the ego from the Great Mother, is at once an inner and an outer "act": primal repression and primal alienation go hand in hand. The commencement of latency, therefore, is at the same time the achievement of libidinal object constancy. That is, it is the beginning of dualism in both its inner (egoic-nonegoic) and outer (self-other) expressions. Dualism remains stable until puberty, at which time it is challenged both intrapsychically (by sexual awakening, which destabilizes primal repression) and interpersonally (by the emergence of sexually driven intimacy needs, which destabilizes primal alienation). Following adolescence, dualism is restructured in both its inner and outer dimensions and typically is not challenged again until midlife.

The unity of the inner and the outer is also evident in midlife transvaluation and the stages leading to integration. The midlife loss of interest in the world and ambivalent attraction to the deep unconscious is at the same time a loss of interest in others as "inauthentic" personas and an ambivalent attraction to others as beings possessing powerful hidden depths (e.g., charismatic personalities, psychopomps, anima-animus figures). The ego's "breakthrough-breakdown" reopening to the nonegoic core is at the same time an ambivalent reopening of the ego to others, a reopening riddled with borderline approach-avoidance, disclosure-exposure, connection-contraction countertendencies. The defenseless vulnerability of the ego to the "return of the repressed" during regression in the service of transcendence is at the same time a defenseless vulnerability of the ego to others, a vulnerability to being seen and taken advantage of by "bad objects." The healing rerooting of the ego in the nonegoic core during regeneration in spirit is at the same time a healing reconciliation of the ego with others, a reconciliation that transforms the ego's vulnerable openness to others into an intimate openness through which the ego is able internally to connect and bond with others. And, finally, the attainment of intrapsychic integration is at the same time an attainment of stable I-Thou intimacy: the higher union of the ego and the nonegoic core is at the same time a transegoic intersubjectivity of ego and "object," of self and others.

Every major step of human development, from the earliest preegoic step to the final transegoic step, has mirror-image inner and outer, intrapsychic and interpersonal, depth-psychological and object-relational sides.

Having set forth the notion of the nonegoic core of the psyche and having seen how the psychoanalytic and Jungian conceptions of the unconscious can be rendered consistent as stage-specific expressions of the nonegoic core, we can now turn to the more proper topic of this chapter: the sources of experience during infancy. In what follows, I shall propose that the nonegoic core of the psyche is a primary source of the infant's experience. The infant's experience consists not only of stimuli arriving from without but also of a wide range of nonegoic potentials upwelling from within. These outer and inner sources of the infant's experience flow together as one, especially in the infant's experience of the primary caregiver as Great Mother.

The Traditional View of the Infant's Experience

We have long been fascinated by the mind of the infant. A primary reason for this is that we have assumed that the infant possesses a type of consciousness significantly different from our own. In the traditional view, the infant's consciousness is, as William James so famously put it, a "blooming, buzzing confusion." It is a form of consciousness with little or no cognitive structure. The infant, in the traditional view, is unable to distinguish one thing from another and is even unable to distinguish itself from the world. The infant's consciousness, that is, lacks both object discrimination and ego differentiation. According to the traditional view, the infant's experience is a stimulus field without discriminable entities and without inner-outer, subject-object, self-other boundaries. To cite a typical example of the traditional view, René Spitz, in his influential *The First Year of Life*, gave this description of the neonatal condition: "At this stage the newborn cannot distinguish one 'thing' from another; he cannot distinguish an (external) thing from his own body, and he does not experience the surround as separate from himself. Therefore, he also perceives the need-gratifying, food-providing breast, if at all, as part of himself. Furthermore, the newborn *in* himself is not differentiated and organized either . . ." (1965, p. 36). According to

Spitz, and the traditional view generally, the newborn enters the world in a completely unstructured state, a primitive state of undifferentiated unity.

If the newborn's state is primitive and undeveloped, it is not for that reason, according to the traditional view, a state plagued by a sense of deficiency. For the traditional view holds that the infant's consciousness is not only unstructured and undifferentiated but also, and by virtue of these very facts, undivided and seamlessly whole. Freud's (1930) account of the newborn as enjoying a limitless "oceanic" feeling, a sense of expansive unity with all existence, is the most influential statement in the psychological literature of this side of the traditional view. An even more idealized statement is to be found among the Jungians. Erich Neumann, for example, describes the newborn as existing in a state of preegoic bliss: "The ego germ still exists in the pleroma, in the 'fullness' of the unformed God, and, as consciousness unborn, slumbers in the primordial egg, in the bliss of paradise" (1954, pp. 276–277). The traditional view sees the infant as being immediately in touch and undividedly at one with experience, intimately immersed in a sensoridynamic world of color, sound, smell, sensation, energy, and affect. The infant, in the traditional view, is not separated from experience in any way and therefore is unfettered by the many dualistic divisions (e.g., subject versus object, mind versus body, thought versus feeling) that tend to plague adult life.

In sum, the traditional view sees the newborn's consciousness as both unstructured and undivided, undifferentiated and full, primitive and whole. Accordingly, in the traditional view, the infant's consciousness has represented something that is not only primordial but also, in its own way, perfect. It has represented not only an aboriginal form of consciousness long ago left behind but also a pristine form of consciousness for which we experience a strong nostalgia.

The traditional view of the infant's experience has been subject to considerable criticism in recent decades. One major criticism is that the view is mistaken in holding that the infant's consciousness is a cognitively undifferentiated field. Contradicting this view, research in the last twenty-five years has revealed that infants are much more cognitively focused and developed than hitherto had been recognized. We now know that the child is born not only with perceptual systems already in operation but also with a remarkably sophisticated cognitive program already loaded and running and with considerable powers of learning and memory ready to add to or modify this program.

For example, virtually from birth, babies exhibit visual preference for the human face (Fantz 1963; Haaf and Bell 1967; Sherrod 1981) and are attuned to the rhythmic movements of human speech (Hutt et al. 1968; Demany, McKenzie, and Vurpillot 1977; Condon and Sander 1974). Also, infants in the first months of life are capable of discriminating and exercising preference for a wide variety of sensory stimuli, not only stimuli bearing upon immediate biological needs but also stimuli of a seemingly purely cognitive sort, for example, patterns, shapes, colors, and sounds (Fantz and Nevis 1967; Tronick and Adamson 1980; Kagan 1984). Furthermore, as parents have known for a long time, and as research has more recently confirmed (Brazelton, Koslowski, and Main 1974; Stern 1974; Trevarthen 1977, 1979; Bower 1979; Kaye 1982; Schaffer 1984), the infant is a social creature who comes into the world preadapted to distinctively human interactions. This social character of the infant is expressed, for example, in the differential perception of the human face and voice, in subtle interactional coordinations and synchronies, and in turn-taking imitation interchanges between the infant and caregivers.

Infants arrive in the world not only with preexisting cognitive programs but also with the ability to alter and add to these programs. From the very beginning, that is, children are able to learn from experience. T. G. R. Bower states this point in an emphatic manner: "This notion [of infant learning] was controversial in the early 1960s but is surely no longer so, complex learning in newborns being no longer thought worthy of particular mention" (1989, p. 150). Bower stresses that babies are capable of discerning contingent connections among stimuli, for example, of recognizing that changes in one stimulus produce changes in another. Grasping connections of this sort is learning in the strict sense of the term. Also, infants in the first months of life habituate to repeated stimuli and therefore are capable of memory of a rudimentary sort (recognition memory). This initial kind of memory can be extended rapidly, even in babies as young as three months, by the employment of reinforcement procedures (Rovee-Collier et al. 1980).

The traditional view of the infant as a completely passive blank slate has been decisively overturned. The infant, we now know, enters the world already gifted with considerable powers of discrimination, attunement, communication, learning, and memory.

A second major criticism of the traditional view is that it too easily assumes that the newborn has no sense of itself as an ego, subject, or self distinct from its environment. This point is controversial and perhaps undecidable. Freud, as we noted, held that the newborn exists in a completely undivided "oceanic" state, a state of egoless absorption that he called *primary narcissism*. This classical psychoanalytic view has been followed and reformulated in many ways, notably by psychoanalytic ego psychologist Heinz Hartmann (1939; Hartmann, Kris, and Loewenstein 1946), who hypothesized that psychic life begins as an undifferentiated matrix that is prior not only to the ego but also to the id, and by psychoanalytic infant researcher Margaret Mahler (Mahler, Pine, and Bergman 1975), who concluded from her studies that approximately the first month of life is lived in a completely undivided autistic state.

This classical view, however, has been criticized or rejected by many developmental theorists. Melanie Klein (1952b, 1958, 1959), for example, argued long ago that a rudimentary ego and object relations exist at birth. Among Jungians, Michael Fordham (1980, 1981), has strongly criticized Neumann's notion of an original infant-caregiver fusion. And more recently, in the psychoanalytic community, Joseph Lichtenberg (1981, 1983, 1987) and Daniel Stern (1985) have challenged the classical view. Lichtenberg, drawing on the most recent results of neonatal research, has argued that the newborn, although lacking a symbolic self-representation, is nonetheless highly differentiated, object related, and interactive in its modes of experiencing. And Stern has argued that the newborn enters the world already situated in a context of self-other differentiation and relationship. Stern, for example, counters the classical psychoanalytic view in emphatic terms. He says:

> Infants begin to experience a sense of an emergent self from birth. They are predesigned to be aware of self-organizing processes. They never experience a period of total self/other undifferentiation. There is no confusion between self and other in the beginning or at any point during infancy. They are also predesigned to be selectively responsive to external social events and never experience an autistic-like state. (1985, p. 10)

The traditional view that the newborn's consciousness is altogether without ego-nonego, subject-object, and self-other boundaries has, then, been seriously challenged. Contemporary opinion seems to favor the view that babies enter the world already differentiated, related to objects, and aware of themselves to some degree.

These criticisms of the traditional view have significantly changed our understanding of the infant, who is now seen to be much more cognitively competent, socially interactive, and ego or self-differentiated than had previously been realized. In fact, by the late 1970s the consensus among experts in the field of infant research had moved so far away from the traditional view as to reject it entirely. This position is forcefully expressed by Robert Emde, who said that "the 'study babies' of today and the 'thought babies' of just twenty years ago are so dissimilar we might mistake them for members of two different species" (Tronick and Adamson 1980, p. 9). By the late 1970s, the prevailing view had become that the growing body of experimental findings had decisively invalidated the traditional view and had demonstrated that infants are *not at all* like the traditional view had thought.

In 1982 Kenneth Kaye maintained that the movement of consensus away from the traditional view had gone too far. He said:

> Ten years ago, this chapter would have reviewed traditional descriptions of the young infant as disorganized, victimized by the "blooming, buzzing confusion" all around, and a passive recipient of nurturance; and then would have proceeded to debunk those myths by discussing the evidence then beginning to accumulate. The evidence indicated that infant behavior is organized in certain respects right from the start, that the newborn's visual and auditory apparatus bring a degree of order to bear upon the stimulus world, and that the behavior of mothers and other caretakers is influenced by their babies' behavior.
>
> Now these recent findings have themselves become the prevailing myths that need to be at least partly debunked. We should try to do so without letting the pendulum swing all the way back again, for the truth lies somewhere in the middle. (1982, p. 30)

As Kaye says, the truth lies somewhere in the middle between the traditional and antitraditional extremes. This middle ground, I suggest, is one from which the traditional view can be restated in relative terms. We must remember that the traditional view was formulated from the adult's perspective. The point of the traditional view was that, relative to the consciousness of the adult, the consciousness of the infant is unstructured and undifferentiated, open and whole. Unfortunately, the relative nature of this point was not emphasized and, consequently, the traditional view was formulated in absolute terms. Rather than simply saying that the infant is radically less structured and differentiated, closed and divided than adults are, the traditional view said that infants are completely unstructured and undifferentiated, open and whole. This overstatement has been deservedly criticized. Regrettably, however, the criticism led to an equal but opposite overstatement rather than to a qualification of the traditional view. In responding to the exaggeration of the traditional view, the criticism dismissed the relative truth implicit in the traditional view.

The relative truth implicit in the traditional view is assumed in the discussion that follows. Accordingly, when I speak of the infant as being unstructured, undifferentiated, open, whole, and spontaneous, I should be understood as speaking of the infant as being *radically but relatively* unstructured, undifferentiated, open, whole, and spontaneous.

THE NONEGOIC CORE AS A SOURCE OF THE INFANT'S EXPERIENCE

According to both classical psychoanalysis and Jungian psychology, most if not all of the potentials of the nonegoic core of the psyche are spontaneously active at birth, if not before. The newborn's state of undivided openness allows nonegoic potentials to express themselves without psychodynamic inhibition. To be sure, nonegoic potentials express themselves in the newborn in a manner that is as rudimentary as it is spontaneous. Although many nonegoic potentials are functionally related to objects at birth, nonegoic potentials in general are at first lacking in significant articulation and, of course, culturally derived meaning. Despite this rudimentary character, however, nonegoic potentials *are* powerfully active in the newborn. Psychoanalysts, Jungians, and other psychologists studying early childhood acknowledge that the newborn experiences discharges of energy, instinctual responses, upwellings of unnuanced affect, and perhaps primitive imaginal formations. With the possible exception of the imagination and archetypal processes dependent thereon, all nonegoic potentials are active at birth, plying the newborn with a profusion of primitive but powerful experiences.

Theorists of infant cognition differ on whether the imagination is active at birth. Freud (1911a) held that infants respond to unmet instinctual demands by hallucinating objects that would satisfy those demands. Melanie Klein espoused an even stronger view, holding that the imaginal process is active from the very first assertion of the instincts. This view is implicit throughout Klein's work (see Segal 1964, 1991) and is given explicit statement by Susan Isaacs (1943), whose formulation was endorsed by Klein. In Isaacs's account, fantasy is a natural mode of expression of the (object-directed) instincts and spontaneously represents the objects of the instincts from the moment the instincts assert themselves. Accordingly, Isaacs interprets Freud's hypothesis about hallucinatory instinctual satisfaction in infancy to mean that the infant's first tendency is to satisfy an instinctual demand in an hallucinatory manner. For Isaacs, then, the instinctual demands themselves, rather than accumulated tension from *unmet* instinctual demands, cause hallucinatory images. In fact, she argues, such accumulated tension, rather than causing hallucinatory images, is what causes such images finally to break down. According to the Klein-Isaacs view, then, the imaginal process is active from the very beginning of life.

If the imaginal process is not active at birth, it is unclear just when it comes into play. Jean Piaget argued that the infant does not begin to produce mental images until significant progress has been made in understanding the object concept, and object permanence in particular. The infant, he argued, must first have some comprehension that objects have an enduring and independent existence before the infant can reproduce in the imagination an object that is no longer within the field of experience. Piaget's studies (1954) indicated that the first major step toward understanding object permanence occurs at about eight or nine months of age, because this is the age at which a child begins to look for objects that it has observed being hidden from view. Full understanding of the independence of objects, however, is not achieved until around sixteen to eighteen months, because, as Piaget's studies demonstrated, only at this age do children begin to understand that objects have an existence in no way tied to or determined by the child's present of past sensorimotor experience. Accordingly, for Piaget, mental images are not even possible until near the end of the first year and can appear at this point, if at all, only as fleeting reproductions grounded in the child's more or less immediate sensorimotor interactions with objects.[6] Piaget (Piaget and Inhelder 1971) believed that in fact images likely appear later than this, near the middle of the second year, and that in any event images do not become adequate object representations until approximately this later time. It is only at about sixteen to eighteen months, Piaget held, that images can arise without being tied to specific sensorimotor stimuli and, therefore, can be evoked voluntarily as symbolic representations of fully independent objects.

Selma Fraiberg (1969), in a classic paper, explicitly applied Piaget's views to the psychoanalytic hypothesis of hallucinatory image production in infancy. Following Piaget's account of the learning of object permanence, Fraiberg dated the possible first appearance of images at about eight months and argued that any images appearing at this early point are tied to immediate or near-immediate stimuli in the child's experience. Fraiberg's position, however, diverges from the general Piagetian perspective in stressing that the stimuli in question need not be only sensorimotor stimuli but can be instinctual stimuli (as emphasized by psychoanalysis) as well. According to Fraiberg, initial images are either images of objects that have just exited from the sensorimotor field or images of objects needed to satisfy occurrent instinctual demands. Whether produced by sensorimotor or instinctual causes, however, initial images, according to Fraiberg, are stimulus bound and short-lived, coming into existence only in response to stimuli and vanishing soon after the stimuli that prompted them have ceased to exist. Fraiberg agreed with Piaget that voluntarily evocable, stimulus-free, images do not appear until about eighteen months.

We may never know the exact age at which the child begins producing images. The Klein-Isaacs view probably estimates this age too early, and recent research indicates that Piaget's view may estimate it too late. T. G. R. Bower (1982) reports on studies indicating that infants possess some sense of object permanence as early as five months, before they are able to express this understanding in motor behavior by looking for objects that have been hidden from view. Renée Baillargeon (1987) has conducted studies that have detected a presumption of object permanence as early as three and one-half months. And, in general, a growing number of researchers have become critical of the narrowly sensorimotor focus of Piaget's studies of infant cognition as wrongly presupposing that cognitive achievements cannot precede the action schemes and motor capacities through which these achievements are outwardly expressed. Jean Mandler (1990) reviews the evidence accumulating against the Piagetian view and concludes specifically that cognitive achievements relating to object permanence and mental imagery occur much earlier than Piaget had thought, perhaps as early as the first months of life.

Whenever images initially appear, they are likely at first extremely primitive: fragmentary, transient, vague, and idiosyncratic. The first images produced by the child are probably merely partial images bound to short-term perceptual or instinctual cues. And these images probably incorporate not only visual but also auditory, olfactory, and other sensory elements that happen, accidentally, to have been conjoined in the child's experience. Images only gradually become more complete, stable, exclusively visual, and adequately representative of objects. Although Piaget may be mistaken in his view on the sensorimotor origins of images, he is probably correct in holding that images do not become adequate object representations until well into the second year.

Although the imagination (and archetypal processes dependent thereon) may not be active at birth, most nonegoic potentials are. Indeed, some nonegoic potentials are probably active *in utero*. And even if the imagination is not functioning at birth, it likely comes into play within the first year, and perhaps within the first months, of life. Accordingly, if not at birth, then not long thereafter, the infant experiences the full range of nonegoic potentials, which express themselves spontaneously in a virtually free play of sensations, energies, feelings, images, and archetypal perceptions and projections. The infant's experience, then, includes not only externally derived stimuli but also a wide variety of indigenous contents, contents that emerge from the nonegoic core of the psyche. The infant of course is unable to distinguish the internal from the external elements of its experience; nevertheless, both of these elements are present.

THE NONEGOIC CORE AND THE PREOEDIPAL "OBJECT"

In focusing on the nonegoic core of the psyche, I have so far been giving primary attention to the inwardly derived content of the infant's experience. In this section I shall shift the focus and consider the outer side of the infant's experience and in particular the principal outer "object" with which the infant interacts: the primary caregiver. At the very outset of life this object has probably not yet been brought into focus as a fully formed entity with object permanence, that is, as a single and enduring entity. At first, the infant probably perceives the primary caregiver, if at all, only as loose groupings of sensory stimuli tied to basic caregiving functions. The infant, however, soon begins to gather these fragments together and, thereby, to bring the caregiver into focus. This initial discernment of the caregiver gives the infant's experience two distinct points of reference, which Margaret Mahler and John McDevitt describe as follows: "In other words, we assume the infant has two basic points of reference from which he builds up his self-schemata: (1) his own inner feelings (or states)—forming the primitive core of the self [viz., the nonegoic core of the psyche], on the one hand—and (2) the care-giving by the libidinal object [i.e., primary caregiver], on the other hand" (1982, p. 837).[7]

The infant is as intimately at one with the external dimension of its experience as it is with the internal dimension. The infant's intra-psychic openness to the nonegoic core of the psyche is at the same time an interpersonal openness to the primary caregiver. The infant therefore experiences a unity or symbiosis with the caregiver, who is not just an object but, to use Heinz Kohut's term, a *selfobject*, that is, an object that is integral to the infant's experience and rudimentary-narcissistic sense of self.

The infant is completely unaware that some elements of its experience have an inner and others an outer origin. In consequence, the inner nonegoic content and the outer caregiving object of the infant's experience are predifferentiatedly fused and apprehended as a single reality. The infant, open to and at one with both of these sides of experience, knows no distinction between them. Accordingly, non-egoic potentials are from the very first associated with the modes of manifestation of the primary caregiver, and the primary caregiver, in turn, is imbued with the qualities and powers of nonegoic potentials. This fact is of immense significance because it is the primary basis for the archetypal association of nonegoic potentials with femaleness and, conversely, of women with nonegoic potentials. Because non-egoic potentials and the primary caregiver are initially experienced as intimately interfluent aspects of a *single* experience, each acquires a deep and permanent association with the other.

The primary caregiver, who is perceived by the infant as the embodiment of the nonegoic, is a being whose function in relation to the infant is, ironically, to a great extent egoic: the caregiver is the infant's external or auxiliary ego (Spitz 1951, 1965). The infant, without a sufficiently developed ego of its own, is unable to perform its own life-sustaining functions. It needs the caregiver to perform these functions for it and in general to provide a "facilitating environment" (Winnicott 1963a, 1963b). The primary caregiver is for this reason not only a selfobject with which the infant is symbiotically merged but also, to use Christopher Bollas's (1987) term, a *transformational object* that stimulates and guides the infant's growth. If the caregiver did not test reality for the infant and attend to its biological and growth needs, the infant of course could not survive. The caregiver, then, performs a role in relation to the infant that is at once indispensable and, ironically, in many respects the opposite of what the child perceives in the caregiver. The infant depends upon the caregiver to serve as a surrogate ego; at the same time, however, the infant is completely unaware of the ego functions performed for it by the caregiver and instead perceives the caregiver entirely in nonegoic terms.

To repeat, the infant's experience of the caregiver is at first fragmented and only gradually coalesces into a configuration that the infant recognizes as a recurring pattern tied to an enduring object. At the outset of life, the infant perceives the caregiver only as an array of impermanent and disconnected objects or stimuli: face, breasts, enveloping embraces, nurturing gazes, comforting intonations. Four or five months may pass before fragments such as these begin to be grouped in the form of a recognizable gestalt grasped as an enduring entity.[8] The integrated object that emerges in this way is at first extremely vague, possessing indefinite boundaries and inconstant properties. Nevertheless, this object is a reality of immeasurable importance to the infant, for it is the central focus of the infant's attention and the primary "other" of the infant's world.

The object that emerges in this way is not just the caregiver: it is the archetypal Great Mother. This Great Mother is a complex being possessing both outer and inner, personal and prepersonal, human and superhuman aspects.[9] Because the infant does not distinguish between the outer and inner elements of its experience, the Great Mother is not just the outer caregiver but also all of the inner (nonegoically derived) experiences elicited by the caregiver's attentions. Accordingly, the Great Mother is a gestalt consisting of both outer, object-derived, and inner, depth-psychological, elements. The Great Mother is a gestalt composed of both the caregiver as the source of infant-directed actions and the myriad sensations, dynamisms, feelings, and images that the infant experiences in conjunction with these actions. The Great Mother is a complex reality embodied in an outer being and drawing upon the deepest of the infant's internal sources: the nonegoic core of the psyche.

In addition to having both outer and inner dimensions, the Great Mother has both personal and prepersonal aspects. A considerable body of research indicates that infants, virtually from birth, respond differently to persons than to nonhuman objects and, therefore, that infants can at some level discriminate between personal and nonpersonal qualities. I referred to some of this research in the last section in noting that newborns respond preferentially to the human face and voice and that infants as young as just a few weeks participate in interactional synchronies and turn-taking interplays with the primary caregiver. These behaviors indicate that infants in some sense have a differential perception of the caregiver as a person.

If, however, infants have such a perception, they are still unaware of many if not most of the caregiver's personal qualities. For, as noted previously, infants need several months to integrate their experience of the caregiver, and even then the "person-object" brought into focus is far from a complete human being. We of course cannot know exactly how infants perceive the caregiver. Nevertheless, we can reasonably assume that their perception is both indefinite and primitive, only minimally personal. The perception of the caregiver's personal qualities is likely limited to such basic human expressions as communicative gazes, vocalizations, facial gestures, and embraces. Except for preferential response to expressions such as these, infants probably perceive the caregiver primarily as a prepersonal being, a being who is less than human, a "mere" source of warmth, food, and comfort. The experience of the caregiver at this point lacks many distinctively human qualities.

In perceiving the caregiver as a being who is less than human, the infant, paradoxically, also perceives the caregiver as a being who is more than human. For the preoedipal child perceives the caregiver as a vast and magical being. The caregiver qua Great Mother is a being who omnipotently meets the child's every need and who manifests herself to the child in extraordinary, nonegoically empowered and elaborated, ways. Among the Great Mother's powers and guises are (1) numinosity, which makes the caregiver awesome and enchanting; (2) magnetic-solvent love, which makes the caregiver not only irresistibly attractive but also inescapably tractive, not only enveloping but also engulfing; and (3) imaginally and archetypally accentuated appearances, which reconstellate and exaggerate the caregiver across all dimensions. These powers and guises quite evidently derive not only from the caregiver but also from the child's nonegoic responses to the caregiver. The caregiver qua Great Mother is a being who, outwardly embodied, is amplified and embellished by forces, feelings, and images that arise from within the child. The child is astir with nonegoic potentials and, as yet unable to distinguish inner from outer, experiences these potentials as emanating from the primary "object" of its world: the Great Mother. The child's primary "object" is thus an amalgam of elements derived not only from the "object" itself but also from the nonegoic core of the psyche.

The Great Mother is, then, both less than and more than a human being. This primary reality of the preoedipal child's world is a *subhuman goddess*, a being with minimal personal qualities but extraordinary nonegoic powers and appearances. The Great Mother, as we shall see in the next chapter, is also a being subject to being split in two, that is, to being perceived as two opposed and seemingly independent beings: the Good Mother and the Terrible Mother. The cause behind this splitting is the child's growing ambivalence toward the Great Mother. Beginning in the second half of the second year, as Margaret Mahler (Mahler, Pine, and Bergman 1975) has shown, the child experiences a crisis in its relationship with the primary caregiver. The child begins at this point to develop feelings for the caregiver that are so sharply ambivalent that the child is prone to divide its representation of the caregiver—or rather, as I am formulating it, its representation of the Great Mother—into separate all-good and all-bad representations. The child relates to these two representations as if they were representations of two separate beings: a Good Mother and a Terrible Mother. Like the original Great Mother, these split-off Good and Terrible Mothers are, for the child, subhuman goddesses. The Good Mother is a benevolent being incorporating all of the Great Mother's positive qualities; the Terrible Mother is a malevolent being incorporating all of the Great Mother's negative qualities.

The child must endure the conflicting influences of these Manichaean semigoddesses until sometime in the fourth year, which by most accounts is the time when the child finally achieves the maturity to perceive the caregiver in integrated and realistic terms: as a single, neither all-good nor all-bad being, as a being who is at once fully human (i.e., a complete person) and merely human (i.e., no longer a bearer of special nonegoic powers and guises). The child's primary object representation at this point becomes both unified and demythologized. The representation ceases being a split representation of the Great (= Good-Terrible) Mother and becomes a unified representation of, simply, the caregiver. In psychoanalytic parlance, this development is what is known as the achievement of libidinal object constancy.

Conclusion

The infant's experience has both a distinctive inner content and outer "object." The inner content derives from the nonegoic core of the psyche and its varied potentials; the outer "object" is the primary caregiver. These two sides of the infant's experience coalesce and are indistinguishable at the outset of life, and they remain intimately interlinked throughout the preoedipal period of development. The result of this undifferentiated confluence of the intrapsychic and the interpersonal is the Great Mother, a larger-than-life presence that is at once less than and more than a human being.

I have noted that the relationship between the young child and the Great Mother is an ambivalent and unstable one, a relationship subject to conflict and splitting. In the next chapter I shall discuss the unfolding of this relationship during the preoedipal and oedipal periods of development. The instability of the relationship, I shall argue, has momentous consequences for the child: it leads the child finally to break its intimate bond with the Great Mother and thereby to divorce itself from both the outer and inner sources of the Great Mother's being. That is, it leads the child simultaneously to sever its symbiotic ties to the caregiver and to close itself to the spontaneous play of nonegoic potentials. The child at once withdraws into itself, thereby putting a distance between itself and others, and seals the nonegoic core of the psyche, thereby quieting nonegoic potentials and submerging them into unconsciousness. In other words, the child commits itself to both primal alienation and primal repression. In short, the child commits itself to dualism.

2 | Ego Formation and the Origins of Dualism in Early Childhood

The emergence of psychoanalytic object relations theory, with its focus on the preoedipal period of development, has markedly changed our understanding of the development of psychic structure. Freud paid scant attention to the preoedipal period, although, late in his career (1931), he did acknowledge that the preoedipal period loomed as a sort of undiscovered Minoan-Mycenaean civilization behind the civilization of classical Greece. Psychoanalysts focusing on object relations—from Melanie Klein and W. R. D. Fairbairn to Margaret Mahler and Otto Kernberg—have explored this previously unknown territory and have discovered the crucial role it plays in the formation of psychic structure and therefore in the genesis of "normalcy" and psychopathology, especially such serious psychopathologies as the narcissistic and borderline disorders and the psychoses.

The findings of the object relations theorists are of special importance to transpersonal theory because, as I shall try to explain in this chapter, the preoedipal period plays a paradoxical double role in relation to transegoic possibilities. The preoedipal period at once (1) significantly prefigures transegoic possibilities and (2) culminates in an organization of the psyche that obstructs these very possibilities. The radical openness and spontaneity of the preoedipal child significantly prefigure transegoic possibilities. On the other hand, the manner in which the child resolves the serious countertendencies of the preoedipal period results in a dualistic division of the psyche that not only consolidates the ego but also closes it and, therefore, that forfeits openness and spontaneity. This dualistic (egoic versus nonegoic, self versus other) division emerges as a protective posture late in the second or early in the third year of life; it is gradually entrenched as a defensive stance during the third and fourth years of life; and it is consolidated as a psychic structure at the end of the oedipal period. The preoedipal period, then, both foretokens and forecloses on possibilities that are essential to transpersonal realization.

Although I shall in this chapter be drawing primarily on psychoanalytic object relations theory, I shall continue, in Jungian fashion, to speak of the child's primary object representation as the Great Mother. I shall do so to stress the fact that the Great Mother is a representation that, in emerging out of the child's interaction with the primary caregiver, draws significantly on inner nonegoic resources. The term *Great Mother* indicates that the child's original "object" is much more than an outer personal presence as experienced through the crude lens of infancy. It indicates that this "object" is a personal presence enlarged, empowered, and imaginally embellished by nonegoic potentials. Melanie Klein is virtually alone among psychoanalysts in having appreciated the role played by nonegoic potentials, and the autosymbolic process in particular, in the fashioning of the child's first object representation. Most of the credit goes to the Jungians for having made us aware of this important aspect of early childhood experience.

THE EARLY PREOEDIPAL PERIOD

In discussing early object relations, I shall follow Margaret Mahler's (Mahler, Pine, and Bergman 1975) account of the stages of preoedipal development, because her account has received wide acceptance in psychoanalytic circles.[1] In the ensuing pages, then, Mahler's framework will serve as the basic context of the discussion, and I shall formulate my own and other views, as relevant, in terms of her framework. Briefly, Mahler divides preoedipal development into the following phases and subphases.

Autism (birth to one month)
Symbiosis (one month to four or five months)
Separation-Individuation (four or five months to thirty-six
        plus months)
    Differentiation (four or five months to eight months)
    Practicing (eight months to fifteen months)
    Rapprochement (fifteen months to twenty-four months;
        with a rapprochement crisis at eighteen months to
        twenty-four months)
    Transition to object constancy (twenty-four months to
        thirty-six plus months)

Mahler believes that the first month of life is lived in a completely undivided and self-encapsulated state, which she calls *normal
autism*. The newborn, she holds, is in a sleeplike state that is ante-
cedent to all differentiation and responsiveness to external influences. In this state, Mahler says:

> There is a relative absence of cathexis of external (especially
> distance-perceptual) stimuli. This is the period when the stim-
> ulus barrier . . . , the infant's inborn unresponsiveness to out-
> side stimuli, is clearest. The infant spends most of his day in a
> half-sleeping, half-waking state: he wakes principally when
> hunger or other need tensions. . . cause him to cry, and sinks
> or falls into sleep again when he is satisfied, that is, relieved of
> surplus tensions. (Mahler, Pine, and Bergman 1975, p. 41)

Mahler's notion of normal autism is fashioned after Freud's notion of
primary narcissism. According to both, as Mahler acknowledges, the
newborn is like a chick still in the egg, undifferentiatedly immersed
in an inner reservoir and completely unaware of the external world.

The view that the newborn is completely undifferentiated and
closed to the world is by no means generally accepted. In the last
chapter I noted that authorities disagree on whether the newborn is
in an absolutely undivided state or in a state in which ego or self-
differentiation is already present to some degree. Also, I cited a few
of the many recent studies that indicate that the newborn is capable
of significant discriminations of and responses to external stimuli.
The infant, therefore, may never be completely egoless, and it is
probably never completely autistic. Nevertheless, following the relative perspective introduced in the last chapter, we can at least say
that the newborn is only minimally differentiated and object related.
To adopt this relative perspective is in effect to combine Mahler's first

two phases. It is in effect to speak of the first four or five months of life as the period during which the ego begins initially to take form and to respond to the external world, with which, in the person of the primary caregiver, the nascent ego is symbiotically linked.

Symbiosis, according to Mahler, is prior to differentiation proper, because, in the symbiotic relationship, the infant has not yet begun to differentiate itself from the object, the primary caregiver. If, however, the infant has not yet begun to differentiate itself *from* the object, it has at least begun to differentiate itself *as* the object. Symbiosis is a primitive form of duality that the symbiotic infant experiences as a unity, a unity that is the symbiotic infant's precursory self. As Mahler says, "From the second month on, dim awareness of the need-satisfying object marks the beginning of the phase of normal symbiosis, in which the infant behaves as though he and his mother were an omnipotent system—a dual unity within one common boundary" (Mahler, Pine, and Bergman 1975, p. 44).

In Mahler's view, the symbiotic infant has no awareness of itself as a being that is distinct from the primary caregiver. The symbiotic phase therefore is still predifferentiated. The symbiotic infant, however, Mahler stresses, has achieved a vaguely articulated awareness of an infant-caregiver totality, a totality that is at once the symbiotic infant's world and self. To speak paradoxically, we can say that the symbiotic infant has differentiated a not yet differentiated self.

In our terms, the symbiotic infant-caregiver totality is the initial manifestation of the Great Mother. In this initial form, the infant has not yet differentiated itself from the Great Mother; the infant and the Great Mother are one, a dual unity. This original Great Mother is not yet a fully formed object but rather is a complex grouping of experiences deriving from both outer and inner, personal and depth-psychological, sources. Deriving from outer sources are the principal experiences that the infant has of the primary caregiver, for example, experiences of tactile and olfactory sorts involved in the feeding and holding of the infant and experiences of visual and auditory sorts (e.g., experiences of the caregiver's face, look, voice, intonations) associated with communicative interactions with the caregiver. And deriving from inner sources are experiences involving the full range of nonegoic potentials, especially as these potentials are responsive to the influences of the caregiver. Nonegoic potentials, as explained in the last chapter, are the original ingredients of the infant's consciousness. The infant is directly open to the free expression of these potentials, which respond spontaneously to the ministrations of the caregiver, amplifying and embellishing the caregiver in a variety of ways.

The original Great Mother, then, who is the symbiotic infant's world and self, is a set of experiences deriving from two independent but intimately interactive sources. The infant in the symbiotic phase of course has no awareness that this set of experiences draws upon both outer and inner sources. Nor does the infant yet associate this set of experiences with a being distinct from itself. The infant in the symbiotic phase has succeeded only in differentiating a system of experiences; it has not yet begun to differentiate itself from this system. The infant is aware of the Great Mother only as a coalescing group of experiences in which the infant participates and with which the infant is still fused.

Following the symbiotic phase, according to Mahler, at four or five months of age, the process of infant-caregiver differentiation begins. The beginning of differentiation is the beginning of the separation-individuation process, which is the major work of the preoedipal period of development. The separation-individuation process has four main subphases: differentiation (four or five months to eight months), practicing (eight months to fifteen months), rapprochement (fifteen months to twenty-four months), and the development of object constancy (twenty-four months to thirty-six plus months). I shall briefly describe the first two of these subphases in the remainder of this section; then in the next two sections I shall give more extended consideration to the rapprochement and object constancy subphases, which are by far the most important for our concerns.

Mahler describes the differentiation subphase as the hatching subphase, because it is the period during which the infant first begins to break out of the "shell" of symbiotic dual unity with the caregiver (or Great Mother). During this subphase, the infant increases its motor skills and begins actively to explore its own body and the body of the caregiver, especially the caregiver's face. Such explorations indicate that the infant no longer relates to the caregiver merely as a symbiotic extension of self and has begun to relate to the caregiver as an object for a (differentiating) self. Additionally, the differentiation subphase is the period during which the infant first adopts a transitional object (e.g., a blanket or stuffed animal) to which to devote its attention in the absence of the caregiver. The selection of a transitional object is evidence of initial differentiation because this object indicates that the infant has begun to realize that the caregiver is not just a dimension of the infant's own experience but rather is a being who can be absent as well as present and therefore other as well as self.

In terms of cognitive development, the differentiation subphase is the period during which the infant achieves an initial sense of object permanence. That is, the infant during this period begins, vaguely and inadequately, to sense that objects are entities that have an existence beyond the infant's experience of them.[2] This dawning realization is an achievement of great importance. It also, however, is an achievement that has a downside for the infant, because an understanding of object permanence, however inadequate, is at the same time a realization of object independence (the object is other, not self) and object absence. The infant's emerging awareness of object permanence is, then, at the same time an awakening to the fact that the primary caregiver is a being whose nurturing presence is intermittent and uncertain. Awakening in this way to the possibility of object loss, the infant in the differentiation subphase gains a special appreciation for the caregiver, which is reflected not only in the adoption of transitional objects but also, as Mahler reports, in a behavior of regularly checking on the caregiver's presence and in the beginnings of stranger anxiety.

In Mahler's account, the fear of possible object loss that arises in the differentiation subphase subsides at approximately eight months, which is the beginning of the practicing subphase of the separation-individuation process (eight months to fifteen months). For by eight months the infant has grown more accustomed to and less fearful of the caregiver's occasional absences and has shifted its primary interest from the caregiver to the world. Accordingly, the infant in the practicing subphase begins to relate to the caregiver less as a being who must be clung to and more as a safe home base from which to go out and explore the world. The practicing subphase is ushered in by the infant's earliest abilities to move away from the caregiver. These early abilities, prior to walking, typically overlap with the differentiation subphase. For this reason Mahler divides the practicing subphase into early practicing (prior to walking) and practicing proper (after walking).

The most characteristic aspects of the practicing subphase are a sense of grandiosity and omnipotence on the part of the child as an agent-explorer of the world and a need to return to home base to "refuel" in the comforting embrace of the primary caregiver. The practicing child, oblivious to danger and protectively watched over by the caregiver, ventures into the world with reckless abandon. Should the child fall or stub its toe, it takes immediate refuge in the healing attentions of the primary caregiver. The caregiver invisibly oversees the child's actions and is immediately accessible in case of need. This support allows the child to act in the world with a sense of omnipotence that is as bold as it is naive.

The child's actions during the practicing subphase are the means by which the child develops such basic ego functions as motor coordination and reality testing. The child masters bodily movement (e.g., crawling and walking) and, employing these skills of movement, begins seriously to test reality by exploring the terrain, contents, and possibilities of the world. The child takes a special delight in performing certain actions in a repetitive manner, because these actions give pleasure not only in their process or outcome but also in the sense of skill mastery that goes with them. In the practicing subphase of the separation-individuation process, the child is excited by the world and pleased with itself; moreover, it enjoys the primary caregiver as a support system that can be taken completely for granted. The practicing child has a sense of omnipotence and is immensely self-satisfied. As Mahler says, "The child seems intoxicated with his own faculties and with the greatness of his own world. Narcissism is at its peak!" (Mahler, Pine, and Bergman 1975, p. 71).

The differentiation and practicing subphases of the separation-individuation process are periods during which the child makes dramatic progress in cognition and action. Despite this progress, however, the child at the end of the practicing subphase remains significantly merged with and dependent upon the primary caregiver. The child's differentiation from the caregiver is far from complete. The caregiver is still a selfobject inherently tied to the child's experience, as is reflected in the child's omnipotent-narcissistic sense of self. Also, although the child has come to recognize that the caregiver is a being who has some sort of existence beyond the boundaries of the child's experience, the child still perceives the caregiver as the bearer of (nonegoic) potentials that derive from within the child's experience. In other words, the child continues to perceive the caregiver as the Great Mother, a being who is at once personal and nonegoic, external and internal, less than and more than a human being.

Finally, although the child has begun to assert its independence, its efforts in this direction remain utterly dependent upon the caregiver. For the child in the practicing subphase is able to take leave of the caregiver and make bold forays into the world only because the child completely takes the caregiver for granted as both overseer and refuge. The child's independent actions are not, then, actions the child undertakes to free itself from dependence upon the caregiver. These actions presuppose rather than struggle against such dependence. The toddler in the practicing subphase is able fearlessly to venture away from the caregiver only because the caregiver constantly watches out for the toddler as the toddler's external or auxiliary ego. The toddler's presumption of the caregiver's support is of course completely unconscious. From the toddler's perspective, the caregiver's actions are an extension of the toddler's own self. In the practicing subphase, therefore, the child experiences the world as a place in which to act with reckless abandon, as a virtually omnipotent being.

Rapprochement, Ambivalence, and the Splitting of the Great Mother

The toddler's naive self-confidence lasts up to about the age of fifteen months, at which time the toddler begins to awaken to its vulnerability and need of the primary caregiver. This awakening occurs as a result of at least two factors: (1) the toddler's experiences as an agent acting on its own in the world and, as I shall discuss later, (2) an advance in cognition that increases the toddler's understanding of the caregiver's independence and therefore the toddler's own dependence. As the toddler gradually learns that it is not omnipotent and is in fact extremely vulnerable, it begins to reexperience a need for the caregiver, and it therefore initiates attempts to reestablish the sense of closeness with the caregiver that, so important during the differentiation subphase, had been forgotten during the practicing subphase. This felt need to reestablish closeness with the caregiver marks the commencement of the rapprochement subphase of the separation-individuation process.

Signs of the beginning of the rapprochement subphase are a reappearance of stranger anxiety and the need regularly to check on the caregiver's presence. The caregiver at this point ceases being just a safe home base and "refueling" station and becomes, again, the child's principle security object, to which the child begins, again, to cling. The child's sense of need for the caregiver is now more acute than it was during the differentiation subphase, and therefore the child's apprehensiveness about the caregiver's possible absence takes on the more serious form of abandonment anxiety. The rapprochement child no longer takes the caregiver for granted and is fearful of losing the caregiver's attentions. Accordingly, as Mahler explains, the child tests the caregiver's availability by playing "shadowing" and "darting-away" games that force the caregiver at least to watch the child if not chase after the child and pick it up. In general, the rapprochement toddler, unlike the practicing toddler, feels vulnerable and needy, and consequently the rapprochement toddler hangs on the caregiver and tries in every possible way to command the caregiver's undivided loving attention.

The toddler's desire for rapprochement soon runs into conflict with the developmental drive toward independence. It is not long, typically by about the eighteenth month, before the child's growing perceived need of the caregiver becomes a serious counterforce to the child's continuing movement toward independence. At this point, the beginning of what Mahler calls the *rapprochement crisis*, the child begins to suffer acute ambivalence, wanting at one and the same time intimacy with and independence from, closeness to and distance from, the caregiver. The child therefore both wants and does not want the caregiver; it both wants and does not want independence. The child strikes out in the direction of independence only to feel insecure and in need of the caregiver, and it retreats to the caregiver only to feel engulfed and therefore in need of asserting its independence from the caregiver. The rapprochement subphase thus eventuates in a crisis. It leads to strongly contradictory feelings on the part of the child, who expresses these feelings through an approach-avoidance interaction with the caregiver and an advance-retreat syndrome in relation to independence.

The rapprochement crisis, which lasts from about eighteen to twenty-four months, is an extremely difficult period for both the child and the caregiver. The child is pulled in opposite directions, and it consequently gives conflicting messages to the caregiver. In asserting its independence, the child willfully distances itself from the caregiver and at the same time keeps an eye on the caregiver to make sure the caregiver is watching and approving of its deeds. And in returning to the caregiver, the child demands the caregiver's attentions and at the same time refuses the caregiver's loving responses. The child both clings and says no; it cries both to be picked up and, in being picked up, to be let go; it both makes demands upon the caregiver and disobeys the requests the caregiver makes of it. The child finds itself in a double bind, and it places the caregiver in a double bind as well.

The serious ambivalence of the child during the rapprochement crisis causes the child to split its primary object representation and its self-representation into all-good and all-bad representations. The caregiver with whom the child seeks rapprochement is seen as a being who is all good: nurturing, loving, protective. And corresponding to this all-good object representation is an all-good self-representation: the child sees itself as a helpless innocent wholly deserving of the caregiver's vigilant love. On the other hand, the caregiver with whom the child has come into conflict is seen as a being who is all bad: absent, engulfing, angry, punishing. And corresponding to this all-bad object representation is an all-bad self-representation: the child sees itself as a being who is imperious and contrary and wholly deserving of the caregiver's abandonment or punishment. The splitting of these representations means that they are kept separate from each other, as if the caregiver and the child were each two independent, good and bad, beings. This complete disconnection of good and bad is vital. For the child, in sensing its smallness and vulnerability, needs to believe that there is an unfailing, all-good being looking out for it and that it is worthy of this being's love and devotion. Splitting of the primary object representation and the self-representation, that is, is a necessary defense mechanism for the rapprochement child. According to Mahler, and according to object relations theory generally, overcoming this splitting and achieving integrated (i.e., realistic, both-good-and-bad, stable) representations of both the primary object and the self is the chief challenge of the preoedipal period of development.

Stressing the outer-inner, personal-nonegoic, two-sidedness of the child's primary object, I prefer, in Jungian fashion, to describe the splitting that occurs during the rapprochement crisis as a splitting of the Great Mother into a Good Mother and a Terrible Mother. The Good Mother and the Terrible Mother, like the Great Mother from which they are cleaved, are beings magically empowered, mythically elaborated, and otherwise augmented by nonegoic potentials deriving from within the child. They are the primary caregiver as transformed—either transfigured (the Good Mother) or transmogrified (the Terrible Mother)—by the projection and intermingling of nonegoic potentials. The splitting of the Great Mother therefore cuts in two directions; it is a splitting not only of experiences deriving (outside-in) from the caregiver but also of experiences deriving (inside-out) from the nonegoic core of the child's psyche. Accordingly, the Good Mother, as a positive transformation of the Great Mother, is an experiential complex including not only such outwardly derived elements as loving gazes, assuaging vocalizations, protective embraces, and nurturing ministrations but also such inwardly derived elements as soothing and ecstatic bodily sensations, enlivening upwellings and rapturous emanations of energy, contented and blissful feelings, and friendly and beautiful images. And the Terrible

Mother, in contrast, as a negative transformation of the Great Mother, is an experiential complex including not only such outwardly derived elements as angry expressions, sharp intonations, confining embraces, and hostile and cold responses but also such inwardly derived elements as agitated and constricting bodily sensations, abyssal implosions and violent eruptions of energy, terrifying and dreadful feelings, and sinister and ugly images. Just as the Great Mother draws on both outer and inner sources, so, too, do the Good Mother and the Terrible Mother.[3]

The split Great Mother thus has four dimensions: good, bad, outer, and inner. Two of these dimensions are distinguished from each other in the child's experience and two are not. The good and bad dimensions are distinguished from each other; indeed, splitting not only distinguishes these dimensions but makes them appear as two independent and opposing realities. The outer and inner dimensions, on the other hand, remain undifferentiated in the child's mind. The Good Mother is a complex but undifferentiated whole of both outer and inner "good" elements, and the Terrible Mother is a complex but undifferentiated whole of both outer and inner "bad" elements. The separation of the outer and inner dimensions of the Great Mother is not accomplished until the splitting of the good and bad dimensions is overcome. In fact, as I shall argue in the next section, the separation of the outer and inner dimensions is precisely the means by which the splitting of the good and bad dimensions is overcome. Rapprochement splitting, I shall argue, is "resolved" by means of a repressive withdrawal of nonegoic potentials from the caregiver, who, in being decathected and divested of nonegoic projections, ceases being the larger-than-life split Great Mother and becomes a "mere" but stably unified human being, that is, a person with whom stable object relations have been established (object constancy).

THE REPRESSIVE UNDERPINNINGS OF OBJECT CONSTANCY

The central question for object relations theory in relation to preoedipal development is how the child overcomes the ambivalence and splitting that characterize the rapprochement crisis. Does the child yield to the need for intimacy with the caregiver, thereby sacrificing growth and independence? Or does the child pursue growth and assert independence, thereby sacrificing intimacy with the caregiver? According to the standard view, these alternatives constitute a false dilemma because neither alternative is acceptable and both can be avoided. In the standard view, both of the alternatives just mentioned require sacrifices that are too large. In the former case the sacrifice is too large for the quite evident reason that it implies that development comes to a halt, indeed that the child regresses to earlier, more symbiotic levels of development. And in the latter case the sacrifice is too large—or so, at least, it is thought—because it implies a break in the child-caregiver relationship that is greater than is readily discernible to observation or than can easily be explained in theory.

Avoiding both of these alternatives, the child, according to the standard view, begins in the third year of life to develop *object constancy*. Object constancy is to be distinguished from object permanence. These two are similar in that both involve an integration of separate appearances or aspects of an object into an understanding of the object as an integral whole. The Piagetian notion of object permanence is a more purely cognitive notion indicating integration of temporally disconnected appearances of an object into a sense of a single enduring object that exists whether or not it is being perceived. The psychoanalytic notion of object constancy, in contrast, is a notion that connotes both cognitive and affective integration. Object constancy is the integration of an emotionally split object into a single whole object that is recognized as having contrary, good and bad, aspects or sides. Object constancy is a *re*integration of an object that has been emotionally cleaved.

Object constancy (and splitting too, which object constancy overcomes) presupposes some level of understanding of object permanence. It does so for two reasons. First, some level of understanding of object permanence is necessary just for there to exist, in the mind of the infant, the kind of object that can be split and then reintegrated after the fashion of object constancy. Prior to object permanence, objects have no histories, or at least no continuous histories, because, in the mind of the infant, they cease to exist whenever they are not perceived. For the child in the first few months of life, "out of sight is out of mind." Accordingly, unaware that objects have continuous histories, the child of this age is unable to sustain continuous, developing feelings for objects, including ambivalent feelings that might lead to splitting and, eventually, object constancy. Prior to an understanding of object permanence, then, although the infant may well separate many positive and negative *experiences* from each other, the infant probably does not split any *objects* (including the primary libidinal object, the caregiver) along positive and negative lines.

The second reason why object constancy presupposes object permanence is that some level of understanding of object permanence is a precondition of the feeling that is the primary cause of early childhood ambivalence and therefore splitting: fear of object loss, anxiety of losing the primary caregiver. Without some understanding that objects continue to exist when not perceived, a child can have no sense that objects, in exiting from view, are departing to locations beyond the range of perception and may therefore become inaccessible or lost. Conversely, in coming to realize that objects *do* continue to exist when not perceived, a child begins to discern that objects, and the primary caregiver in particular, can exit from view in this sense of going "elsewhere" and may therefore be unavailable to the child. Understanding of object permanence, then, leads to awareness of object absence, which in turn triggers fear of possible object loss. And this fear of possible object loss is precisely the feeling behind early childhood ambivalence and splitting. For in fearing possible object loss, the child, without ceasing to strive for independence, begins to feel a need to retreat and cling to the caregiver. The child in this situation, then, is beset with contradictory feelings toward the caregiver, feelings that, as we have seen, can, if sufficiently strong, precipitate a splitting of experience into all-good and all-bad spheres.

I have already noted that, according to recent studies, the first major step toward understanding object permanence occurs at about four or five months, approximately at the beginning of the differentiation subphase of the separation-individuation process. At approximately four or five months, the child begins both to differentiate itself from the caregiver and, correspondingly, to see that the caregiver is an independent being, a being who can exist beyond the child's experience. This first understanding of the caregiver's independence causes fear of object loss, which is evident in stranger anxiety and the appearance of transitional objects. The fear of object loss and consequent ambivalence that emerge at this point are probably not strong enough to cause significant splitting in the child's experience of the caregiver. In any case the differentiation subphase soon gives way to the practicing subphase, during which separation anxiety disappears and the caregiver is again completely taken for granted, this time as a being who, although frequently out of sight, is nonetheless always accessible as a "home base" to which the child can retreat in order to "refuel." During the practicing subphase, it seems, the child's understanding of the caregiver as an independent entity ceases posing a serious threat to the child. For, apparently, the practicing child has learned—or at least has come to assume—that the caregiver's absences are always only temporary and never completely separate the child from the caregiver. The practicing child, that is, has come to assume that the caregiver, although frequently absent from view, is always close by and available to the child when the child is in need.

This confidence of the practicing child may be based not only on learning (the caregiver does almost always return) but also on cognitive limitations. For the practicing child still conceives of the caregiver (along with objects generally) as a being who remains connected with the child's field of experience even when not being perceived. Studies by Piaget and others (see Bower 1982) show that, prior to about sixteen to eighteen months, children assume that objects absent from view exist at specific proximate locations, either at locations where they are usually found or at locations where they were last seen. Between approximately six and ten to twelve months of age, children will look for an object at the location where the object has been found on repeated occasions in the past. Children tie the object to this location so strongly that they will look for the object there even when they have just seen the object being hidden in another place. By about ten to twelve months children cease making this particular placement error but continue nonetheless to assume that objects are bound to specific locations in space. This assumption is evident in children between ten or twelve and sixteen or eighteen months in a failure to understand invisible displacements of objects. For example, if a child in this age range sees an apple being placed under one of two cloths and then watches as the positions of the two cloths are transposed, the child will look for the apple under the cloth that has been shifted to the place where the apple was hidden. The child makes this mistake even though the cloth with the apple under it has a conspicuous lump in it, whereas the cloth that the child lifts is flat.

Prior to about sixteen to eighteen months, then, children assume that objects out of view, including most importantly the primary caregiver, remain close by and can be found at familiar locations within the child's field of experience. Children in the practicing subphase therefore believe that objects that are unperceived are still effectively present. They assume that objects exist where they have previously been found or were last seen. Although objects are understood to have an existence beyond the child's immediate experience, the location of this existence, it is assumed, is still tied to the child's larger and accessible experience. Accordingly, objects, when absent from view, are assumed to be within reach. This assumption is what allows the practicing toddler to act with such heedless confidence. The toddler "knows" that the caregiver is never far beyond the periphery of awareness.

Sometime between sixteen and eighteen months—that is, around the beginning of the rapprochement subphase—this presumed knowledge begins to be undermined. For by this age, as Piaget (1954) demonstrated, children begin to understand that absent objects are not necessarily tied to specific locations in space. Accordingly, by this age, children begin to search for objects beyond the locations where the objects were last seen or were previously found. This untying of objects from specific locations is the last major step in the development of the object concept and is therefore an important advance in cognition. It is an advance, however, the immediate effects of which are decisively negative. For this lifting of spatial restrictions from the object concept transforms the child's world from a safely circumscribed field into a vast and unknown realm, a realm in which objects can be "anywhere," remote as well as proximate, inaccessible as well as accessible. The awakening to this new and larger world is a terrifying experience for the rapprochement child, much more terrifying than was the initial awakening to object permanence and object absence that occurred during the differentiation subphase of the separation-individuation process. For this awakening ushers in an awareness that the primary caregiver, when exiting from view, might be exiting altogether from the child's known universe. For this reason the child during the rapprochement subphase begins to suffer from *abandonment* anxiety, from a fear that the primary caregiver might leave the child's range of vision and *never be seen again*.

This experience of abandonment anxiety—the fear of being alone in a world that has suddenly grown large and unfamiliar—is the primary cause of the ambivalence and splitting of the rapprochement crisis. In achieving an understanding of the full extent of the caregiver's independence as an object, the child at the same time is hit with a realization of the full extent of its own dependence. The child suddenly realizes that the caregiver could be anywhere in a vast and uncharted space and that there is no guarantee that the caregiver can be reached if the caregiver moves beyond the limits of the child's awareness. This realization is a rude insight that jolts the child into a recognition of how small and vulnerable it is and how desperately it needs the caregiver. In suffering this insight, the child becomes insecure and begins to cling to the caregiver—without, however, giving up its claim on and continuing drive toward independence. Accordingly, the child begins to experience the strongly ambivalent feelings toward the caregiver that, as we saw earlier, are characteristic of the rapprochement crisis. The child begins to experience the caregiver as both a supportive presence and a terrifying absence, as both a safety object to which to cling and a domineering-engulfing being against which to assert independence. These ambivalent feelings are so strong that they split the child's representation of the caregiver (or, rather, of the Great Mother) and the child's representation of itself in the ways described earlier. The last major step in the development of the object concept thus has a shattering effect upon the rapprochement child's world. It suddenly enlarges the child's world, sweeping the rug out from under the child's naive self-confidence, riddling the child with intensely contradictory feelings, and fissuring the child's world in a Manichaean fashion.

To repeat, the hypothesis of object constancy is attractive because it provides a way of avoiding an unwanted dilemma. It provides an explanation of how the child can surmount the splitting of the rapprochement crisis without suffering a radical loss of either intimacy or independence, relationship or individuation. Rather than sacrifice either of these vital goods, the child, it is thought, integrates its split part objects (viz., the good object and the bad object, the Good Mother and the Terrible Mother) into a single, neither wholly good nor wholly bad whole object. The child, that is, achieves a balanced and stable understanding of the caregiver as a being who is not omnipotent or perfect but who is nonetheless basically good. The child, in integrating the split all-good and all-bad representations, arrives at a less stormy and more secure relationship with the caregiver, who is now seen as an imperfect but fundamentally positive being.

This view seems straightforward, but it raises difficult questions, in particular questions about how it is possible for a child in the third year of life to accomplish a stabilizing integration of split objects. J. Alexis Burland acknowledges that the possibility of such integration is not yet theoretically understood.

> The healing of this [rapprochement] split is an essential accomplishment of the adequate resolution of the rapprochement subphase, and involves blending the split images into more or less homogenized images of mother and self, with positive and negative affects attached but of a less extreme, all-or-nothing sort.

> This is a developmental phenomenon clinically observable, but
> not yet adequately explained theoretically, perhaps due to
> shortcomings in theoretical conceptualizations at this time.
> (1980, p. 413)

Many questions concerning rapprochement splitting and the achievement of object constancy have not been adequately explained.
Among these, I shall consider three that I think pose the most serious
challenges to the standard account of how the child achieves object
constancy.

The first question is this: How can a child about two years of
age possibly make progress toward integrating its split objects when
(1) the ego at this age is so immature and (2) the split objects to be
integrated are so powerfully charged? Expecting a child in the third
year of life to integrate the Good Mother and the Terrible Mother into
a single stable object representation seems a bit like expecting a mere
mortal to integrate matter and antimatter into a single stable compound. The child-caregiver bond is the most intimate and intense
bond there is. How, therefore, can we expect a young child to achieve
object constancy in its relationship with the caregiver, or Great
Mother, when many emotionally stable and mature adults (not to
mention persons suffering from borderline and narcissistic disorders) are unable to overcome serious love-hate ambivalences and
consequent splittings in their intimate relationships and basic life
projects? The difficulty, then, is that the accepted view seems to imply that the child graduating from the rapprochement subphase
has greater maturity, ego strength, and powers of integration than
many adults.

The second question for the standard view of object constancy is
this: How can the child's split objects be integrated without causing
devastating insight and consequent psychological injury? Adults are
frequently devastated when they are forced to confront a dark or un-
savory side of a love object. Adult children, for example, are frequently devastated when they learn that their parents are not the
paragons of virtue the children had believed them to be. We can only
imagine how much greater the devastation would be for a child in the
third year who, well aware of its vulnerability, is forced to see that *the*
love object, the focus of unconditional trust and good will, the caregiver qua Good Mother, is in fact far from a perfect being. Without
denying that such an insight is possible, the question is whether a
child in the third year of life would be able to experience such an insight without suffering significant psychological injury. I suggest that

a child in the third year of life is not ready for such a disillusionment. Such a "dose of reality" may more likely lead to developmental arrest or regression than, as the standard view assumes, to psychological growth.

The third question for the standard view is this: Supposing that the child is able without psychic injury to integrate its split objects, what happens to the original positive and negative charges of these objects? Do these charges cancel each other out, leaving a resultant that is "constant" or stable only because it has been neutralized, voided of any strong attractive or repulsive power? This neutralization hypothesis, I believe, is not compatible with the standard view of object constancy, even though it has been endorsed by major representatives of the standard view.[4] The difficulty with the notion of neutralization in relation to the phenomenon of object constancy is that it implies the disappearance of strong positive and negative feelings for the primary caregiver, and therefore—because "a strong neutral feeling" smacks of contradiction—a marked *reduction* or *break* in the child's feelings for the primary caregiver. Such a marked reduction or break in feeling, however, is precisely one of the horns of the unacceptable dilemma discussed earlier. The problem with the neutralization hypothesis, then, is that it implies a serious weakening or severing of the child-caregiver bond rather than, as required by the standard view, a new and more mature version of that bond. In a moment I shall argue that the child *is* forced to make a decisive break with the caregiver and, therefore, that a radical decathexis and loss of intimacy cannot be avoided. For the present, however, the point is that a neutralization of the child's contradictory feelings for the caregiver does not seem consistent with the standard conception of object constancy as a strong but stable affective bond.

I believe that the questions just set forth are sufficient to cast doubt on the standard view of object constancy. In registering this judgment, I am not in any way questioning the *fact* that the child achieves object constancy in the sense of achieving a stabilized representation of and interaction with the caregiver. Rather, assuming that the child does achieve object constancy in this sense, my point is that the child does so in some way other than by unifying its split object representations and, thereby, its split affects. The only alternative possibilities, however, are the two dismissed earlier: the (regressive) sacrifice of independence and the (repressive) sacrifice of intimacy. These "unacceptable" possibilities turn out to be the only real options. One must be accepted, and the choice is clear: we must choose the second possibility, for only it is compatible with continued growth on the part of the child. This choice is not a happy one; nevertheless, it is, I think, unavoidable. The child overcomes splitting, then, I propose, not through a straightforward stabilizing integration of opposites, but rather through a repressive withdrawal from and decathexis of the primary caregiver.

Another way to make this point is to say that the child overcomes splitting by closing itself to the caregiver and thereby markedly abating its feelings for the caregiver. If the child were not so deeply and intensely involved with the caregiver, the child, in experiencing ambivalence, would not be prone to the defense mechanism of splitting. Accordingly, I suggest, the child overcomes splitting by withdrawing from involvement, by repressively containing its feelings for the caregiver. Just as we, as adults, frequently need to achieve distance from a person before we can interact with that person in a balanced and evenhanded manner, so the child, I suggest, needs to achieve distance from the caregiver to overcome splitting and be able to interact with the caregiver in a stable, object-constant, manner. The child, of course, cannot achieve this distance by literally removing itself from the caregiver. Instead, the child establishes distance by psychologically removing itself from the caregiver, by retreating inwardly and submerging its feelings, by decisively closing itself to symbiotic intimacy. In establishing distance in this way, the child decathects the caregiver and thereby "pulls the plug" on its strongly ambivalent feelings for the caregiver. Again, the child, I propose, submits to a repressive withdrawal from and decathexis of the caregiver. The child repressively disjoins itself from the caregiver and thereby defuses its powerfully contradictory feelings and overcomes splitting.

This proposal implies that the standard view of object constancy reverses cause and effect: it is not the integration of split object representations that overcomes unstable feelings for the primary caregiver; rather, it is the repressive withdrawal of feelings for the primary caregiver that allows the child to integrate split object representations. The child achieves stable object relations not by *fusing* split object representations but rather by repressively *defusing* the feelings that had led to the splitting. The severing of final symbiotic ties to the caregiver is, I suggest, an act by which the child achieves the composure it needs both to integrate its representations of the caregiver and to achieve stability in its (now much tamer and more manageable) feelings for the caregiver. The child does achieve object constancy in the sense of arriving at stable object relations with the primary caregiver. It does so, however, I suggest, not by forging a synthesis of powerful opposites but rather by repressively distancing itself from the caregiver and closing itself to the feelings it had experienced for the caregiver.

The hypothesis that the child overcomes splitting by repressively distancing itself from the primary caregiver, although at odds with the standard object relations view of how object constancy is achieved, is nonetheless completely in accord with another object relations view; namely, the view that repression replaces splitting as the primary defense mechanism once the rapprochement crisis is resolved and object constancy is achieved. This view is espoused by Otto Kernberg (1976, 1987) and accepted by Mahler (McDevitt and Mahler 1980) and others. Kernberg's principal reason for introducing this view is that repression, he believes, is a mechanism that consolidates the ego. Repression consolidates the ego, Kernberg holds, because it is an act by which the ego asserts itself, even if only in a negative manner, as a singular agency. Repression is an act by which the ego establishes unified boundaries, even if these boundaries are exclusionary, separating the ego from the nonegoic elements of the psyche—which are reorganized as the deep dynamic unconscious, the id. In short, repression consolidates the ego, Kernberg maintains, because it is an act by which the ego defines itself defensively as a self-contained sphere of consciousness. Paradoxically, repression consolidates the ego by creating a division between the ego and the id.

Kernberg makes the following statements in discussing the developmental function and psychic consequences of repression:

> *It is suggested that this consolidation of the ego establishes repression as the central defensive operation, in contrast to splitting of the earlier ego.* (1976, p. 41; emphasis in original)

> *Repression,* by contrast, is a central defensive mechanism of the ego at a later stage [than splitting] . . . . Repression consolidates and protects the core of the ego and contributes crucially to the delimitation of ego boundaries. (1976, p. 45; emphasis in original)

> It [i.e., primitive, split ego organization] further suggests that the quality of dynamic unconsciousness of the id may be closely related to the consolidation of the repressive barrier that reflects the integration of the ego at a certain stage of development. (1987, pp. 5–6)

These statements express Kernberg's view that the primary function of repression is to consolidate the ego and the primary consequence of repression is to separate the ego from the drives, which are reorganized as the unconscious id.

Kernberg, I believe, is correct in holding that repression replaces splitting as the rapprochement crisis is resolved and that the repression introduced at this juncture is, to use Freud's term, primal repression, the deepest defensive barrier separating the system of ego consciousness from the system of the deep dynamic unconscious, the id.[5] Kernberg, however, I suggest, does not offer the best explanation of the transition from splitting to repression. He argues that repression is possible only after and only as a consequence of the integration of split object representations. For example, he says:

> As stated before, the normal fusion of positive and negative introjections [i.e., object representations and self-representations] at the time when repression comes into existence implies a fusion and consequent modification of their affect components. Actually, it is suggested that neutralization takes place quite decisively at this point of combination of libidinal and aggressive drives. *The synthesis of identification systems neutralizes aggression and possibly provides the most important single energy source for the higher level of repressive mechanisms to come,* and, implicitly, for the development of secondary autonomy in general. (1976, pp. 45–46; emphasis in original)

In Kernberg's understanding, the unification of positive and negative split object representations and corresponding affects neutralizes drive energies and thereby frees energy for use by the ego. Empowered by such neutralized energy, the ego, Kernberg maintains, is able to consolidate itself by asserting itself repressively against the rest of the psyche.

Kernberg's account of repression, like the standard account of object constancy, gets the causality backwards: it is not by overcoming split object representations and, thereby, split feelings that repression is possible; it is rather by repression that the overcoming of splitting is possible. The fledgling ego, I have argued, is unable to integrate its split representations and feelings except by first radically diminishing its feelings. This reduction of affect is accomplished not by a neutralizing integration, but rather by repression. It is not, I believe, an alchemical fusion of opposites that frees energy for repression but rather repression that defuses conflicting feelings sufficiently to allow stable object relations.

Something like the position I am advancing is suggested in Melanie Klein's (1934, 1948, 1952a, 1964) notion of the depressive position—provided, that is, that Klein's dating is revised and brought into line with Mahler's.[6] According to Klein, the depressive position is a general orientation that emerges once the child begins to sense that the all-good object and the all-bad object are really aspects of a single, neither all-good nor all-bad object. Klein calls this position *depressive* because it is a state characterized by feelings of mourning and guilt over the loss of the all-good object. The child enjoys greater stability and sense of safety, but it also suffers a definite sense of loss. The child feels that its own greedy and aggressive fantasies have destroyed the original all-good object. The child, in suffering this sense of mourning and guilt, also suffers a quieting of affect generally: the predominant mood shifts from anxiety to sadness. Abandonment anxieties (focused on the all-good object) and persecution anxieties (focused on the all-bad object) are significantly muted as the primary feeling becomes one of "pining for the lost love object" (1940, p. 327). Positive and negative extremes disappear. The child no longer experiences a beatifically good good object and an enormously bad bad object. Rather than two larger-than-life split objects, the child now faces a single disempowered object, an object that, although primarily good, is by no means completely good. And corresponding to this change in the object is a marked diminution of feeling; intense intimacy is replaced by subdued distance. The object is reduced in size and power, I suggest, because the child repressively withdraws its feeling from the object.

To put this in more Jungian terms, we can say that the Great Mother, in both her Good Mother and Terrible Mother forms, disappears and is replaced by a "mere" human being, with whom the child has a much safer, but also a much more distant, relationship. As explained earlier, the preoedipal child's primary object is not just the caregiver, a human person, but the Great Mother, a confluence of outer and inner, personal and psychic, human and nonegoic elements. Accordingly, the act by which the child separates itself from the caregiver is also perforce an act by which the child separates itself from the inner nonegoic domain. Because the child makes no distinction between the outer and inner sides of the Great Mother, any act of the child aimed at the Great Mother is of necessity an act aimed simultaneously at both the caregiver and nonegoic potentials. In withdrawing from the caregiver, then, the child at the same time represses nonegoic potentials. The child not only distances itself from the caregiver but also submerges the feelings and other nonegoic potentials that previously were elicited by or projected upon the caregiver. As this happens, the caregiver is decathected and disempowered. The caregiver is divested of magical powers and images, both positive and negative, and therefore dramatically reduced in stature. The caregiver ceases being the split Great Mother and becomes a whole but "mere" object, an integrated but "mere" human person. In other words, the caregiver becomes, at last, simply the caregiver, a limited but basically good person with whom the child has a secure but much more circumscribed relationship.

The initial achievement of object constancy thus signals more than the achievement of stable object relations. It also signals the end of the child–Great Mother relationship, the end of both radical interpersonal intimacy and radical intrapsychic openness to nonegoic potentials. The initial achievement of object constancy signals that the child has resolved the rapprochement crisis less by means of a developmentally progressive integration of opposites than by means of an escape from the interpersonal-intrapsychic field on which the rapprochement crisis was played out.

In the following comment on Klein, N. Gregory Hamilton criticizes views, like the one I have presented, that see object constancy as involving not only developmental advance but also repression, alienation, and loss.

> Klein's . . . term for the coming together of the good and bad self- and object-worlds is the depressive position. Her phrasing . . . implies a loss of zest, which seems inaccurate. There is a kind of sadness that comes with integration of the good and bad self- and object-images. The grandiose self-images and omnipotent object-images do recede into the realm of fiction, mythology, and dreams. Salvation no longer beckons, but damnation no longer threatens. . . . Yet, the term depressive position implies too much helplessness and too much lack of progress for such an important and creative developmental step. (1988, pp. 110–111)

Note how Hamilton acknowledges that object constancy brings an end to the magical and mythical character of the earlier child-caregiver relationship. In our terms, he acknowledges that the caregiver ceases being the magical but split Great Mother and becomes a unified but merely human person. Nevertheless, like most object relations theorists, Hamilton sees only the developmental advance in this transition (viz., the overcoming of splitting, the achievement of stable object relations) and not the loss that makes possible the advance (viz., the loss of radical interpersonal intimacy and openness to nonegoic potentials). Hamilton, it seems, understands the disappearance of the magical and mythical character of early childhood experience only as a dispelling of illusions and therefore exclusively as a movement to clearer vision. He does not acknowledge that any significant nonillusory aspects of the child's experience are lost in the transition to object constancy.

The initial achievement of object constancy is a crucially important developmental advance. It is, however, an advance predicated on an act of defensive self-closing. This act is bidirectional: it is an interpersonal-intrapsychic act by which the ego closes itself at once to outreaching intimacy and upwelling spontaneity. The ego simultaneously retreats from the caregiver and repressively undergirds itself to protect itself from feelings, images, and energies that otherwise would be elicited by the caregiver. In this way the child overcomes the emotional intensities responsible for splitting and achieves an initial level of object constancy in relation to the caregiver. The caregiver now ceases appearing as two opposed archetypal-numinous powers and becomes a unified but finite and fallible human being, a being who is basically but not exclusively good. Concomitantly, the free play of nonegoic potentials comes to an end. Nonegoic potentials are submerged and rendered latent. The source of these potentials is sealed and becomes the deep unconscious, which in psychoanalysis is the id.

The withdrawal from the caregiver is the first and most basic form of (object-directed) alienation, which, in the last chapter, I termed *primal alienation*. The sealing and submerging of nonegoic potentials is the first and most basic form of repression, which, following Freud, I termed *primal repression*. Primal alienation and primal repression are not two different acts or structures; rather, they are the same act-structure in its outer and inner dimensions. Just as the Great Mother has both interpersonal and intrapsychic dimensions, so, too, does the ego's closing of itself to the Great Mother.

The Oedipus Complex and the Consolidation of Ego Dominance

The Oedipus complex can be fruitfully understood as the closing scene in the childhood rapprochement drama. The resolution of the Oedipus complex, I suggest, significantly reinforces the re-

sponses by which the child resolves the rapprochement crisis. It reinforces—indeed, solidifies into a permanent psychic structure—the
two-sided, interpersonal-intrapsychic, self-closing by which the child
achieves the initial level of object constancy.

Mahler is clear in stating that the resolution of the rapprochement crisis and corresponding development of object constancy are
long-term and open-ended processes. She describes the last subphase of the separation-individuation process as a period *on the way*
to object constancy, and she specifies the time boundaries of this subphase as twenty-four to thirty-six-*plus* months. The "on the way" expression and the "plus" indicate the open-endedness of the
movement toward object constancy. Moreover, Mahler (McDevitt and
Mahler 1980, p. 12) explicitly states that the development of object
constancy extends beyond the preoedipal period into later childhood
and even into adolescence and beyond. Leaving aside the more remote unfoldings, the development of object constancy can at least be
said to extend into the oedipal period, in which, I suggest, it plays a
major role in the Oedipus complex and its resolution.

Interpreting the Oedipus complex in terms of the child's rapprochement conflicts was indirectly suggested by Edith Jacobson a
long time ago and is suggested by Mahler herself as well. Mahler
traces the idea back to the following observations by Jacobson.

> Evidently, this new and advanced type of identifications
> [i.e., selective identifications replacing lines of symbiotic fusion
> with love objects] represents a compromise between the child's
> need to retain the symbiotic situation, to depend and lean on
> the need-gratifying, protective, and supportive love objects,
> and opposing tendencies to loosen the symbiotic ties by way of
> aggressive, narcissistic expansion and independent ego func-
> tioning. Under the influence of oedipal rivalry, this conflict will
> reach its first climax toward the end of the oedipal period and
> will then be resolved by superego formation. (1964, p. 50)

Commenting on this passage, Mahler states: "We are suggesting that
this same conflict reaches an earlier climax in the rapprochement subphase and is slowly resolved by the formation of psychic structure in
the id, ego, and superego precursors. The identifications used to resolve the rapprochement crisis are probably forerunners to those
used to resolve oedipal conflicts" (McDevitt and Mahler 1980, p. 24).

Pursuing this line of interpretation, I shall argue that a chief
function of the Oedipus complex is to force the child to make a sec-

ond and decisive response to the contradictions first experienced during the rapprochement crisis. Specifically, I shall argue that the Oedipus complex makes the child's initial response to these contradictions, repressive withdrawal from the caregiver, irreversible by forcing the child to choose between the mother and the father.

An important difference between the rapprochement and oedipal situations is that the former is dyadic whereas the latter is triangular.[7] Despite this difference in the number of principals, however, the rapprochement crisis and the Oedipus complex can be understood as variations on the same fundamental conflict. The rapprochement crisis is a conflict between a desire for intimacy and a desire for independence. Both of these desires are aimed at the same person, the primary caregiver, typically the mother. The Oedipus complex involves the same conflict between the same two desires with the chief difference being that the secondary caregiver, typically the father, now begins to play an important role in both of the child's two main desires and therefore in the conflict between them.[8]

Specifically, the father emerges both as a model of the independence the child desires and as a rival for the intimacy the child desires. To the child, the father is the exemplary model of independent life—especially in the traditional patriarchal household, where he is not only an independent subject in relation to the mother but also, in important respects, a sovereign master. Accordingly, the child senses that if it can win the father's acceptance it can enter the father's world and thereby share in the father's independence and extricate itself from dependence upon the mother. The father emerges as a symbol and facilitator of the child's growth toward independence. The child therefore seeks to come under the father's wings to free itself from what it senses to be the mother's engulfing-regressive influence. In the oedipal period, then, the child's desire for freedom from the mother acquires a positive focus. It is no longer merely a negative desire exerting itself *against* the mother but also a positive desire leading *to* the father.

The father, however, emerges not only as a figure representing independence but also as someone who competes with the child for the mother's affections. In the conventional household the father is both a self-possessed being and a person who enjoys an intimate relationship with the mother. For this reason the child, in the oedipal period, begins to see the father not only in a positive light, as a model of independence, but also in a negative light, as a dangerous foe. Responding to these conflicting perceptions, the child becomes as ambivalent in its relationship with the father as it is in its relationship with the mother. The child, still suffering from rapprochement ambivalence toward the mother, now begins to suffer from an equal but opposite oedipal ambivalence toward the father. The child is both attracted to and threatened by the father. The child seeks both acceptance from the father as model of independence and safe distance from the father as rival for intimacy with the mother. The dilemma of the rapprochement period is thus projected onto a second person.[9]

The resolution of the Oedipus complex reinforces the resolution of the rapprochement crisis. The route to object constancy once again, I believe, requires a commitment to independence at the cost of intimacy with the mother. The oedipal father seals this decision. He does so because, as model, he provides an added incentive for independence and, as rival, he provides an added disincentive for intimacy with the mother. As a model, the oedipal father provides a positive example of independence to reinforce the child's struggle against dependence. And as a rival, the oedipal father provides a fear of punishment, perhaps even of death, to reinforce the child's struggle against engulfment and regression. The child is already on the way to choosing (growth-promoting, even if repressive) independence over (regressive) intimacy even before the Oedipus complex begins. The confrontation with the oedipal father forces the issue and makes the choice final.

The confrontation with the oedipal father changes the child's choice from a choice for or against the mother to a choice for the mother or for the father. The father wins. The child both rejects and relinquishes the mother, both aspires and accedes to the father. The child rejects the mother by closing itself to the regressive lure of intimacy with her, and the child relinquishes the mother by surrendering rights of intimacy with the mother to the father alone. The child aspires to the father by seeking his acceptance as a model of independence, and the child accedes to the father by capitulating to him as rival. All of the forces at work in the oedipal situation push toward a crucial turning point at which the child is required irreversibly to renounce remaining symbiotic ties to the mother and make a decisive commitment to the father.

The choice of the father over the mother is at the same time a choice in favor of everything the father represents and a choice against everything the mother represents. The mother, as we know, represents nonegoic potentials and the intimate relational experiences associated with them. The father, on the other hand, represents ego functions and the independence and self-initiative associated with them. Accordingly, the choice in favor of the father over the mother is at the same time a choice in favor of egoic self-activity over nonegoic spontaneity and interpersonal merger. The child at this juncture moves decisively in the direction of ego development and fortifies its defenses against nonegoic and interpersonal influences. Primal repression–primal alienation is now solidified as a psychic structure, barring the child from any further return to the preoedipal field.

Concomitant with the consolidation of primal repression and its division of the psyche into disconnected egoic and nonegoic, conscious and unconscious, spheres is the formation of the superego as a functioning intraegoic subsystem. The superego, as Edith Jacobson (1964) explained, consists of a complex array of elements that originate prior to the Oedipus complex but are welded together as a single system only with the resolution of the Oedipus complex. The superego in her view is therefore "heir to the Oedipus complex" not so much in content as in the integration of already existing precursors into a unified agency. Among the superego precursors that Jacobson identifies are (1) a primitive ego ideal of wholeness and perfection (originating, as Freud [1914] hypothesized, in early narcissistic-symbiotic omnipotence experiences), (2) moderated fragments of the earlier split good and bad self-representations (which now, rather than splitting the ego itself, are split off from the ego as praising and punishing superego voices and images), and (3) identifications with the innumerable parental injunctions, admonitions, and pieces of everyday advice to which the child has been exposed during its brief life.

These superego precursors are forged into an integral functioning system under the aegis of the oedipal father. The emulation of the father as model makes the father an exemplar of the narcissistic-perfectionistic strivings of the child's primitive ego ideal: the father's example is accepted by the child as obligatory norm.[10] And capitulation to the father as adversary confers upon the father the power-authority to dictate imperatives of behavior: the father's will is accepted by the child as law. The decisive commitment to the father is thus not only a commitment to egoic self-activity but also a commitment to paternally exemplified and prescribed egoic self-constraint, that is, to rule-governed discipline or self-control. The ego, then, in gaining independence from the mother and her intrapsychic correlate, the nonegoic core of the psyche, at the same time puts itself under the yoke of the father and his intrapsychic correlate, the superego.

Formed under the authority of the oedipal father, the superego is above all an intrapsychic representative of the male parent.[11] Accordingly, the superego judges all things associated with the oedipal father to be good and all things associated with the preoedipal mother to be bad or evil. In general, the superego judges ego functions, independence, self-activity, and self-control to be good, nonegoic potentials, intimate relationship, receptivity, and spontaneity to be bad. Nonegoic potentials are considered dangerous, subhuman, and irrational. They are not only repressed and rendered unconscious but also denigrated as lower forms of life: the forms of life constituting the bestial id. And intimate relationship, receptivity, and spontaneity are similarly devalued. They are seen primarily as the absence or loss of their counterpart egoic "virtues." Intimate relationship is seen as ego weakness, as the absence or loss of independence; receptivity is seen as passivity, as the absence or loss of self-activity; and spontaneity is seen as impulsiveness or instinctual drivenness, as the absence or loss of self-control. The superego, forged under the aegis of the oedipal father, is very much a simplistic Manichaean in its values. The "victorious" father and his domain are good; the "defeated" mother and her domain are bad or evil.

With the final severing of egoic and nonegoic spheres and the concomitant integration of the superego as a functioning system, the structural division of the psyche into id, ego, and superego is complete. The nonegoic potentials of the psyche are repressed and submerged; they are relegated to the deep unconscious and negatively interpreted as the id. The ego assumes a position at the center of consciousness and operates from that position as if it were situated at the center of the psyche as a whole. And the superego is installed within the egoic sphere as a control mechanism to ensure that the ego "stays the course" of egoic independence and does not fall prey to nonegoic-symbiotic "temptations." The psyche is in this way divided at once into two fundamentally opposed spheres and three hierarchically ordered tiers. The psyche is divided into the opposed spheres of ego consciousness on the one hand and the deep (nonegoic) unconscious on the other. And the psyche is divided into the three hierarchically ordered tiers of the id, which is submerged beneath the ego, the ego, which is situated at the center of consciousness, and the superego, which resides atop the ego.

The interpretation of the Oedipus complex and its structural consequences presented in this section is incomplete, because it does not bring gender differences into consideration. I have presented only a general discussion of how the Oedipus complex mirrors the rapprochement dilemma and how the consolidation of ego dominance establishes the tripartite psyche. The points made in this general discussion, I believe, apply to both genders. Both girls and boys,

I believe, experience the oedipal father in terms of their rapprochement ambivalence toward the mother and, in doing so, are forced to make a final, repressive choice in favor of the father (and independence and ego functions) and against the mother (and intimacy and nonegoic potentials). Also, both girls and boys, I believe, form a superego that is fundamentally a representative of the father and the father's domain. This said, however, it is imperative to add that girls and boys differ significantly in the ways in which, and the degrees to which, they separate themselves from the mother (and intimacy and nonegoic potentials) and commit themselves to the father (and independence and ego functions). I shall explore these differences in the next chapter. For present purposes, it has been sufficient to address the oedipal period in terms of its basic choices and general structural consequences.

CONCLUSION

The resolution of the Oedipus complex brings an end to the nonegoic spontaneity and symbiotic intimacy of early childhood and inaugurates a long period of *dualism*. This dualism is at once an intrapsychic (i.e., egoic-nonegoic) dualism and an interpersonal (i.e., self-other) dualism. The intrapsychic side of the dualism is based ultimately on primal repression, the interpersonal side on primal alienation. Primal repression and primal alienation, as I have stressed, are not two different structures but rather are two different (inner and outer) dimensions of the same structure. Correspondingly, dualism is not divided into separate intrapsychic and interpersonal forms; it is a single *bidirectional* division of the psyche.

Dualism commences at the end of the oedipal period and is signaled by the onset of latency. Dualism is then significantly challenged during adolescence by the many powerful drives and needs that emerge during the adolescent process: the awakening of sexuality, the struggle for independence from parents, the search for a new primary "love object," the existential quest for selfhood and identity. Following the turbulence of adolescence, dualism is reconsolidated and, in reorganized form, serves as the foundation for much of adult life. Dualism usually remains the basis of human experience and does not begin to yield to more integrated possibilities until later in life when, if ever, the structures supporting ego dominance begin to give way. Sometimes at midlife, sometimes later, a fundamental psychic reorganization commences: the ego is disempowered, primal repression and primal alienation begin to dissolve, nonegoic potentials and deep intimacy needs are reawakened, and the ego is drawn into a new (inner-outer) rapprochement process. This process, if it unfolds to its end, leads ultimately to a higher reunion of the ego with both nonegoic potentials and other human beings. It leads, that is, to postdualistic integration.

Intrapsychically, the stage of dualism is the period during which the egoic system is disjoined from the nonegoic depth potentials of the psyche. The ego undergirds its own domain in a way that repressively quiets nonegoic potentials. This undergirding is what, following Freud, I am calling primal repression. Primal repression serves at once as a (false) floor that supports the egoic system and a seal that contains and deactivates nonegoic potentials. Accordingly, with primal repression in place, mind is significantly disconnected from body, form from energy, will from instinct, thought from feeling, concept from image, and control from spontaneity. Primal repression, as a structure that separates egoic and nonegoic spheres, is a structure that divides us against ourselves across many dimensions. Ego functions are disconnected from nonegoic potentials, which are submerged and rendered dormant or unconscious. Primal repression, in disjoining the ego from nonegoic life, is a structure that brings an end to the spontaneous and polymorphously charged period of early childhood and inaugurates the more contained, controlled, and subdued period of latency.

Interpersonally, the stage of dualism is the period during which relations with primary others are stable but also, relatively speaking, shielded and distant. Object constancy, which is the object-relational correlate of latency, is possible, as we have seen, only because the relationship with the primary caregiver ceases being internal and symbiotic and becomes external, separated by psychic distance. The ego defines boundaries and erects defenses that guard it as an inner privatized subject. The child adopts a posture of shielded self-possession. This posture is primal alienation. The child alienates the primary caregiver, which means, literally, that the child renders the caregiver "other." In withdrawing from the caregiver in this way, the child a fortiori withdraws from people generally, who become generalized "others." Primal alienation thus relegates not only the caregiver but people generally to the far side of a self-other dualism. Other people are no longer completely accessible, nor is the child completely accessible to them. People in general become self-contained and remote from each other. For the most part they no

longer enter into the radically open, interfluent intimacy characteristic of early childhood.

The stage of dualism is thus a period during which, intrapsychically, we are girded against spontaneity and, interpersonally, we
are guarded against intimacy. To be sure, we, as adults, experience
spontaneity in our more creative expressions and intimacy in our romantic and familial relationships. During the dualistic stage, however, we never open ourselves completely; we never let go of all our
inner supports and outer defenses. Consequently, radical spontaneity and intimacy are beyond the boundaries of possible experience
during the dualistic stage. Such spontaneity and intimacy remain
only as traces of early childhood memory, traces that can afflict us
with a nostalgia for a forgotten past and a yearning for an unknown
future.

Dualism must be considered a definite developmental advance,
because it is a basic structure that protects the ego and ensures its
continued growth. The ego is extricated from conflicting desires and
overawing influences and therefore is allowed to develop itself and its
functions at an accelerated pace. If, however, dualism is a developmental advance, it is not an unqualified advance. For it is an advance
predicated on a serious loss: the sacrifice of radical openness, spontaneity, intimacy, ecstasy, and creativity. The transition from early
childhood to dualism must, then, be counted as a definite but only
net developmental advance. Dualistic psychic structures (primal repression, primal alienation, a stern superego), it seems, are unavoidable preconditions of continued ego development. Later in life, as we
shall see, dualistic structures become obstacles to ego transcendence.
Early in life, however, they serve as indispensable supports for ego
development.

3

Ego and Gender

In the last chapter I discussed early childhood development without consideration of gender differences. In this chapter I shall focus specifically on gender differences as they emerge during the preoedipal and oedipal periods. Consideration of gender differences during these periods is necessary because, as psychoanalytically oriented feminist theorists have argued, gender differences in early childhood are responsible for many of the gender differences, and gender inequities, of later life. As we shall see, the gender differences emerging in early childhood are related in complicated but important ways to the forms of dualism discussed in the last chapter. Moreover, as I shall argue in chapter 10, these gender differences are responsible, later in life, for significant differences in the way women and men experience ego transcendence and the journey to integration.

GENDER ASYMMETRIES IN PREOEDIPAL DEVELOPMENT AND CONSEQUENT GENDER DISPARITIES IN LATER LIFE

Basing her views on psychoanalytic object relations theory, Nancy Chodorow (1974, 1978, 1979) argues that the division of labor assigning responsibility for child care almost exclusively to women has effects that are significantly different for boys and girls. Given the gender identity existing between mothers and daughters, the mother-daughter relationship tends to be closer and to last longer than the mother-son relationship. Mothers identify more with their girl children, and, correspondingly, girls experience a longer and closer connection with the mother and come to identify with the kinds of capacities associated with her. In contrast to the mother-daughter relationship, the mother-son relationship involves more differentiation and opposition. Although mothers are of course intimately involved with their infant sons, they also are aware, according to Chodorow, that they are opposite in gender to their sons. Accordingly, Chodorow believes that mothers treat their sons differently from their daughters. In respect to gender, mothers treat their sons as "other." They insert gender-based difference into their relationships with their sons and, in doing so, help to propel their sons' movement away from the mother-child dyad. Sons, in turn, in becoming aware of their gender opposition to the mother, begin to disidentify and dissociate from her and the kinds of capacities she represents.

Chodorow's analysis of preoedipal gender differences can be summarized as follows:

1. Gender identity between mothers and daughters causes girls to separate from the mother later and less completely than boys do. Gender difference between mothers and sons causes boys to separate from the mother sooner and more completely than girls do.
2. For girls, differentiation from the mother is moderated by gender identity with the mother. For boys, differentiation from the mother is exaggerated by gender opposition to the mother. Girls individuate themselves while remaining associated with the mother; boys individuate themselves in part by dissociating themselves from the mother.
3. Girls, in remaining associated with the mother, continue to identify with the relational, affective-nurturing capacities that the mother represents. Boys, in contrast, in dissociating themselves from the mother, also dissociate themselves from these capacities.

Chodorow offers a straightforward and plausible hypothesis: Because, historically, the primary caregiver has been a woman, the separation-individuation process has been inhibited for girls and exaggerated for boys. According to this hypothesis, the separation-individuation process, for girls, has been bridled by gender identity with the mother and, for boys, has been overdriven by gender opposition to the mother. Because girls share the same gender with the primary caregiver, as mother, their movement toward independence from the caregiver, and from the qualities represented by the caregiver, is decelerated by an associative "pull" back toward the mother. Because boys, on the other hand, are opposed in gender to the caregiver, as mother, their movement toward independence from the caregiver, and from the qualities represented by the caregiver, is accelerated by a dissociative "push" away from the mother.

Chodorow's analysis of gender differences in preoedipal development has many implications. Among these, Chodorow and others applying Chodorow's perspective (Flax 1983, 1990) have stressed those implications that bear upon the negative bases of male selfhood and the conditions that perpetuate female mothering. For example, they have taken note of the following: (1) Men's sense of self is based at the deepest level on a stance of dissociation. (Preoedipal boys see themselves as "not female" before they begin defining themselves as "male.") Women, in contrast, have an original identity to which they always remain linked. (2) Men are prone to stress gender differences. (Gender difference is an original and integral part of boys' sense of self.) Women's sense of gender differences, in contrast, based on an original experience of gender identity, is more understated. (3) Men have rigid and exclusive ego boundaries. (Boys, in dissociating themselves from the mother, dissociate themselves from the relational and affective capacities of the mother.) Women, in contrast, have more open and inclusive ego boundaries and are more rooted in relationship and outreaching affect. (4) Male misogyny has roots in the earliest phases of development. (Boys' gender dissociation from the mother predisposes boys to denigrate women.) And (5) female mothering has roots in the earliest phases of development. (Girls' gender identity with the mother, and with the relational and affective capacities of the mother, is the source of a predisposition in females to provide nurture to the young.)

Dorothy Dinnerstein (1976) presents an analysis of preoedipal gender development that complements Chodorow's account. Dinnerstein, like Chodorow, bases her analysis on the fact that women, historically, have done the primary job of caring for children. And Dinnerstein, like Chodorow, argues that this fact, together with girls' gender identity with the mother and boys' gender opposition to the mother, results in significant gender disparities in later life. In sharing these views with Chodorow, Dinnerstein differs from Chodorow in using these views to explain a different set of adult gender dispar- ities. Whereas Chodorow focuses on the negative dimensions of male selfhood and women's predisposition to mother, Dinnerstein focuses on the systematic disadvantages and internal conflicts that women suffer in male-dominated society. Specifically, Dinnerstein's focus is on the double standard that afflicts adult gender relationships.

Dinnerstein, influenced heavily by Melanie Klein, stresses the powerful ambivalence that both girl and boy children experience to- ward the preoedipal mother, who is both a nurturing-loving presence and a terrifying-engulfing power. Given the magnitude of the mater- nal power, children, according to Dinnerstein, must eventually seek to distance themselves from the mother if they are to have lives and wills of their own. Children accomplish this separation by means of a repression that closes them to both the exuberance and fear, imme- diacy and insecurity, life and death, that were inherent aspects of preoedipal, maternally based, experience. If, however, both girl and boy children perpetrate this repression, boy children, given their gender opposition to the mother, do so more completely. Girl chil- dren, given their gender identity with the mother, always remain linked, however slightly and unconsciously, with the realm of pre- oedipal, maternal, experience. This link, Dinnerstein argues, works against women in a double way. It both haunts them with a sense of their own incompleteness and makes them symbols of, and therefore displacement objects for, the repressed ambivalent feelings that were originally aimed at the preoedipal mother.

The fact that women serve as symbols of the repressed preoe- dipal mother is, according to Dinnerstein, the crux of the double standard that pervades adult gender relationships. Women, although themselves alienated from the preoedipal mother, are nonetheless symbolic surrogates for the preoedipal mother. As such surrogates, women are seen—primarily by men but also, secondarily, by them- selves—as beings of flesh and feeling who are weak or lacking in rea- son, as providers of love and nurture who do not themselves need love or nurture, and as bearers of an awesome power that needs to be controlled, "tamed," "domesticated," that is, repressed. The pre- oedipal mother is a specter that haunts the patriarchal world, stirring infantile perceptions and feelings and provoking hostile, repressive, actions, almost all of which are aimed against women.[1]

Both Chodorow and Dinnerstein base their analyses on the fact that women are alone in the nursery. Accordingly, they maintain that the gender disparities that derive from preoedipal development as a consequence of this fact can in principle be eliminated by bringing men into the nursery as well, as equal nurturers with women. This position has met with criticism. Miriam Johnson (1988), for instance, has challenged it on the ground that the fathers who would be brought into the nursery would be products of the very patriarchal system that, theoretically, they would be helping to transform. That is, they would be caregivers who would be deficient in the nurturing and relational capacities that are essential to caregiving. Moreover, many critics have noted that social circumstances in addition to the division of labor in child care need to be addressed if deep-seated gender disparities are to be overcome. In registering these criticisms, no one is recommending that men stay away from the nursery. Almost everyone acknowledges that equally shared caregiving responsibilities would be a significant net good, for both the women and men providing the care and the children receiving it. There is, however, considerable (and, I believe, warranted) skepticism about whether such a change would be sufficient to eliminate the major forms of gender inequality that plague our society.

Also, I suggest, bringing men into the nursery is unlikey to alleviate some the deeper problems discussed by Dinnerstein, namely, the problems of preoedipal ambivalence, ensuing repression, and consequent "human malaise." Dinnerstein herself acknowledges that bringing men into the nursery should not be considered a panacea. Such a move would indeed have great benefits. It would bring about a more equitable division of gender responsibilities, and it would redistribute more fairly the long-term rewards and liabilities that derive from caring for preoedipal children. Bringing men into the nursery, however, is unlikely to solve the deeper problem of "human malaise."

In the last chapter I concluded that both boys and girls resolve the rapprochement crisis and then the Oedipus complex by choosing independence over intimacy, repression over spontaneity, and the father over the mother. Both boys and girls, I concluded, decide to commit themselves to the father as model of egoic independence rather than submit any longer to the radical instabilities that stem from the splitting of the Great Mother. If, however, both boys and girls choose independence over intimacy, repression over spontaneity, and the father over the mother, they do so, we can now say, in significantly different ways. The analyses presented by Chodorow and Dinnerstein reveal these differences: Boys make the choices indicated in a manner that is both exaggerated and infected with misogyny, because boys, in being opposite in gender to the mother, dissociate themselves from the mother and, later in life, denigrate women as symbolic surrogates of the mother. And girls make the choices indicated in a manner that is both qualified and beset with long-term negative consequences for themselves as women, because girls, in being the same gender as the mother, are unable to separate themselves completely from the mother and, later in life, must suffer the consequences of being adult representatives of the mother. Both boys and girls, I suggest, undergo a decisive shift sometime during the rapprochement and oedipal periods of development. This shift, however, is one that, owing to the gender asymmetries of early childhood, has a different character and different long-term consequences for boys and girls. It is a shift that, for boys, is more emphatic and negatively directed against women and that, for girls, is more ambivalent and conflictually weighted against themselves.

Gender Variations in the Oedipus Complex

Although, as I have argued, the Oedipus complex has the same general outcome for both boys and girls, there are important variations in the way this outcome is achieved by boys and girls. Although both boys and girls relate to the oedipal father as both a model of egoic independence and a rival for the mother's affections, they do so in ways that are significantly different owing to differences of gender. We have just seen that gender opposition to or gender identity with the mother is responsible for significant variations in the preoedipal separation-individuation process. Similarly, gender opposition to or gender identity with the father is responsible for significant variations in the Oedipus complex.

Because boys experience a gender identity with the father, the commitment to the father that resolves the Oedipus complex is at the same time a gender assimilation that admits boys directly to the father's domain. Because girls, on the other hand, experience a gender opposition to the father, the commitment to the father takes the form of an intergender partnership modeled after the mother's relationship with the father, a partnership based not only on commitment to the father but also on difference from him. For boys, then, independence from the mother results in direct and full membership in the world of fatherly independence. For girls, in contrast, independence from the mother results in an indirect membership in the father's world, a secondhand independence that, as we shall see, turns out to be a new form of dependence.

The boy's commitment to the father occurs in a well-known manner. As Freud explained long ago, the boy's oedipal rivalry with the father strikes a fear of dismemberment, of castration or perhaps death, in the boy. The boy deals with this fear by capitulating to the father and emulating him as model (defensive identification). The boy ceases challenging the father for favored status with the mother and submits to the father as to a power that is better joined than fought. The boy at once forgoes his love relationship with the mother and begins acting like the father. In doing this, the boy ceases being a "mother's boy" and becomes a "little man."

The girl's commitment to the father is less obvious and much more complicated. The girl's situation is similar to the boy's in that the girl, during the oedipal period, begins to experience the father as a rival for the mother's affections. The girl's situation is also similar to the boy's in that the girl capitulates in this rivalry and concedes rights of intimacy with the mother to the father alone. However, the girl's situation differs markedly from the boy's in that, in capitulating to the father, the girl cannot join the father's world in the same way the boy does. For whereas the boy joins the father's world by way of a direct gender emulation, the girl must follow an indirect route of opposite-gender affiliation. Whereas the boy joins forces with the father simply by acting like the father, the girl, constrained by gender opposition, can join forces with the father only by establishing a facsimile of an adult male-female relationship with the father. That is, the girl can enter the father's world only by entering into a relationship with the father that is similar to the relationship that the mother has with the father.[2] The mother is not only the girl's original "love object"; she is also an adult who is intimately associated with the father. The girl therefore believes that if she can be like her mother in the mother's relationship with the father, then she, too, can be admitted to the father's world.

The girl's way of making the commitment to the father has three primary ramifications. First, the girl's commitment is a commitment of identity *conceived as difference*. In becoming a partner of the father like the mother is a partner of the father, the girl cannot, like the boy, simply emulate and be accepted by the father as a (lesser) equal. The girl, in striving to be independent like the father, must accept a partnership with the father that is predicated on difference. Accordingly, the girl's emulation of the father is a striving for likeness that is conceived as unlikeness, indeed as opposition. Emulating the father in this indirect way can be compared to emulating a right-handed person while at the same time maintaining a posture of left-handedness. No matter how right-handed one might become by such emulation, one would maintain a stance of being less right-handed than the person being emulated, and indeed of being, by comparison, left-handed. Such an identity conceived as difference allows the girl to enter the father's world, but only as an outsider in this world. The girl *is* accepted, but only as someone who possesses a nature inherently different from that of the father and who therefore, irrespective of her actual accomplishments in the father's world, can never truly meet the standards of that world.

A second ramification of the girl's commitment to the father is that the girl is put in a position of permanent submission to the father and to his surrogates in later life. For the girl, in committing herself to a standard that by definition she can never meet, enters the father's world as a second-class citizen. The girl is not accepted, as is the boy, as a lesser but potential equal but rather as a person who will always remain unequal. The girl is accepted not only as an outsider but as an inferior. This aspect of the girl's situation is already evident in the mother's relationship with the father that the girl emulates. For the mother, in being a partner of the father, is typically a subordinate partner. In the standard oedipal-patriarchal configuration, the father is master of the household and the mother is second in command, chief assistant to the sovereign power. Accordingly, the girl, in seeking to be like the mother in the mother's relationship with the father, aims at a form of independence (from the preoedipal mother) that is in fact a new form of dependence (upon the oedipal father).

The boy, in contrast, in directly emulating the father and being accepted as a "little man," becomes heir to the full privileges of patriarchy. The boy's oedipal capitulation to the father makes the boy a gender ally rather than gender subordinate of the father. In committing himself to the father, then, the boy wins a genuine independence and becomes a (junior) member of the patriarchy. Whereas the girl wins an independence from the mother that is at the same time a dependence upon the father, the boy wins an independence that makes him a true potential peer of the father.

The third ramification of the girl's commitment to the father is that the girl commits herself to the father in a way that involves not only a submissive but also a *heterosexual* aspect. This is not to say that the girl undergoes a "change of object" in the sense meant by psychoanalytic theory, that is, in the sense of a change of *love* object (i.e., partner in intimacy or cosubjectivity). For although the girl relinquishes the mother as love object, conceding the mother to the father in this regard, the girl might not adopt the father as love object (with which, internally, to merge) so much as *role model* (to which, externally, to submit and conform). The girl's commitment to the father need not be based primarily on love of, much less sexual attraction to, the father; it might be based primarily on admiration of the father and a desire to be accepted by the father in the father's role as exemplar of independence. Nevertheless, however the "change of object" is to be interpreted, the girl's relationship with the father does assume at least a minimal heterosexual aspect in that it is an opposite-gender relationship patterned after a heterosexual model (viz., the mother-father relationship). The girl tries to relate to the father in the same manner the mother does. In this sense, the girl becomes a rival of the mother for the father's favor and imitates the mother's role in her relationship with the father—perhaps even to the extent, as psychoanalytic theory maintains, of wanting to have a baby with the father.[3]

If the girl's "change of object" from the mother to the father need not, from the girl's perspective, involve love of, much less sexual attraction to, the father, the matter is frequently quite different from the father's perspective. Miriam Johnson (1988) makes this point in convincing fashion. Contrary to Chodorow, she holds that it is less the preoedipal mother than the oedipal father who responds to children in a gender-differentiating way. The oedipal father, Johnson explains, responds very differently to boy and girl children. He relates to a son as a little man and accepts a son as such once the oedipal rivalry is finished. Once a son has capitulated to the father's authority, he is accepted by the father as a member of the male peer group fraternity. This father-son interaction is in sharp contrast to the father-daughter interaction. For the father does not treat the daughter as a potential member of *his* peer group; rather, the father treats the daughter in an opposite-gender, heterosexual, manner. If the daughter does not romanticize or sexualize the father-daughter relationship, the father frequently does. The daughter, Johnson explains, frequently becomes the father's "little princess"; she becomes "daddy's girl." The father characteristically relates to the daughter in terms of what he perceives as her femininity, frequently flirting with the daughter and behaving seductively in relation to her. Tragically, a significant number of fathers even engage in explicit sexual activity with their daughters. Whether explicitly or implicitly, however, many fathers definitely heterosexualize their relationship with their daughters. In doing this, fathers play a primary role in the process of conventional, patriarchal, gender differentiation.

GENDER DIFFERENCES AND SUPEREGO FORMATION

Many of the points that have just been made concerning differences in the ways boys and girls commit themselves to the father apply as well to differences in the ways boys and girls relate to the superego, which is the internal representative of the father. In the last chapter I discussed how superego precursors are integrated into a single intraegoic agency at the time of the resolution of the Oedipus complex. These precursors, which derive from preoedipal as well as oedipal, maternal as well as paternal, sources, are unified under the authority of the "victorious" oedipal father. Unified in this manner, the superego, as Freud (1923) stressed, is above all the internal voice of the father. Speaking in the father's voice, the superego is inherently biased in favor of everything the father represents and against everything the mother represents in the opposition between these two that, in the child's mind, occurs during the oedipal period. The superego, that is, affirms the values of the "victorious" oedipal father and rejects the values of the "defeated" preoedipal mother. Accordingly, the superego is an advocate of ego functions, independence, self-activity, and self-control and a harsh critic of nonegoic potentials, fusional and symbiotic experiences, receptive openness, and spontaneity. Given this strong gender bias, boys and girls quite understandably relate to the superego in significantly different ways.

Boys, given their gender identity with the father, relate to the superego much as they do to the father himself. They submit to the superego as to an authority that represents what the boy senses to be his own nature. Just as the boy, in capitulating to the oedipal father, at the same time strives to emulate the father, so, too, the boy, in submitting to the superego, at the same time strives to embody the ideals and norms the superego affirms. For the boy, to conform to the superego is to become like the father the superego represents; it is, for the boy, to become his own mature "masculine" self. Although the superego speaks in a voice that is not the boy's own voice, it nonetheless speaks in a voice that is similar to the boy's. The superego's voice is the same gender as the boy's. It is a voice, therefore, that affirms the boy *qua boy*.

Girls, given their gender opposition to the father, relate to the superego in a significantly different way. To be sure, girls, in committing themselves to the father and to the things he represents, at the same time submit to the superego as the internal representative of the father. Girls do not, as Freud so infamously speculated, have weaker superegos than boys. The difference, rather, is that girls experience a gender conflict in relation to the superego that boys do not. The superego, in being biased against the values associated with the preoedipal mother, is biased against values that, by simple fact of gender identity, are associated with females. The girl's gender identity with the mother entails a life-long association with these values. Hence, although girls, like boys, resolve the Oedipus complex by withdrawing from the mother and committing themselves to the father, part of their identity continues to be linked with the mother and the values she represents. This continuing link means that girls are bound to experience more conflict than boys in both the commitment to the father and the submission to his internal voice, the superego. For boys, the voice of the superego is closer to their own voice. For girls, in contrast, this voice has an opposite-gender and even hostile quality. In submitting to the superego, therefore, girls experience ambivalence. They not only feel that they are striving to meet worthy ideals; they also sense that, at some level, they are betraying themselves.

Submission to the superego is a condition of continued growth for both boys and girls. Both boys and girls submit to the superego as a way of asserting themselves, as a condition of freeing themselves from subordination to the Great Mother and thereby consolidating their independence and self-activity in the world. The superego, therefore, serves the cause of development, ego development in particular, for both boys and girls. It does this, however, with significantly different effects for boys and girls. For the boy, the superego motivates not only ego development but also gender development. The superego, for the boy, is like an internal coach or drill sergeant who pushes and disciplines the boy to transform him into a man. For the girl, in contrast, the superego motivates ego development but not gender development. Because the superego is biased against gendered qualities with which the girl is always to some degree identified, the superego does not operate entirely in the girl's interest. It operates in the interest of her ego, to be sure, but not in the interest of her whole self. For the girl, the superego not only pushes and disciplines the ego but also, on a deep level, inflicts further injury upon her original mother-identified nature.

Narrow versus Wide Gender Differences

Thus far I have argued that female preoedipal mothering in conjunction with traditional oedipal fathering is responsible for some important, enduring, and mostly regrettable gender differences. These gender differences, I shall now add, are, in an important sense, narrow rather than wide.

By a narrow difference I mean, in general, a difference that is less than, and that therefore is outweighed by, relevant corresponding similarities. And by a wide difference I mean, just the opposite, a difference that is greater than, and that therefore outweighs, relevant corresponding similarities. If things differ in a narrow sense, that means they are more similar than different with respect to a standard of comparison. If things differ in a wide sense, that means they are more different than similar with respect to a standard of comparison. To return to an example used earlier, two people who differ in degree of right-handedness differ in a narrow sense, whereas two people who differ in that one is right-handed and the other left-handed differ in a wide sense.

In saying that the gender differences arising from the preoedipal relationship with the mother and the oedipal relationship with the father are narrow rather than wide, I am assuming as the standard of comparison an axis one end of which represents the modes of experience associated with the preoedipal mother (viz., intimate relationship and the nonegoic potentials originally experienced in such relationship) and the other end of which represents the modes of functioning associated with the oedipal father (viz., independence and the ego functions requisite to independence). Because the direction of early childhood development is from the mother to the father, from original relationship to initial independence, and from nonegoic potentials to ego functions, I shall call the axis in question the NPR-EFI axis (NPR = nonegoic potentials and relationship; EFI = ego functions and independence). Now assuming the NPR-EFI axis as standard of comparison, the point I am proposing is that female preoedipal mothering and traditional oedipal fathering cause women and men to relate to the poles of the NPR-EFI axis in ways that are at once importantly different and yet predominantly similar.

Let me stress that this point is made only with respect to the NPR-EFI axis. The "narrow rather than wide" thesis I am proposing is not a thesis about gender differences generally. It is rather a thesis that is limited to the gender differences that arise out of the differing ways in which boys and girls resolve the contradictions of the preoedipal and oedipal periods by choosing the father over the mother, independence over intimacy, and ego functions over nonegoic potentials.

Figure 3.1 represents an example of the type of narrow difference that, I am suggesting, separates women and men on the NPR-EFI axis. In figure 3.1 the extreme EFI endpoint of the axis represents the most extreme possible state of ego function dominance and self-contained independence, and therefore also the most extreme possible state of repression of nonegoic potentials and alienation from

FIGURE 3.1
Women's and Men's Positions on the NPR-EFI Axis

other people. This extreme EFI state is a condition of maximal dualism. It is a limit state that, although approximated in some respects in extreme instances of narcissistic and schizoid disorders, is not itself a viable position, because some degree of openness to nonegoic potentials and some degree of intimate contact with other people are necessary for life in any meaningful sense. In contrast, the extreme NPR endpoint of the axis represents the most extreme possible state of undifferentiated immersion in nonegoic life and undifferentiated merger in intimate relationship, and therefore also the most extreme possible state of egolessness and lack of self-boundaries. Newborn infants may approximate this extreme NPR state as a normal condition. For people at other stages of development, however, such a state would indicate serious ego retardation, pathological regression, psychosis, or a radically altered (temporary) state of consciousness. The points on the NPR-EFI axis that represent nonpathological forms of experience are consequently points between but not including the endpoints, or the points near the endpoints, of the axis.

The points on the NPR-EFI axis lying within the nonpathological range represent a spectrum of states in which both ego functions and nonegoic potentials, both independence and intimate relationship, are in play to a significant degree. Near the midpoint of the NPR-EFI axis, ego functions and nonegoic potentials, independence and intimate relationship, can be said to be approximately equally in play; that is, neither side of these paired opposites is dominant over the other. Positions moving away from the midpoint of the NPR-EFI axis in the EFI direction are positions of increasing ego dominance at the sacrifice of nonegoic life and increasing independence at the sacrifice of relationship. Conversely, positions moving away from the midpoint of the axis in the NPR direction are positions of increasing nonegoic dominance at the sacrifice of ego functions and increasing relationship at the sacrifice of independence.

Before interpreting figure 3.1, five points need to be clarified:

1. *Figure 3.1 presupposes that the poles of the NPR-EFI axis are in antagonistic rather than complementary opposition.* Figure 3.1 presupposes

that the two poles of the NPR-EFI axis are mutually exclusive, that is, that they are poles of an antagonistic dualism rather than a complementary duality. This assumption reflects the developmental bases of the axis, namely, the child's choice of the father *over* the mother, independence *over* intimacy, ego functions *over* non-egoic potentials. Presupposing dualistic opposition in this way, the fact that the positions of both women and men are on the EFI side of the NPR-EFI axis reflects the early childhood "victory" of the oedipal father over the preoedipal mother. Were the position of either women or men at or near the midpoint of the NPR-EFI axis, that, dualistically understood, would indicate a condition of maximum *ambivalence* between the two poles of the axis, an ambivalence derived originally from the conflicting feelings felt by the child toward the preoedipal mother (NPR) and oedipal father (EFI). Although the NPR-EFI axis presented here presupposes dualistic opposition, it is possible to conceive an NPR-EFI axis that is not dualistic. Specifically, it is possible to conceive an NPR-EFI axis with poles that are complementary rather than antagonistic and with a midpoint that is a point of maximum integration rather than maximum ambivalence. Such a nondualistic NPR-EFI axis, however, I maintain, does not represent development during the first half of life, which, based on the oedipal challenge and resulting decisive choice of EFI over NPR, *is* dualistic in character. Such an axis would represent possible later stages of development, stages leading beyond the "mature dualism" of early adulthood toward postdualistic, transegoic, integration.

2. *Figure 3.1 represents only one example of narrow difference.* Figure 3.1 represents only one of many different possible examples of narrow difference. Unambiguous examples of narrow difference are all cases in which the lines representing women and men are on the same side of the NPR-EFI axis, whichever side that might be and no matter how close or distant from each other the lines might otherwise be. Any case in which both lines are on the EFI side of the NPR-EFI axis is a case of narrow difference because, in such cases, similarities outweigh differences by virtue of both genders being primarily committed to ego functions and independence. And any case in which both lines are on the NPR side of the axis is a case of narrow difference because, in such cases, similarities outweigh differences by virtue of both genders being primarily given to nonegoic potentials and relationship. In contrast, most cases in which the lines representing women and men are on opposite sides of the NPR-EFI axis are cases of wide difference because, in such cases, differences outweigh similarities by virtue of one gen-

der being primarily committed to ego functions and independence, whereas the other gender is primarily given to nonegoic potentials and relationship. However, not all cases in which gender lines fall on opposite sides of the axis are clear examples of wide difference. Some cases of this type are ambiguous, namely, those in which the lines representing women and men, although on opposite sides of the NPR-EFI axis, are situated near the midpoint of the axis. For these cases can be interpreted in two ways. They can be interpreted in the manner just stated, as indicating that one gender is more EFI than NPR, whereas the other is just the opposite; or they can be interpreted as indicating that, despite these opposing (slight) predominances, the two genders are more similar than different because, situated near the midpoint of the NPR-EFI axis, both genders are very nearly equal in the extent to which both EFI and NPR are in play. Fortunately, we can leave these latter cases uninterpreted, because, if I am right, they are exceptional cases and do not represent the actual situation of most women and men.

3. *Figure 3.1 represents differences between genders, not among individuals.* With the exception of the extreme endpoints, or points near the endpoints, individual women and men can be situated virtually anywhere on the NPR-EFI axis. The lines in figure 3.1 therefore represent women and men collectively rather than individually. Accordingly, nothing can be inferred from figure 3.1 about the behavior or dispositions of any individual person, female or male.

4. *Figure 3.1 represents points around which variations occur.* The fact that figure 3.1 assigns women and men a single point each on the NPR-EFI axis does not mean that women and men are locked into the positions indicated. The positions indicated in figure 3.1 should be understood as *set points*, that is, as stabilization or equilibrium points around which variations occur. Both genders can be more or less egoic or nonegoic, committed to independence or given to relationship, at different times and in different circumstances. For this reason the lines representing women and men must be understood as marking their primary or characteristic, not exclusive, positions on the NPR-EFI axis.

5. *Figure 3.1 implies nothing about "inherent" or "natural" gender differences.* Finally, in assigning men a position on the NPR-EFI axis that is closer to the EFI endpoint of the axis and women a position that is closer to the NPR side of the axis, I am not suggesting that men, in general, are inherently better at exercising ego functions and inherently more disposed to independence than women or

that women, in general, are inherently better at expressing non-egoic potentials and inherently more disposed to relationship than men. Figure 3.1 neither affirms nor denies this or any other account of inherent or natural gender differences. Figure 3.1 represents gender differences only insofar as they can be understood as consequences of the conditions of early childhood development that we have discussed in this chapter. Accordingly, figure 3.1 implies only that women and men differ in the manners in which they have *learned* to relate to ego functions and independence on the one hand and nonegoic potentials and relationship on the other.

Turning now to interpretation, two principal features of figure 3.1 need to be discussed: (1) the position representing men is farther to the EFI side of the NPR-EFI axis than is the position representing women, and (2) the positions representing women and men are both on the EFI side of the axis. The first of these points indicates that men are more identified with ego functions and independence than women are and, correspondingly, experience less conflict in exercising ego functions and asserting independence than women do. Or changing the focus, this point indicates that women are less estranged from nonegoic potentials and relationship than men are and, correspondingly, experience less conflict in expressing nonegoic potentials and yielding to relationship than men do. As we have learned, boys, in being opposite in gender to the mother, have an extra incentive for dissociating themselves from the mother and from the nonegoic potentials and intimate relationship she represents; and boys, in being the same gender as the father, are able to identify with the father completely and to emulate directly the ego functions and independence he represents. In contrast, girls, in being the same gender as the mother, retain an identity link with the mother and with the nonegoic potentials and intimate relationship she represents; and girls, in being opposite in gender to the father, are unable completely to identify with the father and are able only indirectly, in a gender-opposite way, to emulate the ego functions and independence he represents. The first point, then, is the point of difference: women and men relate to the poles of the NPR-EFI axis in importantly different ways.

The second point, on the other hand, is the point of similarity. It indicates that, although there are important gender differences of the types just noted, these differences are outweighed by corresponding similarities. It indicates that both women and men are primarily committed to ego functions and independence and significantly out of touch with nonegoic potentials and relationship. This point reflects the overriding gender-common consequences that, as we have seen, emerge from the resolutions of the rapprochement and oedipal struggles of early childhood: Both boys and girls distance themselves from the mother and from the nonegoic potentials and intimate relationship she represents; and both boys and girls commit themselves to the father and to the ego functions and independence he represents. The second point, then, indicates that, significant differences notwithstanding, women and men are more similar than different with respect to the poles of the NPR-EFI axis.

In sum, the first point indicates that the differences between women and men with respect to the poles of the NPR-EFI axis are *significant* and therefore historically, socially, and psychologically of great importance. The second point indicates that these differences, although significant, are *narrow* and therefore should be understood within a larger context of similarity.

GENDER DIFFERENCES IN THE CONTEXT OF PATRIARCHAL DUALISM

In the last section I considered gender differences with respect to the *common* reference frame of the NPR-EFI axis. In this section I shall consider how these same gender differences appear when they are perceived from the *relative* positions of women and men on the NPR-EFI axis.

The most important difference between the common and relative perspectives just described is that only the common reference frame supports the distinction between narrow and wide differences. From the relative perspectives of women and men, there are no narrow gender differences; all gender differences appear wide. The reason for this is that women and men, in perceiving each other from the standpoints of their respective positions on the NPR-EFI axis, can see only the distance between these positions and not any of the distance beyond the positions. In relative perspective, that is, the positions of women and men on the NPR-EFI axis inevitably appear to be the endpoints of the NPR-EFI axis. Consequently, women and men perceive each other as representing the endpoint of the NPR-EFI axis from which they, as perceivers, are the most distant, irrespective of actual distances. Accordingly, because the position of women on the NPR-EFI axis is farther from the EFI endpoint than the position of men, women perceive men as exemplars of ego functions and independence. Conversely, because the position of men on the NPR-EFI axis is farther from the NPR endpoint than the position of women, men perceive women as exemplars of nonegoic potentials and relationship—even though, as I have argued, the position of women is actually on the EFI side of the NPR-EFI axis. In other words, the actual differences between women and men are exaggerated by relative perspective. Women perceive men as if they occupied the EFI endpoint of the NPR-EFI axis, and men perceive women as if they occupied the NPR endpoint.

Women and men, therefore, are prone to misperceive each other. They are not, however, prone to misperceive each other to the same degree: men's misperception of women is greater than women's misperception of men. For if, as I have argued, both women and men are situated on the EFI side of the NPR-EFI axis, it follows that men commit a greater error in perceiving women as exemplars of nonegoic potentials and relationship than women do in perceiving men as exemplars of ego functions and independence. Men's perception of women, then, is more distorted than women's perception of men. Moreover, men's perception of women, as explained earlier, has highly detrimental consequences for women.

Gathering together the threads of the discussion, we can say that gender differences on the NPR-EFI axis are in fact narrow but are nonetheless perceived to be wide. Women and men are prone to exaggerate their differences on the NPR-EFI axis. Although the positions of both women and men are on the same (EFI) side of this axis, women and men perceive each other as occupying the opposite endpoints of the axis. This exaggeration of narrow differences into wide is an exaggeration of unsameness into complete unlikeness; it is an exaggeration of gender difference into NPR-EFI dualism. It is an exaggeration that makes the two genders appear to stand in the same kind of antagonistic opposition to each other as the endpoints of the NPR-EFI axis that the genders are perceived to represent.

Patriarchal dualism is a vertical (superior-inferior) dualism rather than a horizontal (opposite but equal) dualism. Patriarchy stands for an elevation of the ego and ego functions over the nonegoic core and nonegoic potentials: of mind over body, will over feeling, operational cognition over imaginal-intuitive cognition, reason over spirit, and so forth. Correspondingly, patriarchy stands for an elevation of independence over relationship. Patriarchy defines selfhood in terms of independence and denigrates relationship as a lack of differentiation. And of course patriarchy stands for an elevation of men over women.

The assimilation of men to the EFI endpoint of the NPR-EFI axis and women to the NPR endpoint is at the same time a valorization of men and devaluation of women.

The patriarchal perception of gender differences as wide differences, although a misperception of women's and men's positions on the NPR-EFI axis, is nonetheless an accurate perception of gender organization in patriarchal society. That is, it is an accurate perception of patriarchal social practices and, therefore, social structures and institutions. The misperception of gender differences as wide differences gives rise to actions that translate this misperception into social reality. Accordingly, although gender dualism is a distortion and illusion, patriarchal dualism is not. Patriarchy has exploited the illusion of wide differences to perpetuate a one-sided egoic-over-nonegoic, self-over-other, man-over-woman division within society. This division cuts deeply into the fabric of social experience, affecting virtually everything we say and do, especially when we interact as women and men.

CONCLUSION

Feminists have followed three primary strategies in responding to the patriarchal interpretation of gender differences. One strategy, followed by most liberal feminists, is simply to reject patriarchal dualism and hold that women and men are fundamentally the same. This strategy advocates the complete assimilation of women into existing society and holds that any differences between women and men are insignificant and should be discounted insofar as women's participation in economic, political, and cultural life is concerned. In advocating the assimilation of women into existing society, followers of this strategy quite understandably minimize gender differences. Some, however, in doing this, tend not only to deemphasize gender differences but also to underestimate them. That is, some tend, in arguing against wide gender differences, in effect to argue against narrow gender differences as well.

A second strategy opposes liberal assimilationism and argues that, culturally if not politically and economically, women should not seek to become part of *man's* world but should rather seek to establish networks of relationship among themselves in order to rediscover themselves *as women*.[4] Feminists of this perspective do not minimize gender differences. Rather, they maintain that women and men are fundamentally different. In our terms, they maintain that women and men differ from each other in a wide rather than narrow way. In espousing wide gender differences, however, these feminists completely overturn the patriarchal valuation of such differences. They invert patriarchal values, devaluing "phallocentric" reason and will and valorizing women's depths, which, when recovered, they maintain, will express themselves as a superior life of the body, energy, feeling, imagination, and intimacy, a women-centered life of mystery, magic, goddess power, interwoven selves, and love.

A third strategy—to be found, for example, in the work of Catherine Keller (1986)—attempts to combine aspects of both the first two strategies. It holds that women need both to empower themselves in society and discover their own deeper nature as women. According to this strategy, women's empowerment in society is not merely a matter of equality of opportunity or compromising assimilation. It is rather a matter of simultaneously changing society and opening avenues of self-expression for women. And according to this strategy, women's self-expression does not require turning away from men. For women's self-expression is understood as leading to the recovery of potentials and capacities that, although more intimately associated with women, also in principle belong to men. This strategy, then, acknowledges significant gender differences but does not take them to imply insurmountable or unbridgeable differences between women and men. Significant gender differences are neither overlooked nor exaggerated. Rather, they are seen, in the terms I have been using, as being both real and narrow. I shall explore this third strategy later in the book, in chapter 10, when I turn to the subject of gender and transcendence.

4

Ego Development and
Dualism in Latency

Primal repression brings an end to the free expression of non-egoic potentials that is characteristic of preoedipal and, to a lesser extent, oedipal childhood. The egoic-nonegoic dualism that emerges with primal repression is one in which the ego, still dependent upon the nonegoic sphere, is nonetheless girded against the potentials of this sphere, which potentials are repressed and rendered unconscious. The child in this way sacrifices much of the power, magic, and richness of its earlier experience. In suffering these sacrifices, however, the child also gains relief from nonegoic upheavals. The psychic storms that had troubled the initial years of life subside, and the child, although inwardly girded and divided, is also, relatively speaking, composed and in control.

Primal alienation, the outer correlate of primal repression, brings an end to the child's symbiotic ties to the primary caregiver. The self-other dualism that results from primal alienation is one in which the child, still supported in existence by its parents, is nonetheless disjoined from them and shielded within an inner sphere: emerging mental-egoic subjectivity. The child in this way sacrifices the radical intimacy with the primary caregiver that it had experienced earlier. The child, however, in sacrificing this intimacy, also achieves its independence and gains relief from interpersonal vulnerabilities and conflicts. The struggles of the rapprochement and oedipal periods are over, and the child, although inwardly withdrawn, is also, relatively speaking, self-possessed and at peace.

These observations indicate that primal repression and primal alienation have both negative and positive consequences. On the negative side, primal repression and primal alienation are responsible for a loss of power, spontaneity, and intimacy. On the positive side, however, they consolidate the ego by serving as bases for ego independence and self-control. Both of these sets of consequences are of great significance. At this early development juncture, however, it is, I suggest, the positive consequences that are the more important. For primal repression and primal alienation are the means by which the child wins its freedom from forces that had been holding the child in thrall. Primal repression, then, is initially more an act that lays a solid underfooting and clears the inner atmosphere for the ego than it is an act that divides and disempowers the psyche. And primal alienation is initially more an act that protects the ego against overawing interpersonal influences than it is an act that forfeits interpersonal intimacy.

The negative consequences of primal repression and primal alienation are not to be underestimated, especially because, later in life, they become primary issues on the developmental agenda. Nevertheless, for the young child who has just resolved the rapprochement and oedipal crises, primal repression and primal alienation are developmentally progressive steps, steps to be judged more in terms of their immediate benefits than in terms of their long-term costs. At this developmental juncture, primal repression and primal alienation have more the character of triumph than defeat. They represent more a consolidation than a retreat of the ego. At first, then, primal repression and primal alienation bring about a net developmental advance.

Primal repression and primal alienation usher in the period of latency. Psychodynamically, latency is a period during which primal repression quiets the potentials of the nonegoic core of the psyche. This quieting is evident psychosexually in that the primarily genital ("phallic") but also still polymorphously sensual experience of the late prelatency period comes to an end and psychic energy is arrested in its somatic expression and limited to a dormant genital organization. The quieting of nonegoic potentials, however, is not limited to sexuality. Psychodynamically, as we shall see, latency ·
ing which, owing to primal repression, all nonego
subdued or rendered dormant. From the point of vi

lations, latency is a period of object constancy, a time during which the ego, having safely distanced itself from others, enjoys a primarily harmonious relationship with parents and their internalized imagoes. The rapprochement and oedipal struggles are over and the child, established in its own psychic space, enjoys a primarily positive interaction with parents, submitting to them as sources of authority and relying on them as sources of support. In ego-developmental perspective, latency is a period during which the ego, protected from nonegoic upheavals, defended against interpersonal vulnerabilities, and disciplined and guided by the superego, is able to develop at an accelerated rate. Finally, in its existential dimension, latency is a period during which the activity of play is the primary way of relating to the world.

I shall speak briefly to each of these features of the latency period, focusing the discussion in each case on how these features can be understood in terms of the underlying structures of primal repression and primal alienation.

Psychodynamics

Freud conceived of latency primarily as a stage of psychosexual development; namely, as a stage during which instinctual (and especially sexual) energy is repressed and kept inactive in a dormant genital organization, lying latent in this fashion until it is later stirred into activity with the onset of puberty. This view, I suggest, is better formulated in more general terms to state that latency is a period during which psychic energy generally, and not just instinctual or sexual energy, is repressed and rendered inactive (for the most part). In this more general formulation, latency can be described as a period of energic dormancy, a period during which both the erotogenic zones and the body more generally are deenergized and therefore desensitized. Latency, I suggest, is a period during which psychic energy no longer flows freely in the body because psychic energy has been repressively deactivated at its point of origin in the sexual system.

This modified notion of latency fits the hypothesis of primal repression and has important implications about primal repression as a countercathectic structure exerting focused lines of force. The shift from a genital but also still open and polymorphous expression of psychic energy to a fixed and dormant genital organization implies that primal repression is a structure of a psychosomatic sort that is aimed against an underlying source of energy. It points to the fact that primal repression is a physical structure that in some way opposes the flow of energy and, in doing so, deenergizes the body, transforming it from an ecstatically alive sensorium into a relatively quiescent sensorimotor instrument. Primal repression, I suggest, is an act-structure by which the ego mobilizes the body against itself, and in particular against the dynamic source located in the sexual system, to reduce markedly the amount of energy released from that source into the body.

Primal repression, in mobilizing the body against itself in the way just described, radically changes the ego's relation to the body. For primal repression, in using the body to disconnect the ego from the dynamic center in the lower body, at the same time disconnects the ego from the body itself. The body ceases being a dynamically charged field of the ego's own experience and becomes a "thing" that protectively separates the ego from upwelling energy. The body is in this way demoted in status from something that is primarily a subject to something that, although still intimately related to subjectivity, is now primarily an object for a subject (an incipient mental ego). Latency thus involves both a deanimation of the body and an initial separation of the ego from the body. The body ceases being a sensuously alive field of subjective experience and becomes a sensorimotor instument by which the ego, now significantly disidentified from the body, perceives and acts upon the external world.

Corresponding to this change in the ego's relation to the body is a shift in the ego's boundaries. I shall consider this shift in more detail later. For the present suffice it to say that the ego ceases being coextensive with the body as a whole and becomes associated with the upper body, especially the head. The ego ceases being the body itself and becomes something that, inaccessible to sense perception, exists within the body. It becomes an inner entity of some vague sort that, typically, is assumed to exist in the area of the "pilot's seat" behind the eyes and ears. The ego at this point undergoes a basic transition from being a primarily passive ego of somatosensuous feeling to being a primarily active ego that takes up residence in the region of the head, an ego that, from this lofty perch, takes control of the underlying body, appropriating it for egoic purposes.

Primal repression is in this way the root cause of mind-body dualism. Primal repression is a structure that both deanimates the body and disjoins the ego from the body, elevating the ego to a position (literally) above the body. As will be explained later in the chapter, the mental ego that emerges at this point is by no means a fullfledged dualistic or Cartesian ego. The child during latency continues to think of itself in vaguely material terms and is not yet explicitly self-conscious or introspective in the fashion of the Cartesian *cogito*. The dualism of the latency period is more an implicit dualism of head-centered subjectivity over lower-body objectivity than it is an explicit Cartesian dualism of *res cogitans* versus *res extensa*. Nevertheless, the seeds of Cartesian dualism have at this point been sown.

Two models are useful in explaining how primal repression might work as a somatic structure: (1) the hydraulic (or pneumatic) model—primal repression works like a cap or seal that keeps psychic energy contained within its sphere of origin by exerting a counterforce that arrests the movement of psychic energy; and (2) the thermostatic model—primal repression works like a thermostat that decreases the amount of energy "combusted" and thereby released into the body. Each of these models expresses an important idea; both models, however, are inadequate, although for opposite reasons. The hydraulic model—which, in its role in psychoanalytic theory, has been much criticized—provides effective expression of the notion of repression as a countercathectic force or barrier but not of the notion of latency as a state of dormancy or inactivity. The thermostatic model does just the opposite.

The hydraulic model expresses the psychodynamic idea that repression is a mobilization of energy against the expression of a threatening force, impulse, or idea. Specifically, it expresses the idea that primal repression is a mobilization of psychic energy against the very source of psychic energy, a mobilization that, consolidated as a structure, markedly reduces the amount of psychic energy that can be released from its point of origin in the sexual system. Regrettably, the hydraulic model suggests, and is usually taken to imply, that the body is locked in a potentially explosive posture of pressure versus equal counterpressure, of upsurge versus repressive counterthrust. Because there is no evidence that the body is locked in such a highly charged posture, the hydraulic model has been deservedly criticized. If it is to be useful, it must be reconceived in a way that does not imply the posture in question.

The thermostatic model is immune to the criticisms that have been brought against the hydraulic model, because the thermostatic model stipulates that the amount of psychic energy "combusted" is reduced, not that a constant amount of energy is contained under pressure. The thermostatic model nicely conveys the idea of psychic energy as a mostly dormant force, a force that for the most part is kept in an inactive state. Unfortunately, the thermostatic model does not convey the idea of primal repression as a protective structure that keeps the ego safely disjoined or insulated from the nonegoic sphere of the psyche. It does not convey the idea that primal repression is the product of a defensive mobilization of energy (i.e., a counter-cathexis) by the ego against the dynamic potentials of the psyche's nonegoic core. The notion of countercathexis cannot be eliminated from a proper understanding of primal repression. And the thermostatic model does not contain this notion.

The shortcomings of the hydraulic and thermostatic models can, I suggest, be remedied by integrating what is essential to these models. To see this, consider the example of a fire that has been covered by a dome-shaped lid in which there is only a small hole through which the fire can breathe. The lid over the fire, representing countercathexis, works against the fire in two ways: (1) by confining the fire to a restricted sphere and, as a consequence of this, (2) by cutting back on the combustion process. That is, the lid has both hydraulic (or pneumatic) and thermostatic effects. It works not only to contain the fire but also to reduce its intensity. The lid works by means of a double causality. Primal repression, I suggest, does so as well.

The double causality just described is expressed in the fable of the genie in the bottle. According to one version of this story, the genie lies asleep in the bottle until the cap is removed, at which point the genie awakens and manifests itself as a prodigious, miraculous—and potentially dangerous—power. This active manifestation of the genie continues until the genie is enticed back into the bottle and the cap is put back on the bottle, at which point the genie goes back to sleep. Putting the cap on the bottle thus works not only to confine the genie within the bottle but also, precisely in doing this, to change the genie's power from actual to potential power. Putting the cap on the bottle does indeed "bottle up" the genie, but not, as it were, under great pressure. The genie's power is indeed suppressed, but it is also—and this is perhaps the more important point—rendered dormant. Primal repression, I suggest, works in a similar double manner. It is a countercathexis that contains psychic energy not only by blocking the release of psychic energy into the body but also, precisely in doing this, by deactivating psychic energy and rendering it, relatively speaking, latent (i.e., merely potential, "uncombusted").

It is no accident that the fable of the genie in the bottle is useful for our purposes. For this fable is a story about the very phenomenon with which we are here dealing: dynamic latency (and possible dynamic reawakening). Another story that attempts to express this phenomenon—this one deriving from Tantrism—is that of the serpent power *kundalini*. In the Tantric tradition *kundalini* is said to lie coiled at the base of the spine, where it sleeps until it is awakened through yogic practice. Upon awakening, *kundalini* is said to manifest itself as the goddess Shakti, the power of psychospiritual transformation. Both the genie story and the *kundalini* story convey the idea that a dormant power lies hidden within our field of possible experience, a power that, under certain conditions, can be stirred into activity. Both stories also convey the idea that the power in question is an immense one possessing a magical, numinous character. Accordingly, both stories stress that this power is one the awakening of which carries with it not only the promise of supernormal possibilities but also very real dangers.

As I am interpreting these stories, the power in question is the numinous dynamism that issues from the psyche's nonegoic core, the dynamism that originally manifests itself as the power of the Great Mother. This power, I am suggesting, is put to sleep at the onset of the latency period. Primal repression not only blocks this power but also, to a significant degree, deactivates it. This power therefore remains dormant throughout the period of dualism, that is, so long as primal repression remains in place. Only after primal repression has begun to give way—or after the power in question has otherwise been reawakened—does this power begin once again to manifest itself within consciousness. The return of this power to the field of consciousness is treated in chapter 9.

If the account of dynamic latency just presented is correct, it follows that primal repression has a definite somatic infrastructure but not necessarily one of great countercathectic force or weight. The interpretation of primal repression that I am proposing therefore does not imply that the body is petrified in a highly charged posture of pressure versus equal counterpressure. It does imply that the ego mobilizes a psychosomatic countercathexis. This countercathexis, however, is one that works not only in a hydraulic but also in a thermostatic way. It is a countercathexis that not only contains energy at its point of origin in the sexual system but that also, in doing this, keeps energy in a mostly dormant or potential state. Such a countercathexis, which is aimed at the base of the spine, may involve a constriction of lower bodily muscles, including, most proximately, the anal sphincter and the muscles of the lower abdomen.[1] Whatever parts of the body are brought into play, however, the effect is that the release of psychic energy from the sexual system is throttled and, I propose, psychic energy is reduced to a mostly inactive condition.

The somatic infrastructure of primal repression serves as an undergirding for the ego, which, as we saw earlier, is now a nascent mental ego, an ego that has taken up residence in the region of the head. At the beginning of the latency period, then, the ego is both undergirded and elevated. It is both trussed from below and perched on high. Primal repression serves not only as a cap or seal that covers over the nonegoic sphere but also as a base that supports the mental-egoic system. As a psychosomatic countercathexis, primal repression is a way in which the mental ego at once bears down constrictively on the lower body and propels itself upwardly into the region of the head. The latency ego is by no means cut off from the body completely; it still enjoys the sensations of the body. The body, however, is no longer the polymorphously sensual body of the prelatency period. The body is no longer open to upwelling energy, and it is no longer the primary abode of the ego subject.

So far I have proposed that the classical notion of latency be expanded from a concept of instinctual dormancy to a more general concept of energic dormancy. Now I shall propose that the classical notion be expanded further and be redefined as the concept of *nonegoic* dormancy. For primal repression, I have argued, is a protective structure by which the ego insulates itself from all of the potentials the psyche's nonegoic core. In committing the act of primal repression, the ego cuts itself off from what, intrapsychically, is beyond itself. The ego takes possession of itself and at the same time frees itself from nonegoic "interferences." The ego abandons the body, which had been a field for the free play of nonegoic potentials, and takes up residence in the "control center" behind the sensory instruments located in the head. Primal repression therefore has effects far beyond those we have discussed so far. It not only deenergizes the body; it also (1) attenuates feelings, (2) curtails the creative imagination or autosymbolic process, (3) eliminates archetypal figures and complexes from consciousness, and (4) depotentiates the general atmosphere of experience, thereby disenchanting the world.

Primal repression attenuates feelings. Affective experience is essentially somatic in character. Feelings express themselves by rising and rippling, pulsating, or exploding in the body. Accordingly, the deenergization of the body is at the same time a deenergization of feelings, which are markedly reduced in intensity. Moreover, the ego's constricted-elevated stance, its countercathectic "bearing down" on the lower body, is antithetical to the free movement of feelings. Feelings, therefore, are impeded in their expression. They are forced to move against the grain of the body's newly acquired repressive posture. To be sure, feelings still well up in strong surges and sometimes overwhelm the ego. Nevertheless, relatively speaking, feelings are now both subdued (deenergized) and held in check (inhibited). It is no longer the norm for the ego to be passively played upon by strong feelings; feelings are now "tame" and express themselves in a manner that is subject to the ego's control.

The creative imagination or autosymbolic process undergoes a similar transformation. In having less energy to draw upon, the imagination produces images that are less vivid. And in being inhibited by mental-egoic constraints, the imagination operates in a manner that is less spontaneous. Images, therefore, cease having the character of apparitions, dramatically realistic and unexpected manifestations, and become mere images, figments that to a significant extent are a product of egoic fabrication or at least manipulation. The ego of course never gains complete control of the imagination—or of feelings or any other nonegoic potential. Nevertheless, the ego at this point is able to direct the imagination rather than simply be witness to it. The ego now begins to exercise "its" imagination; the ego acquires a "fantasy life."[2] The original power, spontaneity, and symbolic creativity of the imagination are thus for the most part lost to consciousness and remain evident primarily in the realm of sleep and dreams.

The loss of imaginal spontaneity brings an end to the archetypal activity of early childhood, and in particular the archetypal activity involved in the child's interaction with the Great Mother. The larger-than-life representations that had been elicited in the child's interaction with the primary caregiver recede from awareness. The caregiver therefore ceases being magnified and endowed with the extraordinary qualities of the Great Mother (whether in her Good Mother or Terrible Mother form). The primary caregiver, that is, ceases being a goddess and becomes simply a human being. To a lesser extent, something similar probably happens to the secondary caregiver, usually the father, who, in the child's perception, may undergo a transformation from being an ideal but wrathful deity to being a merely human exemplar and judge. The father remains a model to emulate, as I have argued in the previous two chapters; nevertheless, the father probably becomes a model of much more realistic, human, proportions. The disappearance of the Great Mother and the oedipal father as archetypal deities is equivalent to the achievement of object constancy.

Finally, primal repression has the effect of depotentiating experience across all dimensions. The marked reduction of energy released from the sexual system affects not only the body, feelings, and creative imagination but also the general atmosphere of the lifeworld. The child's experience is no longer empowered with freely moving energy. Such energy, which, prior to primal repression, had magnetized and amplified objects of perception (for good or ill), is now withdrawn from experience. Accordingly, the world at this point loses its numinous quality, and the ego ceases being enthralled and transfixed. The world is "disenchanted." This is not to say that the world of the latency child becomes arid and uninviting; on the contrary, it is very much a playground. The point, rather, is that the world of the latency child is no longer a dauntingly enchanted realm, a realm of awesome power, invisible presences, and mysterious transmutations. Just as the transition to latency transforms parents from overawing archetypal deities into safe human beings, so this transition transforms the child's life-world from an overawing supernatural realm into a safe natural order. It is *because* the world of the latency child has been disenchanted, not despite this fact, that the child is able to enjoy the world as a safe field for uninhibited play.

Psychodynamically, latency is a period in which nonegoic potentials of all types are repressively weakened or deactivated by primal repression. Energically, latency is a period in which psychic energy is confined and reduced to a mostly dormant state within the sexual system: the genie goes to sleep at the base of the spine. Somatically, latency is a period in which the body is repressively constricted, desensitized, and reduced in status from subject to object. Affectively, latency is a period in which feelings are "tamed" and brought under the ego's control. Imaginally, latency is a period in which images are transformed from self-manifesting apparitions into figments of the *ego's* imagination, that is, into phantasms that to a significant degree are products of egoic activity rather than nonegoic spontaneity. Archetypally, latency is a period in which powerful collective representations of the parental figures are withdrawn and these figures are finally seen in their "true" proportions, as human beings rather than gods. And in its general ambience, latency is a period in which the atmosphere of the world loses its dynamic charge and becomes disenchanted and "unhaunted." In sum, primal repression has radical and far-reaching effects. It creates a condition of latency that is evident not only in the organization of libido but also in the expression of all dimensions of nonegoic life.

OBJECT RELATIONS

Primal alienation is the object-directed correlate of primal repression, and object constancy is the object-directed correlate of latency. In relation to the world of primary others and their object representations, the latency child is one who has withdrawn from symbiotic intimacy (primal alienation) and, in doing so, has achieved self-other independence, integration of previously split object representations, and corresponding steadiness in primary relationships (object constancy). The child of early dualism is not only protectively separated from the nonegoic sphere, which is now the dynamic unconscious, but is also shielded from significant others, who are now externalized others, beings from whom the child has achieved safe distance. The intimate openness of the predualistic child is lost. So too, however, are the entanglements with the archetypal parents that had given rise to debilitating splitting of object representations and self-representations.

Primal repression, as we have seen, is the basis of dualistic (egoic versus nonegoic) psychodynamics. Correspondingly, primal alienation is the basis of dualistic (self versus other) object relations. Primal repression is a way in which the ego separates itself from the nonegoic sphere by "girding the loins" and ascending to the region of the head. Correspondingly, primal alienation is a way in which the ego retreats from its primary object by creating an outer shell and withdrawing into interiority. Psychodynamically, primal repression is a constriction of the lower body that weakens or deactivates nonegoic potentials; object relationally, primal alienation is a contraction of the outer body that keeps the primary object at bay. Primal repression, I suggested, may involve a constriction specifically of muscles in the anal and lower abdominal areas. Primal alienation, I conjecture, may involve a tensing of muscles in the neck, shoulder, and chest areas, because these muscles are brought into play when we retreat from others. The tension in these muscles can be quite subtle, and in any case the child soon becomes habituated to it. The posture of primal alienation, like the posture of primal repression, very soon petrifies and becomes part of the unconscious infrastructure of the mental-egoic system.[3]

If primary effects of primal repression are to depotentiate and elevate psychic space, corresponding effects of primal alienation are to internalize and privatize psychic space. Primal repression transforms subjectivity from dynamically alive whole-body subjectivity into dynamically quiescent upper-body, head-centered, subjectivity. Correspondingly, primal alienation transforms subjectivity from open symbiotic subjectivity into closed interior subjectivity. The combined posture of primal repression and primal alienation therefore is one of doubly braced (constricted and contracted, undergirded and shielded, elevated and privatized) self-encapsulation. The ego braces itself against both inner nonegoic and outer interpersonal influences and, in doing so, confines itself within a limited but protected sphere: elevated interiority, private mental space. The ego in this way takes the first step in the direction of Cartesian dualism.

Object constancy goes hand in hand with primal alienation, because, in withdrawing from symbiotic intimacy with the preoedipal mother, the child achieves a significant degree of independence and stability in its primary relationships. As explained previously, archetypal object representations are withdrawn at this point, with the consequence that the mother and father cease being seen as split Manichaean deities and become integrated but lesser (i.e., "merely" human) beings. The mother ceases being the split Good Mother–Terrible Mother and becomes an integrated but "merely" human nurturer. And the father ceases being a split ideal-wrathful god and becomes an integrated but "merely" human model and authority. The severing of symbiotic connections, together with the withdrawal of nonegoic-archetypal projections, allows the child the distance needed to relate to parental figures in a realistic, consistent, and basically positive manner. The latency child thus experiences relative peace and predictability in its primary relationships. It achieves object constancy.

In addition to being a period of relative harmony and stability in relation to parents, latency is a period of submission to parental authority. For latency is ushered in by means of a capitulation to the oedipal father and an internalization of his authority in the agency of the superego. Children entering latency commit themselves to the father not only as model of egoic independence but also as the sovereign (albeit "merely" human) power. In this way the father becomes the ultimate authority in the ego's life—and the mother, who is "second in command" in the patriarchal family, becomes a collateral authority. The latency period is, then, a time during which the ego is not only at peace with the parents but also willingly acquiescent to them.

The internalization of parental authority in the form of the superego is part of the latency child's consolidation of its own sense of self. The superego is by no means merely a foreign implant. It is an agency that enforces norms and values that the child has made its own. Indeed, as we learned in chapter 2, the latency child's ego ideal is one of the elements of the superego.[4] To be sure, the voice of the superego is the voice of an "other" (the father). But the voice of the superego is also a voice of the child's own self, and in particular of the child's potential ideal self. The exhortations of the superego have a double character deriving from the double nature of the child's commitment to the oedipal father: they are both external imperatives deriving from the child's capitulation to the father and immanent ideals deriving from the child's emulation of the father. By the beginning of the latency period, then, the child's self-strivings coincide harmoniously with oedipally based parental authority. This happy synthesis lasts until the beginning of adolescence.[5]

The latency child's acceptance of parental norms and values is at first more implicit and extrinsically motivated and then gradually becomes more explicit and intrinsically motivated. In the earliest phases of the latency period—corresponding to the first stage of what Lawrence Kohlberg (1969, 1976, 1984) designates *preconventional morality*—parental norms and values are incompletely understood and therefore are accepted in a mostly implicit manner as "whatever the parents command." Moreover, the commitment to parental norms and values is motivated primarily by fear of punishment. The child in early latency is lacking not only in understanding but also discipline and therefore is frequently in jeopardy of being punished for "misbehaving." Also, the child at this point, having only recently escaped the arena of oedipal conflict, is prone to reexperience the fear of oedipal wrath.

In the middle years of the latency period—corresponding to the second of Kohlberg's stages of preconventional morality—the child achieves a better understanding of parental requirements and begins accepting them on a more explicit level and for more positive reasons, not only to avoid punishment but also to obtain praise and rewards. Finally, beginning around ten years of age—which is the approximate age at which the child achieves what Kohlberg designates *conventional morality*—the child's acceptance of parental norms and values becomes predominantly explicit and intrinsic. In the first stage of conventional morality, the child conforms to parental norms and values to seek approval as a "good girl" or "good boy." Then, in the second stage, the child begins to show an appreciation of conventional morality for its own sake as defining "the right thing to do." The second stage of conventional morality is the period of greatest agreement between ego ideal and superego, between self-representation and parental imagoes. Ironically, this stage immediately precedes the difficulties of adolescence.

In sum, the object relations of the latency period are founded on supportive object representations. The parents are internally represented as both loving providers and exemplary authorities. The mother, of course, is the primary symbol of love, and the father is the primary symbol of authority. If, however, the mother is the primary symbol of love, she is also a symbol of authority, because, as we have seen, the mother is "second in command" in the patriarchal family. And if the father is the primary symbol of authority, he is also a symbol of love, because, in the patriarchal household, he is the secondary caregiver. The child thus enters latency with object representations that provide a sense of being both lovingly supported and authoritatively guided by the primary people in the child's life.[6] For this reason Peter Blos (1967) aptly describes the latency child as living on "borrowed ego strength."

EGO DEVELOPMENT

The quiescent psychodynamics and harmonious object relations of the latency period constitute optimal conditions for ego development. Primal repression, to be sure, submerges nonegoic potentials and thereby impoverishes experience significantly. In doing so, however, it also frees the ego from overwhelming influences and establishes intrapsychic conditions under which the ego is better able to gain effective self-control and, therefore, control of ego functions. And primal alienation, to be sure, brings an end to freely interfluent intimacy and creates a posture of defensive inwardness. In doing so, however, it also confers upon the ego an independence that allows the ego to exercise its own will without being overawed or undermined by others in the process. The ego of the latency period is protectively buffered from both nonegoic and interpersonal influences that previously had held the ego in thrall. Moreover, the ego of the latency period enjoys both the nurture and leadership that, according to the child's basic object representations, are provided by the parents. Latency is for these reasons a stage of both ego freedom and ego support and therefore also a stage of accelerated ego development. It is a stage during which the ego is able much more rapidly than hitherto was possible to develop such ego functions as synthesis, self-reflection, ego-initiated cognition, and active volition.

Synthesis

Synthesis is the most basic of the ego functions. It is a precondition of all other ego functions, for without a synthesis of succeeding moments of experience into a single sustained experience, no experience would last long enough to be subject to any of the other ego functions. Without synthesis, consciousness would be a disconnected, and therefore uncomprehended, succession of episodes.

A passive precursor of synthesis seems to be present very nearly from the outset of life and is evident in the infant's ability to follow the movement of salient stimuli. Such "tracking" of stimuli reflects sustained attention over time. Active synthesis—which is synthesis more properly speaking—is progressively developed during the first and second years as the object concept is gradually achieved. Development of the object concept, and of a sense of object permanence in particular, indicates active synthesis because the ability to hold an object in mind in the absence of the object itself implies a corresponding active ability to hold experience together over time. To the degree that it understands object permanence, the child no longer needs the presence of an enduring stimulus object to have an enduring, integrated consciousness. As understanding of object permanence is achieved, the child is progressively better able, actively and on its own, to hold awareness together. The full understanding of object permanence thus marks a developmental juncture of great importance so far as the ego function of synthesis is concerned.

Although an initial sense of object permanence has been detected as early as four or five months (Bower 1982; Baillargeon 1987), full understanding of object permanence, as Piaget (1954) demonstrated, is not achieved until about sixteen to eighteen months. For it is not until this age that a child is able to evoke representations of absent objects without the aid of sensory cues. Sixteen to eighteen months therefore marks the age at which the ego function of synthesis can be said to be significantly developed. Speaking of this age (and the months that follow), Jerome Kagan draws the following conclusion from his studies of the second year of life: "I believe that a central change of this period is the ability to sustain ideas and action plans. The psychological stage on which schemata interact and guide action does not collapse every half-minute or so as it did previously" (1989, p. 237). By the middle of the second year, then, the child is able actively to maintain the continuity of experience for significant stretches of time. Experience can be held together without the aid of sensory cues and therefore is not so liable to collapse into disconnected segments or episodes.

The middle of the second year, however, is a time at which synthesis is not only significantly developed but also significantly challenged. For eighteen months is the approximate age at which the child, in achieving a full understanding of object permanence, also achieves a full understanding of object independence and therefore possible object loss. Accordingly, eighteen months is the age at which the child begins to experience abandonment anxiety and the acute ambivalence and splitting of the rapprochement crisis. The active synthesis of experience achieved with the full development of the object concept is challenged by rapprochement splitting of the primary object representation into all-good and all-bad halves. As we saw in chapter 2, rapprochement splitting causes the child to suffer radical reversals and discontinuities in its experience. At one moment the child is the good self in the lap of the Good Mother only, at the next moment, to be the bad self in the clutches of the Terrible Mother. Reversals like these fracture the child's world; they divide the child's experience into suddenly changing, disconnected frames and therefore seriously interfere with the synthesis process.

The consolidation of the synthetic function requires the overcoming of preoedipal splitting. It requires, that is, the achievement of object constancy. This point is suggested in the following observation by Otto Kernberg: "At this point [the achievement of object constancy], the final condition of consciousness mentioned earlier, namely, the establishment of full continuity of self-awareness, is fulfilled, and, by the same token, an integrated structure of the self emerges within the ego" (1987, p. 11). As we know, object constancy is initially achieved at the end of the rapprochement crisis and is then reinforced at the end of the oedipal period. Only at the end of the oedipal period, then—that is, only at the beginning of latency—is the ego able finally to consolidate the synthetic function and thereby begin effectively to develop the other ego functions. The consolidation of the synthetic function, curiously, is predicated on (egoic-nonegoic, self-other) dualism.

Self-Reflection

Self-reflection presupposes synthesis and therefore appears only after synthesis has been developed. The child's ability actively to synthesize experience, as we have just seen, can be measured by the degree of development of the object concept, which is not fully achieved until about the middle of the second year. Correspondingly, self-reflection makes its initial appearance approximately at the middle of the second year. A considerable body of research (see Lewis and Brooks-Gunn 1979; Kagan 1981, 1989) demonstrates that the period between the fifteenth and twenty-first months is the principal developmental time for the occurrence of the first acts of self-awareness. During this time, children begin to exhibit self-conscious behaviors such as bashfulness and coyness, to recognize themselves in mirrors, and to use personal pronouns. They also, as Kagan (1989) has shown, begin during this time to exhibit such other signs of self-awareness as smiling upon completing an act or mastering a skill, engaging in symbolic play in which a toy plays the role of the child, and using a variety of self-descriptive phrases. The evidence indicating an important advance in self-awareness during the second half of the second year is sufficiently decisive for Michael Lewis and Jeanne Brooks-Gunn to draw the following conclusion from their extensive research: "Clearly, self recognition is well established by 21 months of age, and from this age onward, self recognition increases across all representations" (1979, p. 215).

Early self-reflection prior to latency is a *perceptual* self-reflection of a *body* ego. It is an awareness of a corporeal self that reflects on itself simply by watching itself in a mirror, looking at itself in a photograph, or observing its body in motion. This straightforward, unproblematic form of self-reflection ceases being possible after the complex posture based on primal repression and primal alienation has been set in place, because, as discussed earlier, this posture significantly alters the ego's relation to the body. The body is constricted, contracted, deenergized, and objectified; simultaneously, psychic space, the sphere of subjectivity, is elevated, sealed, and privatized. Primal repression and primal alienation transform the original body ego into an inner psychomental subject, a subject assumed to reside in the region of the head. Beginning with latency, then, the self of self-reflection ceases being an outwardly perceivable entity and becomes an entity within the body that is inaccessible to the outer senses. Accordingly, self-reflection at this point turns inward in a implicit and vague way.

Children already have a sense of psychological (as distinct from physical) states near the end of the second or early in the third year of life (Kagan 1981). At this young age, however, children do not yet think of themselves as *mental* subjects possessing psychological states. Rather, they see themselves as bodily beings who happen to possess psychological as well as physical states, emotional and cognitive as well as strictly behavioral dimensions. For example, children in the third year of life see themselves as beings who can see as well as be seen, who can be happy or sad as well as big or little. Children at this age have only a very limited grasp of psychological states and virtually no vocabulary with which to express what grasp they have. Nevertheless, children at this age are able to make and give indirect expression to basic psychological discriminations. Children understand the most fundamental forms of psychological subjectivity, which forms they attribute to themselves and to others as *bodily* rather than as inner, psychomental, subjects.

Primal repression and primal alienation abolish this perspective, changing the child's view of itself from a *double-aspect* view to a *two-entity* view. After primal repression and primal alienation are in place, the child ceases seeing itself as a single bodily being with both physical and psychological aspects and begins seeing itself as a composite of two entities, a primarily psychomental subject (associated with the head or brain) on the one hand and a merely physical object (the larger body) on the other. By the beginning of latency, then, a fundamental ontological division has occurred: the child no longer *is* the body but rather is an emerging mental ego that *has* a body. This division is at first made in only the crudest and most primitive way. The division is, however, detectable, as John Broughton's (1978, 1980, 1982) studies of the development of the mind-body concept have shown. Broughton's studies have shown that a vague "head-body" dualism emerges between four and seven years of age and that a sharper "brain-body" dualism emerges between eight and eleven years of age. Reporting on Broughton's studies, Lawrence Kohlberg states: "At around age 6–7 children reorganize their experiences around the distinction between the mind (or mental) and the body (or physical). . . . This new clear distinction of two separate entities in each person, the mental and the physical, gives rise to many important changes in children's relation to reality, to the values they attach to themselves and to other people" (1987, p. 25).

The emerging mental ego of the latency period is by no means a fully differentiated Cartesian ego aware of itself as such. On the contrary, the latency ego, although disjoined from the larger body and interiorized in the region of the head, still continues to think of itself in vaguely material terms. As just noted, Broughton's studies indicate that children between four and seven conceive of the mind-body division as a head-body division and that children between eight and eleven think of the mind-body division as a brain-body division. The latency child, that is, only partially differentiates itself, qua mind, from bodily existence. To be sure, by age eight the latency child has developed a quite definite idea of its mind as an inner entity that exercises distinctively psychomental functions and that possesses thoughts that are invisible to the outer world. Nevertheless, in conceiving of its mind in this way, the latency child still conflates the mind with the brain or part of the brain and, when asked, describes the invisibility of its thoughts in terms of them lacking solidity or tangibility rather than, as Descartes did, in terms of them lacking corporeality altogether (Broughton 1978, 1980). The latency child is not yet capable of thinking of itself in abstractly immaterial terms, and consequently it thinks of itself as something that is nonbodily but also still vaguely (and inconsistently) material.

Moreover, this self-conception is almost entirely implicit. The self-reflection of the emerging mental ego does not involve actual introspection. It is a merely tacit self-understanding. Latency children can be induced to think explicitly about themselves by posing questions like those asked in Broughton's studies. Responding to such questions, however, can be considered a form of self-reflection only in a very indirect sense. Besides, even when questions like these are posed, the cognitive development of latency children does not allow them to understand the vagueness and inconsistency of their answers. Practically speaking, latency children are aware of themselves as psychomental subjects only in a tacit and prereflective manner. Latency children are indeed insatiably curious about themselves in a wide variety of ways. They are not yet, however, introspectively self-conscious or concerned about what it means to exist as "a thinking being." Reflections such as these, as we shall see in the next chapter, are preoccupations of adolescence.

Ego-Initiated Cognition

Ego-initiated cognition is an ego function in a very general sense. As I shall be conceiving it, ego-initiated cognition includes all forms of cognition in which the ego is active in making discriminations, exploring connections, and exercising cognitive schemes, routines, or operations. Understood in this wide sense, ego-initiated cognition includes most of the forms of cognition studied by Piaget, from the sensorimotor cognition of the infant to the formal operational cognition of the adolescent and adult.[7] To be contrasted with ego-initiated cognition is ego-receptive cognition. Ego-receptive cognition, unlike ego-initiated cognition, is not a product, or at least a direct product, of ego activity. Indeed, ego-receptive cognition usually involves some degree of suspension or disengagement of the ego. Whereas ego-initiated cognition is transacted by the ego alone, ego-receptive cognition draws upon nonegoic sources and is spontaneous in expression. In ego-receptive cognition the ego is at least in part a receiver and therefore not exclusively an agent of cognition.[8] Examples of ego-receptive cognition are all forms of imaginal cognition (in both its primary process and higher visionary expressions), spontaneous intuitive disclosure or reconstellation, and infused contemplation (*samadhi, jhana,* enstasy[9]).

Because latency has an indefinite starting point, which can be as early as four or five years of age and as late as six or seven, the exact cognitive stages involved vary in individual cases. Assuming an earlier commencement, we can say, following the Piagetian account, that latency is a period that passes through two major phases of ego-initiated cognition: (1) the intuitive substage of the stage of preoperations (four to seven years) and (2) the stage of concrete operations (seven to twelve years). The stage of preoperations, in both its preconceptual (two to four years) and intuitive (four to seven years) substages, is a transitional stage during which the child develops the rudiments of conceptual thinking and gains an initial sense that things belong to classes and represent general types. The stage of concrete operations is the period during which the rudiments of conceptual thought are mastered sufficiently that the child can begin to grasp, albeit only on a concrete level, the basic logical relations that obtain among classes and types. Logical operations are at this point performed on particulars as representatives of classes and types rather than on the classes and types themselves. Logical operations on classes and types—or on any other sort of abstraction (e.g., axioms, principles, hypotheses)—are part of formal operational thinking. Such abstract cognition is not attained until adolescence.

Prior to latency, in the preconceptual substage of the stage of preoperations, the child begins to learn language and begins to relate to things not only as individuals or particulars but also as instances of general kinds. The child begins in the most basic ways to structure its experience into a system of classes. Unfortunately, during the preconceptual substage, the classes that the child learns are loosely and often inconsistently articulated and therefore cannot be fitted neatly into stable networks involving lateral exclusion or intersection and hierarchical subsumption. Moreover, the distinction between the particular and the general is only tenuously grasped during this period. Consequently, the child in the preconceptual substage of the stage of preoperations is susceptible to all manner of mistaken identifications and faulty inferences.

The preconceptual substage of the stage of preoperations is frequently described as a period of magical thought because it so easily mistakes a particular for its general type, and therefore particulars of the same type for each other, that it is prone to serious logical condensations and displacements. Silvano Arieti (1967) has explained that such condensations and displacements both inflate the child with a sense of magical omnipotence and afflict the child with a sense of defenselessness and vulnerability. The child is inflated with a sense of omnipotence because, in failing to make a clear distinction between the particular and the general, and therefore between similarity and identity, the child believes that actions that it takes upon particular things extend in their effects throughout the classes to which the things acted upon belong. And the child is afflicted with a sense of defenselessness and vulnerability because, by the same logic, the child believes that actions taken upon things that are members of classes to which the child belongs are actions taken upon the child as well. The child has magical access to the whole world, which has magical access to the child in turn.

The intuitive substage of the stage of preoperations, coinciding approximately with the transition to latency, brings the wild condensations and displacements of the preconceptual substage to an end. Concomitant with the beginning of latency is a markedly improved ability on the part of the child to distinguish between the particular and the general and a much sounder intuitive sense of class boundaries. The child at this point also exhibits a more effective intuitive sense of basic spatial and causal relationships. The child ages four or five to seven, then, lives in a world that is considerably more orderly than did the child of ages two to four. In the early phases of latency, the child develops a much more consistent and constant sense of the general natures of things and the general patterns of experience. This improved intuitive sense allows the child to test reality and interact with the world in a much more effective manner.

It is noteworthy that this dramatic forward step in cognition coincides approximately with the beginning of latency. For, I believe, the advance from the preconceptual to the intuitive substage of the stage of preoperations is facilitated by primal repression and, specifically, by the deactivation of the autosymbolic process that is one of the consequences of primal repression. The transition from preconceptual-magical to intuitive-conceptual thought is, I believe, accomplished in part by a repressive disengagement of thought from the spontaneity of the imagination. Let me explain.

The imagination is the initial medium of conceptual thought. Prior to latency, during the preconceptual substage of the stage of preoperations, the imagination spontaneously forges "ikonic representations" (Bruner 1966) or "paleosymbols" (Arieti 1967). These products of the imagination are primitive symbolic expressions of the conceptual meanings that the child, with the initial acquisition of language, is just beginning to learn. The imagination thus plays an indispensably important role in the initial phase of conceptual development. However, the concrete and ideographic character of imaginal representations places limits on conceptual understanding. For instance, imaginal representations can depict conceptual meanings only so far as such meanings involve visually discriminable properties (e.g., size, shape, position in space, distinctive motion, color, pattern). Moreover, because imaginal representations are still as much particulars as they are universals, they relate to each other not only as (implicit) representatives of classes but also as individuals, which means that they are subject to accidental and merely local associations and to the illogical condensations and displacements explained a moment ago. During the preconceptual substage, then, the spontaneous imagination or autosymbolic process works both for and against the child. It takes the child's thought halfway from particularity to universality *and keeps it there.*

If, then, the child is truly to master conceptual thought, it is necessary that the child eventually free cognition from the limitations of the imagination. This point is stressed by Bruner, who says: "For the child who still searches for the vivid perceptual cue the task of attaining conceptual meanings is necessarily made more difficult. . . . The results point clearly to the . . . conclusion: *the inferior conceptual performance of children with imagery preference is a result of their use of surface features in grouping*" (1966, pp. 27–28; italics in original). If the ego is to begin thinking for itself in an effectively conceptual way, it must, it seems, be weaned from the imagination.

This surmounting of the imagination is accomplished with a vengeance by primal repression, which not only disengages but *dissociates* the ego from the nonegoic source of imaginal creativity. Primal repression, in submerging the nonegoic sphere, disconnects the autosymbolic process from consciousness and thereby deprives the ego of spontaneously forged symbolic images. The ego, severed in this way from autosymbolic spontaneity, is forced to begin making conceptual discriminations without the aid of autosymbolic images. Primal repression, that is, forces the ego to begin disembedding universal from particular, conceptual meaning from perceptual or imaginal exemplification. Curiously, primal repression works as a negative means to a positive developmental end. In disconnecting the ego from the autosymbolic process, it forces the ego to do what Hegel calls the "hard work of the concept."

In moving from preconceptual-imaginal-magical to fully conceptual thought, the child at first develops only a vague intuitive "sense" or "feel" for conceptual meanings and their logical relationships. Such a "sense" or "feel" is distinctive of the intuitive substage of the stage of preoperations, which, as we have seen, coincides with the transition to latency. In time, however, by about the age of seven, the child becomes sufficiently familiar with conceptual boundaries and logical interconnections that it begins to be able to talk about them and perform operations on things in terms of them. This improved understanding remains, however, on a concrete level. That is, the child, although able to make proper class discriminations and perform effective logical operations, is able to do these things only in relation to particular things and events. The child is not yet able to conceive conceptual meanings or perform logical operations in the abstract. For this reason the child's thought at this stage is described by Piaget as concrete operational thought. This is the type of thought that prevails throughout most of latency.

Active Volition

Closely related to ego-initiated cognition is the ego function of active volition. The latter is the practical correlate of the former. Active volition is ego-initiated action, action that issues from conscious exercise of will. It is action that derives from egoic intention or choice rather than (exclusively) from nonegoic drives, impulses, or feelings.[10] Active volition is "self-will." Active volition includes all forms of ego-initiated action from the most basic forms of sensorimotor intentionality and impulse control on the one hand to the most elevated forms of rationally legislated conduct on the other.

Active volition, like the other ego functions, undergoes accelerated development during latency. Primal repression and primal alienation, in freeing the ego *from* the powerful influences of the pre-latency period, free the ego *to* exercise itself, both cognitively and practically, in a relatively unencumbered way. The ego, accordingly, experiences greatly increased impulse control. The ego not only grows stronger and therefore more able to exercise its will; it also experiences fewer and less powerful influences acting upon its will. Moreover, the development of intuitive-conceptual and, then, concrete operational thought during latency greatly increases the options and range of the ego's will. Initially, in the intuitive substage of the stage of preoperations, the child's self-willed actions involve very little if any forethought. The child merely senses that one course of action is the best and immediately affirms that course. Later, however, once intuitive-conceptual thought is superseded by concrete operational thought, the child is able to consider multiple options and calculate consequences. This deliberation, however, remains on the concrete level. It is conducted in terms of specific actions that the child might pursue and specific consequences that the child might enjoy or suffer. In terms of moral action, as we saw earlier, the child here acts in more or less immediate preconventional or conventional ways. The child is not yet able to deliberate abstractly and therefore is not yet able to conceive or apply moral principles. The ability to employ moral principles presupposes formal operational thought, which is not achieved until adolescence.

EXISTENTIAL ORIENTATION: PLAYFUL EXPLORATION OF THE WORLD

Despite being forms of negation, primal repression and primal alienation have the immediate positive effect of freeing the child from the overawing nonegoic influences, the psychic splitting, and the interpersonal conflicts that plagued the later preoedipal and oedipal periods. The period of latency, then, is not a time of insecurity or anxiety. On the contrary, it is a time of stability and fundamentally positive prospects. Latency is a time characterized by rapid ego development, as we have already discussed, and by playful exploration and pursuit of enjoyment, as we shall now discuss. The world is no longer the daunting and dangerous realm that it was prior to latency, and it is not yet the arena of serious commitments that it will be in late adolescence and early adulthood. Rather, the world is at once a school and a playground, a place to master basic ego skills and a field of pleasure and adventure.

Soren Kierkegaard (1945, 1959) divides human development into three stages: the aesthetic stage, the ethical stage, and the religious stage. His account of the aesthetic stage nicely describes the period of latency—although Kierkegaard himself saw the aesthetic stage as typically being of longer duration and as having no set chronological boundaries. Kierkegaard uses the term *aesthetic* in its original etymological meaning of sensation. Accordingly, the aesthetic stage is the period during which the primary aim of life is the pursuit of enjoyable sensations or of enjoyable experiences more generally. Kierkegaard describes the aesthetic stage as having the following features: immediacy, freedom, lightness, and egoism.

Aesthetic life is immediate in the sense that it is lived for the day or the moment rather than for a future that must be prepared for. Aesthetic life has no predefined agenda or long-term goals; rather, aesthetic life is a series of experiences: encounters, adventures, tasks, delights, surprises. Parents may set long-term goals for their children, but latency children rarely set serious long-term goals for themselves. Aesthetic life has no overarching plan or unifying purpose. It is a sequence of episodes, most of which, the child hopes, will be enjoyable ones.

Aesthetic life is free in the sense that it is not fettered by commitments. To be sure, latency children submit to the dictates of the superego and accept the limits and responsibilities set by parents and teachers. Moreover, older latency children, who have a more conventional moral perspective, typically take pride in meeting the requirements imposed by such authoritative agencies and figures. For this reason latency, as Erik Erikson (1963) explains, is a period of industry as well as play, a period during which children strive to achieve social and educational norms in order to meet the expectations and gain the approval of superiors. However, despite responding in this way to the responsibilities set for them by others, latency children typically do not impose major responsibilities on themselves. Latency children, therefore, although obedient to superego, parental, and conventional constraints, are relatively free of self-constraints. Relative to adults, latency children are not bound by commitments, which means that they are free to pursue enjoyment and to play—which is just what they want to do. Latency children characteristically perform their assigned duties in a conscientious manner; they also, however, characteristically perform these duties with one eye on the clock, looking forward to the moment when they can put these duties aside and lose themselves in the delights of play. For latency children, play is the basic and preferred mode of relating to the world.

Lived primarily in the mode of play, the latency child's life is characterized by lightness. Life is not a serious matter; it is not afflicted, to use Nietzsche's expression, with a spirit of gravity. For the child of the latency period, life is not supposed to be earnest or effortful; it is rather meant to be fun. To be sure, life is frequently not fun, because unwanted work and boredom are inevitable and sometimes tragic life circumstances prevail. Nevertheless, the lightness characteristic of youthful enjoyment is characteristic of the latency period generally. This lightness is evident even in areas we ordinarily think of as laden with seriousness. Children, for example, make every effort to transform work into play; they are extremely creative in finding ways of turning tasks into games. Also, children during latency approach the existential "concern" of self-identity in a playful spirit. Children tend to be more curious than anxious about who or what they are. They frequently pursue identity possibilities through exploratory play, by pretending to be heroes and by acting out character types and role scripts. By means of playful explorations such as these, children test a wide range of identity possibilities without having to make serious identity commitments. Children's make-believe performances are ways in which children form identifications that, as Erikson (1956, 1963) has explained, will later serve as the bases for the identity experiments of adolescence.

Aesthetic life, Kierkegaard believes, is egoistic in that it consists of the pursuit of enjoyment *for oneself*. Unlike a life of commitment and responsibility, which postpones or sacrifices enjoyment, frequently for others, aesthetic life seeks enjoyment as often as possible. In being egoistic in this sense, however, aesthetic life need not be egoistic in any other sense of the term. Specifically, latency children need not be excessively self-interested, selfish, or self-important. Children of the later latency period (ten and older), as we have seen, grow beyond a merely individual-egoistic outlook and achieve a more conventional-social perspective. Moreover, latency children can be dramatically generous and unselfassuming. Still, the primary focus for latency children is the pursuit of enjoyment. Latency children, it might be said, are "greedy" for enjoyment.

Kierkegaard stresses that boredom is the nemesis of aesthetic life. Accordingly, aesthetic life comes to an end when old sources of enjoyment become stale and boredom becomes a dominant mood. The child who is otherwise healthy but no longer delights in play, the child for whom "there is nothing to do," is about ready to leave the playing fields of latency and begin the "serious business" of adolescence and early adulthood.

CONCLUSION

Latency is a period of psychodynamic quiescence, peaceful object relations, rapid ego development, and playful pursuit of enjoyment. Primal repression frees the latency child from psychic upheavals by subduing nonegoic potentials and relegating them to the unconscious. Primal alienation provides the latency child with safe distance from primary others, distance that extricates the child from the interpersonal struggles of the preoedipal and oedipal periods and earns the child a sense of protected self-possession. Benefiting from these intrapsychic and interpersonal realignments, the ego is able to develop at a pace that is much more rapid than hitherto was possible. Latency is a period that roughly corresponds to the years that, in our society, are set aside for primary education. During these years, the child not only learns basic facts about the world but also masters basic ego functions and rudimentary skills of action and relationship. Finally, latency is a time that, free of upheavals and conflicts, and bolstered by "borrowed ego strength," is existentially secure and playful in spirit. The latency child suffers little anxiety, is full of curiosity, and experiences enjoyment in play and adventure.

Ruthellen Josselson (1980) has compared the latency period with the practicing subphase of the separation-individuation process of preoedipal development. She notes that the latency period is like the practicing subphase in that the child is at once thoroughly dependent upon its parents and thoroughly unaware of this dependence. Utterly taking for granted the support and guidance provided by parents and parental imagoes, the latency child explores the world with reckless abandon, taking delight in the world and in itself. The latency child, like the practicing toddler, uses the parents as a "home base" from which to proceed and to which to return for "refueling" and nurture. The pervasive and absolutely indispensable support provided by the parents is invisible to the latency child just as it is to the practicing toddler. Again, this invisible support is the "borrowed ego strength" on which, according to Peter Blos, latency is founded. This borrowed strength is in significant measure forfeited when latency gives way to adolescence.

From a transpersonal perspective, the latency period is the stage of early dualism. It is the time during which egoic-nonegoic and self-other dualisms initially emerge. These dualisms, however, are not problematic for the latency child. In fact, as already noted, primal repression and primal alienation perform positive developmental functions throughout latency and, indeed, throughout much of adult life. The latency child does not, then, suffer from a sense of loss of spontaneity and intimacy. Instead, the latency child experiences relief from intrapsychic storms and interpersonal battles. The negative side of dualism is not manifested during latency. It does not surface until adolescence, when the ego is beset with a regressive recapitulation of prelatency difficulties and with existential anxieties focused on ego identity. After adolescence, the negative side of dualism again disappears and typically does not resurface until midlife, when it can manifest itself in a wide variety of psychological difficulties. The negative side of dualism as it manifests itself during adolescence is discussed in the next chapter. The negative side of dualism as it manifests itself at midlife is discussed in chapter 7.

5

Ego Development and Dualism in Adolescence

Adolescence is the transitional period between youth and adulthood. The upheavals of the adolescent years are symptomatic of a process of awakening, destabilization, and restructuring that prepares the way for adult life. The equilibrium of the latency period is upset by the activation of sexuality and consequent stirring of nonegoic life, by a need to struggle for independence from parents and their internalized representations, by a search for a person or persons with whom to establish a sexually intimate relationship, and by existential concerns focused on emerging selfhood. Adolescence is in these ways a period of serious disequilibrium. Adolescence, however, is not only a period of upheaval; it is also a period of continued rapid ego growth. It is an ordeal of change that involves both regressive and progressive movements, both of which work to prepare for a new equilibrium that is achieved at the end of adolescence and serves as the foundation for early adult life.

I designated the period of latency *early* dualism because it is the first stage of life based on primal repression and primal alienation and the egoic-nonegoic and self-other dualisms that those structures bring into being. In this chapter I shall treat adolescence as a transitional stage between the early dualism of the latency period and the mature dualism of early adult life. As such a transitional stage, adolescence characteristically involves a challenge to primal repression and primal alienation. These dualistic structures are put to the test as significant psychodynamic transformations and interpersonal realignments occur. The stresses applied to primal repression and primal alienation weaken these bases of the mental-egoic system without, however, radically undermining them—except in pathological cases. Accordingly, once the adolescent process is complete, primal repression and primal alienation are refortified, and new forms of nonegoic latency and interpersonal object constancy emerge. Early adulthood is thus a new and more mature form of dualism.

Psychodynamically, adolescence is a period during which sexuality is awakened and, consequently, primal repression is loosened and nonegoic potentials of all types are stirred into activity. From the point of view of object relations, adolescence is a period during which primal alienation is relaxed and long-buried intimacy needs reassert themselves in distinctive ways, namely, by triggering a recapitulation of early childhood object relations and a search for a new primary "love object." In ego-developmental perspective, adolescence is a stage characterized by continued rapid development of ego functions and most notably by the attainment of transcendental self-reflection and formal operational cognition. And in its existential dimension, adolescence is a time of narcissistic preoccupation with and anxious uncertainty about emerging selfhood. Repeating the approach of the last chapter, I shall discuss each of these features of adolescence, focusing specifically on how these features can be understood in terms of the underlying structures of primal repression and primal alienation.

Psychodynamics

The most obvious of all phenomena associated with adolescence is the awakening of sexuality. Puberty marks the beginning of adolescence, and in this respect adolescence is punctuated not only by a psychosexual but also by a physiological transformation. The beginning of adolescence is conspicuously evident not only in the emergence of new sexual interests and behaviors but also in the beginning of menstruation in girls and ejaculatory capacity in boys and in the appearance of secondary sexual characteristics in both girls and boys. These physiological changes indicate just how powerful and pervasive a transformation adolescence is. No other period of human development is introduced by physiological changes as dramatic as those that introduce adolescence.

Psychodynamically, the awakening of sexuality has two principal effects. First, this awakening, as an upsurge from the nonegoic sphere, has the effect of loosening primal repression. The power of the sexual drive is such that it weakens primal repression sufficiently to allow sexual feelings to express themselves within consciousness. Primal repression is in this way rendered permeable without, however, as noted earlier, being radically undermined. And second, the awakening of sexuality has the effect of arousing nonegoic life generally. Nonegoic potentials, long dormant, are reactivated and, along with sexuality, begin to exert an influence within consciousness. This renewed activity of nonegoic potentials is evident across virtually the entire range of these potentials: the body, energy, instincts, feelings, and the creative (imaginal-autosymbolic-archetypal) process.

Bodily changes, as just noted, are conspicuous. The profound physiological transformations taking place make adolescence a time of acute bodily awareness. Rapid overall growth, sexual maturation and corresponding new sexual sensations, and dramatic changes in shape, voice, and complexion make the body a central focus of attention. Puberty involves an awakening of the body in ways that, for the adolescent, are both fascinating and frightening. Many adolescents become obsessively focused on the body, on both its changing internal "feel" and its changing external appearance.

Energic awakening is apparent in a shift from "object libido" to "narcissistic libido" and in corresponding experiences of estrangement and narcissistic self-absorption. Peter Blos, the preeminent psychoanalytic writer on adolescence, describes this cathectic shift in the following way:

> The narcissistic quality of the adolescent's personality is well known. The withdrawal of object cathexis leads to an overvaluation of the self, to heightened self-perception at the expense of reality testing, to an extreme touchiness and self-absorption, and generally, to self-centeredness and self-aggrandizement. The adolescent's withdrawal of cathexis from the object world can lead to narcissistic withdrawal and loss of reality testing . . . . (1962, p. 90)

The dynamic upsurge of adolescence disrupts the cathectic equilibrium of latency. It supercharges the ego, making the ego the dynamic center of gravity of the psyche and thereby causing the ego to withdraw preexisting object cathexes. The ego is in this way both infused and turned in upon itself. The energic awakening of adolescence both inflates and introverts the ego, rendering it susceptible to narcissistic self-absorption.[1]

Phenomenologically, the withdrawal of object cathexes is expressed in a sense of indifference to the world. The teenager, for example, frequently withdraws from persons who previously were figures of value. Many friendships come to an end or are redefined, childhood heroes are cast aside, and parents are perceived as old-fashioned or otherwise not "with it." The teenager also experiences indifference toward activities that previously were of great importance. These activities are now perceived as "childish" or "boring." The withdrawal of object cathexes estranges the teenager both from persons who previously were primary others and from activities that previously were primary enjoyments. It causes the teenager to experience a generalized alienation from the world.

As the withdrawal of object cathexes causes the adolescent to experience this alienation, the upwelling of energy into the ego causes the adolescent to experience a heightened, almost voluptuous self-consciousness. The inner world of subjectivity is lit up and amplified, and the adolescent becomes introspectively self-absorbed. In extreme cases this self-absorption can become almost solipsistic in its inwardness. The adolescent experiences a growing preoccupation with self that is inversely proportional to the loss of interest in persons and activities associated with "childhood." As the teenager's outer world is divested of charge and significance, the teenager's inner world is invested with charge and significance.

The instinctual awakening of adolescence is most evidently an awakening of sexuality. It is, however, an awakening of aggression in some sense as well. Classical psychoanalytic drive theory, of course, holds that sexuality and aggression are equiprimordial instinctual drives that are present at birth or begin differentiating themselves soon thereafter. According to the standard two-drive theory, sexuality and aggression are uninhibitedly active during infancy and early childhood; they are quieted significantly as a consequence of the repression that brings an end to the Oedipus complex; and they are reawakened powerfully with the onset of puberty. According to this standard view, sexuality and aggression are instincts of equal status that develop along parallel lines.

A criticism sometimes brought against this view is that it does not give sufficient recognition to the unprecedented nature of sexuality and aggression as they emerge in puberty. The desire-anger, love-hate ambivalence experienced by the infant and young child and the sexuality-aggression ambivalence experienced by the adolescent are indeed analogous, but they may not be expressions of the same underlying drives. The sexuality that awakens during adolescence is so strongly connected with physiological maturation and hormonal changes as to suggest an important difference between it and the desire-love side of infantile and early childhood ambivalence. And the aggression that emerges during adolescence, it seems, has psychodynamic underpinnings that are not found in the anger-hate side of infantile and early childhood ambivalence. That is, adolescent aggression seems to derive not only from interpersonal tensions between child and parents but also from intrapsychic tensions between instinctual impulses and countercathectic inhibitions, inhibitions not present during infancy and early childhood. I shall pursue this suggestion in chapter 9. For present purposes it suffices to note that adolescence is a period punctuated by a relatively unprecedented upsurge of sexuality and aggression.

The instinctual awakening of adolescence generates compelling impulses and ideations. Freud's term *drive* (*Trieb*) applies perhaps most fittingly to the sexual urgency experienced by the adolescent. The adolescent feels relentlessly driven, as if under the influence of an irresistible need. This experience is threatening to the ego, which, during latency, was not seriously challenged by nonegoic potentials. The ego therefore sometimes tries to reassert itself by means of extreme defensive maneuvers. Anna Freud (1946, 1958) pointed to asceticism and intellectualism as defenses to which teenagers are prone in responce to threatening instinctual importunings. And Blos (1962) notes that excessive self-control in general is a defense that is typical of adolescents in the throes of instinctual awakening. Owing to powerful somatopsychic transformations, many teenagers fear that they are on the brink of losing control. And, responding to this fear, some teenagers place themselves under severe regimens (e.g., diet, study, physical exertion, involvement in activities) to keep a rein on themselves.

The instinctual eruption of adolescence triggers a dramatic outpouring of emotions. The teenager is flooded with feelings. Some of these feelings are reactivations of dormant prelatency feelings and others are feelings not experienced before, including a whole range of yearnings, enthusiasms, and anxieties that accompany the awakening of sexuality, the emergence of self-consciousness, and the struggle for personal independence. The teenager's emotional life is expanded in these and other ways. It also is intensified and destabilized. For the teenager's feelings are amplified by narcissistically introverted energy and, as we shall see, frequently split into conflicting opposites by contradictions implicit in adolescent object relations. The teenager's emotional life is therefore both volatile and labile. The teenager is prone to experience feelings that are both exaggerated and inconsistent, for example, passions and rages, ecstasies and agonies, yearnings and loathings. To be sure, the teenager experiences a good deal of emotional level ground. The teenager, however, also experiences many emotional peaks and valleys.

Finally, adolescence is a period of quickened imaginal activity. It has been well known for a long time (Spiegel 1958; Blos 1962) that adolescence is for many people the most creative period of life. It is a period during which, for example, many people keep diaries, write poems or stories, begin novels, develop an interest in art or music, embark upon mechanical or intellectual projects, or invent games or other recreational diversions. These creative endeavors serve both expressive and defensive purposes. They are ways in which the adolescent is able to give expression to a wealth of new experiences and at the same time gain better understanding or control of these experiences. They are creative expressions that bring greater coherence or order to the teenager's burgeoning internal life. Adolescence is a time of creative-emotional efflorescence. Regrettably, this flowering is frequently nipped in the bud when adolescence gives way to early adulthood.

According to Peter Blos (1967, 1968), the awakening of nonegoic life that occurs during adolescence is not an awakening pure and simple; it is rather an awakening accompanied by regression of a distinctive sort. This regression, Blos holds, is both a necessary and normal part of the adolescent process:

> In contrast, adolescent regression, which is not defensive in nature, constitutes an integral part of development at puberty. This regression nevertheless induces anxiety more often than not. Should this anxiety become unmanageable, then, secondarily, defensive measures become mobilized. Regression in adolescence is not, in and by itself, a defense, but it constitutes an essential psychic process that, despite the anxiety it engenders, must take its course. Only then can the task be fulfilled that is implicit in adolescent development. (1967, p. 154)

Adolescence involves what Blos calls a regression in the service of development. The ego undergoes a regression to make possible a higher state of (egoic) integration. Adolescent regression, in Blos's view, is not a pathological regression but rather is a regression that facilitates development toward a more inclusive equilibrium.[2]

Adopting Blos's notion of adolescent regression in the service of development, I suggest that the principal cause of this regression is the weakening of primal repression that occurs during adolescence. Primal repression is the deepest infrastructure of the mental-egoic system, and therefore the weakening of primal repression has the effect not only of reopening consciousness to nonegoic potentials but also of destabilizing the ego. It has the effect of rendering the ego vulnerable to being decentered, disoriented, flooded, and dissolved. To be sure, the ego, in being reopened to the influence of nonegoic potentials, is greatly enriched in its interior life. It becomes sensitive to a wide range of new sensations and feelings, and it sometimes becomes significantly more creative. The ego, however, is not only enriched but also regressed by the influence of nonegoic potentials, because the ego's openness to these potentials destabilizes it in the ways just mentioned and, as we have seen, renders it prone to both narcissistic self-absorptions and defensive self-contractions. Moreover, the ego, in being subject to powerful nonegoic spontaneities, tends to suffer some loss of discernment in reality testing and to fall prey to flights of fantasy and enthusiasm.

Again, these regressive phenomena are normal rather than pathological. They can of course be a matter of considerable distress for the adolescent and are responsible for many instances of poor judgment. In most cases, however, they are not symptomatic of psychic impairment. They reflect a turbulent but noninjurious transformation of the adolescent psyche. Accordingly, the ego almost always survives the adolescent process and, in the end, is able to regroup in a way that makes it stronger and more integrated than it was before the process began. Primal repression is weakened but rarely collapses. Rather, it is partially deconstructed and then reconstructed in a way that integrates awakened sexuality and corresponding intimacy needs.

The restructuring of primal repression brings about a new equilibrium, the attainment of which is one of the chief indications that the transition from adolescence to adulthood has occurred. This new equilibrium differs from the equilibrium of the latency period in that, as just noted, it allows awakened sexuality and corresponding intimacy needs to be expressed within the field of consciousness. This new equilibrium therefore is more inclusive than was the equilibrium of the latency period. Nevertheless, this new equilibrium remains similar in many respects to the preadolescent condition it replaces. For, as Blos (1968) notes, postadolescent psychodynamic equilibrium is not only a move forward to a more inclusive form of structural stability but also, in most respects, a return to preadolescent dormancy. It involves not only an integration of awakened sexuality but also a requieting of most of the rest of nonegoic life. In our terms, the restructuring of primal repression consolidates in new form the constraints of egoic-nonegoic dualism. It reasserts the dualistic separation of the ego from the nonegoic sphere. Primal repression, as restructured, allows the expression of awakened sexuality and related interpersonal feelings but otherwise reinforces the repression of the nonegoic sphere, which is once again deactivated and returned to latency. The new equilibrium of early adulthood can therefore be described as an equilibrium of "sexually active latency."

OBJECT RELATIONS

Adolescence is a time of complex object relations. The following aspects or phases are most noteworthy: (1) primal alienation is relaxed, and the adolescent consequently experiences a gnawing longing for intimacy; (2) the adolescent struggles for independence from parents and their internal imagoes and begins to search for a person who, as a new primary object choice, can satisfy the reawakened longings for intimacy; (3) the struggle for independence triggers a recapitulation of the major positions of preoedipal and oedipal object relations; and (4) this struggle simultaneously disempowers the superego (as a source of parental interdictions) and promotes the emergence of the ego ideal (as a source of individualistic strivings). Adolescent object relations involve a rekindling of the need for intimacy and a simultaneous shift of primary cathexis away from parents toward new "object" possibilities. These developments trigger a replay, in new form, of the conflictual object relations that plagued the late preoedipal and oedipal periods. Concomitantly, these developments weaken the intrapsychic representative of parental authority (the superego) and facilitate the emergence of the intrapsychic agency driving the ego toward fulfillment and self-perfection (the ego ideal).

The instinctual upsurge that loosens primal repression relaxes primal alienation as well, because, as we know, these two are the inner and outer dimensions, respectively, of the same fundamental structure. Adolescence, therefore, is a period characterized by a stirring not only of nonegoic potentials but also of longings for intimacy. The adolescent begins to experience a restless sense of incompleteness and a corresponding need to share subjective life with someone else. These feelings revivify experiences tied to preoedipal object relations. The adolescent's rekindled need for intimacy reactivates feelings, both positive and negative, for the mother that were last experienced when the adolescent, as a young child, was still symbiotically connected with the mother as primary caregiver. The adolescent, however, is headed in a developmental direction leading away from parents, and therefore the intimacy needs that the adolescent experiences undergo a shift away from their original object toward a new object choice. Moreover, because the adolescent's need for intimacy is driven by awakened sexuality, the tendency is for the adolescent to move, ultimately if not immediately, in the direction of a new object choice that can satisfy intimacy and sexual needs at the same time.

The struggle for independence from parents can be a painful ordeal. The adolescent, to become a "complete" person, must sever lines of emotional dependence upon parents. In the early teenage years, the first steps that a young person takes in this direction are typically to seek out a small group of same-sex friends and to join a larger peer group. The young person ages twelve to fourteen or fifteen characteristically selects one or two people of the same sex with whom to have a confidential, an intimate but nonsexual, relationship. The young person confides thoughts, desires, and hopes with this select friend or group of friends. At the same time, the young person may cease communicating with parents in these ways. Also, the young person at this point usually joins a peer group, a cohort exploring common values, styles, and points of view. If the purpose of the select friend or friends is to facilitate an initial refocusing of intimacy needs away from parents, and from the mother in particular, the principal purpose of the peer group, it seems, is to serve as an initial replacement of the parents, and the father in particular, as authority figures, as judges of standards and norms.

Ruthellen Josselson (1988) rightly cautions against exaggerating the adolescent's break with parents, noting that the separation from parents is almost always a process that occurs within a larger context of continuing relationship. The separation from parents is rarely an all-or-nothing movement. The young adolescent wavers back and forth, sharing some confidences with parents and others with friends, submitting for the most part to parental authority while dressing and talking in ways prescribed by the peer group, relying predominantly on parental support and nurture while stressing self-possession and searching for ways to assert independence. The adolescent's relationship with the parents almost always remains the basis of the adolescent's life. Nevertheless, it is a basis against which the adolescent necessarily struggles in attempting to become an autonomous individual.

According to Blos (1962), early adolescence ends and adolescence proper commences when the teenager begins to search for a relationship that is intimate not only in the sense of confidential sharing but also in the sense of romantic and sexual mutuality. The teenager's newfound sexuality impels the teenager in this direction, inexorably transforming the need for intimacy into a need for sexual intimacy. Consequently, the teenager usually becomes less exclusively devoted to friends and the peer group that had been so important in early adolescence and begins to invest primary attention and energy in romantic-sexual prospects. This further shift of object focus most often passes through a period of exploration and trial (dating, "going steady," courtship, engagement) and leads toward a final object choice, which, when it occurs, is usually made at the end of adolescence or in early adulthood. Commitment to such a final object choice is one of the markers indicating that the adolescent struggle for independence from parents has achieved successful completion.

The struggle for independence from parents triggers a recapitulation of prelatency object relations. This fact was recognized long ago by Ernest Jones (1922) and was reemphasized by Anna Freud, who said:

> The danger [i.e., the anxiety experienced by the adolescent] is felt to be located not only in the id impulses and fantasies but in the very existence of the love objects of the individual's oedipal and preoedipal past. The libidinal cathexis to them has been carried forward from the infantile phases, merely toned down or inhibited in aim during latency. Therefore the reawakened pregenital urges, or—worse still—the newly acquired genital ones, are in danger of making contact with them, lending a new and threatening reality to fantasies which had seemed extinct but are, in fact, merely under repression. (1958, p. 268)

In addition, then, to experiencing an awakening of sexuality and a consequent stirring of the "id" (i.e., nonegoic potentials), the adolescent experiences a return of desires and conflicts that, having afflicted the preoedipal and oedipal child, were long ago "swept under the rug." These desires and conflicts now spring back to life, and the adolescent is forced to deal with them again, on a new level and in search of a superior resolution.

Although the manner in which the Oedipus complex is replayed during adolescence was investigated early on in psychoanalysis, the manner in which preoedipal desires and conflicts are replayed during adolescence has been investigated only in recent decades. Studies of preoedipal influences on adolescent development were made possible by the wide acceptance of Margaret Mahler's (Mahler, Pine, and Bergman 1975) account of the separation-individuation process. Many psychoanalysts have applied Mahler's ideas to adolescence, showing how stages of adolescence can be understood in terms of subphases of the separation-individuation process. Blos (1967) led the way in applying Mahler's ideas, and many others (e.g., Brandt 1977; Esman 1980; Josselson 1980; Kroger 1985, 1989) have followed his lead.

Those who apply Mahler's work to adolescence interpret the adolescent's struggle for independence in terms of some or all of the subphases of the separation-individuation process: differentiation, practicing, rapprochement, and the transition to object constancy. Representatives of this perspective disagree on just how to correlate these subphases with specific time frames within the teenage years, and they differ as well on which one of the subphases is to be correlated with the beginning of adolescence. Most, however, agree that a recapitulation of the rapprochement subphase and a renegotiation of the resolution of the crisis of this subphase are essential challenges of the adolescent period.

Aaron Esman (1980) correlates the differentiation or "hatching" subphase with early adolescence, which is the period during which the young person takes the first steps toward independence from parents. During early adolescence, Esman notes, the young person seeks to achieve psychological distance from parents, perhaps, as I have suggested, by withdrawing from confidential communication with them and selecting a friend or friends with whom to communicate in this way. Following this initial distancing from parents, the young person enters a period similar to Mahler's practicing subphase. Esman and Ruthellen Josselson (1980) agree that much of early adolescence is like the practicing subphase in that, during this period, the young person participates in peer groups and explores new personal and social possibilities while at the same time unconsciously presupposing parents as a support system on which to rely and to which to return in time of need. David Brandt (1977) compares this adolescent practicing period to what Erik Erikson calls the *psychosocial moratorium* of adolescence, because this practicing period is a sort of "time out" during which the young person can explore new roles without having to face serious commitments or responsibilities.

By middle adolescence or adolescence proper, however, the young person begins to sense being at a crossroads. This crossroads is a juncture at which the increased independence from parents brings into focus and begins to call into question the young person's continued dependence on parents. This crossroads is also a point at which the adolescent's intimacy needs are especially acute and therefore at which the adolescent is resensitized to residual lines of intimacy with the mother, lines that lead all the way back to preoedipal symbiosis. The sense of being at this crossroads marks the beginning of a period similar to Mahler's rapprochement subphase. The adolescent, still committed to the course of independence, begins at this point to sense the degree and force of the underlying emotional bond with parents, especially the mother. Accordingly, the adolescent begins to feel caught between opposing forces, forces pushing forward toward greater independence and distance and forces pulling backward toward continued dependence and attachment. Caught in this way, teenagers, as Blos (1967) stresses, become strongly ambivalent toward their parents. Although some of this ambivalence, as we shall see, is reawakened oedipal ambivalence directed primarily at the father, much of it is reawakened preoedipal ambivalence directed at the mother as original love object.

Depending on the intensity of the ambivalence experienced, the teenager may be forced to resort to the defense mechanism of splitting, a mechanism that, if we remember, is characteristic of the preoedipal rapprochement crisis. The teenager is here prone to split parents, individually or collectively, into all-good and all-bad caricatures that reflect the positive and negative sides of the teenager's ambivalence. The mother may once again be split into a Good Mother and a Terrible Mother, and the father, as symbol of oedipal authority, may be split into a Wise Ruler and a Ruthless Tyrant. Also, as frequently happens when critical decisions are at stake, the teenager may make a mutually exclusive division between all-good peers and all-bad parents. The adolescent at this crossroads experiences strongly conflicting desires and sharply divided loyalties, desires and loyalties that frequently cause the adolescent to split primary object representations.

Brandt (1977) notes that the teenager at this rapprochement crossroads is vulnerable to the Eriksonian identity crisis and to the acting out of unrealistic or merely negative identity possibilities. I shall discuss the matter of adolescent identity anxiety later. Brandt's observation is well placed here, however, because the strong ambivalence experienced during middle adolescence can cause a splitting not only of object representations but also of the self-representation. The adolescent is torn between two senses of self, an old, parentally grounded sense and a newly emerging sense; and both of these senses are repeatedly valued, devalued, and revalued as the teenager oscillates between the opposing sides of his or her ambivalence toward parents. Torn between these two senses of self, the teenager suffers from serious self-doubts and is prone to extreme, if not desperate, self-expressions. Most teenagers probably do not experience difficulties such as these to a degree sufficient to warrant applying the term *crisis*. Nevertheless, most do experience considerable ambivalence and even some splitting, and most suffer painful uncertainty about themselves.

Successful navigation of the straits of middle adolescence leads, in Mahler's terms, from rapprochement ambivalence and splitting to object constancy. Blos (1967), as noted earlier, explicitly compares the transition from adolescence to early adulthood to the achievement of a second level of object constancy. Discussing a clinical case, he says:

> A secondary object constancy in relation to the mother of the adolescent period became established. The omnipotent mother of the infantile period was superseded by the son's realization of her fallibilities and virtues. In short, she became human. Only through regression [i.e., regressive recapitulation of pre-oedipal separation and individuation] was it possible for the boy to re-experience the maternal image and institute those corrections and differentiations that effected a neutralization of his preoedipal ambivalent object relation. (p. 165)

Adolescent splitting is finally overcome when the adolescent, now a young adult, has achieved a sufficient degree of independence no longer to be caught in the contradictory predicament of "dependent independence." Upon achieving this level of independence—which usually involves an intimate relationship with a new primary other or others—the young adult is able to integrate feelings for parents and enter into a relationship with parents as more or less equal human beings, that is, as fallible but lovable persons rather than as spilt (caring-cruel, omniscient-ignorant) sovereign powers. Contradictory feelings and split object representations begin to be resolved, and the young adult begins to experience a new level of psychic equilibrium. From a psychodynamic perspective, as we saw earlier, this new level of equilibrium is a new level of latency; from an object-relational perspective, it is a new level of object constancy.

The full attainment of this second level of object constancy requires that a new resolution be found not only for preoedipal but also for oedipal conflicts. The timing of the adolescent replay of preoedipal and oedipal interactions is not sequentially ordered in any clear way as is the original occurrence of these interactions during early childhood. Rather, the contradictions of middle adolescence simultaneously rekindle preoedipal ambivalence toward the mother and oedipal ambivalence toward the father. Both of these ambivalences plague the adolescent during the middle teen years, and both ambivalences must be surmounted for stability and equilibrium—the second level of object constancy—to be achieved.

In the case of oedipal ambivalence, the adolescent once again experiences the father as both a model and adversary. In the original oedipal situation, if we remember, the father is both a model in being an exemplar of egoic independence and an adversary in being a rival for intimacy with the mother. The original oedipal situation refocused preoedipal ambivalence toward the mother onto the father: the preoedipal child's need for independence from the mother found a positive focus in the father as model of egoic independence, and the preoedipal child's desire for continuing symbiotic intimacy with the mother found a negative focus in the father as rival for the mother's primary affections. The ambivalence that is redirected upon the father in these ways, as we know, was finally overcome in childhood by means of a double commitment to the father. The child made a positive commitment to the father in decisively accepting him as model, either by directly emulating him (boys) or by establishing a relationship with him patterned on the mother's relationship with him (girls). And the child made a negative commitment to the father in decisively capitulating to him as rival for intimacy with the mother. This double commitment brought an end to child-parent ambivalence, which remained buried until its reawakening in adolescence.

The reawakening of the oedipal struggle during adolescence causes the father once again to be experienced as both a model and adversary. These two roles, however, are now fused, because it is precisely *as* a model that the father is now also experienced as an adversary. In being experienced as a model, the father is no longer perceived solely as an exemplar of egoic independence, as a model to emulate in pursuing independence. Rather, the father is now perceived as a person whose example exerts a dominating influence upon the adolescent, an influence from which, therefore, the adolescent feels impelled to break free. Emulating the father as model is no longer perceived as a way of asserting selfhood. Rather, emulating the father is now perceived only as conformity and capitulation to the father. The father's egoic independence no longer represents the child's need for independence from the preoedipal mother; rather, it now represents the adolescent's need for independence from the father himself. The teenager is still very much under the sway of the father's oedipal authority, and the need to break away from this authority causes feelings of guilt. Because, however, the teenager's movement toward independence has developmental priority, the teenager cannot help experiencing a strong, negatively weighted ambivalence toward the father as the focus of both fear and hostility, submission and rebellion, loyalty and betrayal. As noted previously, ambivalent feelings like these can lead to a splitting of the father into exaggerated opposites such as Wise Ruler on the one hand and Ruthless Tyrant on the other.

The overcoming of this ambivalence toward the father, like the overcoming of adolescent ambivalence generally, requires the attainment of a sufficient degree of independence on the part of the adolescent to cease being a "dependent independent" and become, simply, an independent person. Once genuine independence is achieved, the adolescent, now a young adult, can establish a new relationship with both parents. Residual symbiotic longings for the mother subside once an intimate, maturely sexual relationship has been established with a significant other or others. And residual oedipal fear of the father subsides once real autonomy and self-responsibility have been won. Prelatency object relations are thus once again laid to rest.[3] Early adult life is a second period of object constancy, a period of interpersonal stability that is relatively untroubled by the contradictory object relations of early childhood.

Adolescent ambivalence, and oedipal ambivalence in particular, is played out internally in a conflict between the ego ideal and the superego. Blos (1962, 1972, 1974) especially has stressed the important role played by the ego ideal in adolescence. Blos agrees with Edith Jacobson (1964) that the ego ideal is significantly restructured during adolescence. Generally, they hold that the ego ideal, which during latency is a part of the superego, emerges during adolescence as a structure that is significantly independent of the superego. Their main point is that the harmony that exists between the ego ideal and superego during latency is disrupted during adolescence, with the consequence that the ego ideal is disembedded from the superego and begins to function as a semi-independent source of motivation.

Because the superego is an intrapsychic representative of parental, and especially paternal, authority, the adolescent's struggle for independence from parents is at the same time a struggle for independence from the superego. The growing tensions that afflict the adolescent's relationship with parents undermine the adolescent's confidence in parents as moral paragons. Parents, accordingly, as we have seen, become objects of intense ambivalence, and the teenager seeks to establish distance from them. Intrapsychically, this means that the teenager experiences ambivalence toward the superego, the voice of which now takes on an ego-dystonic tone, and begins to experience individualistic strivings that challenge the imperatives of the superego. As Jeanne Lampl-de Groot (1960) explains, the strivings for individual fulfillment and perfection generated by the ego ideal at this point cease supporting the imperatives of the superego and begin pushing the adolescent in new directions. The nucleus of the ego ideal begins to separate from the superego complex and begins to take on a voice of its own as a semi-independent psychic agency. This new psychic voice is initially unclear; the ego ideal's strivings are at first little more than longings for some vague ideal condition. If, however, the strivings of the ego ideal are vague, they are nonetheless powerful in their effect. They fill the adolescent with implacable yearnings and fervors, and they provide the stimulus for abstract idealisms and utopian dreams.

This conflict between the ego ideal and superego lasts throughout the period of middle adolescence and is not resolved until the adolescent's ambivalence toward parents, and toward the father in particular, is resolved. I have already noted that a precondition of the overcoming of ambivalence toward parents is that the young person make real progress toward independence. Correspondingly, a precondition of the reconciliation of the ego ideal and the superego is that the young person make an initial commitment to an identity project. I shall discuss the matter of ego identity extensively in the next chapter. For the present suffice it to say that commitment to an identity project provides a common ground on which the ego can reintegrate the ego ideal and superego. Accordingly, once the adolescent has made an initial commitment to an identity project, the intraegoic conflict between the ego ideal and superego can begin to subside and these two egoic subagencies can begin to work in harmonious unison.

The interpersonal and intrapsychic struggles just discussed are pervaded by a feeling of *guilt*. For the teenager's struggle for independence from parents involves in a very real sense an unprovoked turning away from the persons who have been and continue to be the teenager's principal benefactors. To a significant degree, the struggle for independence from parents requires the teenager to reject his or her parents as ideal models, to withdraw from them as love objects, and to challenge them as authority figures. Parents are the most important people in the teenager's life, and yet the teenager, frequently, is impelled to devalue them, rebuff their loving solicitations, and contest their well-intentioned guidance. This turning away from parents, which can be either overtly rebellious or subtle and "polite" (passive aggression), happens without the parents having done anything that would "justify" the teenager's new attitudes and actions. The adolescent's treatment of his or her parents, although developmentally necessary, is therefore "unjustified" and carries with it a burden of guilt. It is a version of the archetypal "sin" of rejecting one's creator(s), of defying and denouncing the gods. The guilt incurred by this "sin" is difficult to bear, and teenagers frequently engage in exaggerated devaluations of parents and self-deluding rationalizations of their own actions to keep this guilt from view.

The guilt that the adolescent experiences in relation to parents can be compared to the guilt that, according to Melanie Klein (1934, 1948, 1952a, 1964), the preoedipal child experiences in relation to the mother. Klein holds that the preoedipal child's aggressive-destructive fantasies involving the mother cause the child to experience feelings of loss, mourning, guilt, and need to make reparations, as if the child's fantasies had caused injury to the mother. Similar feelings, I suggest, are experienced by the teenager as a result of the teenager's turning away from parents. The teenager both loves and hates, both respects and rejects his or her parents. And precisely because of this ambivalence, the teenager experiences feelings of sorrow and remorse. The struggle for independence from parents saddles the adolescent with a sense of guilt that lasts beyond adolescence into adult life. Following adolescence, most people experience a need to establish a new relationship with parents and a need to justify their independence from parents by succeeding in life in ways that will make parents proud. In Klein's terms, these felt needs are guilt-driven desires to make reparations to parents that arise as a consequence of earlier actions perpetrated against parents.[4]

In sum, the object relations of adolescence can be said to have two chief dimensions: (1) a growth-motivated but guilt-ridden struggle for independence from parents and their internalized representations, and (2) a sexually driven search for a new primary object choice. The struggle for independence from parents is at once an outer struggle with the parents themselves and an inner struggle with parental imagoes. Outwardly, the struggle involves a replay of prelatency object relations and in particular a recapitulation of the separation-individuation interaction with the preoedipal mother and a reenactment in new form of the emulation-competition interaction with the oedipal father. And inwardly, the struggle involves a conflictual separation of the ego ideal from the superego. Both of these outer and inner struggles, as we have seen, are burdened with a sense of guilt, because the adolescent, in struggling against the parents and their internal representations, is unilaterally turning away from what hitherto were exemplars of perfection, love, and proper authority. The guilt that is incurred in this way, although significant, is rarely sufficient to abort the adolescent process, which pushes forward until independence is achieved, typically in conjunction with commitments to an identity project and a new object choice. The young adult embarks on a self-chosen identity project and, typically, a self-chosen primary relationship. These expressions of independence are the primary goals of the adolescent process and therefore bring adolescent object relations to a close. Accordingly, at the beginning of adulthood, the difficulties of adolescent object relations disappear and a new stage of object constancy begins.

Earlier, I noted that the second level of latency achieved at the end of adolescence is preceded not just by a resurgence of nonegoic potentials but by a *regressive* resurgence of nonegoic potentials. Correspondingly, the second level of object constancy achieved at the end of adolescence is preceded not just by a recapitulation of the primary positions of early object relations but by a *regressive* recapitulation of these positions. Peter Blos (1967, 1968) puts a special emphasis on this latter side of adolescent regression. According to Blos, the psychic equilibrium of early adulthood is possible only by means of a regressive reexperience of the object relations of both the preoedipal and oedipal periods.

The reencounter with the positions of early object relations is a regressive process because the ego, to a certain extent, is actually drawn back to these positions, becoming entangled in the ambivalences these positions originally engendered. To be sure, the adolescent, in reexperiencing prelatency object relations, does not simply revert to earlier levels of development. Instead, the adolescent reexperiences prelatency ambivalences from the standpoint of a considerably more mature understanding and life context. That is to say, the adolescent reexperiences these ambivalences *qua adolescent*. The regressive recapitulation of prelatency object relations is therefore a real regression but not a pathological regression. It is, as Blos says, a regression in the service of development. Or, to borrow a term from David M. Levin (1985, 1988, 1989), the adolescent's regressive reexperience of prelatency feelings and dilemmas is a *hermeneutical* regression, a regression that reexperiences the past from the perspective and within the context of the present. The hermeneutical nature of the regression is what makes it a regression that serves positive rather than pathological ends.

The regressive recapitulation of early object relations and the regressive resurgence of nonegoic potentials (discussed earlier) go hand in hand. They are two sides of the same regressive-transformative process, just as the second level of object constancy and the second level of latency that emerge from this process are two sides of the same state. From the perspective of psychodynamics, the regressive-transformative process of adolescence is one in which the ego undergoes a turbulent resurgence of nonegoic potentials, an alienating decathexis of the world, and a narcissistic infusion-inflation of subjectivity. And from the perspective of object relations, this process is one in which the teenager undergoes a distressing reencounter with object representations, feelings, and imaginal productions last experienced in early childhood (resurgence); an alienating withdrawal from parents and their internalized imagoes (decathexis); and an idealistic-narcissistic emergence of the ego ideal (infusion-inflation). The regressive-transformative process of adolescence is a single bidirectional process leading to a single bidirectional end: the new level of (inner-outer, latent–object-constant) equilibrium of early adulthood.

The psychodynamic and object-relational sides of the adolescent process are united in one more way: the restructuring of primal repression leading to the second level of latency is at the same time a restructuring of primal alienation leading to the second level of object constancy. Because primal repression and primal alienation are dimensions of the same structure, the loosening of the former during adolescence (leading to a psychodynamic regression of the ego in relation to nonegoic potentials) is at the same time a loosening of the latter (leading to an object-relational regression of the ego in relation to preoedipal and oedipal object representations). And, in turn, the restructuring of the former at the end of adolescence (leading to the second level of latency) is at the same time a restructuring of the latter (leading to the second level of object constancy). The adolescent process involves a bidirectional regression that is brought to an end by a bidirectional reclosing. Primal repression is restructured in a way that integrates awakened sexuality but otherwise is closed to nonegoic potentials, and primal alienation is restructured in a way that integrates relationship with a new primary other or others but otherwise is closed to deep intimacy. Early adulthood thus is characterized not only by a new equilibrium but also by a renewal of dualism, a reassertion of both the egoic-nonegoic dualism rooted in primal repression and the self-other dualism rooted in primal alienation.

Ego Development

Joseph Adelson and Margery Doehrman (1980) observe that adolescence is intriguing in that it is a period of human development during which the ego undergoes regression and dramatic forward development at the same time. It is a period, they note, characterized simultaneously by serious instability and remarkable advances in cognitive and moral growth. Having just discussed the upheavals and regressions experienced by the ego during adolescence, I shall here briefly consider the principal advances made by the ego during this time.

The advances in cognitive and moral growth during adolescence have one important element in common: understanding of abstract universality. This understanding is fundamentally a cognitive achievement, an achievement, specifically, of formal operational cognition. The attainment of formal operations therefore has profound consequences for all of the principal ego functions. I shall discuss these consequences in a moment, but before doing so it is necessary to make the following cautionary observation: Although the understanding of abstract universality is first possible in adolescence, not all adolescents achieve this understanding. Piaget (1972) believed that most people achieve formal operations by the end of adolescence. This view, however, is optimistic. Evidence now indicates that a significant percentage of people do not achieve formal operations by this time.[5] Accordingly, the discussion of ego functions that follows, although meant to be representative, is by no means descriptive of all adolescents. The discussion is more ideal-typical than simply typical.

Synthesis

If we remember, the synthetic unity of experience is consolidated just prior to latency with the overcoming of rapprochement and oedipal splitting and the attainment of the first level of object constancy. The integration of object representations and, even more, of corresponding self-representations mends the main fissures in the child's world and makes possible the unification of the child's experience into a single temporally unfolding consciousness. This unity of experience is challenged during adolescence by the recurrence of ambivalence and splitting and by the conflict between the emerging ego ideal and the superego. These challenges cut deeply into the fabric of experience but do not tear it as deeply as did the conflicts of the late preoedipal and oedipal periods. The tear is not as deep because, given the abstractly universal perspective of formal operations, adolescents achieve an awareness of themselves as conscious subjects and begin to see that, as such, they remain undivided even when, as persons in the world, they are torn by contradictions in their life circumstances.

The unity we possess as conscious subjects is what Immanuel Kant (1929) called the *transcendental* unity of consciousness. In designating this unity transcendental, Kant held that our abiding unity as conscious subjects is a necessary condition of consciousness properly so called. For if consciousness were not held together in a unity over time, he argued, it would be only a disconnected sequence of frames. New moments of consciousness would have no relation to preceding moments, and therefore no enduring and interconnected objects, no world, would exist. Consciousness without transcendental unity would be completely fragmentary and chaotic. In clinical terms, such a consciousness would represent the limit case of psychotic disintegration.

According to Kant, the transcendental unity of consciousness must be distinguished from the empirical unity of personal selfhood: the transcendental unity of consciousness is a universal *form* of consciousness, whereas the empirical unity of personal selfhood is a particular *content* of consciousness (viz., the self-representation). As such a content, the empirical unity of consciousness can be divided or dissolved without necessarily dividing or dissolving consciousness itself. The empirical self or self-representation is subject to the conflicts of lived experience and can be rent by these conflicts without thereby dissolving the unity of consciousness as such. The transcendental unity of consciousness can remain intact even when one's self-representation is seriously divided. Awareness of this underlying transcendental unity first emerges during adolescence.

The preoedipal child's consciousness is also bound up in a synthetic unity—or at least, as we learned in the last chapter, it begins to be so bound up as the small child, in the first year and one-half of life, makes progress in the development of the synthetic function. The preoedipal child, however, is completely unable to discern this unity of itself as conscious subject. The preoedipal child has no understanding of the unity of consciousness, much less any understanding of the transcendental as opposed to empirical unity of consciousness. Accordingly, when splitting cleaves the preoedipal child's experience, it does so in a way that affects the child *in toto*. The small child is blind to the underlying unity that holds experience together even when experience is sundered by ambivalent feelings and contradictory object relations. The adolescent, on the other hand, upon achieving formal operational cognition, *is* able to distinguish abstract from concrete, transcendental from empirical, and so splitting does not affect the adolescent in such a thoroughgoing manner. The adolescent is able to discern the unity of consciousness that lies behind inconsistencies and splits in the self-representation. In fact, precisely such inconsistencies and splits may be what first throws this transcendental unity into relief for the adolescent.

Self-Reflection

We learned in the last chapter that self-reflection turns inward during the latency period, although only in an implicit way. The latency child, owing to primal repression, is no longer a body ego that can be aware of itself simply by looking in a mirror or at a photograph but rather is an emerging mental ego or inner psychomental subject. The latency child, however, although identified with inner psychomental subjectivity, is so only implicitly and unconsciously. The latency child assumes that it is an inner subject but does not undertake introspectively to explore subjectivity to find the inner subject that it assumes itself to be. Moreover, despite being disidentified from the body, the latency child still continues to think of itself in vaguely material terms. The latency child is not yet capable of thinking of itself abstractly as a purely psychomental subject, and consequently it continues to think of itself as an entity with a vaguely material nature. The mental ego as it emerges in the latency period is incompletely differentiated from the head or brain and therefore, to a certain extent, is still inconsistently conflated with its embodiment.

The mental ego is dramatically reconceived during adolescence. Specifically, it ceases being a merely assumed entity and becomes an explicit focus of introspective inquiry. Simultaneously, it ceases being conceived in a vague and contradictory way and begins being conceived in a way that thoroughly distinguishes it from the body, and from the head or brain in particular. Self-reflection during adolescence becomes the explicit inward search by the mental ego for itself conceived as a psychomental subject that cannot be identified with any part or organ of the body. In other words, as experimental studies have confirmed (Broughton 1978, 1980, 1982), adolescence is the period during which self-reflection becomes consciously and consistently dualistic.[6] The mind is no longer confused with the head or brain. It is rather thought of as a sphere of experience that is inherently invisible and inaccessible (i.e., except through introspection) and, therefore, that is radically distinct from the body. Correspondingly, the transcendental unity of consciousness is interpreted as a completely nonphysical unity, as the unity of a purely psychomental subject. Self-reflection during adolescence is thus Cartesian self-reflection. It is the completely introspective self-reference of the Cartesian *cogito* or "I think." In Kant's terms, it is *transcendental apperception*, consciousness of the unity of consciousness as such.

Cartesian or transcendental self-reflection is intriguing in that it has two opposing existential consequences. Initially, this self-reflection provides a sense of existential security. For, as we have seen, it reveals an abiding center of subjectivity that lies behind and is unaffected by the vicissitudes of the adolescent process. According to Augusto Blasi (1988), the adolescent's most fundamental sense of self is as an inner, active, unified self-reflecting subject. Adolescents enjoy a self-awareness and self-certainty well expressed in the Cartesian formula "I think therefore I am." Their existence as inner subjects is something that they know immediately and incontrovertibly. As Broughton (1978) says, "There is immediate and complete self-knowledge, and no unconscious" (p. 88). Adolescents have no doubt *that* they exist (qua transcendental subject or mental ego) even when they are most in doubt about *who* or *what* they are (qua self-representation or ego identity). In extreme cases, as Lawrence Kohlberg and Carol Gilligan note, adolescents may even be more sure of their own existence then they are of the existence of the external world. "The external is no longer the real, 'the objective,' and the internal the 'unreal.' The internal may be real and the external unreal. At its extreme, adolescent thought entertains solipsism or at least the Cartesian cogito, the notion that the only thing real is the self" (1972, p. 157). For the adolescent, the inner subjective realm, centered in the transcendental ego, has the character of a self-certain refuge from an uncertain world.

Moreover, this realm is where the adolescent feels most at home, most like his or her "true" self. It is the location of what the adolescent considers the authentic core of selfhood, the innermost center of the self hidden behind outer social "masks." Self-reflection for the adolescent is therefore in a sense twofold. It is divided into inner-transcendental-"authentic" self-reflection on the one hand and outer-social-"inauthentic" self-reflection on the other. Broughton describes this divided self-reflection. He says:

> The metaphysical form of the self is like that description of schizoid alienation presented in Winnicott and Laing. This *divided self* has a real inner core, masked, protected and stifled by an outer social role-self, an appearance or affected "personality" put on for the benefit of others.
>
> Two kinds of self-consciousness are here juxtaposed without being integrated. There is immediate, intuitive awareness of the "real me" . . . and relational or interpersonal awareness of self disguising itself to the other . . . . (1982, pp. 247–248)

Broughton's description of the two types of self-consciousness is a bit extreme. Nevertheless, the point is that the dualistic division between mind and body is at the same time a division of self-reflection into inner and outer, immediate and indirect, "as-I-am-in-myself" and "as-I-am-for-others" types of self-reflection. The latter of these types of self-reflection is frequently a source of acute insecurity for the adolescent, because this type of self-reflection is predicated on outer "performances" and the consequent judgment of others. The former type of self-reflection, on the other hand, is a source of a sense of inviolable security, because this type of self-reflection is inherently self-confirming: the inner self is immediately certain of its existence and the reality of its thoughts and feelings.

Cartesian or transcendental self-reflection, however, is a source not only of security but also, paradoxically, of anxiety. For the very transcendental subject that initially provides the adolescent with a sense of abiding and authentic existence is eventually experienced as a lack, an absence, a "nothing." The transcendental subject that is the intended "object" of self-reflective inquiry, it turns out, is nowhere to be found. David Hume (1888), the eighteenth-century Scottish philosopher, made this point long ago by saying that when we look inward we never find the self itself but rather only "perceptions" (i.e., percepts, sensations, feelings, ideas) that, we believe, are perceptions *of* the self. Kant went further and held that it is impossible in principle to find the transcendental subject because the transcendental subject is always presupposed as a condition of consciousness and cannot therefore be an object for consciousness. Accordingly, whereas the body ego is tangibly and visibly present to itself, the mental ego is inherently absent to itself; it cannot find itself through introspection. From the adolescent's point of view, this fact is seriously disturbing, because it bears the meaning that the transcendental unity of consciousness is an *empty* unity. The adolescent rarely grasps this fact in an explicit manner. Usually, the adolescent grasps the emptiness of transcendental consciousness only in unsettling intimations. Vaguely and prereflectively, the adolescent senses that at the center of subjectivity, at the focal point behind the fluctuating contents of consciousness, at the place where the most intimate and true self is supposed to be, *nothing* is to be found.

Whatever the ultimate ontological status of the transcendental subject—an actual entity or agency always behind the scene of consciousness, a merely formal and therefore empty unity of consciousness, or, as Hume, Jean-Paul Sartre (1957), and all Buddhists believe, a mere fiction or illusion—it is at least true that the transcendental subject or purely mental ego is inaccessible to itself as an object of consciousness. The adolescent awakens to a clear and consistent conception of itself as a psychomental subject only, upon looking for this subject, to find "nothing." Primal repression, in decorporealizing the ego, also, it seems, "deentifies" it. The ego ceases being a thing that can be perceived, or even introspected, and becomes a mysteriously elusive, if not completely illusory, subject. The adolescent, then, is anxiously surprised to learn, or at least suspect, that the inner self-reflecting subject that it takes itself to be cannot be found at the center of subjectivity. The adolescent's transcendental self-reflection, which begins so self-certainly, ends in anxiety: it comes up empty. This encounter with "nothingness" is an integral part of the so-called adolescent identity crisis, which I shall discuss later.

Ego-Initiated Cognition

The understanding of abstract universality distinctive of adolescence is fundamentally a cognitive achievement. It is an achievement of formal operational cognition. In Piaget's (Inhelder and Piaget 1958; Piaget 1972) well-known view, adolescence is the developmental period during which cognition moves from the level of concrete operational thinking to the level of formal operational thinking. Whereas prior to adolescence, thought is tied to concrete observable objects and situations; beginning with adolescence, thought frees itself from the observable and begins to consider hypothetical possibilities and abstract structures and relationships. Beginning with adolescence, the young person begins to develop an experimental attitude and to generate hypotheses about things not yet observed, to manipulate not only things but also symbols of things, to do abstract thought problems, and to engage in logical argument and purely theoretical explanation. All of these developments are characteristic of a formal, abstract-universal, perspective.

The advance to formal operational cognition dramatically improves the range and power of thought. Whereas the concrete operational thought of the latency child is limited to the entities and events at hand, the formal operational thought of the adolescent is able to explore "what-if" alternatives and to comprehend the general types of which given entities and events are instances. Whereas concrete operational thought is able to perform cognitive operations only on particulars, formal operational thought is able to perform cognitive operations on the universals under which particulars fall. Whereas concrete operational thought can know what is true or what will happen only in the present case, formal operational thought can know what is true or what will happen in every case of like kind. Formal operational thought treats whole classes at once rather than treating members of classes one at a time. Formal operational thought is a powerful shorthand that traces patterns that hold in general and therefore hold for all particulars that happen to exemplify the patterns. Formal operational thought is not interested in particulars qua particulars; it is interested in particulars only as verifying instances, examples, or special cases of general principles. Formal operational cognition, as Piaget frequently puts it, is "thought about thought."

The attainment of formal operational cognition is at the basis of the advances that the adolescent makes in the other ego functions. The ability to think abstractly is clearly required for grasping the formal synthetic unity of consciousness and for engaging in transcendental self-reflection in search of a purely psychomental subject. And, as we shall see, the ability to think in terms of universals rather than just particulars is essential to the kind of volition distinctive of adolescence. To be sure, the adolescent might not be prompted to make these advances in the synthetic, self-reflective, and volitional functions were it not for the specific character of adolescent psychodynamics and object relations. The attainment of formal operational cognition, then, may be only a necessary and not a sufficient condition for corresponding changes in the other ego functions. Nevertheless, formal operational cognition is at least a principal necessary condition for these changes; it is a basic factor that, although not guaranteeing these changes, nonetheless renders them possible.

Active Volition

Formal operational cognition, in clearly abstracting universals from particulars, opens the way for the distinction between conventional morality (the particular morality of one's own community or society) and universal or ideal morality (what should be the moral requirements of all communities and societies). The achievement of formal operations allows the young person to see that the mores and norms that happen as a matter of fact to obtain do not necessarily reflect what is right and good in itself. The achievement of the universal perspective allows the young person to see that the way things are done locally is only *a* way things can be done and not necessarily *the* way things should be done. This new perspective, then, opens up new possibilities for the exercise of will, which no longer needs to be confined to convention and can now reach beyond convention toward universal moral principles and ideal moral possibilities. For the teenager, the awareness that convention is "merely" particular rather than universal typically arises first in relation to the family, then the immediate community, and then the larger society. The teenager's new universal perspective allows the teenager to see that his or her family, community, and society are but examples of organized social life, examples that might well fall considerably short of an ideal standard.

Two chief consequences follow from this initial insight into the difference between the conventional and the ideal: cynical relativism and naive idealism.[7] Cynical relativism and naive idealism are of course complete opposites. Nevertheless, they go together in the adolescent's ethical thinking, for in being able to see that de facto social arrangements might fall considerably short of an ideal standard, the adolescent at once looks *down* on conventional actualities and *up* to ideal possibilities. The movement of thought away from the concrete and toward the abstract predisposes the adolescent harshly to prejudge conventional actualities as "merely" conventional (if not worse) and uncritically to embrace ideal possibilities as "the way things should be." These hasty conclusions frequently underappreciate convention (by which, for the most part, the teenager continues to live) and overestimate ideals (which tend to be vague, remote, and unrealistic). Consequently, the adolescent is prone repeatedly to return to convention and to change ideals. In terms of the exercise of will, this means that the adolescent is prone repeatedly to stoop to relativistic expedients and to take flight in idealistic hopes.

This oscillation between relativism and idealism is nicely described in the following statement by a student interviewed by Carol Gilligan and Lawrence Kohlberg:

> During my sophomore year, I rejected morality completely. I did, in the freshman year and in the sophomore year, a lot of talking about huge theoretical moral constructs and systems, and during the end of my sophomore year, I got into some experiences which led me to the conclusion, not very much based on reasons, that morality was by and large a lot of bunk, that there was no right or wrong whatsoever, that people did things that were givens of experience and it was beyond anyone's judging power not only to determine whether any person's acts were right or wrong, but to determine whether there was a right or wrong. I read a lot of Kant, obviously, so he really got to me in those days, and I don't think that is a position I have totally rejected either . . . after the relativism, I started to read Marx a lot . . . and stopped thinking in moral terms, or I stopped thinking in abstract moral terms as I had been thinking. I think during the first couple of years, I went from a position of very abstract, sort of universalistic moral concepts to, on the other hand, a sort of nihilistic rejection, to sort of worrying about more immediate problems. (1978, p. 132)

The student who made this statement undoubtedly exceeds the norm in intelligence and self-understanding. Nevertheless, the statement provides a dramatic example of the kinds of shifts between relativistic denigration of convention and flights of idealistic abstraction that can occur during adolescence.

Adolescent relativism and idealism can also be explained in terms of the struggles, discussed earlier, between adolescents and their parents and between the emerging ego ideal and the superego. If adolescents are already prone to denigrate convention on cognitive grounds, they are all the more prone to do this given the connection between convention on the one hand and parents and their internal voice, the superego, on the other. And if adolescents are already prone to glorify ideals on cognitive grounds, they are all the more prone to do this given the connection between ideals in general and the emerging ego ideal in particular. Not only on cognitive grounds, then, but on object-relational and structural grounds as well, adolescents are prone to turn away from conventional actuality and toward ideal possibilities. They are prone to see conventions not only as "mere" particulars but also as constraints that stifle selfhood and bind the will. And they are prone to see ideals not only as "higher" universals but also as goals that facilitate selfhood and liberate the will. To some degree, adolescents experience convention as a violation of autonomy; therefore, to some degree, they feel that the assertion of will requires a rejection of convention. Adolescents experience a disjunction between convention and ideal and interpret this disjunction as a conflict between heteronomy and autonomy of the will.

EXISTENTIAL CONCERNS: IDENTITY TESTING AND IDENTITY ANXIETY

A variety of factors converge during the teenage years that make adolescence a time of awakening to self. Adolescence is above all a time of self-consciousness, self-exploration, and self-doubt. As Erik Erikson (1950, 1956) has shown, it is the time when the question of identity arises and becomes the central focus of attention. Of the features of adolescence we have discussed, the following are among those that converge to make the self the primary focus of the adolescent process: (1) the narcissistic cathexis of the ego, (2) the struggle for separation from parents, (3) the emergence of the ego ideal, and (4) the attainment of transcendental self-reflection. I shall here draw together some of the strands of our earlier discussion to show how these four features of adolescence work together to make emerging selfhood and identity anxiety the primary existential concerns of the adolescent years.

The narcissistic shift of cathexis from world to self interiorizes the adolescent's awareness. The external world, from which energy is withdrawn, loses its appeal, and subjective life, which is infused with energy, becomes larger than life, fascinating, engrossing. The teenager spends a good deal of time engaged in fantasy. The inner world of subjectivity becomes the primary field of awareness, sometimes, as we have seen, almost solipsistically so. This inward turn is a turn toward self that initiates a preoccupation with self. It is what first throws subjectivity into relief as an inner, seemingly self-contained realm, the realm in which the mental ego resides.

The struggle for independence from parents provides a powerful impetus for self-assertion and exploration of new modes of self-expression. As a second separation-individuation process, adolescence is a time during which young people are impelled to distance themselves from parents and explore ways in which they can be persons in their own right. In moving away from parents, teenagers make a break from their own previous implicit sense of self, which was tied to the parents, and embark upon an exploration of new possibilities of selfhood. Sometimes this transition from old to new can cause distressing splitting of the self-representation, which can divide into an old "childish," "parent-dominated," "inauthentic" self on the one hand and a new hyperindividualistic, idealistic, "authentic" self on the other hand. However, even when the move from an old to a possible new form of selfhood is not afflicted with serious splitting, this transition, and therefore the phenomenon of emerging selfhood, is still the central preoccupation of the adolescent. Separation from an old parent-based self-representation and exploration of new identity possibilities are the principal existential tasks of adolescence, and therefore the issue of selfhood is the main concern of the adolescent even when an identity crisis in the Eriksonian sense does not occur.

Inwardly paralleling the adolescent's separation from parents is the ego ideal's separation from the superego. The adolescent's need to break with the old parent-based self-representation is played out not only against the parents themselves but also against their internal representatives, the superego in particular. And the adolescent's need to test new identity possibilities is played out not only through a peer group but also through the emerging ego ideal, which stirs the imagination to explore ideal selves to which the adolescent might aspire. As we know, the selves explored in this way tend to lack realism; they are idealistic fantasies. The teenager therefore is prone not only to try on such imagined selves but also to have them dashed. The teenager is for this reason susceptible to repeated enthusiasms and disillusionments, to oscillations between idealistic hopes and relativistic cynicisms or despairs. These dramatic mood shifts compound the other conflicts that trouble this difficult developmental period and work to intensify the teenager's anxious concern with self.

The attainment of transcendental reflection is another important factor that, for the adolescent, works to throw the self into relief and to call it into question. If we remember, the discovery of the transcendental subject brings with it both self-certainty and self-doubt. It brings self-certainty because merely to conceive of this subject is to be sure of its existence: *cogito ergo sum.* Despite experiencing internal conflicts of many sorts, adolescents can assure themselves of their existence as subjects merely by engaging in transcendental reflection. The discovery of the transcendental subject, however, also brings self-doubt, because this subject has no intuitable content. The mental ego, as transcendental subject, is inaccessible to instrospection. Introspection reveals only a formal unity to which nothing corresponds. Transcendental reflection, then, not only provides confirmation of existence; it also, eventually, induces a fear of being a nonentity, of being a self-certain *illusion.* Needless to say, such a fear of "nothingness," however vague and prereflective it might be, heightens the teenager's concern with self.

When the factors just considered converge, the adolescent is prone to suffer the most acute identity anxiety. For each of these factors contributes a contradiction to the adolescent process. The narcissistic cathexis of the ego makes the adolescent both self-absorbed and hypersensitive to others. The struggle with parents makes the adolescent both defiant and submissive. The separation of the ego ideal from the superego makes the adolescent both self-aggrandizing and self-denigrating. And the emergence of transcendental reflection makes the adolescent both self-certain and ontologically insecure. The adolescent's fledgling self is to some degree beset with all of these contradictions. For this reason the issue of selfhood is the adolescent's primary existential concern.

The adolescent must eventually make a commitment to an identity project. For only through an identity project can the contradictions of the adolescent self be reconciled. An identity project is a type of involvement with self that is open to the critical and confirming responses of others. It is a form of self-assertion that submits to norms and limits. It is an endeavor that aims at an ideal goal that, although never completely attainable, is nonetheless in touch with realistic possibility (i.e., the goal of perfectly achieving one's chosen identity). And it is a way of establishing ontological security by giving outwardly recognized form and definition to one's inner or transcendental subjectivity. The contradictions of the adolescent process concur in driving the young person toward making a commitment to an identity project. And in finally making such a commitment— frequently in conjunction with a commitment to a new primary "object choice" or "love object"—the young person passes from adolescence to young adulthood.

I have been careful to speak of commitment to an identity *project* rather than to an ego identity or self-concept, because the former alone occurs at the end of adolescence. Commitment to an identity project is only the first step in achieving an ego identity; the actual work of forging the identity comes after the commitment. If, then, commitment to an identity project is the proper goal of adolescence, the work of following through on that commitment and actually creating an ego identity is the proper business of the first half of adult life. Accordingly, having spoken of the factors leading to commitment here, I shall discuss the identity project itself in the next chapter.

CONCLUSION

Adolescence is a stage of development facilitated by a nonpathological regression. I return to this point here because I believe that adolescence is the first of two stages of human development that involve such a "progressive regression." The other stage, which I shall discuss in chapter 9, is a stage that I ([1988] 2d ed. in press) have called *regression in the service of transcendence*. The regression of adolescence is a regression in the service of the ego. For during adolescence the ego submits to the regressive upsurge of nonegoic life and the regressive recapitulation of prelatency object relations in order later to reestablish its own ascendancy on a more integrated and stable plane. The end of adolescence, as we have seen, involves a restructuring of primal repression and primal alienation, which are the bases of dualistic ego dominance. Early adulthood is ushered in by a new level of latency and object constancy. Adolescence is therefore a "progressive regression" of limited, egoic, scope. The progress achieved is primarily progress for the ego, which remains a mental ego undergirded and encapsulated by dualistic structures.

In contrast, the regression in the service of transcendence that I shall discuss in chapter 9 involves a much more thorough psychic reorganization and leads to a much more thorough psychic integration. For during this regression, primal repression and primal alienation are not only loosened; they are *dissolved*. The ego undergoing this regression therefore loses its position of psychic ascendancy and yields to extraegoic powers and possibilities. Psychic life ceases being in the service of the ego, and the ego begins to be in the service of "greater" ("deeper," "higher") psychospiritual forces. This is not the place to pursue a discussion of regression in the service of transcendence. The process is mentioned here only to emphasize that adolescence is not the only developmental stage to involve a regression in the service of development. As human development unfolds, first in the direction of ego development and then in the direction of ego transcendence, it is twice punctuated by "progressive regressions."

The first such regression, occurring during adolescence, is a necessary preliminary to the last phase of ego development. The second such regression, sometimes occurring at or after midlife, is an integral part of the "journey to wholeness."

6 | *Ego Development and Dualism in Early Adulthood*

Early adulthood to midlife is the last phase of ego development. The ego, having been nurtured, sheltered, and educated during latency and adolescence, is ready at the beginning of adulthood to exercise its powers and express itself in the world. The ego therefore steps forth into the world by embarking upon an identity project, a project aimed at "being-in-the-world" and "being-with-others." This identity project is the primary vehicle of adult ego development. Young adults resolve, embrace, reaffirm, or otherwise commit themselves to such things as family relationships, intimate partnership, gender, ethnicity, job, career, personal appearance, life-style, ethical values, and religious faith. These commitments carry with them responsibilities requiring young adults to sustain courses of action they have been embarked upon and to cultivate relationships and social networks they have embraced or reaffirmed. The ego is in this way tested and matured by experience. Through the vehicle of the identity project, the ego learns how to take effective action in the world and how to share life with and care for others. The ego actualizes potentialities, masters skills, takes root in relationships, grows emotionally, and learns the ways of the world.

This maturation of the ego occurs within dualistic constraints and protections. Although the ego in early adulthood is open to the expression of sexuality and enjoys sexually based intimacy with a primary other or others, it is otherwise still repressively insulated from nonegoic potentials and defensively shielded from other people. Egoic-nonegoic and self-other dualism, introduced at the beginning of latency and challenged during adolescence, are reconsolidated at the end of adolescence and thereafter usually remain in place at least throughout the first half of adult life. These forms of dualism place significant limits on what the young adult ego can experience. They also, however, protect the ego, in the final stage of its development, from powerful influences to which it is not yet ready to be exposed.

Once ego development has been completed during early adulthood, dualism ceases performing a necessary role and can in principle be transcended. Once the ego has completed its development, it no longer needs to be insulated from nonegoic potentials or shielded from other people. It no longer needs primal repression or primal alienation. Accordingly, at midlife or thereafter these dualistic structures sometimes begin to give way, thereby creating an opening for a transformative return of the ego to nonegoic and interpersonal possibilities that long ago were buried and lost to experience. Early adulthood, then, is the time during which ego development is completed as the final step that prepares a person for entering postdualistic, transegoic, stages of life.

The passage from adolescence to adulthood is marked by many discernible changes. Erik Erikson (1950, 1963) focused on intimacy (development of relationships) and generativity (providing for the next generation, making a contribution to society, being creative) as the primary distinguishing characteristics of early adult life. In a report published in 1968, the Group for the Advancement of Psychiatry listed the following changes as being principal among those that usher in adult life:

> (1) The attainment of separation and independence from the parents; (2) the establishment of sexual identity; (3) the commitment to work; (4) the development of a personal moral value system; (5) the capacity for lasting relationships and for both tender and genital sexual love in heterosexual relationships [or, I would add, in partnership relationships generally]; and (6) a return to the parents in a new relationship based on relative equality. (pp. 93–94)

Peter Blos (1976), focusing more on matters of emotion and character, proposed that the transition to adulthood can be understood best in terms of such changes as (1) a decrease in mood swings, (2) a channeling of emotions to select private relationships, (3) character stabilization, and (4) a division of interpersonal relationships into public and private spheres. And Herman Staples and Erwin Smarr (1980), after reviewing several accounts of the differences separating adulthood from adolescence, stressed the central importance of participation in social life: the adult, unlike the adolescent, assumes a place, adopts a role and values, and earns an identity in the public domain.

All of the proposed changes just noted point to important distinguishing features of adult life. Most of these features will be discussed in the account that follows. Following the format of the last two chapters, the discussion in this chapter will be divided into four sections focusing, in order, on psychodynamic, object-relational, ego-developmental, and existential considerations.

Psychodynamics

Virtually all accounts of the transition from adolescence to early adulthood stress such things as consolidation and equilibrium. Many factors are responsible for this new state of stability. Basic among them is the restructuring of primal repression and primal alienation that occurs at the end of adolescence. The weakening of primal repression and primal alienation during adolescence leads eventually to a restructuring of these root dualistic defenses. Primal repression is restructured in a way that allows for the expression of sexuality while otherwise quieting (i.e., rerepressing) nonegoic potentials. And primal alienation is restructured in a way that allows for sexually based intimacy while otherwise reinstating, and sometimes even increasing, the psychic distance of self-other dualism. The restructuring of primal repression and primal alienation in these ways brings an end to the regressive resurgence of nonegoic potentials and the regressive recapitulation of early object relations characteristic of adolescence and leads to a state that is dualistically circumscribed but also, relatively speaking, firm and abiding. In the last chapter, following Peter Blos's suggestion, I described this new level of equilibrium as a new level of latency and object constancy.

Calling early adulthood a second period of latency is not just a remote analogy or metaphor. For early adulthood is similar to latency in being a period during which nonegoic potentials are markedly reduced in activity, if not rendered dormant, by the countercathectic weight of primal repression. In particular, early adulthood is similar to latency in being a period during which the body is, relatively speaking, quiescent and limited in its arousability. At the beginning of latency, the child loses the general bodily arousability or polymorphous sensuality that, despite earlier oral, anal, and genital predominances, had obtained throughout the prelatency period. In the transition to latency, psychic energy ceases circulating freely in the body and is repressed, deactivated, and reduced to a dormant genital organization. Similarly, in the transition to early adulthood, the general dynamic-sexual-somatic eruption of puberty subsides and the body, physically and sexually mature, becomes much more constant and subdued in its internal "feel." Admittedly, there is the major difference that the body of the young adult is a sexually excitable body: psychic energy is now actively rather than dormantly organized in the sexual system. This active sexuality, however, is restricted in its expression. The mature adult body, although sexually arousable, is otherwise dynamically abeyant, at least to a significant degree. Differences of course exist among individuals and perhaps between genders on the strictness of the genital organization of psychic energy. Accordingly, to say that psychic energy is genitally organized does not mean that psychic energy is completely confined to the sexual system and, therefore, that all of the body except the genitals is dynamically dead and unexcitable. On the contrary, most adults are stimulated to some degree by general body caressing. What is meant, rather, is that bodily excitability has a distinct sexual tone and a distinct sexual progression leading in the direction of genital arousal.

Freud tended to equate latency with sexual latency, and consequently the idea of a sexually active latency, which I am here attributing to early adulthood, sounds like a contradiction in terms. The idea, however, makes perfectly good sense if the notion of latency is expanded to connote *nonegoic* latency. For then the idea of a sexually active latency conveys the entirely unproblematic meaning of a state or stage that is sexually active but otherwise nonegoically abeyant. Such a nonegoic latency is just the kind of condition that, I propose, obtains in early adulthood.

In the transition from adolescence to adulthood, the body (excluding sexuality) and nonegoic potentials generally (including affective and imaginal-creative potentials[1]) are rerepressed and muted or deactivated. The nonegoic upsurge of adolescence comes to an end and inner experience becomes less active and, therefore, more calm. The stirring of nonegoic potentials during adolescence makes the teenage years a time that is both painful and powerfully alive. The experiences triggered by nonegoic potentials can be distressing, and some are truly overwhelming. At the same time, however, these experiences are engrossing and exciting, even intoxicating. For this reason the requieting of nonegoic potentials that occurs at the end of adolescence makes early adult life not only more stable but also less rich, not only more peaceful but also less potent than adolescence. The agonies of adolescence disappear, but the fecundity and power of adolescence are lost in the process. Sensing this loss many people look back on adolescence as the time of life when they felt most intensely alive. This retrospective appraisal is in part merely nostalgia, to be sure; it also, however, is to a significant extent a reflection of something real that has been lost.

Also part of the psychodynamics of early adulthood is a rechanneling of psychic energy to the external world. The narcissistic introversion of energy that obtains during adolescence gives way to a stable recathexis of the physical, interpersonal, and social domains. This recathexis, as we shall see, occurs in conjunction with the primary commitments of the identity project, including commitments to occupation or social function and to primary relationship. In making the commitments of the identity project, young adults refocus their energy, investing it in the responsibilities and loving or nurturing activities that are distinctive of adult participation in the world. Energy is refocused away from self and toward "being-in-the-world" and "being-with-others." As this cathectic shift occurs, the narcissistic self-absorption and the sense of estrangement characteristic of adolescence tend to be replaced by outwardly focused attention and a new sense of interest in and belonging to the world.[2]

Corresponding to this cathectic shift from narcissistic to object libido is a shift in the use of ego functions from defensive to constructive assignments. For example, ego-initiated cognition, which during adolescence is sometimes used for defensive intellectualization, begins more regularly to be put to "real" work as the young adult prepares for entering the world. Similarly, active volition, which during adolescence is sometimes used defensively to control emerging sexuality, is now brought into the service of the identity project. The restructuring of primal repression, the corresponding subduing of nonegoic life, and the making of worldly commitments bring about a general redirection of both energy and ego functions. Energy ceases being narcissistically introverted and begins being reinvested in world, and ego functions cease being defensively deployed and begin being put to work in the service of worldly responsibilities and relationships.

OBJECT RELATIONS

Object relations in early adulthood have two principal aspects. First, early adulthood is, again, a second period of object constancy; and second, early adulthood is a period during which one typically makes a new primary object choice.

The second level of object constancy of early adulthood is like its counterpart in childhood in being a condition of relative interpersonal stability based on a realistic integration of previously split parental imagoes. It is a time during which the conflicts experienced in relation to parents during adolescence are significantly resolved and a new relationship with parents begins to evolve. In achieving independence from parents, young adults are able to relate to parents in a more realistic way. No longer beholden to parents, they are no longer prone to split parents into all-good and all-bad part objects. Young adults have the perspective to see that parents are people who, like everyone else, have both good and bad sides. Concomitantly, as this more realistic perception emerges, young adults experience a need to reestablish a solid, mutually caring relationship with parents. Accordingly, young adults typically seek a new kind of closeness with their parents. Typically, they make efforts to repair any damage remaining from adolescent conflicts, and they strive to succeed in life in ways that will make their parents proud.

Another factor contributing to a resolution of residual conflicts with parents is the young adult's new primary object choice. This choice helps resolve remaining conflicts because it shifts the focus of primary interpersonal investment away from parents to another person. Conflicts that arose out of the mother being the first love object and the father the first person to whom an unconditional commitment (viz., the oedipal emulation-capitulation commitment) was made are to a great extent resolved by the new primary object choice. For as a *primary* object choice, this choice transfers primary affections from the mother to the person with whom a loving relationship is being established. And as a primary object *choice*, this choice is, typically, an unconditional commitment, whether the commitment is made official by marriage vows or whether it remains unofficial or even tacit. By making a new primary object choice, the young adult at once finds a new "love object" to replace the preoedipal mother and a new "commitment object" to replace the oedipal father. The mother and father cease for the most part playing these roles. Concomitantly, the relationship of the young adult to parents is for the most part relieved of long-standing needs and corresponding tensions. The young adult for this reason can begin relating to parents in a way that is much less ambivalent and much more stable. This new way of relating is the new level of object constancy that emerges in early adulthood.

The intimacy needs that were reawakened during adolescence do not disappear. They are, however, rechanneled. These needs are now met almost entirely in and through the relationship with the new primary other. The young adult experiences intimacy almost exclusively within a narrowly circumscribed domain: the domain of the new primary relationship and the nuclear family that typically derives from this relationship. To be sure, a secondary level of intimacy extends to the original family, to other kinship relations, and sometimes to a small circle of same-sex friends. This secondary level of intimacy, however, is usually much more superficial than the intimacy that obtains with the primary object choice (i.e., one's love partner) and with offspring, if any. For the young adult, then, the range of truly intimate relationship is very restricted; it is limited, typically, to a primary other and children.

The narrow range of the young adult's sphere of intimacy is a main cause of the division of adult life into public and private domains.[3] The exclusive character of adult intimacy creates boundaries that divide the private sphere in which this intimacy occurs from the public world in which safe psychic distance and clear ego boundaries are maintained. Intimacy in the sense of open confluence of feelings and sharing of basic life experiences is restricted to the private domain. Relationships outside this domain are usually nonintimate, predicated on psychic distance and projected appearances. Relationships in the public world tend to hide rather than share subjective life; they tend to maintain separateness rather than to allow states of confluence or merger.

The intimacy characteristic of young adult life is thus an intimacy of a limited sort: it is a private and exclusive intimacy based, typically, on a sexual tie. It is intimacy within the limits of dualism. The fact that this intimacy is circumscribed in these ways does not, however, take away from the fact that it *is* a form of intimacy. The intimacy of young adult life involves (growing degrees of) openness, transparency, vulnerability, sensitivity, attunement, outreaching feeling, and deep emotional resonance and bonding. Perhaps the best way to describe the limited nature of this intimacy, then, is to say that it is a form of intimacy that takes place within the *safety* of a private and exclusive relationship. Young adult intimacy is an intimacy within the protective boundaries of a cocommitted relationship, a relationship in which each party is committed to being faithful to the other. This form of relationship allows each party to trust the other and therefore to feel safe in the "risks" of intimacy. The young adult relationship with a primary other is a secure context for *learning* intimacy. This relationship, especially when it widens to include children, is the context in which we first learn to be authentically open and caring.

Erik Erikson (1950, 1963) held that the two major tasks of the first half of adult life are (1) intimacy versus isolation and (2) generativity versus stagnation. The first of these tasks is the task just discussed, the task of learning intimacy within the safe boundaries of privacy. According to Erikson, failure to accomplish this task, perhaps out of fear of ego loss, leaves a person in a state of self-absorbed isolation. People who have not learned intimacy have not learned how to live beyond themselves and are therefore locked within themselves. They are subject to a completely unyielding self-other dualism. Unable to open themselves to others, people such as these lead lonely lives. They are cut off from others and unable to get their own intimacy needs met.

Following the task of intimacy versus isolation is the task of generativity versus stagnation. This task coincides approximately with the latter part of the first half of adult life. According to Erikson, generativity has the core meaning of providing for the next generation and the wider meaning of productivity and creativity in general. In its core and more specifically interpersonal meaning, then, generativity is the task of learning how to nurture or mentor those who by some connection are dependent upon us. If learning how to be intimate with a new "primary object choice" is the first major interpersonal task of adulthood, learning to give of oneself to one's offspring or other representatives of the next generation is the second major such task. In learning intimacy, we learn how to get outside ourselves and share our lives with another person; in learning generativity, we learn how truly to go beyond ourselves and give ourselves to other people. Granted, generativity, like intimacy, typically occurs within the confines of privacy. It is typically limited to our own children and our parents as they age. Nevertheless, even within these limits, profound lessons are learned, lessons that, later in life, some people begin to put into practice without any longer being limited by private versus public (or any form of we versus they) boundaries.

EGO DEVELOPMENT

The primary ego functions continue to develop during the first half of adult life. Because early adulthood is the final stage of ego development, ego functions achieve their full power and range during this stage. Early adulthood prepares the ego for stages of transegoic development, stages during which ego functions are reconnected with nonegoic potentials.

Synthesis

We learned in the last chapter that the adolescent process both develops and divides the egoic system. It develops this system by disclosing the transcendental unity of consciousness and facilitating the emergence of the ego ideal from the superego. In doing these things, however, the adolescent process at the same time divides the egoic system because the egoic elements it differentiates—transcendental consciousness, the ego ideal, and the superego—are left disconnected. The transcendental unity of consciousness, as a merely abstract unity, is disclosed as a necessary but empty center of consciousness, a center that represents only the fact and not the "substance" or "content" of the ego's existence. The ego ideal, as the agency of individual fulfillment, emerges as a source of inspiring but unattainable ideals. And the superego, given its connection with the parents, becomes alien to the ego. It comes to represent what the ego was but no longer is. Accordingly, although the ego is certain *that* it exists (*cogito ergo sum*), it is perplexed about *what*, if anything, it is. The adolescent ego is clear about what it has been and no longer wants to be: the superego becomes alien to the ego. It is full of grandiose visions about what it would like to be but never could be: the ego ideal spawns unrealistic self-projections. And although enjoying an immediate sense of its existence as a transcendental subject, it suffers from anxieties that, as a transcendental subject, it may be no more than a vacuous self-reference, an "I think" to which nothing corresponds.

Given this intraegoic fragmentation, the principal work of the synthetic function during early adulthood is to integrate the egoic system by unifying the transcendental unity of consciousness, the ego ideal, and the superego. This synthesis is accomplished by means of the identity project. As we shall see, the identity project creates a self-representation that effectively reintegrates the superego and ego ideal and, in doing so, creates an "object" (a surrogate or adopted content or "body") that the mental ego, as transcendental subject, can take itself to *be*.

Commitment to an identity project reconciles the superego and ego ideal because an identity project is a long-term undertaking that (1) demands sustained effort and therefore needs the disciplining motivation of the superego, and (2) aims at an ideal (viz., the perfect realization of the core aspects of the chosen identity) and therefore needs the inspiring motivation of the ego ideal. The identity project requires both perseverance and continuously renewable hope. The former requirement is met by the superego, which, therefore, the ego now reowns; and the latter requirement is met by the ego ideal, which, therefore, the ego now more realistically redefines. The identity project needs to be pushed from behind and therefore is in need of the superego; and the identity project needs to be pulled from ahead and therefore is in need of the ego ideal. The identity project creates new functions for the superego and ego ideal and therefore serves as a mediating ground on which the superego and ego ideal can be reunited and synthesized, now as truly complementary agencies.

In being reunited by the identity project, both the superego and the ego ideal are transformed. The superego is transformed because it ceases being so exclusively associated with its parental origins and begins speaking more in the ego's own voice. This change is brought about in part simply through the young adult's achievement of independence from parents. This change, however, is also brought about by the ego's commitment to the identity project. For this commitment, as just noted, creates a new function and, therefore, need for the superego. The identity project, as a long-term commitment, needs a disciplining overseer to keep it on track, and discipline of course is precisely the superego's job. The ego, then, in committing itself to the identity project, ceases feeling like it must free itself from the superego and begins, once again, feeling a need to yoke itself to the superego. Accordingly, the ego ceases experiencing the superego primarily as a parental adversary and begins reexperiencing the superego as part of its, the ego's, own self. The ego begins reexperiencing the superego as a voice of *self*-discipline. The superego becomes the ego itself as it exhorts itself to persevere in working toward the ideal to which it aspires. Once again, as happened at the end of the oedipal period, the ego submits to the superego as a way of asserting and establishing itself.

The ego ideal is transformed too. It ceases being naively idealistic, as it was during adolescence, and becomes realistic. The commitment to an identity project makes the ego ideal both specific and approachable. The ego ideal no longer aims at vague utopian possibilities and now aims instead at a clear goal: the perfect fulfillment of the chosen identity, for example, being the best possible life partner, mother, father, writer, accountant, socialist, conservative, Buddhist, Christian, or representative of one's gender, race, family, nationality, or ethnic group. Granted, it is impossible to become a completely perfect anything; nevertheless, the ego ideal, as tied to the identity project, becomes realistically *approachable* even if never completely *reachable*. Erikson (1956, p. 149) explains the difference between ego identity and the ego ideal by describing ego identity as the "actually-attained-but-forever-to-be-revised sense of the reality of the self within social reality" and the ego ideal as "the set of to-be-strived-for-but-forever-not-quite-attainable ideal goals for the self." The ego ideal is now a concrete goal rather than an abstract wish, and as such it becomes the telic cause of the ego's identity project.

As transformed and reunited through the identity project, the superego and ego ideal become effectively interactive agencies. The superego "pushes" the ego in the identity project, the ego ideal "pulls" the ego. The superego is the stick, the ego ideal the carrot. The superego is the propelling cause of the identity project, the ego ideal the telic cause. Thus integrated with the identity project, the superego is no longer just an intrapsychic representative of the parents, and the ego ideal is no longer just a source of unrealistic aspirations. The superego never completely loses its association with the parents, and the father in particular.[4] And the ego ideal, by definition, never ceases being ideal and, therefore, unreachable. Nevertheless, both the superego and the ego ideal are transformed into effectively interactive *egoic* sources of motivation. The superego becomes the ego itself as it commands itself to sustain its discipline, and the ego ideal becomes the ego itself as it envisions the ideal goal toward which it strives.

The synthesis of the egoic system requires not only an integration of the superego and the ego ideal but also an integration of these two with the transcendental unity of consciousness. This latter integration is also accomplished by means of the identity project. For in forging an identity in the world, the ego forges a sense of being that fills in the abstract emptiness of transcendental consciousness. The ego identity brought into being by the identity project is, as it were, a surrogate body for the mental ego; it is something the mental ego can be said to *be*. The identity project thus serves not only to mediate the superego and the ego ideal but also to instantiate the transcendental subject. The transcendental subject, which is the mental ego's most interior and essential self, becomes a "thing" in assuming an ego identity. In forging an ego identity, the transcendental subject ceases being a nonentity, a distressing "nothingness," and becomes something that exists in and is recognized by the world. The identity project thus synthesizes all three agencies of the egoic system by creating at once a common ground for the superego and ego ideal and a concrete embodiment for the transcendental subject.

Self-Reflection

The identity project changes the nature of self-reflection. Self-reflection ceases being the vacuously self-certain self-reflection of the mental ego as transcendental subject and becomes the self-reflection of the mental ego as embodied in an unfolding identity project. This new form of self-reflection involves all of the agencies we have been discussing, each of which has a voice in an internal self-reflective dialogue. The superego speaks in expressions such as "I should do . . . ," "I must do . . . ," "It is good that I did . . . ," "I am remiss or deficient for not having done . . . ," and "It would be wrong if I did not do. . . ." The ego ideal speaks in expressions such as "If I persevere, I will be a success as . . . ," "If I find the right . . . , I shall be happy," and "If only I could achieve . . . , I would be fulfilled." Finally, the transcendental subject as embodied in its unfolding ego identity speaks in such expressions as "I just did . . . , therefore I am a . . . ," "No one (or everyone) appreciates me when I do . . . , therefore I am . . . ," and "I just achieved (or failed at) . . . , therefore I am a. . . ." This dialogue of voices is the inner medium through which the mental ego conducts the identity project and in doing so both forges and reflects upon itself.

Although ego identity serves as a surrogate body for the transcendental unity of consciousness, it is not an object in the sense of being an entity already formed and ready to be discovered by thought. Rather, ego identity is a constantly evolving self-*understanding* or self-*concept*. It is an epistemic rather than ontic entity that, as such, exists only *as* a distinctive process of thought rather than as an object that could be given *for* thought. Ego identity exists only in being conceived, that is, only in the act of self-conception; and it continues to exist only so long as it continues to be conceived, and reconceived. (Remember Descartes's addendum to "I think therefore I am": "At least so long as I continue to think.") This epistemic status of ego identity helps account for the virtually incessant nature of internal dialogue. An almost continuous flow of inner talk is necessary because one can exist as an ego identity only by thinking one's identity, only by monitoring, appraising, and updating it. Self-reflection upon identity, then, is more than a merely passive act of introspective observation. It is not a purely cognitive apprehension of an independent entity; it is rather an act by means of which a special kind of object, an epistemic object, is forged and kept in existence. Self-reflection helps create the very object it reflects upon.

The fact that the mental ego thinks that it *is* an "object" that the mental ego itself creates is a curious inversion indeed, as I have noted elsewhere (Washburn and Stark 1979). Because consciousness, including self-reflective consciousness, is a power of the ego, it follows that consciousness is a power of the "object" that the ego is. However, because the "object" that the ego is, or at least takes itself to be, is an "object" that the ego itself creates, it follows that consciousness is both the producer and a power of the same "thing," a "thing" that, moreover, exists only as an ever-unfinished epistemic construct within the stream of consciousness. This subordination of consciousness to an object that consciousness itself creates is contradictory; nevertheless, it is inherent to the adult mental ego's reflection upon itself. For the adult mental ego, to be is to be conceived—even though the mental ego itself must do the conceiving!

Ego-Initiated Cognition

Piaget believed that cognitive development is complete by the end of adolescence. The formal operational cognition achieved during adolescence, he believed, represents the final level of cognitive growth. In the last two decades, cognitive-developmental theorists have challenged Piaget's view by arguing that a distinct new level (or levels) of cognition emerges during adulthood. These theorists point to a number of ways in which formal operational cognition falls short of the cognition that is, or at least can be, achieved during adulthood. For example, they argue that formal operational cognition is limited in being closed, static, detached, linear, abstract, and absolutistic. Adult cognition, according to these theorists, surmounts these limitations by moving in a direction that is more open, evolving, contextual, holistic, inventive, and pragmatic or "relativistic."

Klaus Riegel (1973) and Michael Basseches (1980, 1984a, 1984b, 1989), for example, have argued in favor of a dialectical conception of postformal cognition.[5] This conception stresses the dynamically unfolding character of thought. Dialectical thought, originally described by Hegel in the nineteenth century, is a type of thought that moves through contradictions to higher syntheses. It is a type of thought, therefore, that aims at progressively more differentiated and integrated structures that transcend the inherent limitations of earlier, more primitive structures. Dialectical thought is holistic and dynamic. Rather than focusing on isolated propositions and the formal operations that can be performed on them, dialectical thought focuses on theoretical systems as evolving wholes, as constructs that grow through assimilation-accommodation exchanges and ensuing negations and radical restructurings. Dialectical thought moves in the direction of increasing inclusiveness and unification; each transcending phase of dialectical thought subsumes and integrates previously independent or fragmented theoretical structures—for example, as relativity theory subsumes Newtonian theory.

Francis Richards and Michael Commons (1984) have stressed the metasystematic aspect of postformal thought. Similar to those espousing a dialectical conception, Richards and Commons argue that postformal thought moves in the direction of increasing inclusiveness and unification. Whereas formal operational thought performs operations on the propositional or conceptual components of theoretical systems, postformal thought performs operations on theoretical systems as wholes. Moreover, Richards and Commons propose, postformal thought moves beyond single systems and works toward integrating independent theoretical systems into unified supersystems. In this movement toward inclusiveness and unification, postformal thought reaches ultimately toward integrating, or at least bridging, the most basic paradigms of inquiry. Richards and Commons acknowledge that many adults do not attain these higher levels of postformal cognition. They maintain, however, that such levels are inherently achievable by adults.[6]

Another proposal is that postformal thought, in contrast to formal operational cognition, is thought of a distinctively inventive sort. The major exponent of this view is Patricia Arlin (1975, 1977, 1984, 1989), who contrasts the problem-*finding* orientation of postformal thought with the problem-*solving* orientation of formal operational cognition. Formal operational cognition provides effective procedures for the solution of a wide variety of problems. These problems are solved deductively or inductively, logically or empirically, according to the rules of inference and testing that form the canon of hypothetico-deductive thought. However, if formal operational cognition is effective in solving problems in these ways, it is of little use, according to Arlin, in discovering problems. Formal operational thought is a powerful tool but is not itself a source of new ideas. The generation of new ways of seeing things occurs beyond rather than within formal operational thought. Such inventive thought, according to Arlin, is for this reason distinctive of postformal cognition.

Carol Gilligan and Michael Murphy (Gilligan and Murphy 1979; Murphy and Gilligan 1980) have criticized formal operational thought for ignoring the concrete contexts in which "facts" are embedded and the multiple interpretations and uncertainties inherent to such contexts, especially contexts that situate moral decisions. Formal operational cognition aims at univocal clarity and unassailable demonstration or confirmation; in contrast, postformal thought, according Gilligan and Murphy, allows a multiplicity of perspectives and acknowledges that ineluctable uncertainty is inherent to human understanding. No one is a completely detached anonymous subject; everyone is a bearer of gender, class, and culture. Everyone brings a point of view to bear upon "objects of knowledge." Gilligan and Murphy draw upon the work of William Perry (1970), who describes development in the college-age years as progressing from an absolutistic "either-it's-true-or-it's-false" dualism through intermediate positions to, finally, a contextual relativism sensitive to the perspective, ambiguity, uncertainty, and therefore inescapable commitment intrinsic to belief.

Jan Sinnott (1981, 1984, 1989) has explicitly proposed that postformal cognition be understood as a kind of relativistic thinking. She argues that postformal thought is always based on a frame of reference and therefore always has a relative, perspectival, element. Sinnott's postformal relativism, unlike the relativism characteristic of adolescence, is by no means a merely negative or skeptical relativism. It is rather a pragmatic relativism that conceives of knowledge as a functional exchange between consciousness and the world, an exchange that always involves, to some degree, subjectivity and a multiplicity of possible points of view. As a pragmatic relativism, postformal relativism, according to Sinnott, is socially grounded. Although individual subjectivity always plays a role, intellectual communities take precedence in setting the standards of thought.

Theoretical discussion of adult postformal thought is still in its early phases. None of the proposals just reviewed has won the day, and most theorists agree that all of these proposals have something important to contribute. The consensus at present is that adult cognition involves dialectical, metasystematic, inventive, contextual, and relativistic-perspectival aspects. No one knows exactly how these aspects are related or how, if at all, they interconnect as dimensions of a fifth Piagetian stage. In fact, the very idea of extending the Piagetian program to include a fifth, postformal, stage has met with serious criticism (Broughton 1984). Nevertheless, the trend at present is to investigate how the aspects of postformal thought that have been proposed so far might presuppose each other or otherwise be understood as developmentally collateral or interdependent aspects of a higher stage of adult cognition.

In being stage-related to the first half of adult life, which is the final stage of ego development, the types of postformal thought just discussed should be considered the highest forms of ego-initiated cognition. These types of thought however, I propose, should at the same time be considered precursors of transegoic cognition. For the dynamically integrative, holistic, and inventive aspects of postformal cognition suggest that the ego is not only active in performing cognitive operations and following preestablished rules and routines but is also receptive to spontaneously emerging insights into new patterns, models, and metaphors. These aspects of postformal cognition suggest, that is, not only that cognition continues to be centered in the ego but also that it has begun to draw upon nonegoic potentials. Because primal repression usually remains in place throughout the period of early adulthood, nonegoic potentials typically do not play a major role in cognition during this period. However, for those whose cognition advances from formal operational to postformal modes of thought, it seems that some significant degree of egoic-nonegoic interactivity has begun. If, then, the types of postformal thought that we have reviewed are to be grouped together as dimensions of a distinct cognitive stage, this stage should be recognized as a *transitional* stage. Ken Wilber (1980a, 1990) places forms of holistic-synthetic thought right at the transition between egoic and transegoic modes of cognition. I agree with him in this judgment.

Theory inevitably reflects its cultural milieu. For example, many people have observed that Piaget's conception of formal operational cognition was influenced by the positivist philosophy of science of his time. Similarly, conceptions of postformal cognition seem to reflect postpositivist, nonfoundationalist, neopragmatist, and postmodern trends in recent thought. In noting this, my point is not to cast suspicion on these conceptions. The fact that conceptions of cognitive-developmental stages reflect their historical contexts is not inherently problematic. After all, Socrates's philosophy of the concept, an innovation in its own time, made it possible to understand that people had been thinking in concepts *all along*. Similarly, post-positivist and postmodern trends in philosophy and other disciplines have allowed us to see that people, that is, adults, have been thinking in postformal ways *all along*.

Active Volition

We have already seen that belief in face of uncertainty is stressed in the notions of mature or postformal "relativism" set forth by Perry, Gilligan and Murphy, and Sinnott. Correspondingly, *commitment*, I believe, is the mode of volition most characteristic of early adulthood. Unlike the skeptical relativism characteristic of adolescence, which condemns "oppressive" convention as "merely" particular, contingent, and uncertain, the mature "relativism" of early adulthood realizes that there is no escape from particularity, contingency, and uncertainty. Mature "relativism" is therefore prepared to make a commitment to a particular course of life. The commitments of early adulthood typically commence with the commitment to occupation (be it in the public or private domain) and to a relationship with a primary other. These commitments belong to the larger identity project, which includes not only commitments to occupational and relational identity but also to sexual orientation, personal life-style, ethical values, political and religious point of view, and familial, ethnic, cultural, and racial inheritance or heritage. I shall consider the identity project in more detail in the next section. For present purposes it suffices to make the following two general points about the commitments of early adulthood: (1) they are of two principal types, and (2) they are limited in two chief respects.

The commitments of early adulthood are of the following two principal types: (1) commitments to new possibilities, and (2) affirmations or denials of what one has been. The first type of commitment is the type with which we are most familiar. The commitments to occupation and relationship with a primary other, the two chief commitments of the identity project, are commitments of this type. These commitments place us in new roles and bring us new aspects of identity. However, although it may sound paradoxical, we can also make commitments with respect to what we already are or have been. For example, a member of a large family may at some point explicitly address the issue of "being a member of the family," either affirming or denying such membership as an identity commitment. Similarly, people can embrace or disown their sexual orientation, ethnicity, race, and nationality. These kinds of commitments are ways in which we deepen or sever our roots to our heritage and existing relationships. To use Martin Heidegger's (1962) apt expression, we are all "thrown" into existence ("thrownness": *Geworfenheit*). We already have a history and belong to relationship networks before we even begin to inquire about our identities. The second type of commitment is the way in which we affirm or deny our history and inherited networks of belonging.

The commitments of early adulthood are limited in two main ways. First, they are limited in that, as explained earlier, they are made in the face of uncertainty. Young adults, for example, do not know if they are making the "right" occupational choice, the "right" relationship choice, the "right" choice with respect to their inherited circumstances. No guarantees exist before the fact, and therefore young adults have to take a "leap of faith" in making commitments. This leap is by no means a leap into the total unknown, because there are examples all around of how others have fared in making commitments like the ones that the young adult is about to make. Nevertheless, these examples provide no sure indication of how such commitments will turn out for the young adult who is approaching a decision juncture. Adult commitments are by nature uncertain and therefore involve an element of risk. For some people this risk seems great enough to inhibit commitment or even to make commitment impossible. For most people, however, this risk poses no insurmountable obstacle to commitment and in fact works to enhance the existential significance or individual authenticity of adult life. The commitments of early adulthood individualize life: the life to which I have committed myself is *my* life.

The second principal way in which the commitments of early adulthood are limited is that they are inherently tied to the specific life contexts of the persons making the commitments. This is obviously true of those commitments that either affirm or deny inherited circumstances. It also, however, is true of commitments to future possibilities. For the future possibilities among which we choose are almost always options suggested by or feasible in terms of the conditions of life from which we emerge. Moreover, our commitments are tied not only to the conditions from which we emerge but to future conditions as well. For commitments, once made, evolve or fail as a consequence of how reinforcing the world is of the commitments, how fortunate we are in escaping unforeseeable accidents and unwelcome twists of fate, and how able we are to sustain the kinds of effort required by the commitments. A commitment to a primary relationship, for example, is dependent upon a cooperative partner, upon contingencies of compatibility and unpredictable circumstances, and upon continual work on the relationship. Such a commitment—and therefore one's identity as a person in relationship—can be dissolved by separation or by the accidental death of one's partner. We are never in complete control of our commitments. Commitments always involve an ongoing exchange between the ego and the world.

EXISTENTIAL PROJECT: EARNING BEING AND VALUE—THE IDENTITY PROJECT

The identity project is the fundamental existential project of early adulthood. Following initial identity commitments at the end of adolescence, the young adult engages in the long-term effort of following through on those commitments and accomplishing the goals set by them. Although the adolescent has a self-representation in which basic trait characteristics are nucleated, the adolescent is as yet undefined in terms of the world. The identity difficulties of adolescence, so well described by Erik Erikson, are precisely difficulties that arise in preparing for commitments to such a social definition. Once the adolescent has weathered the difficulties, and perhaps "crises," of the teenage years and has finally made initial identity commitments, the work of early adulthood begins. The real work of forging and maintaining an identity takes place during the first half of adult life.

The identity project has both negative and positive motivations. The project is negatively motivated insofar as it is an attempt to overcome the anxieties of "nothingness" and "guilt" that emerge in adolescence. In flight from the feared "nothingness" at the core of consciousness, the young adult embarks upon a project to *be* something in the world. An ego identity is something definite and socially recognized and therefore something that confers upon the mental ego a sense of concrete existence or being. In response to the question "What am I?," the mental ego can respond, "I am a wife, husband, mother, father, member of a particular family or ethnic group, electrician, doctor, accountant, social worker, Buddhist, Christian, Jew, socialist, conservative, and so forth." These elements of identity are social roles or categories that the mental ego commits itself to or otherwise adopts as it own and, in doing so, forges a sense of concrete, defined existence.

In forging such a sense of existence, the mental ego is gradually relieved of the anxiety of "nothingness." To the extent that an ego identity is successfully established, the young adult is freed from the sense of ontological insecurity that afflicted the adolescent. This insecurity recedes and a sense of existential cohesion and even solidity arises. Adolescent self-doubts are not always laid to rest, because some people fail in their commitments and goals and therefore fail to become what they set out to be. Nevertheless, even these people achieve a negative identity, an identity by default if not by success, and consequently even they usually suffer less existential anxiety than the adolescent.

Jean-Paul Sartre (1956) more than anyone else has focused on ontological insecurity as a motivation behind the identity project. Flight from "nothingness," he maintains, is *the* motivation of our "fundamental project," the project to *be*. In seeking to forge a sense of being, Sartre says, we are attempting to be self-creators. Sartre believes that we all pursue a nuclear identity that is our self-posited essence. This nuclear identity is the meaning of our "being-in-the-world," and, according to Sartre, everything we say and do can be properly understood only as an expression of the quest for this core identity. Sartre contends that this quest for being is ultimately an impossible one, a "useless passion." For no matter how hard we may strive to forge an identity and no matter how successful we might be in this endeavor, the "nothingness" of consciousness is always one step behind us, ready to reclaim us. According to Sartre, the anxiety of "nothingness" not only motivates the identity project; it also lurks in the immediate background as an ever-present danger in our lives.

Sartre makes, but also exaggerates, an important point. He brilliantly describes how the anxiety of "nothingness" can motivate the identity project. In doing so, however, he seriously overstates the role of this anxiety, making it both the sole motivation behind the identity project and an unappeasable fear that could at any time expose the identity project as a "useless passion." Moderating Sartre's view, I suggest that the anxiety of "nothingness" is not the only motivation behind the identity project and that this anxiety, although always implicit, does not always pose as serious, or at least as immediate, a threat as Sartre maintains. The identity project, as we shall see shortly, has positive as well as negative motivations; moreover, the positive motivations gradually become more evident and the negative less evident as the identity project gets in gear and begins making progress toward its goals. Sartre seems unaware that, following adolescence, most people do make progress in establishing identities and that these identities frequently confer a solid sense of being, at least for significant periods of time. The anxiety of "nothingness" never disappears entirely; it remains an implicit fear and, as Sartre maintains, an ultimate Achilles' heel of the identity project. These important points acknowledged, the fact remains that the anxiety of "nothingness" does tend to move into the background as the young adult mental ego immerses itself in the identity project and begins to make progress in "being-in-the-world" and "being-with-others."

Although the anxiety of "nothingness" recedes into the background, it can still be detected indirectly in the seeming life-or-death, "being-or-nothingness," quality of decisions or events that have a major impact on identity (e.g., saving or losing a primary relationship or a job, being accepted or rejected by a kinship or ethnic group). The anxiety of "nothingness" can also be detected in the compulsiveness of the adult mental ego's internal dialogue. We have already seen that internal dialogue is the medium through which the mental ego forges its identity. For the adult mental ego, to be is to be conceived. The adult mental ego must reflect upon itself in order to maintain its existence as an epistemic object, a "thought thing," an identity. The mental ego cannot see itself through introspection but it can, it fancies, *hear* itself as it talks to itself in internal dialogue. Accordingly, the mental ego, when not engaged in activity, tends to talk to itself in compulsive fashion to guard against gaps or voids in consciousness. The mental ego is frightened by periods of internal silence. Such periods tend to dissolve the identity that the mental ego has forged and to reexpose the mental ego to the underlying "nothingness" of transcendental consciousness.

A second negative motivation behind the identity project is the sense of "guilt" that emerges during adolescence as a consequence of the adolescent's breaking away from parents. The adolescent's assertion of independence involves an alienation from parents that repeats in significant respects the young child's primal alienation from the preoedipal mother. This severing of ties with one's primary benefactors is the primordial "sin" of rejecting the love of one's "creators," and it therefore carries with it, however unconsciously, a burden of guilt and a corresponding sense that one is in need of justification for one's independent existence. For this reason young adults feel a need to justify their independent existence by proving their worth as individuals, both to themselves and to their parents.

Young adults attempt to prove their worth in the same way they attempt to establish a sense of being: by pursuing the identity project. The identity project is a means to both of these ends because to succeed in establishing the identity to which one aspires is also to earn a sense of value. To achieve success in what one has set out to do, and be, earns one self-esteem. A well-established identity therefore confers not only being but also justification for being. It is satisfying to know that one is keeping to one's commitments and succeeding in one's goals. This satisfaction involves a sense of *earned* value, a sense of merit that accrues as a result of "good works." The person who meets with success in the identity project thus gains not only a sense of being to placate the anxiety of "nothingness" but also a sense of worth to placate the anxiety of "guilt."

Interestingly, a sense of value can be earned even with an identity that transgresses social norms if that identity is sufficiently extreme to bring with it a sense of specialness. For example, being dramatically unconventional or especially wicked can give one a sense of standing out from others and, therefore, of being superior, even if sometimes in an inverse-perverse sort of way. Bohemians and gangsters, for example, enjoy a sense of value of this sort. In diverging from the norm by a wide margin, some people believe that they are extraordinary rather than just nonordinary. The sense of value that goes with being distinctive in this way, although problematic in certain respects, is nonetheless existentially rewarding in much the same manner as a sense of value based on an identity embodying social norms.

Both of the negative motivations behind the identity project recede into the background as progress is made in the project. We usually establish a sufficient sense of being and value not to be plagued by chronic ontological and moral anxieties. To be sure, the anxiety of "nothingness" is implicitly evident in the ways noted previously. And the anxiety of "guilt" or lack of justification is implicitly evident in the feeling that justification is never complete, that the jury remains out, that additional "good works" are always required. Nevertheless, the severity and frequency of ontological and moral self-doubts decrease as progress is made in the identity project. Typically, a more or less solid sense of being is forged and a more or less adequate sense of worth or value is earned during the first half of adult life.

The anxieties of "nothingness' and "guilt" also recede into the background because the identity project has positive motivations that gradually take precedence over the negative motivations. If at first we embark upon the identity project to forge a sense of being and value, it is not long, typically, before we become involved in the project for the satisfactions it brings. The identity project has its own rewards. It is the means by which we develop our potentialities and give shape and expression to our character. Adult commitments admit us to the "school of the real world." This school is a testing ground in which we face challenges and grow. Our faculties are engaged, our personal resources are tapped, and our powers are thereby revealed and enhanced. We learn our abilities and limits by means of the identity project. The identity project therefore is not just a mode of flight from "nothingness" and "guilt"; it is also a vehicle for growth and authentic self-expression. Moreover, if at first it is primarily the former, it usually does not take long before it becomes primarily the latter. The negative motivations behind the identity project, which initially are at center stage, withdraw into the background as initial identity commitments lead to real identity accomplishments. This direction of change typically holds at least until midlife, when, as we shall see in the next chapter, the negative motivations sometimes resurface and begin once again to get the upper hand.

In addition to having both negative and positive sources of motivation, the identity project has both inner and outer frames of reference. We have already addressed the inner frame of reference in discussing the interior dialogue the mental ego carries on with itself as it monitors the identity project and thereby maintains a continuous sense of existence. The outer frame of reference corresponding to this interior dialogue is *other people* as observers and judges of the mental ego's identity performances. The indispensable role played by others in identity formation has been recognized for a long time (Cooley 1902; Mead 1934; Goffman 1959). Not only sociologists but also social psychologists and existential philosophers have long understood that a person's identity in the world is mediated through other people. Other people are the audience before whom we act to gain recognition and confirmation of the identity we are trying to be.

On this point, Barry Schlenker says:

> The theme that emerges from these analyses is that identity is forged, expressed, maintained, and modified in the crucible of social life, as its contents undergo the process of actual or imagined observation, judgment, and reaction by audiences (oneself and others). People's ideas about themselves are expressed and tested in social life through their actions. In turn, the outcomes of these "tests" provide a basis for crystallizing, refining, or modifying identity based in part on how believable or defensible these identity images appear to be. (1986, p. 24)

Sartre (1956) stretched this point to the limit, stating that "to be is to be perceived." This statement, although exaggerated, throws into relief the essential role played by the other. The existence of identity as an epistemic object depends not only on identity being conceived (inner frame of reference) but also on it being perceived (outer frame of reference). And, indeed, the former presupposes the latter, because the mental ego can convince itself of its identity (through internal dialogue) only if it has first convinced others (by receiving their recognition and confirmation). This priority of the other is evident in internal statements such as these: "They accepted my manuscript; therefore, I am an author." "No one will go out with me; therefore, I am undesirable." "No one will give me a job; therefore, I am a failure." "They laughed at my jokes; therefore, I am a funny person."

The role played by the other is especially conspicuous in the early stages of the identity project when the anxieties of "nothingness" and "guilt" play a larger role. To the extent that one is afflicted with a sense of lack of being and value, one turns to others to provide a *reflected* sense of being and value. In the early stages of the identity project, this mediating role played by others can lead to a narcissistic solicitousness of others' attentions. However, as progress is made in the identity project, and as the negative motivations behind the project give way to the positive motivations, the role played by others becomes less evident. The role played by others is never eliminated completely; no mental ego ever achieves a completely self-grounded identity. Moreover, as we shall see in the next chapter, the role played by others tends to return to the fore at midlife.

If other people play an essential role in the identity project, so too do social roles and categories. The identity project is an attempt to establish a *socially recognized* sense of being and value. Erikson (1956) stresses this fact, holding that ego identity is as much society's definition of the ego as it is the ego's conception of itself. The social aspect of the identity project involves affirming or assuming social roles and categories and thereby becoming (i.e., instantiating, embodying) those roles and categories. This aspect of the identity project is what Soren Kierkegaard (1945, 1959) referred to as *ethical choice*, the choice to submit oneself to the "universals" of social life. Kierkegaard (1941) stressed that ethical choice properly speaking is sustained choice. To be a father, for example, one must not only help conceive a child but also be responsibly involved in the child's life. To embody any of the roles or categories that society has defined, one must not only make initial identity commitments but also follow through on those commitments. Only by following through on the commitments does one truly live up to and, therefore, exemplify the social roles and categories to which one has submitted oneself.

Sustaining identity commitments is no easy matter. For identity commitments, like all commitments, are subject to the vicissitudes of lived experience. Susan Whitbourne and Comilda Weinstock (1986) make this point in Piagetian terms, explaining that an identity is an unfolding construct that engages experience in both assimilative and accommodative ways. To the extent that an identity has been forged, that identity assimilates experience by structuring and interpreting it according to a preestablished pattern. Whitbourne and Weinstock give as an example a woman who as part of her identity believes she is a "leader," a person who quickly understands and can take effective charge of difficult situations. This identity assimilates experience by leading the woman both to assert herself in difficult situations and to expect others to defer to her in such situations. On occasions when this assimilative style does not work, the woman feels that she is somehow not herself and that others are not recognizing her for what she truly is. When this happens, rationalization and distortion frequently occur as ways of preserving a threatened identity. Sometimes, however, the dissonance between identity and experience becomes sufficiently great that identity assimilation gives way to identity accommodation. Ego identity has to be restructured to adjust to changing experience so that, once restructured, it can begin assimilating experience again. According to Whitbourne and Weinstock, an optimal equilibrium between assimilation and accommodation can be achieved. Ego identity is an unfolding construct that under optimal conditions both assimilates experience and makes ongoing accommodations to experience. When an assimilation-accommodation equilibrium obtains, identity is both solid and flexible; it not only provides an ongoing sense of being but also adjusts to changing life circumstances.

The assimilation-accommodation interplay between identity and experience is one among many ways in which identity is a joint product of ego-world exchange. We noted earlier that identity commitments are inherently tied to life circumstances, both to past circumstances from which they emerge and to future circumstances toward which they unfold. The writings of existential phenomenologists contain many accounts of this interconnection of self and world. The best account, I believe, is that provided by Maurice Merleau-Ponty (1962) in his debate with Sartre on the extent to which we are free in defining ourselves.

Sartre (1956) believes that we are "self-creators," the sole authors of what we will be. For Sartre, existence precedes essence; we exist as undefined consciousness, as "free nothingness," before we posit the fundamental project that defines our being. Sartre's position, as always, is extreme, and Merleau-Ponty offers the needed counterpoint. Merleau-Ponty explains that what we are is as much given as "self-created," as much inherited as self-legislated. By the time the identity project is conceived, the ego already finds itself molded by society. It realizes, for example, that it is already rich or poor, female or male, sister or brother, Hispanic or Asian, Catholic or Buddhist. The ego does not create itself *ex nihilo* but rather forges an identity on the basis of an already-given reality. Moreover, in forging its identity, the ego not only sets out from an inherited situation but also moves toward future situations that it cannot completely foresee or control. These future situations will either reinforce or obstruct, facilitate or thwart the ego's identity project. The ego is continually moving from the embedded past into the unknown future. Accordingly, for Merleau-Ponty, our worldly selfhood is never completely self-possessed or final. It remains an ongoing interchange between consciousness and the world.

The identity project is thoroughgoingly two-sided. It has both negative and positive motivations, both inner and outer frames of reference, and both individual and social dimensions. It is a project by which the ego seeks, negatively, to overcome a sense of "nothingness" and "guilt" and, positively, to exercise its powers and give expression to itself in the world. It is a project by which the ego attempts inwardly to convince itself of its being and value by outwardly seeking the recognition and confirmation of others. And it is a project by which the ego attempts to define and realize itself as an individual by adopting or affirming shared social roles and categories. The two-sided nature of the identity project creates tensions that can destabilize and even jeopardize the project. These tensions, however, usually pose no serious difficulties during the early phases of the project. These tensions usually do not become severe until midlife or later when, sometimes, the resurfacing of the negative motivations behind the identity project brings the opposing sides of the project into explicit conflict with each other.

CONCLUSION

The first half of adult life is the last phase of ego development. The ego is given a new foundation with the restructuring of primal repression and primal alienation. The ego's primary "parts"—the superego, ego ideal, and transcendental unity of consciousness—are unified as effectively interactive elements of a single system. The ego grows cognitively and volitionally with the development of postformal thought and the emergence of the self-discipline needed for long-term commitments. And the ego actualizes potentialities and gives form and expression to itself by forging an ego identity or worldly self. By these means and in these ways, the ego continues to undergo development during the first half of adult life.

Ego development is usually complete by midlife. By midlife, typically, the ego has actualized its potentialities and established itself in the world. Accordingly, the ego at midlife, or later, sometimes begins to feel as though it is no longer moving forward and even that it is losing ground. If and when this happens, the ego usually resists acknowledging that anything is wrong and attempts to carry on in the accustomed fashion. In some cases, however, the ego begins to suffer disillusionments that throw into question its goals, its accomplishments, and even its very being. These self-doubts, should they emerge, signal that the long period of dualism has run its course and is in its final days. They indicate that mature dualism has given way to late dualism. Late dualism, as we shall see in the next chapter, is a period during which the mental ego, in its last days, is vulnerable to a wide range of existential "maladies" and psychological "disorders."

7

Midlife Transvaluation and Pathologies of the Self

Late dualism is the period of the mental ego's decline.[1] The ego, having achieved full development sometime in early or middle adulthood, no longer needs to be protected by primal repression and primal alienation. The ego is at this point ready to return to the sources from which it has long been in flight, and it begins to sense its separation from these sources in feelings of unwholeness. If, however, the ego is ready for a return to sources and has begun to yearn for transcendence, it nonetheless fears what lies beyond the safe boundaries of the mental-egoic domain. The ego, as mental ego, is for this reason resistant to changing its basic stance in being. The mental ego of late dualism, then, frequently finds itself at once drawn and resistant to unknown possibilities lying beyond its own domain.

The mental ego's resistance to change is entirely understandable. Nevertheless, this resistance must be judged a negative holding action, because, by late dualism, the protectively encapsulated life of the mental ego has become developmentally retrograde. Notwithstanding its resistance, then, the mental ego in late dualism is prone to undergo a deep shift in its sense of how it stands in existence. It is prone gradually to lose the feeling of being safely self-contained and to begin feeling dualistically dissociated, to lose the feeling of being autonomous and self-sufficient and to begin feeling alienated and empty. This shift in feeling signals that primal repression and primal alienation have ceased serving as necessary foundations of ego development and have become obstructions to ego transcendence. The mental ego, then, despite being prone to maintain its stance in being, is also prone to feel that this stance is somehow self-defeating or unwarranted.

Because we are dealing with tendencies and countertendencies here, no invariant pattern is followed during the period of late dualism. The decline of the mental ego can unfold in many ways. It is not surprising, therefore, that the phenomenon of the mental ego's decline has been subject to so many interpretations. The current fashion is to interpret the shift from feelings of security and autonomy to feelings of alienation and emptiness as being symptomatic of a "midlife crisis" leading from the more externally derived motivations of early adulthood to the more internally derived motivations of later maturity. In the 1940s and 1950s, atheistically oriented existentialists interpreted this shift in feelings as a prelude to an unhappy acknowledgment of the "groundlessness" or "meaninglessness" of existence. Spiritually oriented thinkers have interpreted the shift as a prelude to religious conversion or spiritual awakening. Kierkegaard, for example, interpreted the shift in question as a transition from the ethical to the religious stage of life. Jung interpreted it as a midlife turn toward individuation, the spiritual odyssey. And in India the shift is interpreted as a transition from the stage of the householder to that of the forest dweller (spiritual seeker). The developmental process of late dualism moves in a direction away from worldly engagement and toward unknown, hidden possibilities. In moving in this direction, however, the process does not produce any regular, much less necessary, sequence of experiences. Consequently, the decline of the mental ego during late dualism follows an unpredictable course and has been subject to a wide variety of understandings.

In using the term *midlife* to describe late dualism, I do not mean to suggest that late dualism occurs within a clearly bounded time period. The term *midlife* is chosen because the process of decline distinctive of late dualism typically occurs only after the ego has completed the identity project, which, as we have seen, is the project of early adulthood. Accordingly, late dualism is most accurately described as a stage that, for those who experience it, typically commences at midlife *or later*. I am not, then, using *midlife* in a literal chronological sense to designate the middle years of the normal life span. This point needs to be emphasized as strongly as possible. Rather, I am using the term in a more general developmental sense to designate a life stage that people can but need not experience, a stage that, for those who do experience it, typically begins only after the developmental work of early adulthood is complete.

Midlife, as I shall be using the term, then, designates the transitional period between egoic maturity and transegoic awakening. The ego, having completed its development in early adulthood, begins to sense that something is amiss at the very (dualistic) bases of its being. This sense of dis-ease grows into an existential malaise, into, as Kierkegaard put it, a "sickness unto death." The ego begins to "die to the world" and in doing so is brought slowly to the "precipice of faith," that is, to the threshold of transegoic possibilities. It is a perplexing fact that not all people—and perhaps only very few—are brought to this threshold. Many if not most people who experience some aspects of the mental ego's decline are not affected radically enough to be dislodged from mental-egoic existence. Accordingly, not only transegoic stages of life but also the midlife transition leading to them must be considered possible rather than likely, expectable, stages of human development.

Late dualism involves a decline of the mental ego leading to the possibility of transcendence rather like, for Marx, late capitalism involves a decline in the rate of profit leading to the possibility of a collapse of the capitalist system. Late dualism, that is, does not follow a necessary course. Too many countertendencies and short-term expedients exist to allow meaningful predictions in particular cases. The dualistic bases of the mental-egoic system are deeply entrenched. Moreover, the mental ego is able to bail itself out, prop itself up, and rationalize itself in myriad ways. Accordingly, even if the mental ego begins to undergo decline, it need not become consciously aware that this is happening, much less aware of the deep significance of the process it is undergoing. Even if the mental ego begins to be afflicted with "sickness unto death," it need not become acutely ill, much less "die." "Sickness unto death" is potentially a fatal illness for the ego, qua mental ego, but the stress needs to be put on *potentially*.

THE DISILLUSIONMENT OF THE MENTAL EGO

The identity project characteristic of early adulthood may occupy a person for the whole of adult life. Factors, however, work against the project that can lead to its abandonment. Paradoxically, the project can be abandoned either as a result of failure or success. Failure can obviously lead to the abandonment of the project. A person can spend years devoted to commitments and goals only, in the end, to fail to establish a secure sense of being and worth by, for example, failing in relationships, in parenting, in career, or in legal or ethical obligations. Clearly, a person failing in any of these ways might easily become dejected and conclude that the identity project is impossible. Less evident, but also possible, is that a person might arrive at this same conclusion as a result of success, by meeting commitments and achieving goals. This possibility exists because to succeed in the identity project is to realize that the identity project promises more than it can deliver. To succeed in the identity project is to realize that more than worldly being and value is needed to find fulfillment in life. I am not denying that genuine satisfaction comes with accomplishing the life objectives implicit in the identity project. My point is rather that, contrary to the assumptions of the identity project, the completion of these objectives does not suffice to bring completion to life itself. To succeed in the identity project is therefore to face the question "Is this all there is?"

The reason why the identity project cannot deliver what it promises is that the fulfillment that presumably would be achieved through the project does not involve the whole psyche. It involves only the mental ego. The identity project is an attempt to achieve fulfillment *as a mental ego*. A fulfilled mental ego, however, is a contradiction in terms. For the mental ego exists in disconnection from the nonegoic and interpersonal roots of its being and is therefore inherently incomplete. The mental ego of course strives to hide this incompleteness from itself. The mental ego is committed to the idea of its independence and self-sufficiency. Indeed, the identity project is the principal way in which the mental ego attempts to *demonstrate* its independence and self-sufficiency. However, because the mental ego is inherently incomplete, the attempt to demonstrate the contrary is doomed to failure. In this sense I agree with Sartre's (1956) claim that the identity project is an impossible project. Ultimately, the identity project is an attempt to turn disconnection into self-sufficient independence, isolation into wholeness.

The mental ego typically does not begin to understand why the promises implicit in the identity project cannot be met until after it has succeeded in completing the specific life goals of the project. Just as, typically, only a wealthy person can know that wealth cannot buy happiness, so, typically, only a person who has achieved the specific goals of the identity project can know that accomplishing these goals does not by itself bring fulfillment to life. The identity project is motivated by the ego ideal as telic cause. The ego ideal aims at a condition of perfect fulfillment and wholeness. This condition is not impossible per se, but it is not a condition that can be attained through the identity project. The identity project can achieve only full ego development, not full psychic (egoic-nonegoic, self-other) development and integration. The mental ego, however, is typically blind to the fact that the identity project cannot achieve the ultimate end that motivates it until after the project has been completed *without achieving that end*. The mental ego usually needs to complete its own development through the identity project before it can learn that its own completeness is, paradoxically, incomplete. The paradox is that the mental ego usually must fulfill itself to discover that, by itself, it cannot be fulfilled.

The identity project, then, can fail both by failing and by succeeding in its specific life goals. And when it fails, it fails more profoundly through success. For people who fail in the project simply by failing in specific life goals tend to put all of the blame on themselves, whereas people who fail in the project despite succeeding in specific life goals sense, correctly, that something is fundamentally wrong with the project. In either case, however, whether through failure or success, people who lose faith in the project suffer a serious disillusionment in life. The identity project is the meaning of the adult mental ego's life. To abandon this project, therefore, is, for the mental ego, to abandon hope in life itself.

If and when the mental ego begins to sense the impossibility of the identity project, the negative motivations behind the project begin to return to the fore. The sense of "nothingness" and the corresponding felt need to establish being, together with the sense of "guilt" and the corresponding felt need to justify independent existence, begin once again to plague the mental ego. So long as the mental ego is making progress in the identity project, still believing that the being and worth earned through the project are sufficient for fulfillment, the negative motivations behind the project remain in the background and the positive motivations and compensations stay at center stage. So long as the mental ego is still moving forward with faith in the identity project, the mental ego remains motivated by possibilities of growth, self-expression, and achievement and continues to enjoy a relatively solid sense of being and worth. However, once the mental ego begins to sense that it cannot succeed in the identity project—whether this realization arises from failing or succeeding in specific life goals—the mental ego begins to be less inspired by the positive motivations of the project and more disturbed by the negative motivations. The mental ego begins once again to suffer from ontological and moral insecurity, from the anxieties of "nothingness" and "guilt."

The anxieties of "nothingness" and "guilt" are stirred by a deeper source as well. As noted earlier, primal repression and primal alienation undergo a revaluation at midlife, a revaluation that throws these basic structures of the mental-egoic system into question. Primal repression and primal alienation cease performing positive developmental functions and therefore lose their developmental warrant. The repressive infrastructure underlying the mental-egoic sphere and the defensive shields outwardly fortifying this sphere cease serving the mental ego as invisible protective structures and begin being experienced by the mental ego, vaguely and prereflectively, as self-limiting exclusionary structures. Accordingly, at the same time the mental ego begins to lose faith in its worldly being and value, it also begins to sense that its inner foundations and self-boundaries are somehow suspect. At the same time the mental ego begins to suffer disillusionment in the identity project, it also begins to feel uneasy about its basic stance in being.

The mental ego is therefore susceptible at this point to begin feeling very different about itself. It is prone to begin feeling less like a self-subsistent incorporeal subject and more like an ungrounded, disembodied witness, less like an autonomous mind and will and more like an isolated consciousness cut off from other people, less like a "thing that thinks" (res cogitans) and more like a nonentity incapable of feeling, creative imagination, and outreaching openness. To be sure, these uneasy feelings are at first extremely vague and virtually unconscious. The mental ego is still a long way from explicitly encountering primal repression and primal alienation as embedded obstructions to higher development. Nevertheless, the feelings stirred by the revaluation of primal repression and primal alienation are quite real, and they exacerbate the mental ego's sense of "nothingness" and "guilt." They amplify the fears, the negative motivations, behind the identity project.

The reemergence of "nothingness" and "guilt" besets the mental ego with a feeling that it is on the run and losing ground. Haunted by this feeling, the mental ego's response is typically to step up its efforts to demonstrate its worldly being and value, that is, to increase its efforts to succeed in the identity project. These efforts, however, do not lessen the mental ego's self-doubts. In fact, they have the effect of making the mental ego's self-doubts more severe. At this point, increased efforts to succeed in the identity project only make the impossibility of the project more evident. The mental ego therefore eventually begins to suspect that no amount of effort or success could possibly allay its anxieties and even that the very attempt to quell these anxieties by pursuing worldly being and value is somehow problematic, counterproductive, "wrong." These suspicions can lead the mental ego to question its basic life objectives and thereby set in motion a process of reflection that can lead only to unwelcome insights. At this juncture all developmental factors are working against the mental ego: The impossibility of the identity project is about to be exposed, and primal repression and primal alienation have lost their warrant. Accordingly, if and when the mental ego begins to question itself in the manner indicated, it is led ineluctably to strongly negative conclusions. It is led to conclude that its basic life objectives are misguided and that they are so because they aim only at escaping "nothingness" and "guilt."[2]

The mental ego resists this conclusion, this sobering realization, as long as possible. Such resistance can take many forms. The mental ego may engage in even more strenuous efforts to establish a sense of being and worth, narcissistically exaggerated efforts designed to command the confirming attention of other people. These efforts, however, are no solution to the mental ego's problems; they are, rather, desperate expressions of the problem. In addition to such exaggerated efforts, the mental ego may indulge in fugitive diversions, escapades, affairs, or perhaps the use of chemical substances to achieve distraction from or to numb the inner sense of lack and fault. These measures, however, are only palliatives that leave the underlying conditions unchanged. They may delay the moment of reckoning, but they are unlikely to postpone it permanently. Despite its resistance, then, the mental ego is headed toward the unhappy realization that its basic life project is an impossible one. The moment of this insight is the moment of the mental ego's disillusionment.

Pathologies of the Self

The revaluation of primal repression and primal alienation, the reemergence of feelings of "nothingness" and "guilt," and the dawning disillusionment of the mental ego all have an undermining effect on the mental ego's worldly being. They can therefore cause a variety of serious psychological difficulties. These difficulties are "pathologies" or "disorders" of middle and later adulthood, and in particular "pathologies" of the mental ego's sense of self. Because there is no definite age at which late dualism comes to an end, nor even any indefeasible reason or cause why it must come to an end, the "pathologies" of the stage typically appear as a seemingly unrelated array rather than as a coherent sequence of expressions of a developmental process. Reflecting this fact, I shall in this chapter consider the "pathologies" of midlife simply as a set of difficulties that can afflict the mental ego that is in decline. I shall discuss the phenomenology and etiology of these conditions without focusing explicitly on their developmental interconnections or transpersonal implications. Then, in the next chapter, I shall discuss how these "pathologies" can be seen as stages of a developmental process leading to transcendence.

To avoid misunderstanding, the following point needs to be stressed: The difficulties to be described—depression, narcissism, existential syndrome, the divided or schizoid self, and the borderline condition—are treated only insofar as they arise and can be understood as stage-specific difficulties of midlife. All of these difficulties have other, often chronic and seriously pathological forms. I stress this point as a caution against two contrary misunderstandings— namely, (1) that difficulties like those to be discussed are always and only pathological in nature and therefore are never properly conceived as developmental trials occurring on the way to higher stages of growth; and (2) that, on the contrary, such difficulties are frequently if not usually developmental in nature and therefore are in many if not most cases properly conceived as trials on the way to higher stages of growth. These two misunderstandings are well represented in the psychological literature. The former is found in most psychoanalytic accounts of the major personality disorders and the latter in many existential, Jungian, and transpersonal accounts of these disorders. The truth lies somewhere between the extremes. People suffering from serious psychological disturbances are frequently tempted to fantasize that their sufferings are really trials of growth and, possibly, transcendence. Conversely, people undergoing developmental difficulties on the way to higher stages of growth frequently fear that they are succumbing to serious, permanent psychopathologies. A discerning eye is needed to tell the difference between merely pathological disorders on the one hand and phenomenologically similar but developmentally propitious difficulties on the other.[3] This difference, although difficult to discern in many individual cases, is crucial to the discussion that follows, especially the discussion of the divided or schizoid self and the borderline condition.

Depression

Depression takes many forms and has many causes. Among the causes are not only exceptionally unhappy or tragic life circumstances but also biochemical imbalances and psychodynamic abnormalities that can work irrespective of life circumstances. Most clinical cases of depression probably have a complex etiology involving combinations of these factors. The type of depression discussed here is distinctive in that its primary cause is to be found not in any exceptional circumstances or in any specific neurochemical or psychiatric conditions but rather in the adult mental ego's basic objectives in life. In this sense, the type of depression discussed here can be considered an existential depression specific to the adult mental ego. It is a type of depression that arises out of the mental ego's life project: the identity project.

The identity project is inherently susceptible to ups and downs, elations and dejections, because the actions of the identity project are judged successful or unsuccessful depending on how they are received by the persons (significant others, reference groups, boards, media, institutions) to whom the actions are addressed or pertain. Actions that earn recognition of the right kind are successful, because by such actions a person receives confirmation of the larger identity that the person is seeking to establish. On the other hand, actions that fail to earn recognition, or that earn recognition of a kind different from that intended, are unsuccessful, because by such actions a person fails to receive confirmation, or actually receives disconfirmation, of the larger identity that the person is seeking to establish. In confirming a person's identity, successful actions validate a person's sense of being and value and create a sense of confidence and self-satisfaction. Contrariwise, in failing to confirm a person's identity, or in actually disconfirming a person's identity, unsuccessful actions provoke worries about being and value and stir feelings of self-doubt and depression.

The depressions inherent to the identity project tend not to be serious in the early and middle stages of the project. So long as the mental ego has faith in the identity project and feels as though it is making progress in the project, unsuccessful efforts and corresponding disconfirmations of being and value are experienced more as temporary setbacks than as lasting defeats. They are experienced as disappointments that can be overcome by renewed efforts. And in fact, when renewed efforts do lead to the right kind of recognition from others, the mental ego soon forgets past setbacks. In the early and middle stages of the identity project, the mental ego is strongly confirmed in its being and value by efforts that are favorably received by others, and the mental ego anticipates ultimate success or vindication in the identity project sometime in the indefinite future. Accordingly, setbacks and consequent depressions tend to be occurrences of short duration. Setbacks are stinging blows that cause the mental ego intense unhappiness, to be sure; nevertheless, they are blows that typically have the effect of increasing the mental ego's resolve to succeed in the identity project.

This fundamentally optimistic outlook disappears as the mental ego approaches midlife. For the reemergence of the feelings of "nothingness" and "guilt" begins to erode whatever sense of being and value the mental ego might have earned from past accomplishments and to diminish the satisfaction that can be taken in present accomplishments. At midlife, the tendency is for successes in the identity project to cease being as cumulative and confirmatory as they were during early adulthood. Accordingly, the mental ego begins to feel that greater efforts than before are needed to maintain a sense of being and value and that, irrespective of past record, unsuccessful efforts provide serious and lasting disconfirmation of being and value. Affected by these apparent changes in its life prospects, the mental ego is prone to experience depression more and more frequently and for longer periods of time. Depression can even become the rule rather than the exception. Fears of "nothingness" and "guilt" lurk ominously in the background, and a steady string of successes is needed just to keep a step ahead of these fears. Not to succeed, or actually to fail, is to allow these fears to disclose themselves, however vaguely and faintly. In late dualism, the negative motivations behind the identity project tend to become more pronounced, and consequently successes in the identity project gradually diminish in significance and lasting effect and setbacks in the identity project gradually increase in significance and lasting effect.

This state of affairs leads the mental ego toward disillusionment. The mental ego senses that its efforts have diminishing returns and, therefore, that the identity project cannot be brought to a fulfilling conclusion. As the mental ego approaches disillusionment in this manner, it is afflicted with deeper and more tenacious depressions. Depression ceases being a merely passing mood associated with temporary setbacks in the identity project and becomes more a chronic mood associated with life prospects generally. Depression tends to manifest itself less in discrete episodes of dejection and widens to shroud life as a whole in a dark cast. It ceases being the affective expression of specific life misfortunes and becomes the affective expression of a waning of hope in the very possibility of good fortune. In other words, as the mental ego approaches disillusionment, depression turns into despair. Depression, then, especially as it becomes more subtle and pervasive, is an index of the gradual disillusionment of the mental ego. As such, it is a symptom of late dualism.

Narcissism

Our current understanding of narcissism is highly indebted to the work of Heinz Kohut (1971, 1977), who proposed that narcissism is inherent to human development and has both normal and pathological variations. Briefly, Kohut held that the child comes into the world merged with the primary caregiver, who is, for the child, an ideal selfobject. The caregiver is an ideal selfobject because (1) the caregiver devotes undivided loving attention to the child and omnipotently meets the child's every need (the caregiver is an *ideal* selfobject), and (2) the caregiver is a being in whom and through whom the child experiences it own self (the caregiver is an ideal *self*object). Merged with such a selfobject, the infant is utterly supported in its being and knows no limits to its powers. Accordingly, the infant expresses itself assertively and spontaneously, indeed grandiosely and exhibitionistically, as if it were the center of the universe. This condition of primitive narcissistic merger is not only our original condition but also, according to Kohut, the condition that determines our life-long developmental objectives: to express ourselves assertively and spontaneously under the supportive, facilitating influence of selfobjects.

Development after infancy is not, then, for Kohut, as it was for Freud, a matter of leaving narcissism behind, but rather of attaining more mature forms of narcissism. The assertive-spontaneous self is not denied, and selfobjects are not abandoned. The assertive-spontaneous self, if appropriately mirrored and nurtured, continues to grow and express itself in new ways, but with increasing appreciation of its limitations and its place in the world as one self among others. And selfobjects continue to be sought out as empathic mirrors and confirmers of the self, but with increasing appreciation that these selfobjects are persons in their own right with narcissistic needs and assertive-spontaneous selves of their own. As infantile narcissism unfolds into mature narcissism, then, what was originally an unrealistic (i.e., grandiose-omnipotent) and one-sided (i.e., exclusively infant-centered) merger of self and selfobject becomes a realistic mutuality of selves and selfobjects, a mutuality in which each assertive-spontaneous self is supported by selfobjects and is selfobject for others in turn.

In Kohut's view, narcissistic disorders emerge when a person fails to receive proper empathic mirroring during childhood. Lack of such mirroring prohibits the child from growing beyond infantile narcissism and attaining a mature narcissism capable of both expressing itself realistically and appreciating and confirming others. Narcissistic pathology, according to Kohut, can express itself in a variety of forms; nevertheless, he holds, all forms of this pathology involve a fixation of narcissistic development at the archaic, infantile, level. Despite having achieved the outlines of a nuclear self, the person afflicted with narcissistic personality disorder continues to live at the archaic level of grandiose self-expression and one-sided selfobject dependency.[4] Functioning at this level, the pathological narcissist is someone who is at once *excessively* needy of the supportive mirroring of others and *exaggeratedly* self-demonstrative and self-important. Paradoxically, the pathological narcissist is someone who desperately needs other people to confirm a sense of being special and superior to other people. The pathological narcissist is a person who chronically acts in an exaggerated or exhibitionistic way in order to win the one-sided attention and approval of others in order, in turn, to have the kind of selfobject support needed to sustain the archaic sense of being the center of the universe.

Kohut's conception of narcissism broadens the idea of narcissism in such a way that narcissistic disorders can be seen as distortions of normal narcissistic needs. In explaining how normal narcissistic processes become distorted, Kohut, as we have seen, focuses on early childhood, stressing the pathological consequences that can ensue if significant selfobjects fail to provide the child with proper empathic mirroring. Most psychoanalytic object relations theorists agree with Kohut in tracing the etiology of pathological narcissism to early childhood.[5] Without disagreeing with this general perspective, I would add that narcissistic dysfunctions can also be explained in terms of vicissitudes distinctive of midlife.[6] Specifically, I suggest that normal narcissistic dependencies can become exaggerated at midlife, or thereafter, when, for the reasons discussed earlier, faith in the identity project begins to wane. For in losing faith in the identity project, the mental ego begins to sense that its efforts in life have reached a point of diminishing returns. At this point, "nothingness" and "guilt" lurk threateningly in the background, and the mental ego begins to feel that extraordinary narcissistic efforts are needed to demonstrate worldly being and value.

As we have seen, the resurfacing of feelings of "nothingness" and "guilt" amplifies the negative motivations of the identity project. This amplification has the effect, frequently, of shifting the identity project into narcissistic overdrive. The mental ego, to escape awakening fears of nonbeing and lack of justification, may feel impelled to make extraordinary efforts to demonstrate its being and value. If so, the mental ego becomes narcissistically self-concerned and excessively focused on others as mirrors in which it can see its own identity and worth. The world becomes a stage on which the mental ego is the principal actor, and other people become an audience that provides confirmatory responses to the actor's performance. The mental ego in this situation relates to other people almost exclusively as supportive selfobjects, as people whose purpose is to help the mental ego believe the opposite of what it is beginning to suspect about itself.[7]

As the mental ego approaches disillusionment, the fears of "nothingness" and "guilt" motivating narcissistic performances press closer to the forefront of consciousness. We have seen that, under these circumstances, worldly successes gradually diminish in significance and lasting effect. Consequently, the mental ego begins to realize that individual performances, no matter how appreciative the audiences might be, provide only incomplete and temporary relief from inner insecurities. Successful performances are no longer entirely satisfying and no longer contribute to a lasting sense of being and value; rather, they accomplish only a brief abatement of feelings of "nothingness" and "guilt." The mental ego may respond to this dawning insight by putting on even grander performances to larger and even more appreciative audiences. The results, however, remain unsatisfactory. No amount of confirmation suffices to bring lasting relief from the underlying, growing fears. Eventually, the mental ego reaches a point at which it can no longer keep itself in narcissistic overdrive. It loses energy and will. This point, as explained earlier, is the threshold at which depression begins to change into despair. Sensing that its basic life objectives cannot be met, the mental ego is here on the verge of disillusionment.

Existential Syndrome

Existential philosophers from St. Augustine and Blaise Pascal to Soren Kierkegaard, Friedrich Nietzsche, Martin Heidegger, Jean-Paul

Sartre, and Albert Camus have described various difficulties that they see as inherent to the "human condition" or to our "existential predicament." Included among these difficulties are such experiences as purposelessness, nihilism, boredom, alienation, unhappy consciousness, anxiety, and despair. Some existential philosophers and psychologists (Frankl 1962, 1969; Maddi 1967, 1970; Yalom 1980) have proposed that experiences such as these be recognized as constituting the symptomatology of a distinctively existential syndrome ("existential vacuum," "existential neurosis," "existential sickness"). Adopting this proposal, I shall here discuss existential syndrome as a developmental phenomenon distinctive of midlife transition. As I shall be explaining it, existential syndrome is not rooted in the "human condition" or our "existential predicament" per se but rather is a consequence of the *mental ego's* condition or predicament during late dualism. The symptoms of existential syndrome, I suggest, can be understood as afflictions that plague the mental ego after it suffers disillusionment.

Purposelessness. Clearly, a loss of faith in the identity project brings about a sense of purposelessness. The identity project is the meaning of the adult mental ego's life. To lose faith in the identity project is therefore, for the adult mental ego, to lose faith in life itself. It is to be divested of purpose and reason for being.

Nihilism. Corresponding to the loss of purpose, is nihilism, the loss of worldly values. The mental ego, divested of its reason for being, perceives a world that is barren, neutral, and gray. As Nietzsche (1968) and Heidegger (1982) clearly saw, a nihilistic or valueless world is a world in which everything has been leveled. All gradations of value have been erased. Differences between good and evil, attractive and unattractive, and important and trivial have collapsed. Nothing stands out as necessary or desirable; nothing commands or stirs the mental ego. This nihilistic leveling is indicative of a general withdrawal of psychic energy, a pervasive decathexis of the world. A nihilistic world is one that has lost its charge and significance, its highs and lows. It is a world in which everything is equal by default, equal in the negative sense of being equally uninteresting and devoid of life.

For Nietzsche, a nihilistic world is a world that is without a "tablet of values," a world that no longer reflects the differential preferences of the "will to power." For Heidegger, it is a world in which everything has been stripped of self-nature and intrinsic worth and reduced to what he (1953) calls *standing reserve* (*Bestand*), reduced, that is, to the status of a transformable resource for possible exploitation by impersonal technologies and bureaucracies. Nietzsche and Heidegger, of course, believed that nihilism is a historical phenomenon distinctive of our era. They may be right. Nihilism, however, is not only a historical phenomenon; it is also an individual phenomenon occurring across historical epochs and spanning cultural boundaries. Although a good case can be made that nihilistic tendencies are especially strong in modern Western society, it is not the case that modern Western individuals are alone in suffering from nihilism. Nihilism is something to which the mental ego qua mental ego is susceptible.

Boredom. As the world loses its positive and negative values, the mental ego loses its hopes and fears, its desires and aversions. The world ceases motivating the mental ego, and the mental ego, consequently, ceases responding to the world. The mental ego becomes bored. The mental ego, already disillusioned of its major life objectives, now ceases caring even about small matters. Corresponding to the withdrawal of psychic energy from the world, the mental ego loses its appetite for the world. The mental ego is no longer hungry for experience, and consequently the world is no longer appealing to the mental ego. The mental ego experiences a pervasive indifference or even revulsion. Things either have no effect upon the mental ego, which, like Meursault in Camus's *Stranger,* is an unfeeling spectator, or they actually "turn the mental ego's stomach," causing the mental ego, as Sartre (1949) so powerfully described, to experience nausea. The mental ego is no longer moved by the world and therefore experiences everything with a uniform, flat affect. Confronting a leveled nihilistic world, nothing matters to the mental ego. The disillusioned mental ego is pervasively depressed, and one aspect of this depression is an all-encompassing apathy.

Alienation. Disillusioned and without purpose or desire, the mental ego begins to withdraw from the world. This withdrawal is the phenomenon of alienation so much discussed in existentialist literature. It is a process by which the mental ego not only loses interest in the world but also loses touch with the world. The mental ego withdraws into itself, and the world, it seems, slips away from the mental ego, becoming remote and unreal. Alienation, then, is an apparently two-sided process, a process that, in the mental ego's perception, involves both the mental ego and the world. The mental ego becomes cut off; the world becomes inaccessible. The mental ego becomes a lifeless spectator imprisoned in its own subjectivity;

the world becomes an alien landscape that lies beyond the mental ego's reach.

In clinical terms, the mental ego's alienation can be described as a type of depersonalization-derealization phenomenon. Here are two classic psychoanalytic accounts of this condition:[8]

> Depersonalization consists of an estrangement of the external and internal world. The patient has lost the feeling of the reality of inner and outer perceptions and of sensations. Just as the external world appears to him strange, unreal, "ghostlike," so have his thoughts, his feelings, and the sensations of his own body lost to some extent the quality of being real. (Nunberg 1955, p. 184)

> To the depersonalized individual the world appears strange, peculiar, foreign, dream-like. Objects appear at times strangely diminished in size, at times flat. Sounds appear to come from a distance. . . . The patients characterize their imagery as pale, colorless, and some complain that they have altogether lost the power of imagination. . . . The patients complain that they are capable of experiencing neither pain nor pleasure, love and hate have perished within them. When an individual is in a state of depersonalization libido is withdrawn not only from the environment, but also from the ego, or, at any rate, from certain of the embodiments of the ego. . . . The depersonalized patient characteristically speaks of the impression that his own thinking is not carried on by himself. The alienated, subjective life appears to have been robbed of its personal character and removed into the outside world. The outer world from which the individual has turned away and withdrawn his libido is only capable of alteration in the direction of the unreal. It no longer possesses the full character of reality. The world appears as a dream, objects as though they belonged to the planet Mars. (Schilder 1928, pp. 32–35)

These descriptions point clearly to the two sides of the alienation process, which is at once a derealization of the world and a depersonalization of the mental ego. The world loses its old sense of realness and meaning, and the mental ego loses its previous sense of worldly selfhood. The world loses its closeness and familiarity, and the mental ego feels separated from the world and uncomfortable in its old roles and identity, which no longer fit. The world becomes strange, dreamlike, "absurd," and the mental ego becomes cut off and disconnected, as if situated in outer space. The world is decathected and nihilistically leveled, and the mental ego is demotivated and deenergized. Both the world and the self in the world become remote, flat, alien, dead.

A good analogy to help convey the outer correlate of this experience (i.e., derealization) comes from the domain of the cinema. The experience of derealization is similar to the experience of a moviegoer who loses interest in a film. Let us suppose that a person who is watching a film is suddenly told the ending and that this person finds the ending disappointing. Before learning how the film turns out, we can imagine, the moviegoer was caught up in the action of the film, taking the characters seriously as real people, experiencing real emotions in response to the twists and turns of the plot, and perhaps identifying with the protagonist or some other character in the film. Suddenly, however, upon learning the ending, the moviegoer is disillusioned, and what was the *world* of the film suddenly falls flat and dead. The action now consists of mere events on the screen. The characters become mere actors saying lines, and what was a compelling drama becomes a mere plot or story line. The moviegoer cannot get back "into" the film. The film has ceased being a real world, and the characters in the film have ceased being real people. The moviegoer, in withdrawing from the world of the film, finds that the film ceases being a lived world of experience and is reduced to a two-dimensional screen on which appear a sequence of images. The person undergoing alienation is in a similar situation, except, of course, that this person witnesses the derealization of the "real" world of material and social life rather than of a fictional world of the cinema.

Depersonalization is an inherent correlate of derealization, because withdrawal from the world is at the same time withdrawal from worldly selfhood, that is, from ego identity. Accordingly, as the world becomes alien and inaccessible to the mental ego, so, too, do the various ways in which the mental ego had identified itself with the world. These aspects of the mental ego's identity cease being natural and comfortable aspects of the mental ego's sense of self and become odd, awkward, and "other." The mental ego's identity, most of which was deeply embedded and unconscious, is in this way disembedded and rendered conscious, indeed conspicuously so. The face that the mental ego had unconsciously presented to the world is now disjoined from the mental ego and seen as a flat, lifeless, inauthentic mask: the persona. The mental ego is no longer able to act spontaneously *through* its identity and therefore is put in a position where, for the first time, it begins, frustratingly, to relate *to* its identity. The paradox here is that the mental ego becomes explicitly aware of its worldly identity only as alienation disallows the mental ego any longer to *be* that identity.

Unhappy Consciousness. Depersonalization-derealization is a process that expands the mental ego's awareness and confers upon it insights not available to most people. This expanded awareness, however, to use Hegel's (1967) expression, is an "unhappy consciousness." We just noted that depersonalization causes the mental ego to become aware of its worldly identity, which it sees as an inauthentic persona. The alienated mental ego can take pride in this heightened self-knowledge and can look down on the "ignorant masses" who take themselves so seriously, failing to see that what they take for a self is really only a repertoire of unconscious habits, pretensions, and postures.[9] However, any pride the mental ego takes in its newfound vision is combined with frustration, even humiliation, because the price the mental ego pays for being able to see the "games people play" is an inability any longer to participate in those games.

The alienated mental ego is the unhappy beneficiary of other insights as well. Alienation has the general effect of disembedding the prereflective patterns by which the mental ego organizes experience and participates in the world. It disembeds both cognitive constructions (intentionalities or projected meanings) and valuative-behavioral dispositions (cathexes and conditioned reactions). These patterns of structuring and responding to experience, in being prereflective, are ordinarily part of the invisible background of life. Like the mental ego's identity, they are forms *through* which life is lived rather than forms that stand forth as structures *for* explicit consciousness. These patterns, however, cease being invisible once the process of alienation is set in motion, for the mental ego's withdrawal from the world "pulls the plug" on its preestablished modes of thinking and acting. The mental ego, in undergoing alienation, is no longer able to engage the world in the same prereflective manner. The mental ego's ingrained constructions and valuative-behavioral dispositions no longer effectively engage their objects. Rather, they fall short or fall dead. Torn from the fabric of experience in this way, these embedded patterns become evident—indeed, conspicuous—for the first time.

Another type of unhappy consciousness arises in the form of an encounter with the shadow side of the personality. The shadow, as Jung (1953) explained, is the psychic structure that contains the rejected parts of the personality. The shadow consists of those parts of the personality that are repressed because they are incompatible with the mental ego's identity (the Jungian persona). As the repressed underside of identity, the shadow can be uncovered only if identity is somehow displaced or disempowered. Now alienation, as we know, has just such an effect on identity. Alienation deanimates the mental ego's identity and thereby saps it of repressive power. Accordingly, alienation has the consequence of triggering a derepression of the shadow. Shadow elements are released into consciousness, tormenting the mental ego with unwelcome insights and anguishing self-recognitions. If the alienated mental ego can no longer lay claim to being what it had aspired to be (its identity), it now is forced to acknowledge that it is what it had not wanted to be (the shadow).

Anxiety. Disillusionment and alienation have a subduing effect on the mental ego. The mental ego, as we have seen, is subject to deepening depressions, a sense of purposelessness, and apathy. This subduing of the mental ego, however, is offset by a variety of anxieties that are distinctive of the alienated condition. In addition to the anguish caused by the disclosure of the shadow, the following can be included among these anxieties: anxieties of dissociation, death, radical freedom, "nothingness," and "guilt."

The mental ego is quite obviously troubled by feelings of dissociation, because it is cut off from the world and has lost its worldly identity. The alienated mental ego cannot reengage the world. Its attempts to become involved seem contrived and wooden; they are attempts at acting rather than genuine actions. This sense of being severed from the arena of life is a serious concern for the mental ego, which in desperation may try to "force the issue" by attempting to act in a decisive manner, only to learn that such attempts produce only pathetic caricatures of real deeds. The alienated mental ego finds itself locked in its own subjectivity, exiled from life.

Concomitantly, the alienated mental ego experiences the deanimation of its identity as an inexorable process of death. The mental ego is unable any longer to be its old worldly self. That self is now increasingly experienced as inauthentic, flat, "not me." Waltraut Stein describes this condition of deathlike disidentification, and the panic that goes with it, in striking terms: "And in a very real sense he is dying, as he feels less and less like a real person. This sense of dying can come upon him slowly or suddenly. In either case, panic is possible at any time, should he catch a glimpse of complete dispossession, of death. Then he feels totally disorganized and runs 'every which way' " (1967, p. 270). The alienated mental ego increasingly feels as if it is undergoing a process of separation and death. And it experiences extreme anxiety over its inability to halt, much less reverse, this process.

The mental ego also experiences an anxiety of radical freedom, for disconnection from its old way of life is at the same time—or so, initially, it seems—liberation for possible new ways of life. The mental ego is no longer bound by its old identity and is now free—or so, again, it seems—to do and be whatever it chooses. This freedom is virtually unrestricted, and the sheer number of possibilities can set the mental ego's head spinning, as Kierkegaard (1954a) explains in discussing a feeling of vertigo that accompanies awakening to possibilities. Sartre (1956) adds in his discussion of this subject that such a dizzying discovery of possibilities leaves one altogether "without excuses" and therefore completely responsible for one's deeds. Moreover, because many of the mental ego's new possibilities are suggested by the derepressing shadow, the mental ego is distressed not only by the number but by the nature of its possibilities. The mental ego in this situation can easily be overwhelmed with options it cannot dismiss, and it tends to shudder with a sense of heavy responsibility for its fate.

Underlying the anxieties of dissociation, death, and radical freedom are the deepest anxieties of the mental ego: the anxieties of "nothingness" and "guilt." These anxieties, as we have seen, are inherent to the mental ego. The anxieties of "nothingness" and "guilt" first emerge during adolescence and then subside during early adulthood when the mental ego, in pursuit of the identity project, begins to feel that it is making progress in establishing and justifying itself in the world. The anxieties of "nothingness" and "guilt" typically do not resurface until midlife and specifically not until the mental ego begins to lose faith in the identity project. The reemergence of these anxieties during midlife, as we saw earlier, is evident in the narcissistic disorders that are common in late dualism. The exaggerated need to gain confirmation of being and value is symptomatic of serious insecurities about precisely these matters. Finally, once the mental ego has suffered disillusionment and abandons hope in the identity project, even in its narcissistic forms, the mental ego is no longer able to hide its "nothingness" and "guilt" from itself. "Nothingness" and "guilt" at this point relentlessly press forward and plague the mental ego with deeply disturbing self-doubts.

Despair. The anxieties just discussed are strongest soon after disillusionment, that is, in the early and middle stages of the alienation process. As alienation unfolds into later stages, these anxieties begin to subside and the numbness of despair becomes the mental ego's primary state of mind. The anguish caused by the disclosure of the shadow, the anxieties of dissociation, death, and radical freedom, and even the root anxieties of "nothingness" and "guilt" gradually wane, leaving the mental ego not so much relieved and at peace as, simply, devoid of feeling, affectively dead.

The anguish caused by the disclosure of the shadow abates because one ceases being shocked by the shadow. Moreover, the shadow, as the flip side of identity, or the persona, is itself a form of worldly selfhood; it is the mental ego's alter ego in the world. Consequently, withdrawal from the world forces the mental ego to relinquish not only its identity but also, eventually, the shadow. Having already lost its identity, the mental ego may begin to cling to the shadow out of a perverse and desperate sense that it is better to be something undesirable than to be nothing at all. This state of mind is forcefully expressed by Dostoyevsky's underground man, who flounders in a seriously alienated condition. "Oh, if I had done nothing simply from laziness! Heavens how I should have respected myself then. I should have respected myself because I should at least have been capable of being lazy; there would at least have been one quality, as it were, positive in me, which I could have believed myself. Question: What is he? Answer: A sluggard. . ." (Dostoyevsky 1960, p. 39). The process of alienation is, however, inexorable; and in time it begins to deanimate the shadow, which eventually becomes as defunct as the persona.

The anxieties of dissociation and death subside simply because the mental ego's situation becomes more and more hopeless. The possibility of reengaging the world and reenlivening worldly identity (or even the shadow) becomes increasingly unlikely, and the mental ego becomes increasingly resigned to its incarcerated and lifeless state. The anxiety of radical freedom also subsides, because the mental ego soon learns that the new possibilities that seem to have opened up are really false possibilities, possibilities that cannot be realized. The mental ego's disconnectedness, it turns out, is not only a separation from its old identity and style of life but also a prohibition against new identities and styles of life. The mental ego is not free to do or be anything it chooses, as it had thought. If the mental ego is no longer bound to its old way of life, that is only because it is cut off from life generally.

Even the root anxieties of "nothingness" and "guilt" recede as the alienation process unfolds. Living with a sense of being dead and without value to the world, of being an "unjustified nonentity," is, of course, something that can never be easily accepted. Nevertheless, as the prospects for worldly being and value diminish virtually to zero, the mental ego tends to lose its spirit and intensity, even its anxiety, and to languish in an ever-deepening despair. The end of such a process, if it is ever reached, is a state of completely dead, numb dissociation.

The Divided Self

Divorced from the world and stripped of all worldly selfhood, the ego finds itself at a radical existential impasse. It finds itself in a state similar to an extreme version of the schizoid condition described by the British school of object relations theory (Fairbairn 1940; Guntrip 1952a, 1952b, 1961, 1969; Laing 1960). DSM III-R, the official diagnostic manual of the American Psychiatric Association (1987), recognizes this condition as schizoid personality disorder. Borrowing from the title of R. D. Laing's (1960) book, I shall call this condition the *divided self*.

The divided self is a condition of severe psychic estrangement in which mind is dissociated from body, thought is dissociated from affect, and consciousness is dissociated from the world. Murray Stein (1983) describes this condition as being one of complete marginality, as being a condition in which one is neither in the world nor beyond it, but rather in a "nowhereland" in between. Divorced from the world, one is "nowhere"; dispossessed of all worldly being, one is "nothing"; and stripped of all worldly value, one is "worthless," "unjustified." This existential cul-de-sac is the endpoint of the process of alienation. It is the limit case of total alienation and therefore of maximal dualism. It is the point at which the depersonalization-derealization *process* comes to a halt in a completely dissociated schizoid *condition*. No actual case of alienation may ever unfold all the way to this limit; nevertheless, the process of alienation aims at this limit as its most extreme possibility.

The person who has arrived at this boundary has completely lost contact with the world. Nietzsche (1966, pp. 233–236) employs an apt simile to describe such extreme lifeless disconnection: the divided self is like the moon, a pale, cold reflector, an outsider who witnesses the world but is impotent to interact with it in any significant way. Harry Guntrip offers the following account:

> External relationships seem to have been emptied by a
> massive withdrawal of the real libidinal self. Effective mental ac-

tivity has disappeared into a hidden inner world; the patient's conscious ego is emptied of vital feeling and action, and seems to have become unreal. You may catch glimpses of intense activity going on in the inner world through dreams and phantasies, but the patient's conscious ego merely reports these as if it were a neutral observer not personally involved in the inner drama of which it is a detached spectator. The attitude to the outer world is the same: *noninvolvement and observation at a distance without any feeling . . .* (1952a, p. 86)[10]

The divided self is a disembodied, disidentified witness. It is consciousness in exile, a spectral outsider looking in upon the world.

The divided self has arrived at a dead end. The alienation process has run full course, and the ego is left without any apparent life prospects. Laing says: "The final effect is an overall experience of everything having come to a stop. Nothing moves; nothing is alive; everything is dead, including the self" (1960, p. 87). Although fully conscious, the divided self is immobilized, devoid of affect, despairing, and completely separated from life. The divided self is nothing more than a remote spectator. Stripped of all identity in the world, the divided self has no content; it exists only as the empty unity of consciousness, as an abiding point of awareness without substance or definition. And stripped of all worldly value, the divided self has no reason for being; it exists only as a perspective without purpose, as a completely superfluous point of view. The divided self is a barren witness devoid of both being and value; it exists as "unjustified nothingness."

If, however, the divided self is at a dead end as far as the world is concerned, it is, without knowing it, at a threshold as far as possibilities beyond the world are concerned. The divided self is not only at an impasse but also, unknowingly, at a point of access to a new mode of experience. In Kierkegaard's (1954b) terms, the divided self has arrived at the boundary that serves both as the furthest limit of despair and the precipice of faith. This boundary marks the furthest limit of despair because all hope in the world has been lost; and this boundary marks the precipice of faith because beyond this boundary lies the *mysterium tremendum* to which, eventually, the divided self might be called. The divided self, however, is not yet aware that anything exists beyond the boundary at which it has arrived. It knows the boundary only as dead end, not yet as threshold. It knows only despair; it has not yet been driven to faith.

The Borderline Condition

The divided self is an ego from which almost all energy has been drained. The process of reversal in the flow of psychic energy that Jung (1928) believed was characteristic of the midlife turn toward individuation has, in the case of the divided self, reached its most extreme limit. For the divided self, then, the world is decathected and therefore nihilistically leveled and derealized; the ego is deenergized and therefore depersonalized and deanimated; and psychic energy is concentrated at its source in the nonegoic sphere and therefore lost to conscious experience.

The recession of psychic energy has an implosive effect upon the ego. Psychic energy has an attractive-absorptive "magnetism" that, when working through object cathexes, has the effect of drawing the ego into involvements with objects and, when concentrated in the ego itself, has the effect of drawing the ego into narcissistic self-absorptions. When, however, psychic energy is withdrawn from both the world and the ego and concentrated at its source in the deep psyche, its power of attraction affects the ego by exerting an abyssal suction or gravitational pull. Introverted psychic energy, concentrated in the nonegoic sphere, has a tractional effect on the ego, sapping it of remaining strength and drawing it toward a dark underlying unknown. Once the ego becomes aware of this effect, however faintly, it ceases being a divided self cut off from all feelings and influences and becomes a borderline self that is affected by an invisible power and afflicted with a sinking sense of doom.

The gravitational force acting upon the borderline ego undermines the infrastructure, primal repression, by which the ego, as mental ego, is separated from the nonegoic sphere. We can get a sense of what this would be like by imagining a supermassive particle of matter placed at the center of a large, hollow ball-like sphere (e.g., an immense ping-pong ball). People on the surface of the sphere (like the mental ego) would feel a dreadful gravitational force, and the surface of the sphere (corresponding to primal repression, the mental ego's terra firma) would begin to give way, sinking or collapsing toward the mass acting upon it. Similarly, introverted psychic energy exerts a force that undermines primal repression, causing the ego to feel as if the ground beneath it were beginning to give way. Otto Kernberg (1987), in a discussion of borderline personality disorder, describes the borderline self as one that is without secure repressive shielding from the dynamic unconscious. In a Jungian perspective, Nathan Schwartz-Salant (1989) describes the borderline self as one that has become inwardly exposed to the dark side of the *numinosum*, the awesome power of the deep psyche. The borderline ego, we can say, is no longer safely undergirded; its repressive infrastructure has been subverted, rendering the ego vulnerable to the stirrings of frightening abyssal forces.

The undermining of primal repression strikes terror in the ego. Primal repression, as the boundary between mental-egoic and nonegoic spheres, is the very boundary that a moment ago was described as the boundary between despair and faith. The manner in which the ego experiences this boundary at this developmental juncture, however, in no way suggests faith. The ego does not experience the boundary as a precipice from which it might leap to a celestial destiny but rather as a shaky or collapsing ground giving way to a gravitational abyss. Having lost its footing in the world (its identity), the ego at this point feels as though it is losing its invisible footing within. The ego at this point, then, is no longer the divided self that, although dissociated from the world, is still safely supported by primal repression. It is rather a borderline self that, as Gerald Adler (1985) stresses, suffers from *annihilation anxiety*. The borderline ego feels itself precariously on the edge of an abyss, an abyss from which it cannot escape and to which, somehow, it has not yet succumbed.

The annihilation anxiety of the borderline ego differs from the anxiety of "nothingness" experienced by the alienated mental ego. The latter anxiety is the anxiety that makes itself felt after the "death" (i.e., deanimation) of the mental ego's worldly identity. The divided self has completely lost this identity and therefore exists as barren consciousness, as empty "nothingness," as a mere perspective on the world. If, however, the divided self has altogether lost its worldly identity, it nonetheless continues to exist as an abiding witness. Although the divided self has lost the content, the worldly embodiment, of its selfhood, it nonetheless remains a unitary consciousness, that is, a transcendental subject or "I think" that sews together passing moments of consciousness into a synthetic unity. This unitary or transcendental consciousness, first discovered by the adolescent, is now the last thread of the ego's existence. However, it is precisely this last thread that is threatened in the borderline condition. Whereas the divided self, despite its complete dissociation from the world, remains stable as a transcendental witnessing consciousness, the borderline ego feels that it is in danger of falling prey to forces that would destroy even this final form of individuated existence. The borderline ego's annihilation anxiety is an anxiety of total self-dissolution. It is the primal fear of becoming psychotic, of ceasing altogether to exist as a singular subject of awareness.

In describing this self on the edge of annihilation as a borderline self, I mean to include it within the diagnostic category known as borderline personality disorder. Borderline personality disorder is a complex condition resulting from many causes and afflicting many age groups. In most instances it is a persistent psychopathology, a "stably unstable" form of personality organization.[11] In most instances, then, the borderline condition is not a merely stage-specific developmental difficulty, much less one that may lead to higher levels of growth. This fact notwithstanding, the borderline condition has a place among the difficulties of late dualism, because the symptoms characteristic of borderline disorder are also characteristic of the self on the edge that I have just described.

DSM-III-R lists eight criteria for borderline personality disorder, five of which are needed to warrant diagnosis. I shall briefly discuss these criteria to show how they apply to a mental ego that, having lost its footing in the outer world, finds itself on sinking inner ground and is fearful of being engulfed by a psychic abyss.

Unstable and Intense Interpersonal Relationships. The borderline personality desperately needs interpersonal closeness but is unable to maintain lasting or stable relationships. This fact is usually explained from the perspective of object relations theory by tracing the borderline condition back to the precarious child-caregiver relationship that obtains during the rapprochement subphase of the separation-individuation process.[12] The borderline's difficulties in relationships, however, can also be explained in terms of the energy reversal and consequent intrapsychic effects just discussed. For the introversion of psychic energy and consequent undermining of primal repression and fear of engulfment impel the borderline to reach out to significant others as a way of hanging on to the last thread of existence. Relationships with other people can in this way be seen as lifelines by which the borderline keeps from being swallowed in inner darkness. For the borderline, then, significant others play the role of rescuers, saviors. Significant others are—or so the borderline must believe—solid, stable, and utterly faithful supporters who provide the borderline with the safe ground that the borderline lacks within.

In assigning this role to others, of course, the borderline places completely unrealistic expectations on them. Needing a savior, the borderline cannot help imposing these expectations; being only human, the people on whom these expectations are imposed cannot possibly live up to the expectations. The borderline therefore is inherently prone both to overestimate and be seriously disappointed in significant others. The borderline is predisposed to idealize significant others only later to devalue and condemn them. The borderline desperately needs significant others to be perfect, and when, inevitably, significant others are not perfect, the borderline feels deeply threatened and betrayed.

This idealization-devaluation dynamic splits the borderline's perceptions of significant others into separate all-good and all-bad halves. Needing the other to be a savior, the borderline perceives the other as all good, as a person of unfailing strength and good will. Disappointed and "betrayed" by the other, the borderline perceives the other as all bad, as a person of treacherous character and evil intent. The borderline is unable to integrate these split perceptions, because to do so would be to dash the hope for a savior. To integrate the split perceptions would be to perceive the other as a "mere" part-good–part-bad human being, that is, as an imperfect being who cannot perform the role of savior. Consequently, rather than integrating the all-good and all-bad perceptions of the other, the borderline alternates back and forth between these perceptions, idealizing and then devaluing, worshiping and then condemning the other. This violent inconsistency ruins important relationships and "abandons" the borderline repeatedly to a sense of isolation and doom.

The borderline's fear of inner engulfment and annihilation prohibits stable relationships not only because it sets in motion the idealization-devaluation dynamic but also because this fear is inevitably projected upon the people with whom the borderline becomes intimate. The borderline needs to get as close as possible to significant others to be able to keep from being pulled under by a psychic undertow. The closer the borderline gets to others, however, the more the borderline tends to project onto them the fear of engulfment and annihilation. Accordingly, the closer the borderline gets to others, the less these others seem like supports and the more they begin to seem like dangerous (seductive, deceptive, consuming) powers. The borderline thus suffers from an acute approach-avoidance ambivalence toward others that is reminiscent of the ambivalence experienced by the preoedipal child during the rapprochement subphase of the separation-individuation process. The desperate need for a savior drives the borderline to others and at the same time confers upon them powers that overawe and engulf the borderline. The borderline therefore seeks closeness only, upon obtaining it, to withdraw coldly or strike out violently. Understandably, these contradictory behaviors undermine the borderline's primary relationships.

The borderline's sense of being engulfed by others is probably not a matter of projection alone. It is likely also a consequence of the underlying unity of primal repression and primal alienation. Because primal repression and primal alienation are two sides of a single deep structure of the psyche, any change in one is at the same time a change in the other. When one is weakened, loosened, or dissolved, so is the other. Now in the borderline condition, as we have seen, primal repression is undermined sufficiently to allow the gravitational effect of psychic energy to be felt by the ego, which is beset with a sense of doom. Responding to this fear of annihilation, the ego desperately searches for a "saving" other to be as close to as possible in order to be as far as possible from the danger that is sensed to lie within. This search for maximal closeness is intermittently rewarded, because the weakening of primal repression is at the same time a loosening of primal alienation. The intrapsychic wound that drives the borderline to the other is at the same time an open core that allows the borderline moments of exceptional intimacy with the other. This intimacy, however, so coveted by the borderline, turns out to be the opposite of what had been sought. For the unity of primal repression and primal alienation means not only that the borderline's inner wound facilitates interpersonal closeness but also that interpersonal closeness aggravates this inner wound and the sense of engulfment that goes with it. Accordingly, just as the borderline seems to be escaping inner engulfment, this danger reappears embodied in the very person or persons who were supposed to rescue the borderline from the danger. The borderline is thus caught in a vicious cycle: (1) a sense of inner engulfment drives the borderline to reach out to others; (2) the achievement of interpersonal intimacy paradoxically stirs in the borderline the feeling of being engulfed by others; (3) the borderline therefore withdraws from or undermines the threatening relationships; (4) the interruption or dissolution of these relationships "abandons" the borderline to the original sense of engulfment; consequently, (5) the cycle begins again.

The borderline's relationships with others differ from the narcissist's. Both the borderline and the narcissist relate to others almost exclusively as supportive selfobjects. The narcissist, however, relates to others as selfobjects to gain confirmation of identity and worth. Such confirmation bolsters the narcissist's insecure sense of worldly being and value. The borderline, in contrast, relates to others as selfobjects just to cling to existence, period, that is, simply to keep from dissolving as a unitary consciousness. The borderline has little or no stake in worldly being and value. For the borderline, a sense of identity and value was never established in the first place; or, as in the case of stage-specific borderline difficulties occurring at midlife, whatever sense of identity and value may have been established has been lost. The borderline, then, is not engaged in the identity project; rather, the borderline is just trying to keep from being swallowed by an inner black hole. Both the narcissist and the borderline have special interpersonal needs and suffer serious anxiety when deprived of the selfobjects on which they depend. But whereas the narcissist's problems arise from self-doubts about status or standing in the world, the borderline's problems arise from fears of inner self-dissolution.

Impulsiveness in Potentially Self-Damaging Behaviors. According to DSM-III-R, the borderline is prone to engage in potentially self-destructive behaviors in areas such as spending, sexual activity, substance abuse, shoplifting, reckless driving, and binge eating. Behaviors such as these do a variety of things for the borderline. Sexual activity, for example, is a way of obtaining intimacy with an other, and drugs and alcohol can be used as medication. Despite this variety of functions, however, all of the behaviors in question have one thing in common: they induce experiences sufficiently intense to override, even if only temporarily, the borderline's annihilation anxiety. All of these types of behavior induce experiences that are highly charged and potent in their impact, either because the behaviors trigger strong feelings (sexual activity, use of chemical substances[13]) or because they involve an element of risk (shoplifting, reckless driving) or because they go to excesses or extremes (spending, binge eating). Borderlines cannot tolerate the sinking feeling of doom inherent to their subjective life, and so they seek to escape from subjectivity through intimate relationships and through exciting and even self-damaging behaviors.

Affective Instability. DSM-III-R states that borderlines experience "marked mood shifts from baseline mood to depression, irritability, or anxiety, usually lasting a few hours and only rarely more than a few days" (p. 347). Borderlines are prone to depression because they suffer from an inner sense of doom and because they repeatedly undermine the relationships through which, they hope, this doom can be escaped. Borderline depressions thus have both an intrapsychic and an interpersonal source. They have an intrapsychic source insofar as they are feelings of doom deriving from the gravitational-engulfing effect of introverted energy acting through a weakened buffer of primal repression. And they have an interpersonal source insofar as they are feelings of abandonment deriving from interactions with significant others cast in the impossible role of saviors. Borderlines flee an inner sense of doom by reaching out to others as saviors. When others inevitably fail to live up to the unrealistic expectations imposed upon them, borderlines feel, once again, that they have been "abandoned" to an inner doom.

Exposure to the gravitational pull of the deep unconscious distinguishes the borderline's depressions from the depressions that plagued the mental ego during the later phases of the identity project. These latter depressions were losses of hope, and therefore of interest and motivation, in the pursuit of worldly being and value. The depressions experienced by the borderline, in contrast, are morbid, dense, sunken conditions. They involve feelings of hopelessness, to be sure. They also, however, involve such feelings as being heavy and inert, being unable to think, and being on the edge of engulfment and extinction. The depressions experienced by the mental ego in the later phases of the identity project were for the most part existential depressions resulting from unwelcome incidents or insights bearing upon the mental ego's basic life endeavor. The depressions experienced by the borderline, in contrast, have a powerful psychodynamic etiology, being instances of ego implosion resulting from the ego's exposure to the gravitational pull of the deep unconscious. The borderline is subject to the influence of ominous intrapsychic forces that induce dark and heavy states of mind.

The flip side of the borderline's depression is a susceptibility to sudden outbursts of strong emotion. The borderline can endure the inner gravity only for so long before feeling driven to break free in any way possible. The borderline becomes impatient to find relief from the inner pressure and, consequently, is prone not only to impulsive behaviors, as we have already seen, but also to explosive ventilations. Nathan Schwartz-Salant draws on his clinical experience to make this point:

> The borderline patient's inner, death-like world is rarely satisfying, and the person commonly attempts to waken it in a very noisy way. A patient said: "I am finally able to be a 5, previously I was either a 0 or a 10. I had to have very strong feelings in order to feel alive." . . . Many borderline patients engage in negative interactions with others, and are addicted to such stimuli as self-mutilation, stealing and other self-destructive behav-

ior. They make use of these patterns in order to overcome the omnipresent feeling of inner deadness. (1989, pp. 51–52)

For the borderline, any strong feeling, whether a thrill induced by risk or an unprovoked explosion of anger, provides relief from the relentless feeling of doom.

Inappropriate, Intense Anger. The borderline is prone to anger for several reasons: (1) The borderline idealizes significant others only later to devalue them, becoming angrily or contemptuously disenchanted with them. (2) The borderline feels engulfed by significant others and therefore strikes out against them with defensive aggression. And (3) the borderline is subject to the explosive emotional outbursts just discussed. The borderline relates to others in ways that lead inevitably to eruptions of intense anger, and sometimes, as one of Schwartz-Salant's clients reported, the borderline is driven "to start fights to feel alive" (1989, p. 52).

Suicidal Threats or Self-Mutilating Behaviors. Suicidal threats are made both as an expression of desperate unhappiness and as a way of preventing rejection from others. The borderline fantasizes about suicide as a way of gaining permanent relief from inner misery. Moreover, the *threat* of suicide is something the borderline can use to manipulate significant others to protect against possible abandonment. Also, the borderline is prone to self-mutilating behaviors (e.g., cutting and burning the skin) because behaviors of this sort, like the impulsive behaviors discussed previously, have an intensity that alters consciousness sufficiently to render the borderline oblivious, however temporarily, to inner pain.

Persistent Identity Disturbances. Kernberg (1975, 1980a) borrows the term *identity diffusion* from Erik Erikson to describe a chronic condition of the borderline. In suffering from identity diffusion, the borderline, according to Kernberg, is without a core identity and therefore suffers from fragmentation and inconsistency of the self-representation. For most people suffering from borderline disorder, such identity diffusion is probably the result of never having established a core identity. For people suffering midlife borderline difficulties, however, this identity diffusion is the result of having suffered a deanimation of a core identity already established. In either case, however, the borderline is without a core identity and therefore without a coherent or consistent inner sense of being. Lacking a core identity, the borderline is "many things to many people." The borderline adapts to others like a chameleon in order to be accepted by them. In doing so, however, the borderline feels that the adapted modes of self-presentation are merely masks. Unlike narcissists, who, despite self-doubts, take their identity overseriously, borderlines cannot take their identity seriously at all.

Aggravating the borderline's identity diffusion is a root inconsistency stemming from the tendency to split not only significant object representations but also the self-representation along all-good and all-bad lines. Corresponding to the splitting of primary others into all-good and all-bad part objects is a splitting of self into all-good and all-bad part selves. Corresponding to the perception of others as saviors is a perception of self as a helpless innocent deserving of being cared for by others. And corresponding to the perception of others as betrayers is a perception of self as a worthless nonentity deserving of being abandoned by others. Just as borderlines cannot integrate split object representations, neither can they integrate split self-representations. To integrate split object representations would be to preclude the possibility of finding a savior. To integrate split self-representations would be to give up the belief that one is deserving of a savior's unconditional supportive attention.

Emptiness and Boredom. Unlike the narcissist, who feels an emptiness that is a restlessness to obtain selfobject approval, and unlike the divided self, which feels an emptiness that is a mere lack of feeling, a deadness, the borderline feels an emptiness that is a forsakenness and sense of doom. The borderline's emptiness is a state of oppressive destitution, of heaviness and sunkenness, of grim inner vacancy or absorption. Jerome Kroll (1988) notes that borderlines are subject to morbid semitrance states associated with feelings of emptiness. Such trances are altered states of consciousness that, in the view being presented here, indicate that borderlines are subject to the captivating influence of darkly working inner gravitational forces. The emptiness experienced by borderlines therefore is indeed a state of boredom, but not in any of the usual senses of the term. For this boredom is not a sense of having nothing to do, or a sense of lacking desire to become involved, or even a sense of being unable to become involved, but rather a sense of having to endure a relentless inner gravity auguring engulfment and extinction. This oppressive boredom can be tolerated only for short periods before, as explained earlier, the borderline is moved to try almost any expedient to find relief: sexual activity, chemical substances, reckless actions, fights, self-mutilation.

Fear of Abandonment. We have seen that intimate relationships are the means by which the borderline clings to life. For the border-line, the other is a savior. Without the possibility of such a savior, the borderline is lost, "abandoned" to a dark and oppressive inward-ness. For this reason the borderline is exceptionally needy of relation-ship and hypersensitive to any cues of possible rejection. The borderline fears rejection as total devastation. The fear of rejection is so severe that the borderline sometimes rejects the other just to avoid being rejected by the other. This, of course, is no solution to the bor-derline's predicament, because the need for the other remains every bit as great as it was before. Accordingly, despite rejecting the other, the borderline continues to seek out the other and fear possible re-jection by the other. The borderline condition, quite evidently, is rid-dled with contradictions.

The term *borderline* was originally employed (Stern 1938; Knight 1953) to describe disturbances that were considered more serious than the neuroses but not as serious as the psychoses.[14] This orig-inal intuition is most apt. The borderline lives right at the intersec-tion of the world (representing both normalcy and the neuroses) and the deep unconscious (representing the threat of psychosis). The borderline throws out lifelines to the world and seeks worldly stimulation. These measures, however, do not save the borderline from the inner abyss. Yet somehow the borderline, although exposed without relief to the abyss, does not succumb to the abyss—except for brief periods when under stress. The borderline, again, is "stably unstable."

Although exposed to the deep unconscious and only tenuously connected with reality, the borderline is for the most part effective in testing reality, as Kernberg (1975, 1980a, 1981, 1984) especially has stressed. William Goldstein (1985) reviews the full range of ego func-tions and defense mechanisms and assesses the borderline's mar-ginal status. The borderline, he concludes, suffers chronic deficits (e.g., poor impulse control, identity diffusion, affective instability, primitive defense mechanisms) and yet is relatively intact, even if se-riously troubled, in other important areas (e.g., reality testing, thought processes, adaptation to reality). The borderline, although not psychotic, is weak, unstable, rent in two by a cleaving of the self-representation, and vulnerable to the influence of threatening inner forces. The borderline desperately reaches out to the world to avoid being submerged by a psychic undertow. The borderline finds noth-ing that can be grasped securely and yet, oddly, although occasion-ally pulled under, somehow keeps from being drowned.

CONCLUSION

All of the conditions discussed in this chapter are difficulties to which the mental ego is susceptible during late dualism. Very few mental egos suffer from all, or even most, of these conditions; nevertheless, all of the conditions reflect possible expressions of the mental ego's decline, its "sickness unto death." The developmental revaluation of primal repression and primal alienation, the reemergence of feelings of "nothingness" and "guilt," and the introversion of psychic energy work to undermine the mental ego's standing in the world and to predispose the mental ego to depressive episodes, narcissistic exaggerations, sobering disillusionment, incapacitating existential malaise, despairing dissociation from life, and agonizing borderline instabilities.

The following point should be restated: The conditions discussed in this chapter, although distinctive of midlife, by no means belong exclusively to midlife. On the contrary, all of the conditions discussed here have contributing causes other than the ones I have focused on and in most cases are probably best understood as resulting from such causes as early developmental arrests, structural deficits, biochemical imbalances, or psychodynamic abnormalities. Moreover, as explained at the beginning of the chapter, the mental ego, although inherently prone to the "pathologies" of midlife, is by no means developmentally required to suffer them. The mental ego's decline during late dualism is only a tendency or susceptibility, not an inevitability. The mental ego's decline is not a necessary or invariant process; no definite predictions are possible. Many mental egos in the second half of life do not discernibly suffer from these conditions. Still, the conditions we have discussed belong together as a group of difficulties all of which can be understood as symptoms of the mental ego's decline during late dualism. Accordingly, having in this chapter considered these conditions from descriptive and etiological perspectives, I shall in the next chapter treat them from a strictly developmental standpoint, as coherently unfolding phases of the mental ego's difficult journey to transcendence.

8

The First Stage of Transcendence: The Dark Night of the Senses

Although the difficulties of late dualism appear across the population in isolated and apparently unrelated ways, these difficulties can be fitted together in a developmentally coherent sequential pattern. This pattern has been recognized in spiritual literature as reflecting the process by which the self is gradually stripped of worldly attachments and identifications in preparation for spiritual awakening. Spiritual literature describes this process of being "weaned" from the world in many different ways; for example, as "dying to the world," "the spiritual desert," "death of self," and "sickness unto death." In this chapter I shall examine the account of the process as presented by the great sixteenth-century mystic St. John of the Cross in his masterpiece *The Dark Night*.

John of the Cross distinguishes between the dark night of the senses and the dark night of spirit as earlier and later phases, respectively, of the dark night. Of these two phases, the dark night of the senses is considered in this chapter. The dark night of the senses is the period of purgative withdrawal from the world that is a prelude to the awakening of infused spirituality. The dark night of spirit occurs after the ego has suffered the night of the senses and has experienced spiritual awakening. It is the period during which the ego is purged by the direct, intimately inward action of spiritual power. The dark night of spirit will be discussed in the next chapter.

PRIDE GOETH BEFORE A FALL

John of the Cross begins the *Dark Night* with a discussion of how the seven capital sins of pride, covetousness, lust, anger, gluttony, envy, and sloth manifest themselves in those who have embarked upon the spiritual path. His discussion is not directed to the general population, but rather specifically to members of a spiritual community. He is addressing future contemplatives with the purpose in mind of helping them see how the seven capital sins continue to burden the soul even after one has renounced the world and dedicated oneself to the spiritual life.

John of the Cross focuses on the seven capital sins because, he says, these are the primary imperfections of the soul that are purged by the dark night of the senses. The night of the senses liberates a person from these imperfections by divesting the person of the worldly interests and drives that give rise to the imperfections. The night of the senses dispossesses the ego of its desires, its strength, its sense of selfhood, and its values, priorities, and goals. In being dispossessed in these ways, the ego gradually loses its prideful sense of superiority, its covetousness, its need for sensual satisfaction, its feelings of self-righteous anger, its craving for pleasures and consolations, its envy of the superior achievements of others, and its slothful resistance to spiritual growth. The dark night of the senses purges the seven capital sins not by opposing them with an active exercise of equal but opposite virtues but rather by cutting them off at the root and causing them to wither away. It is an interesting fact that people often become less driven by self-centered impulses and desires when they become ill. Habitual vices frequently disappear during an illness. The dark night of the senses works in just this way; it is a "sickness unto death."

Pride is perhaps the most serious of the seven capital sins, and John of the Cross focuses on what is perhaps the most serious form of pride: spiritual pride. Spiritual pride is so serious because, as pride in spiritual attainment, it is pride in that which is supposed to surmount pride; it is self-satisfaction in that which is supposed to surmount the self. Persons suffering from spiritual pride feel superior in their good works and presumed spiritual advancement. These people, however, are not secure in their feeling of superiority, because, as John of the Cross observes, they need to have others recognize their superiority. Accordingly, people suffering from spiritual pride are impelled to put on a display of their good works and to show off signs of their spiritual advancement. On this point, John of the Cross says:

> So they quickly search for some other spiritual advisor more to their liking, someone who will congratulate them and be impressed by their deeds; and they flee, as they would death, those who attempt to place them on the safe road by forbidding these things—and sometimes they even become hostile toward such spiritual directors. Frequently, in their presumption, they make many resolutions but accomplish very little. Sometimes they want others to recognize their spirit and devotion, and as a result occasionally contrive to make some manifestations of it, such as movements, sighs, and other ceremonies; sometimes, with the assistance of the devil, they experience raptures, more often in public than in private, and they are quite pleased, and often eager, for others to take notice of these. (1991a, p. 363)

This description clearly indicates that the spiritually proud person is really ego hungry rather than spiritually fulfilled. The proud person, despite an overt sense of superiority, suffers from a covert sense of deficiency and need. The proud person suffers from an unconscious sense of inner lack and therefore has a special need for the recognition and praise of other people.

The person suffering from spiritual pride is a narcissist in the sense of the term discussed in the last chapter. The spiritually proud person, like the narcissist, has begun to experience apprehensions of inner emptiness and lack of value. The meaning of these apprehensions is by no means consciously understood; nevertheless, the apprehensions exist and are disturbing. Accordingly, the spiritually proud person experiences a need to make an outer demonstration of precisely the things that are felt to be missing within. People suffering from pride feel a need to prove themselves to others so that, by winning recognition and confirmation, they can convince themselves of the very opposite of what they have begun to suspect about themselves. Pride, as a form of narcissism, is a paradoxical phenomenon: the grander the outer display, the greater is the inner sense of lack. The greater the conscious assertion of superiority, the greater is the unconscious fear of "nothingness" and "guilt."

THE INVERSE LAW OF SPIRITUAL DEVELOPMENT

The *Dark Night* is based on what I shall call the *inverse law of spiritual development*. According to John of the Cross, when one undergoes spiritual purgation, things are the opposite of what they seem. A spiritually purifying process seems like a dark night. Although, in John's view, the purgative process is truly a passage from darkness to light, from sin to grace, from isolation to union, it seems just the opposite to the person undergoing it. The person undergoing spiritual purgation suffers from an aggravated sense of darkness, sin, and isolation.

Applying the inverse law, John of the Cross focuses on the difficulties of spiritual growth. Spiritual development is seen as a long and painful process. The dark night of the senses is a relentless desert experience of exile, aridity, enervation, disorientation, and unquenchable spiritual thirst. According to John, the night of the senses leads ultimately to spiritual awakening, which, in its initial expression, involves extraordinary experiences that overawe the ego and quench—indeed, sate—its spiritual thirst.[1] This awakening, however, provides only temporary relief for those who are destined to continue on the spiritual path all the way to the end: full union with the divine. For these people, according to John, the blessings that attend spiritual awakening eventually disappear and the dark night of spirit sets in. This night of spirit is a direfully painful purgative transition involving feelings of darkness, forsakenness, dread, sin, engulfment, burning, and dissolution. In John's understanding, then, spiritual transformation is much more difficult than people realize. Expectations of sudden peace, bliss, light, and love are ruthlessly dashed, and the person undergoing the spiritual process suffers repeatedly and for long periods from feelings of alienation, worthlessness, darkness, and aloneness. However, it is precisely painful feelings such as these, John believes, that indicate that authentic spiritual growth is occurring. This conjunction of pain and progress is an example of the inverse law.

The inverse law is already evident in the spiritual pride that so frequently precedes the dark night of the senses. As we saw, spiritual pride is paradoxical in that the more a person asserts superiority and solicits the external recognition thereof, the more that person suffers unconsciously from inner needs and insecurities. The inverse law expresses itself here in that spiritually proud people, precisely because they believe they are far along on the spiritual path, are in fact lost. Once the dark night of the senses begins, the inverse law begins to express itself in just the opposite way. The seeker, now rudely disabused of any sense of superiority, begins to feel lost and therefore in fact is finally embarking upon the true path. John of the Cross has a keen sense of paradox, and the *Dark Night*, based on the inverse law, stresses paradox at every step of the spiritual journey.

PASSIVE PURGATION

John of the Cross distinguishes not only between the dark night of the senses and the dark night of spirit but also between active and passive nights of the senses and spirit. The active night of the senses is the period during which, of one's own volition, one attempts to tame the senses and desires and to harness the interior faculties of thought and fantasy. The active night of spirit is the period during which, of one's own initiative, one attempts to live by faith in submission to the divine, for example, by means of ritual, obedience, penance, and devotion. The key phrases here are *of one's own volition* and *of one's own initiative*, which indicate that the active nights of the senses and spirit involve the ego taking charge and responsibility of its spiritual quest—supported, John of the Cross would add, by the aid of ordinary grace. In the active nights of the senses and spirit, then, the ego is the primary agent of the purgative process; it practices purgation. The active nights of the senses and spirit precede their corresponding passive nights. The *Dark Night* treats the passive nights of the senses and spirit.

The passive nights of the senses and spirit typically begin after the ego has taken active purgation as far as it can go. At this point, when it is no longer able to do anything more in its own behalf, the ego begins undergoing purgations that are effected by spiritual power alone. John of the Cross is adamant about the necessity of passive purgation. Active purgation alone cannot fully prepare the soul for union with spiritual power. Passive purgation is needed as well. John writes: "No matter how much individuals do through their own efforts, they cannot actively purify themselves enough to be disposed in the least degree for the divine union of the perfection of love. God must take over and purge them in the fire that is dark for them, as we will explain" (1991a, pp. 366–367).

Passive purgation works at a much more radical level than is possible for active purgation. Active purgation, we can say, tames the senses, desires, and interior faculties without challenging the ego's supremacy within the domain of consciousness. In fact, the ego's ascendant position is even consolidated by active purgation to the extent that the ego achieves independence from the dominating influence of the senses and desires and gains command over interior faculties. Passive purgation, in contrast, challenges the ego's supremacy; indeed, passive purgation completely overthrows the ego and makes it a servant of spiritual power. Passive purgation disempowers the ego, undermines the ego's defenses, submits the ego to direct infusive transformation, and ultimately yokes the ego to spirit. Passive purgation, then, is a process that not only challenges but also takes possession of the ego. No wonder the ego by its own activity is unable to complete this stage of the purgative process.

In laying claim to the ego, passive purgation is a process that works against the grain of the ego's will. This adverse character of passive purgation explains why the passive nights of the senses and spirit are so dark, much darker than their corresponding active nights. The passive night of the senses is the period during which, by the exclusive action of spiritual power, the senses and desires are dulled, interior faculties are deactivated, and in general the ego is disempowered. In turn, the passive night of spirit is the period during which, again by the exclusive action of spiritual power, the ego is assailed and engulfed by dark forces, agonizingly purged of all defenses, disabused of the last vestiges of self-importance, and gradually prepared for union with the divine. In the passive nights of the senses and spirit, the ego is unable to do anything on its own and is the object rather than the agent of purgation. In the active nights, the ego effects purgation; in the passive nights, the ego (and deeper levels of the psyche) undergoes purgation.

As stages of passive purgation, the dark night of the senses and the dark night of spirit differ primarily in the manner in which spiritual power affects the ego. In the night of the senses, spiritual power, hidden deep within the psyche, works invisibly upon the ego in a way that withdraws the ego from the world. In the night of spirit, spiritual power, no longer hidden, works discernibly within consciousness to purge the ego of its deepest and most inward imperfections. In the night of spirit, spiritual power penetrates the ego and works upon it from the inside, affecting it in a wide variety of ways. For example, spiritual power pierces, absorbs, dissolves, ruptures, inflames, and consumes the ego. Given the presence of spiritual power within consciousness during the night of spirit, this stage is a stage of *infused* purgation. In contrast, in the night of the senses, spiritual power has not yet penetrated the seal separating the egoic and nonegoic spheres (viz., primal repression) and consequently still works at a distance from consciousness, exercising influence upon the ego primarily in a gravitational way. In the night of the senses, the ego is "unworlded" by the gravitational influence of a hidden power working from a point beyond the boundaries of consciousness.

As a stage of passive purgation, then, the dark night of the senses is not a stage of intentional or even voluntary spiritual practice. During this stage, the ego does not so much renounce the world as lose it. Despite the ego's efforts to hold onto the world, the world becomes increasingly lifeless, barren, and remote. And despite the ego's efforts to remain active in the world, the ego suffers a gradual loss of motivation, weakening of will, loss of command of faculties, and dissociation from old priorities and sense of self. Despite the ego's efforts to remain a part of the world, the ego is inexorably alienated from the world. It is gravitationally pulled out of the world and into its own subjectivity, all the way to the boundary where consciousness is separated from the deep unconscious, the known from the unknown.

ARIDITY

John of the Cross explains that a major sign of the onset of the dark night of the senses is the drying up of satisfactions and pleasures: aridity. Because he is addressing members of a religious community, he focuses his discussion of aridity on matters pertaining specifically to spirituality. He notes, for example, that the aridity of the night of the senses becomes evident when the consolations of spiritual practice disappear. For those committed to the spiritual life, aridity manifests itself as a loss of feelings of piety and sweetness when meditating, praying, or performing devotional rituals. These disciplines and observances become stale, tedious, and difficult to perform. They lose all appeal and become burdensome routines.

John compares the cutting off of consolations in spiritual practice to being weaned from the mother's breast:

> They cannot advance a step in meditation, as they used to, now that the interior sense faculties are engulfed in this night. He leaves them in such dryness that they not only fail to receive satisfaction and pleasure from their spiritual exercises and works, as they formerly did, but also find these exercises distasteful and bitter. As I said, when God sees that they have grown a little, he weans them from the sweet breast so that they might be

strengthened, lays aside their swaddling bands, and puts them down from his arms that they may grow accustomed to walking by themselves. (1991a, p. 376)

In psychoanalytic terms, the onset of aridity indicates that cathexes have been withdrawn from the world and therefore that worldly activities and goals have lost the power to elicit strong positive or negative feelings. The onset of aridity means that the world has ceased being a vital life-world and has become neutral, flat, and dead.

Although John's discussion of aridity focuses on the specifics of spiritual practice, his understanding of the phenomenon is not restricted to this area of primary attention. He makes it clear that aridity, as a part of the night of the senses, is a condition that cuts across all dimensions of life. This point is made in the context of a discussion of how one can tell whether the experience of aridity is due to passive purgation or to causes such as, he suggests, sickness or sin. John specifies three criteria by which the experience of aridity can be known to be part of the night of the senses. The first is stated as follows:[2] "The first is that since these souls do not get satisfaction or consolation from the things of God, they do not get any from creatures either" (1991a, p. 377). In John's understanding, then, true aridity admits of no exceptions. Not only spiritual endeavors but all of life becomes stale and dead. The desertlike condition of aridity is without oases to which the person suffering from aridity might go to find relief. The world at large is desiccated. In the terms introduced in the last chapter, we can say that the person suffering from aridity experiences a pervasive derealization of the world.

The two other criteria by which, according to John, genuine aridity can be known are (1) that, despite aridity, one continues to be focused on the spiritual life and, therefore, to be worried about backsliding; and (2) that the symptoms of aridity continue to grow worse without interruption. The first of these two criteria is stated in a way that applies primarily to the specific audience to which John was addressing himself. The criterion can, however, be stated more generally, as John himself does later in the Dark Night when he says that aridity causes a thirst for the divine: "Because the enkindling of love in the spirit sometimes increases exceedingly, the longings for God become so intense that it will seem to such persons that their bones are drying up in this thirst, their nature withering away, and their ardor and strength diminishing through the liveliness of the thirst of love" (1991a, p. 383). The drying up of all worldly satisfactions causes a desire for a kind of satisfaction that the world cannot provide. This desire is a thirst for something beyond the world. Although John explains that this thirst is a yearning for authentic spiritual life, he stresses that the person experiencing the thirst has no understanding of what is being yearned for. The yearning is vague and undefined. The thirst is for an "I know not what." Aridity, in desiccating the world that the ego has known, causes the ego to thirst for something unknown.

The third criterion is understandable just as it is stated: aridity grows worse without interruption. True aridity is indeed a "sickness unto death." It grows worse until one has finally died to the world and been opened to spiritual possibilities beyond the world. If aridity were suddenly to disappear and one were again to find satisfaction in the activities that one had previously enjoyed—that is, if one were suddenly to become one's "old self" again—the experience of aridity would have no lasting purgative value. Such a temporary aridity would be like a passing illness, a temporary loss of worldly appetite, not a "sickness unto death." Such an aridity would not contribute significantly to spiritual transformation; old vices or "sins" would spring back to life. For real spiritual transformation, aridity must be total and relentless. One must lose the world without hope or desire of regaining it. One's yearning must become focused entirely on possibilities beyond the world, possibilities of faith.

WEAKNESS OF WILL

In drying up desires and satisfactions, the dark night of the senses saps the strength of the will. It weakens resolve because old priorities no longer seem compelling or even important. Aridity carries with it lassitude, loss of motivation. For the members of John's audience, this erosion of resolve was a source of a fear of backsliding, a fear that one is losing one's commitment to the religious life. In a spiritual community, such weakness manifests itself as an inability to meditate or pray, as difficulty in maintaining the regimen of devotional life. To a person committed to the spiritual life, weakness in these areas is alarming. The fear is that one is forfeiting the highest good and sliding into an insidious indifference. John's point, however, is that this weakness of will and this fear of backsliding are in fact favorable developments. By the inverse law, they indicate that a genuine spiritual transition is occurring, namely, the transition from active to passive purgation.

Shifting John's account from the religious to the secular sphere, we can say that the weakening of will occurring during the night of the senses manifests itself in the primary areas of worldly commitment: career, civic life, family.[3] Success in one's career may suddenly begin to pale in importance, and one may begin suffering a loss of motivation to pursue the career goals that, before, were powerful inducements to action. Civic duties, too, may lose their sense of virtue or seeming obligatoriness. One may begin to suffer a sense of futility, a sense that one's individual efforts make little difference in the larger scheme of things. And even commitments to family life may begin to erode. One may cease experiencing satisfaction in sharing life with another person, or one may cease enjoying the role of parent. Aridity in these primary relationships can express itself in a growing indifference toward, and a corresponding loss of commitment to, the very people who, heretofore, were the closest and dearest people in one's life. Needless to say, such aridity and loss of resolve are disturbing. The fear in this case is that one is forfeiting the primary goods of this world.

Whether in the religious or secular sphere, then, the weakening of will that occurs in the dark night of the senses is experienced as an inability to hold onto life as one has lived it. One experiences a self-destructive slide into indifference, a perverse "not caring" that abandons life's joys and hopes. The perverseness of this process is compounded by the fact that, accompanying the slide into indifference, there sometimes occurs a stirring of impulses to say and do things that previously would have been unthinkable. The assertion of these impulses corresponds to the derepression of the shadow. I shall discuss John of the Cross's treatment of this phenomenon later in the chapter. For the present, the phenomenon needs only to be mentioned as one of the aspects of what seems a perversely self-destructive process. Whether or not one is a member of a spiritual community, the feeling is that one is throwing away the goods that one has achieved and flirting with "evil" inclinations. No wonder John of the Cross, in his own idiom, describes the night of the senses as the work of the devil. But this, again, is an expression of the inverse law.

John of the Cross gives special attention to how weakness of will affects the practice of discursive meditation. People in the night of the senses, he notes, not only lose interest in meditation, which becomes stale and tedious; they also begin experiencing difficulty in controlling mental faculties during meditation. Despite sincere efforts, John explains, attempts to focus the mind on a particular theme or image are useless. The mind and its faculties do not respond obediently. The mind either wanders uncontrollably or falls into an obscure inertness. These difficulties indicate that, to a significant extent, people in the night of the senses lose command of mental faculties. Weakness of will includes loss of power over the mind.

John of the Cross comments that this is just as it should be, for the person in the night of the senses is undergoing the transition from meditation to contemplation proper. Discursive meditation is an active discipline. The night of the senses, in contrast, as we have seen, is a passive process. During the night of the senses, the ego suffers disempowerment and, as a consequence, loses the strength needed to maintain control of interior faculties. Accordingly, the attempt to exercise these faculties in meditation now requires much more effort than before and achieves much poorer results. The exercise of mental faculties becomes both laborious and ineffective.

Moreover, John notes, the exercise of mental faculties actually becomes *counterproductive*. He writes:

> If individuals were to desire to do something themselves with their interior faculties, they would hinder and lose the goods that God engraves on their souls through . . . peace and idleness.
>
> If a model for the painting or retouching of a portrait should move because of a desire to do something, the artist would be unable to finish and the work would be spoiled. Similarly, any operation, affection, or thought a soul might cling to when it wants to abide in interior peace and idleness would cause distraction and disquietude, and make it feel sensory dryness and emptiness. (1991a, p. 382)

In the dark night of the senses, the ego is being acted upon by a gravitational force drawing the ego away from the world and toward eventual union with spiritual power. If the ego is active during this process, trying to regain possession of itself and command of its faculties, it will oppose the force acting upon it. For this reason John of the Cross recommends against the continued practice of discursive meditation and counsels people in the dark night of the senses to allow their minds to rest in a quiet and receptive emptiness.[4]

The weakening of will that goes with the dark night of the senses is symptomatic of a transformative process that disarms and deactivates the ego so that, naked and still, it can be brought into the presence of spiritual power. The ego can fight this process by making extraordinary efforts to exercise self-will. Struggling of this sort, however, is futile, because spiritual power is immeasurably stronger than the ego. The ego, then, must persevere and do what it can to maintain its responsibilities in the world while at the same time striving to release the will and allow the mind to become quietly receptive. Above all, the ego should not panic at its disempowerment and seeming loss of self-possession. Resistance is counterproductive. Later, after being reunited with spiritual power, the ego will be given new strength. However, for the duration of the dark night of the senses—and the dark night of spirit as well—the ego has little choice but to endure a process that works against the grain of its will.

THE BITTER PILL OF SELF-KNOWLEDGE

A particularly anguishing part of the dark night of the senses is the sobering self-knowledge it brings. John of the Cross discusses two types of such unhappy self-knowledge. One of these involves a confrontation with one's own insignificance. The ego, weakened and disabused of its previous sense of self-importance, is lucidly confronted with its "wretchedness." This type of self-knowledge corresponds to what, in the last chapter, I referred to as the mental ego's gradual awakening to its "nothingness" and its lack of justification or "guilt." The second type of self-knowledge discussed by John involves an encounter with dark impulses that begin importuning the ego. This type corresponds to what, in the last chapter, I referred to as the mental ego's encounter with the (personal) shadow.[5]

Concerning the first type of unhappy self-knowledge, John of the Cross says:

The aridities and voids of the faculties in relation to the abundance previously experienced and the difficulty encountered in the practice of virtue make the soul recognize its own lowliness and misery, which was not apparent in the time of its prosperity. (1991a, p. 385)

Now that the soul is clothed in these other garments of labor, dryness, and desolation, and its former lights have been darkened, it possesses more authentic lights in this most excellent and necessary self-knowledge. (1991a, p. 386)

The dark night of the senses is a humbling—indeed, humiliating— experience. The ego, which before was engaged, accomplished, and perhaps even narcissistically proud, is rudely divested of its sense of being and power. Alienated from the world and sapped of strength, the ego is unable to do the things it used to do and therefore be the person it used to be. The ego is stripped of its pretensions and exposed to itself in its vulnerability and smallness. The ego no longer feels satisfaction in its actions and begins to feel useless and therefore lacking in reason for being. The dark night of the senses divests the ego of its sense of identity and worth and ruthlessly reveals to the ego its "nothingness" and "guilt."

John of the Cross discusses the second type of unhappy self-knowledge very near the end of his treatment of the dark night of the senses. In the last chapter of Book One of the *Dark Night*, John notes that some people in the night of the senses are forced to confront wicked impulses. This fact is not discussed until the end of the treatment of the night of the senses because, John says, the impulses in question occur primarily in those select few who are destined later to experience the night of spirit. He says:

> Such is the sensory night and purgation of the soul. For those who must afterward enter into the other more oppressive night of the spirit in order to reach the divine union of love— because not everyone but only a few usually reach this union— this night is ordinarily accompanied by burdensome trials and sensory temptations that last a long time, and with some longer than others.
>
> An angel of Satan . . . ,which is the spirit of fornication, is given to some to buffet their senses with strong and abominable temptations, and afflict their spirit with foul thoughts and very vivid images, which sometimes is a pain worse than death for them.
>
> At other times a blasphemous spirit is added; it commingles intolerable blasphemies with all one's thought and ideas. Sometimes these blasphemies are so strongly suggested to the imagination that the soul is almost made to pronounce them, which is a grave torment to it. (1991a, pp. 392–393)

The person in the dark night of the senses is here beset with "forbidden" thoughts and feelings. Previously, when the ego was strong and actively engaged, such thoughts and feelings were unable to find expression in consciousness. Now that the ego is weak and passively disengaged, however, it is vulnerable to these "evil" importunings, these stirrings of the shadow.

It is interesting that John of the Cross chooses fornication and blasphemy as his examples of shadow manifestations. These choices reveal as much about John and his context as they do about the shadow per se. As we know, the (personal) shadow consists of elements of the personality excluded from consciousness because they are inconsistent with ego identity or the self-concept. The content of the shadow, then, is determined by what the ego rejects. Accordingly, it follows from John giving primary attention to fornication and blasphemy that these impulses, as shadow impulses, represented possibilities that were especially threatening to John's sense of who he was. This fact about John of the Cross should not be surprising. As a devout Christian and member of the Carmelite order, John was strongly identified with the values of chastity and piety. These values were components not only of his ego ideal but also of his ego identity. For John, then, impulses urging fornication and blasphemy were especially forbidden and therefore also especially disturbing. Such impulses posed an especially serious threat to his sense of self.

The dark night of the senses is a process of devastating self-insight. It is a process that brings to light aspects of ourselves that we do not want to see or do not want to own. The self-knowledge gained during the dark night of the senses is at once a harsh antidote to pride and a stern teacher of humility. The person in the night of the senses is given a sober look at the egoic personality, which, alienated from the world, is exposed as impotent and insignificant and, even worse, as hiding forbidden elements. This sober self-awakening is a bitter pill indeed.

ON THE EDGE: TRANSITION TO THE DARK NIGHT OF SPIRIT

The dark night of the senses leads in the direction of complete aridity, complete disempowerment of will, complete disillusionment of self. In leading away from the world in these ways, however, the night of the senses also leads toward direct openness to spiritual power. The ego, having been pulled out of the world and divested of its defenses and foundations, is ready for a breakthrough into consciousness of the power that up to this point has acted upon the ego only from a distance, gravitationally. This readiness for direct openness to spiritual power marks the point of transition from the dark night of the senses to the stage of infused contemplative experience. It marks the point at which spiritual awakening—or the beginning of the illuminative way—occurs. As mentioned earlier, spiritual awakening is typically experienced as a joyous-ecstatic breakthrough of spiritual power. The ego is suddenly filled with wondrous new feelings and transported euphorically by spiritual power. These joyous-ecstatic experiences, however, eventually subside, and the ego once again enters a period of darkness, a period that, indeed, is much darker than the earlier night of the senses. This second and darker night, the night of spirit, will be discussed in the next chapter. The ego's initial experience of this second night, however, is properly considered in this chapter, because it bears significant similarities to the borderline condition discussed in the last chapter.

After the initial joyous-ecstatic breakthrough of spiritual power subsides, the ego, now directly exposed to spiritual power, begins to experience this power as emanating from an inner abyss. The gravitational force of spiritual power no longer acts at a distance and now exerts a suctional force upon the ego from a hole within the ego's own depths. This hole, or "wound," is the point at which spiritual power has ruptured the seal (viz., primal repression) that hitherto had protected the ego from the nonegoic core of the psyche. This hole is like a black hole in psychic space. Potent with spiritual power, it exerts an irresistible tractional force upon the ego, a force that draws the ego into a dense interior darkness, as if to its doom. John of the Cross describes this experience of darkness as being oppressive, consuming, and, it seems, annihilating. He says:

> Under the stress of this oppression and weight, individuals feel so far from all favor that they think . . . that there is no one who will take pity on them. (1991a, p. 403)

> Since the divine extreme strikes in order to renew the soul and divinize it . . . , it so disentangles and dissolves the spiritual substance—absorbing it in a profound darkness that the soul at the sight of its miseries feels that it is melting away and being undone by a cruel spiritual death. It feels as if it were swallowed by a beast and being digested in the dark belly, and it suffers an anguish comparable to Jonah's in the belly of the whale. (1991a, pp. 403–404)

The ego is repeatedly enveloped and absorbed by a dark abyssal power. The ego feels as though it is in danger of being completely consumed. The sufferings endured here are severe, much more severe than the sufferings endured in the night of the senses. For in the night of the senses, the ego suffered a loss "only" of its worldly being and value. Now, however, in the initial phases of the night of spirit, the ego fears that it is about to lose its very "spiritual substance." The ego fears that it is in imminent danger of being absorbed and dissolved without remainder: annihilation, extinction.

This fear, as we learned in the last chapter, is the primary anxiety of the borderline personality. The person entering the dark night of spirit, then, can be said to be susceptible to borderline difficulties. This person is both drawn to and terrified by a mysterious power that acts upon the ego in an ominous way, capturing the ego in morbid absorptions and pulling the ego toward what seems like a lethal enveloping darkness. Although the person in this borderline condition is on a precipice of faith, this precipice, following the inverse law, seems more like an abyss of doom. Accordingly, the person in this situation is prone to feel completely alone and abandoned to darkness. John of the Cross says: "When this purgative contemplation oppresses a soul, it feels very vividly indeed the shadow of death, the sighs of death, and the sorrows of hell, all of which reflect the feeling of God's absence, of being chastised and rejected by him, and of being unworthy of him, as well as the object of his anger. The soul experiences all this and even more, for now it seems that this affliction will last forever" (1991a, p. 404). On the edge of an apparent abyss, the person entering the dark night of spirit feels isolated, cast off, and doomed. Having already been banished from the outer world during the night of the senses, this person is now utterly alone in a menacing inner world.

The pain of abandonment, John of the Cross observes, is felt most acutely in relation to friends. "Such persons also feel forsaken and despised by creatures, particularly by their friends" (1991a, p. 404). The person entering the night of spirit feels abandoned by friends because friends "fail" to rescue this person from the prospect of doom. The person entering the night of spirit expects much too much of friends and therefore is bound to be disappointed by them. Like the borderline, the person entering the night of spirit reaches out to friends—to spiritual advisers, to spouses or life partners, to confidants and other intimate acquaintances—as if they were saviors who could perform superhuman feats. These friends, however, are not superhuman, and therefore they inevitably "fail" the person who has tried to make saviors of them. In being "failed" in this way, the person entering the night of spirit is "abandoned," abandoned by friends and abandoned to an inner doom. The person entering the night of spirit is caught between two alien worlds. The outer world is a lifeless world in which "no one really cares," and the inner world is a terrifying abyss. Sometimes the person caught between these worlds feels like jumping into the abyss, like committing suicide, precisely because "no one really cares."

EMERGENCE OF THE MYSTERY OF FAITH

John of the Cross, following the inverse law, describes faith as dark and mysterious. Faith, according to John, begins in the experience of being lost. This experience is already present in the aridity and weakness of the dark night of the senses. As aridity sets in, a person no longer feels at home in the world, which becomes a desert, a wasteland; and as one becomes weak, previous commitments, including commitments to religious belief and practice, begin to fall away. John of the Cross elaborates:

> We will quote that passage from David in which the great power of this night in relation to the lofty knowledge of God is clearly shown. He proclaims: *In a desert land, without water, dry, and without a way, I appeared before you to be able to see your power and your glory.* David's teaching here is admirable: that the means to the knowledge of the glory of God were not the many spiritual delights and gratifications he had received, but the sensory aridities and detachments referred to by the dry and desert land. And it is also wonderful that, as he says, the way to the experience and vision of the power of God did not consist in ideas and meditations about God, of which he had made extensive use. But it consisted in not being able either to grasp God with ideas or walk by means of discursive, imaginative meditation, which is here indicated by the land without a way. (1991a, p. 388)

The path of faith, according to John of the Cross, is not a path of glory and vision but rather a path of destitution (aridity, dispossession) and seeming loss of faith (weakness of will, lapsing of spiritual beliefs and practices). The inverse law is at work: In feeling destitute, one is on the verge of spiritual riches; in feeling that one has lost one's faith, one is on the verge of finding a deeper faith.

This apparent loss of faith that, paradoxically, is a movement toward a deeper faith involves a "death" of the old god representation. John Welch stresses this point in his recent book on John of the Cross, aptly titled *When God Dies*. Applying Jung's ideas, Welch says:

"The pain and sorrow of the night [of the senses] are the grief that accompanies the death of gods. When gods die, Jung explained, the personality begins to disintegrate. In Jung's understanding, what is needed is a birth of a new and more appropriate image for the god-archetype within the psyche. Projections are withdrawn in the night and the other is allowed to be 'other,' and not a screen for the unconscious" (1990, p. 113). In dying to the world, the ego also dies to the god image it had projected upon the world. The ego's disempowerment is at the same time a decathexis of this image, which ceases being a compelling reality in the ego's life. The night of the senses is therefore a "twilight of the gods"; it involves a loss of faith that is also a "death of god."

The ego's loss of faith is at the same time the birth of a new and deeper faith. This new faith initially manifests itself as the thirst for an "I know not what" that, as discussed earlier, appears in conjunction with aridity and is one of the signs by which aridity can be known to have spiritual rather than psychopathological or "moral" causes. If, before, the ego had been guided by a definite representation of the divine and had been sustained in faith by commitment to this representation, it now seems that both the representation and the commitment have been lost and that the ego is left with nothing but an incomprehensible sense of emptiness and longing. This obscure yearning seems like something completely negative. It is, however, in truth something positive. To modify Pascal's expression, it is a yearning of the heart that reason cannot know. To the mind, this thirst seems like a complete loss of faith. To the heart, however, this thirst is the true awakening of faith.

This thirsting faith accelerates the gravitational process of the night of the senses and leads to spiritual awakening. Spiritual awakening brings the night of the senses to a dramatic end. It creates an oasis in what had been a desert wasteland. Drinking the waters of this oasis, the ego's thirst is quenched for a time. Eventually, however, the rejuvenating interlude passes and the night of spirit begins, bringing the ego to a kind of faith that is even more difficult and mysterious than the earlier thirst for the "I know not what." A darker night sets in. Spiritual power ceases bathing the ego in rejuvenating experiences and begins manifesting itself as the doomful darkness just discussed and as a dark smoldering fire that burns and consumes the soul. In this seemingly hopeless situation, according to John of the Cross, faith takes the form of a will to persevere in darkness even as one is absorbed, dissolved, burned, and consumed. John assures us that what the ego here experiences as an engulfing abyss will eventually become a fount of grace and that what the ego here experiences as a dark and annihilating fire will eventually become a fire of wisdom and love. Faith at this point, then, is the will to persevere until the black hole in the soul becomes a "wound of love."

CONCLUSION

In this chapter I have followed John the Cross's account of the transition that leads from dualism to the emergence of faith. As we have seen, John stresses passive purgation, aridity, weakness, unhappy self-knowledge, a sense of being lost, and, finally, the emergence of faith. More generally, John stresses the inverse law: in the purgative process things are the opposite of what they seem. Although John of the Cross speaks to a narrow audience and gives a specifically religious formulation to most points, he nonetheless presents the essentials of the psychospiritual process by which the ego undergoes withdrawal from dualism. He shows how the difficulties discussed in the last chapter can be part of a coherent process of development with a redeeming spiritual *telos*.

Stressing the inverse law as he does, John of the Cross's understanding of the night of the senses is strongly negative. It is not, however, I believe, overly negative. The night of the senses is an inexorable process of alienation, desiccation, enervation, self-dissociation, and disorientation. Periods of relief may occur, but they are usually of brief duration. For the ego, then, the night of the senses is a thoroughly negative experience; it is a progressively worsening "sickness unto death." As John of the Cross notes, once aridity sets in, if one has truly entered the night of the senses, aridity (along with the other symptoms of this night) simply gets worse. The night of the senses is the experience of outer or worldly death.

The night of spirit is the experience of inner or psychological death. It, too, is an inexorable process that allows only brief periods of relief. The night of spirit, however, must be set in the larger context of infused spiritual transformation to be properly understood. I have already noted that the night of spirit is typically preceded by a spiritual awakening characterized by blissful feelings and euphoric transports; and in the next chapter I shall explain how the night of spirit is followed by spiritual rebirth, regeneration, and higher integration. In the *Dark Night*, John of the Cross gives only scant attention to these periods that precede and succeed the night of spirit. Of the former, he gives only passing mention to the dramatic phenomena that accompany spiritual awakening and then dismisses them as signs of spiritual immaturity. And of the latter, he merely points forward to the prospect of spiritual rebirth and transformation through the inner work of love. He does not elaborate on these in *Dark Night*, as he does in his *Living Flame of Love* and *Spiritual Canticle*. In the next chapter, then, I shall discuss the night of spirit in the larger context of spiritual awakening and regenerative transformation. I shall explain that the night of spirit is the downward or regressive turn of a developmental spiral by which the ego, following spiritual awakening, is returned to, regenerated by, and finally integrated in higher fashion with the nonegoic core of the psyche and with the spiritual power that burns within this core.

9 | *The Spiral Path of Transcendence: Awakening, Regression, Regeneration*

The ego's withdrawal from the world leads to a threshold beyond which the ego confronts the deep unconscious and the potentials that belong to the nonegoic core of the psyche. This threshold is the boundary that separates the natural from the supernatural, the world from the "beyond." If the ego crosses this threshold and moves into the "beyond," it enters an extraordinary, redemptive phase of the human developmental journey. That is, the ego enters such a phase *if* it is developmentally ready to meet the challenges of the deep unconscious. The ego, however, is not always ready. The ego sometimes lacks sufficient strength to withstand the powerful influences of the nonegoic sphere. The potentials of the deep unconscious pose definite dangers to the ego, which must be "seaworthy" if it is to survive the "night sea journey." Even the ego that is constitutionally prepared for this journey is fearful of the fate that lies ahead. Even the strongest of egos clings to dry land and resists being cast into the vast ocean of the unconscious.

The ego that is ready, however, eventually loosens its moorings and allows itself to set sail, or at least its moorings are cut loose and it is set adrift. The ego relinquishes or loses its last contact with dry land, and the night sea journey begins. This voyage is always unique to the individual; nevertheless, it has a common basic itinerary. As Leo Frobenius (1904), Carl Jung (1912), Joseph Campbell (1949), and others have explained, this voyage is a transformative journey that follows a path of descent and higher return. The night sea journey is a voyage that draws the ego into a harrowing encounter with psychic depths so that the ego can rediscover and eventually be reunited with the psychospiritual resources of these depths.

The initial departure from dry land can be exhilarating. The ego may enjoy wondrous new experiences and may be led to believe that it has suddenly arrived at a glorious destiny. Before long, however, the ego is engulfed by the ocean (the unconscious, the abyss, the underworld) and set upon by dark influences. This turn of events is terrifying. The ego's initial enthusiasm vanishes and it finds itself in a life-and-death struggle with overwhelming forces. The ego struggles against these forces with all its strength but finally succumbs and is taken captive by them. It is swallowed up in the "belly of the beast." This engulfment marks the nadir of the night sea journey. Arriving at this nadir, the ego believes that its ultimate destruction is at hand. The "seaworthy" ego, however, survives the nadir experience, and the nadir point turns out to be a positive turning point. For once the ego has submitted itself to the powers of the deep, the manifest nature of these powers and their effect upon the ego undergo a paradoxical reversal. The ego finds that it has somehow—seemingly by miracle—been released from the "belly of the beast" and that the powers of the deep have ceased assailing and engulfing it and have begun regenerating it instead.

Accordingly, in surviving the nadir experience, the ego begins being regenerated by the very powers that had besieged it and held it captive. The ego is not only released from engulfment and returned to the world; it is also transformed. It is rooted in both deeper and higher, psychic and spiritual, sources. It is integrated with the full spectrum of nonegoic life. The ego, in returning to the world, therefore does not return to its point of departure from the world. Rather, it returns to higher ground. The night sea journey, then, is a descent into the unconscious that prepares the way for a higher return to conscious life. In psychoanalytic terms, the descent can be called *regression in the service of transcendence;*[1] in traditional spiritual terms, the higher return can be called *regeneration in spirit.*

The night sea journey of descent and higher return is a psychospiritual journey of regression, regeneration, and higher integration. The ego is regressively drawn into the deep unconscious, where it comes under the irresistible sway of previously repressed nonegoic potentials. The ego is then regeneratively transformed by these potentials, which cease assailing the ego and begin infusing and transforming it instead. Finally, the ego is gradually integrated with these potentials in a way that brings into being a transegoic unified duality of egoic and nonegoic spheres. This journey of regression, regeneration, and higher integration follows a *spiral* course of return and transcending reunion. The ego follows a path that returns it to origins so that, taking root in these origins, it can grow to new heights.

The spiral path of regression, regeneration, and higher integration leads not only to an inner reunion of the ego with psychic and spiritual sources; it leads as well, as we shall see, to an outer reunion of the self with others. The spiral journey is not only a voyage into the deep psyche but also an interpersonal or object-directed process. The spiral journey has these two dimensions because the undoing of primal repression, which opens the ego to the unconscious, is at the same time an undoing of primal alienation, which opens the ego to others. Accordingly, the ego's regressive encounter with the forces of the deep is at the same time a defenseless exposure to others. The ego's regeneration by nonegoic potentials is at the same time a healing reconnection with others. And the ego's higher integration with the nonegoic sphere is at the same time a redeeming reunion with others. Every step of the spiral journey has both intrapsychic and interpersonal, both depth-psychological and object-relational, sides. The inner journey of regression, regeneration, and higher integration is at the same time an outer process of unmasking, retouching, and higher intimacy.

The spiral journey is an archetypal process that has been described in many different ways. For example, in the Judeo-Christian tradition, it is the process that leads the righteous or faithful self through the cataclysm that destroys the fallen world order and brings this self to the New Israel, New Jerusalem, or heavenly kingdom. In Orthodox and Roman Catholic Christianity, it is the period of purgative trial and transformation that precedes final salvation. In much of world mythology, it is the hero's adventure into and return from the underworld. In Hinduism and Buddhism, it is the difficult "passage to the other side" that occurs between initial awakening and final enlightenment. In the Tantric tradition, it is the process involving the arousal of the "serpent power" *kundalini* and the gradual unveiling of this power as the purgative-transformative dynamism of the goddess Shakti. In alchemy, it is the process of reduction and transubstantiation of base metal into gold. In Zen, it is the phase of the spiritual journey during which "there are no mountains" (descent, regression) and then, once again, "there are mountains" (higher return, integration). And, in its most general expression, it is the process of the psychological death and spiritual rebirth of the self.

I shall treat the spiral journey in this and the next two chapters. In this chapter I shall discuss the first two stages of the journey: regression in the service of transcendence and regeneration in spirit. In the next chapter I shall return to the subject of gender differences and suggest some ways in which these differences might manifest themselves in women's and men's experience of the spiritual path, including their experience of midlife transvaluation, the night of the senses, and the spiral journey. Finally, in the last chapter of the book, I shall address the goal of the spiral journey, integration.

Awakening: Rupture of Planes[2] and Encounter with the Numinous

The initial awakening to spiritual power is frequently experienced as a breakthrough of a miraculous and, it seems, redemptive sort. In the last chapter I noted that, in the Roman Catholic contemplative tradition, spiritual awakening (the beginning of the illuminative way) is said to involve an initial period of extraordinary but "immature" phenomena such as transports, ecstasies, and sudden intuitions. Similarly, in Buddhism, the initial awakening of insight is said to involve wondrous sensations, feelings, and visions. Because these preliminary experiences are frequently mistaken for *nirvana* itself, Buddhism refers to initial awakening as *pseudonirvana* and to the ten primary kinds of experiences that go with it as the *ten corruptions*. These "corruptions" are regarded as deceptive phenomena that can distract one from the proper goal of the spiritual journey. Japanese Zen gives emphatic expression to this general Buddhist view by calling the alluring experiences that accompany initial awakening *makyo*, diabolical phenomena that tempt the Zen seeker away from the disciplined practice of *zazen*. All traditions hold that the phenomena that attend initial awakening are not only dramatic but also dangerous in that they lead spiritual seekers to believe that they have finished the spiritual quest when in a sense they have only just begun. The consensus is that these phenomena render spiritual seekers prone to a false sense of realization and perfection and therefore to narcissistic inflation.

Although initial awakening is frequently experienced as a dramatic breakthrough to a higher realm, nothing dictates that it be experienced in this way. For the event is as much a breakdown as it is a breakthrough, as much a rending of the ego's deepest system of defense (primal repression–primal alienation) as it is an opening to new possibilities. Moreover, the opening to new possibilities is as much an exposure to dangerous forces as it is a receptivity to redemptive ones. Nothwithstanding these facts, initial awakening is typically experienced in a decisively positive manner, because, following a period of alienation and aridity, initial awakening has the character of a yearned-for infusion of new life and a manifestation of wondrous new powers. The ego is at first unaware of the trials that lie ahead and easily mistakes the influx of new life and powers for salvation or enlightenment. Having suffered through a spiritual desert, the ego is prone to experience the infusion of new life as an upwelling of rejuvenating waters or as a dispensation of manna from heaven. Having "died to the world," the ego is prone to experience the manifestation of new powers as a sign of the opening of heaven or the attainment of higher insight. Having been utterly lost, the ego is prone to believe that it has suddenly found its ultimate destiny. But it has not. The ego has only begun to set sail on the ocean of the deep unconscious.

In Rudolf Otto's (1958) terms, the breakthrough experience just described is an experience of initial encounter with the *numinous*. The numinous is supernatural energy. It is something that appears to the ego as an immense power arriving from another world. The ego experiences the numinous as an awesome presence that is "wholly other," a transcendent unknown that can either haunt or hallow, besiege or assuage, extinguish or exalt. According to Otto, the numinous is the *mysterium tremendum et fascinans*. In our terms, we can say that the numinous is an ego-eclipsing dynamic reality that emerges when the plane separating the egoic and nonegoic spheres (viz., primal repression) is breached and the ego is suddenly opened to the direct influence of the prodigious power that previously lay latent in the nonegoic core of the psyche.

The darker possibilities implicit in awakening soon begin to emerge. The ego quickly learns that although it is no longer wandering in a desert, neither has it arrived safely in the promised land. It becomes evident to the ego that the rejuvenating waters quenching its thirst are the waters of an ocean that is dark, deep, and "wholly other." As the ego begins to comprehend the daunting immensity of its situation, its feelings toward the numinous become acutely ambivalent. The ego of course remains fascinated by the numinous, but it now also becomes acutely fearful of the numinous. The ego begins to feel that the breakthrough it has experienced is not completely beneficial. Specifically, it begins to sense that its new openness is not only a spiritual receptivity but also a psychic vulnerability or "wound"; and it begins to sense that that to which it is open is not only a source of replenishing energy and wondrous phenomena but also an "abyss" that emits dangerous forces and beckons the ego to a dark destiny. Accordingly, the ego ceases being one-sidedly enthusiastic about the breakthrough it has experienced and begins to suffer seriously mixed feelings about its new condition and prospects.

The ambivalence experienced by the ego toward nonegoic possibilities renders the ego prone to split these possibilities, and its own responses to them, into all-good and all-bad categories. The ego senses that it is perched between heaven and hell and that, pulled in these opposite directions, it is in touch with both what is best and what is worst in itself. Riddled with this acute ambivalence and splitting, the ego is prone to highly inconsistent, borderline, behaviors. The ego is prone to idealize others as all-good saviors who would rescue the ego from the abyss and from its own attractions to "evil." Because, however, idealization is a form of falsification, the persons who are idealized in this manner are eventually unmasked and, with equal but opposite falsification, perceived as uncaring exploiters or as pawns or agents of the very powers from which the ego is trying to be rescued. The ego's situation here is highly unstable.

REGRESSION IN THE SERVICE OF TRANSCENDENCE

The ego's ambivalence toward nonegoic possibilities gradually shifts in a one-sidedly negative direction. Having been perched between heaven and hell, the ego begins to feel that it has been deserted by all persons or agents who might have saved it and has been left abandoned to purely negative possibilities, to the dark forces of the netherworld. This negative turn is to be expected, for the undoing of primal repression triggers a "return of the repressed" and a corresponding "regression of the repressor." Numinous power awakens from dormancy and activates nonegoic potentials. These potentials assert themselves powerfully and lay claim to the ego, which is now powerless to defend itself. The ego, having repressively disconnected itself from the nonegoic sphere, is now forced to confront, and regressively to submit to, what it had repressed. Accordingly, the ego loses its underfooting and is engulfed by the ocean of the deep unconscious. The ego undergoes a *regressus ad originem* that returns the ego to, and ultimately reroots the ego in, the sources from which it originally arose.

Negatively Weighted Ambivalence and the Reawakening of the
Negative Side of Early Childhood Object Relations

The negative shift in the ego's ambivalence toward the nonegoic sphere manifests itself in a negative shift in the ego's relations with others. This latter shift is evident both in a pervasive devaluation of others and in a resurfacing of the negative side of early childhood object relations, that is, in a reencounter in new form with the menacing side of the oedipal father and preoedipal mother.

We have already noted that the person on the verge of regression in the service of transcendence tends both to idealize others as saviors and devalue them as evil. The person who has begun regression in the service of transcendence ceases for the most part oscillating back and forth like this and, deeply disillusioned, tends to see others primarily in devalued "bad object" guises. This change of perspective reflects the fact that the ego at this juncture is no longer perched between heaven and hell. The ego has succumbed to dark forces and therefore feels lost and forsaken, abandoned by all persons who might have saved it from the abyss. Such persons, hitherto idealized, are now devalued and seen in the worst possible light. The ego undergoing regression in the service of transcendence is cynical about others, who are seen as selfish and deceitful, if not demoniacally wicked.

The ego believes that others perceive it in at least as negative a light as it perceives them. Specifically, the ego assumes that the inner darkness that it sees in itself can also be seen by others. This assumption is mistaken in one respect and correct in another. It is mistaken in that most other people, still feeling justified by their ego identities and ignorant of their own dark depths, are insensitive to the kinds of experiences the ego is undergoing. The assumption is correct, however, in that the ego is completely unable to contain or hide the disturbing feelings that afflict it. The "evil" that the ego senses within itself, that is, although perhaps not recognized by others, is not hidden from them either. Regression in the service of transcendence is therefore a period during which the ego feels defenselessly exposed, both to its own inner darkness and to what seems like the penetrating gaze of others. The ego feels that others can see through it, that its dark core is open for all to see.

Another consequence of the negative shift in the ego's ambivalence is a resurfacing of the negative side of early object relations. The ego reexperiences negative patterns of relationship deriving from prelatency childhood. These patterns resurface because the ego is here defenseless like a child and caught in conflicts, both intrapsychic and interpersonal, that are reminiscent of those the child experienced in relation to the negative sides of the oedipal father and preoedipal mother. The ego's situation bears similarities to that of the child both in the child's relation to the wrathful-punishing side of the oedipal father and in the child's relation to the engulfing-abandoning side of the preoedipal mother. These similarities trigger a reactivation of the negative aspects of early childhood object relations, the principal moments of which are now reexperienced in new ways.

Negative oedipal and preoedipal object representations begin to dominate interpersonal relations. The ego begins to see significant others primarily as harsh judges (negative oedipal figures) and consuming-rejecting powers (negative preoedipal figures). Persons undergoing regression in the service of transcendence, in perceiving themselves as "worthless" or "sinful," are prone to see others as hostile witnesses who, like the wrathful oedipal father, would pass ruthless judgment upon them. This negative oedipal posture already resurfaces during the night of the senses when the ego, in suffering deanimation of its worldly identity and derepression of the personal shadow, begins to see itself as "unjustified" and "bad" and to fear that others see it as "unjustified" and "bad" as well. But this posture becomes even more severe during regression in the service of transcendence when the ego confronts the darkness deep within its soul, the archetypal shadow. For in looking into these depths, the ego sees tendencies toward absolute evil, and, again, what it sees in itself it fears that others, as oedipal judges, see in it as well. Accordingly, the ego feels that it stands not only judged but condemned by others.

Additionally, the ego feels seriously imperiled by others, for a resurfacing of the negative side of preoedipal object relations predisposes the ego to see others in the image of the Terrible Mother. The ego is both needy and suspicious of others and therefore perceives others as beings who, like the Terrible Mother, are both irresistible and dangerous. The ego sees others as beings who would entice the ego into vulnerable openness only to "devour" (i.e., take advantage of) the ego and then abandon it. The ego feels rejected by others and completely alone in its misery. It desperately needs understanding and support. The ego is therefore drawn to people even though it has lost faith in them. The ego for this reason feels vulnerable to being seduced, used, and deserted by others, just as, in early childhood, it felt vulnerable to being captivated, consumed, and abandoned by the Terrible Mother. The ego, accordingly, is fearful of others not only as hostile judges but also as dangerous "love objects."

I shall discuss how oedipal and preoedipal themes are replayed in representations of the divine in the next chapter. It is noteworthy here, however, that the negative themes just discussed are present in John of the Cross's account of entry into the dark night of spirit. John, if we remember, states that the soul passing into the night of spirit experiences a feeling of "God's absence, of being chastised and rejected by him, and of being unworthy of him. . ." (1991a, p. 404). Moreover, this soul, John observes, feels as though it is being consumed by a dreadful power that is "absorbing it in deep and profound darkness . . . [as if] swallowed by a beast and being digested in the dark belly. . ." (p. 404). The feelings of being unworthy and rejected reflect the negative oedipal imago: God the Father is experienced as a judge who condemns the soul as being unworthy and punishes it without mercy. And the feelings of being swallowed and absorbed in darkness reflect the negative preoedipal imago: the psychic space beneath the ego is experienced as a maw, abyss, or consuming darkness, a womb-belly that, reminiscent of the Terrible Mother, would swallow and annihilate the ego.

I am not suggesting, reductionistically, that the experiences described by John of the Cross involve only a reactivation of early childhood object relations. The point is not that early object relations determine *what* is experienced during regression in the service of transcendence. The point, rather, is that they determine, to a significant extent, the ego's *manner of representing* what is experienced during this period. The ego is predisposed to interpret its dire experience in terms of its prior most similar experience and specifically in terms of its primal childhood fear of being rejected by the oedipal father and left abandoned to the engulfing power of the preoedipal mother. Accordingly, the ego interprets regression in the service of transcendence as an experience of being condemned by a wrathful father god and left abandoned to the engulfing power of a terrible goddess.

Dread

Dread is the characteristic affective state of regression in the service of transcendence. Dread is not the same as anxiety. Anxiety is similar to fear in being a state of alarm that occurs in response to sensed danger, a state that triggers a response of fight or flight. Anxiety, however, differs from fear, as existential philosophers such as Kierkegaard, Heidegger, and Sartre have explained, in being a dis-ease without a recognizable danger to which it is a response. Anxiety is a response to a sensed but unperceived danger. Anxiety is a state of alarm or hyperarousal that is without an object or at least a known object.

Dread is similar to anxiety in being a state of dis-ease that, frequently, has no perceived object. It differs from anxiety, however, in two main ways: (1) it involves a "shudder" rather than alarm or hyperarousal; and (2) it causes a state of breathless immobility rather than a condition of fight or flight.

Rudolf Otto's account of the numinous emphasizes the experience of the *shudder* or *tremor*. In being exposed to the numinous, one comes into the presence of a vast and eclipsing power that causes one to tremble. This trembling is frequently accompanied by shivers and horripilation. Otto stresses that the shivers and horripilation occurring in response to the numinous can be positive as well as negative. They can, for example, accompany spiritual ravishment and exaltation as well as dread. Nevertheless, he argues, in earlier and more "primitive" experiences of the numinous, shivers and horripilation tend to be the quaking and "goose bumps" distinctive of dread. The quaking of dread involves a queasiness and sense of revulsion; the "goose bumps" involve a clamminess or cold wetness. Unlike anxiety, then, which is a state of heated alarm in face of an unspecifiable danger, dread is a state of queasiness and clamminess in face of something eerie.

Dread also differs from anxiety in being a state that, typically, involves an inability to move. One is said to be caught in the *grip* of dread. One is taken hold of by a power that stops one in one's tracks, takes the breath away, and makes the skin crawl. Dread is not a condition of hyperarousal leading to fight or flight, to aggressive or defensive behavior; it is rather a state of morbid fascination leading to immobility. One is seized and held in thrall by something supernatural. In sum, whereas anxiety is a dis-ease that leads to accelerated activity, dread is a dis-ease that leads to paralysis.

Closely related to dread is the experience of *flooding*, the sense of being infiltrated by an alien power. The ego's vulnerable openness, its deep psychic wound, allows the numinous power of the deep unconscious to affect the ego in a variety of ways. Dread is symptomatic that this power has already "gotten under the ego's skin." Flooding is symptomatic that this power has seeped into the "basement" of the egoic sphere and is immersing the ego in currents of heavy, "unclean" energy. The ego experiences these currents as noxious upwellings. It feels contaminated by them. Flooding therefore adds to the ego's dread. Flooding is the characteristic expression of the infusive movement of numinous power during regression in the service of transcendence. As we shall see later, the ego during this period is for the most part affected by numinous power as it acts upon the ego from a source (the nonegoic core) or from points (cathexis objects) located outside the egoic sphere. The ego's wounded openness, however, does allow numinous power to infiltrate the egoic sphere directly, and this infusive movement is typically experienced in an alien, heavy, and "liquid" way, that is, as flooding.

If dread (including flooding) is the characteristic affective state of regression in the service of transcendence, it of course is not the only affective state experienced during this period. The person undergoing regression in the service of transcendence continues to experience a wide spectrum of feelings, including on occasion some of the intensely positive (eruptive-infusive) feelings that emerged during the period of initial awakening. Nevertheless, feelings other than dread, and positive feelings in particular, tend to be brief or rare. Dread is the baseline affect, the mood most distinctive of regression in the service of transcendence. Correspondingly, as we shall see, states of spiritual excess (i.e., intoxication, tearful rejoicing, ravishment) are distinctive of regeneration in spirit, and feelings of blessedness and bliss are distinctive of transegoic integration.

Strangeness

During the night of the senses, as we know, the ego experiences the world as arid and desertlike. The withdrawal of object cathexes derealizes the world and levels all differences between good and evil, important and unimportant, attractive and unattractive. The world is reduced to a lifeless landscape. In sharp contrast, the world during regression in the service of transcendence is powerfully recharged with energy. During regression in the service of transcendence, the opening of the deep unconscious saturates experience with numinous power, reanimating the world in a way that not only returns things to life but makes things larger than life. Everything in the world is amplified, accentuated in appearance and magnified in significance. That is to say, the world becomes *superreal*. This aspect of superreality is not one quality among others that might be isolated for study. It is rather a pervasive, global, dimension of the ego's new experience. In becoming superreal, experience in general is potentiated. All qualities are enhanced; everything is made more lustrous, rich, or deep; everything becomes more salient, interesting, or fascinating.

If the world is enlivened in this way, it is also haunted. For the saturation of experience with numinous energy gives the world an eerie quality. It makes the world *surreal*. More specifically, it gives the world an alien cast similar to that of dreams. Prior to regression in the service of transcendence, numinous energy is confined almost exclusively to the deep unconscious and therefore is limited to the realm of dreams. With the onset of regression in the service of transcendence, however, this energy pervades the world of waking experience and gives it the shrouded and otherworldly atmosphere characteristic of dreams. In becoming superreal, the world becomes larger than life, more potent than it otherwise would be. In becoming surreal, the world becomes weird, shot through with a darkly preternatural "feel." In becoming surreal, the world is filled with mysterious forces, obscure possibilities, and ominous new meanings and values. Dread is a response to this numinous surreality of the world.

The onset of regression in the service of transcendence opens consciousness to the deep unconscious and in doing so blurs the boundary between waking and dreaming experience. As this happens, the ego suddenly finds itself in a strange new world. If, before, the ego was anxiously alienated from a world that had become flat and dead, it now is dreadfully enthralled by a world that has become "supersurreal," by a world, that is, that has become *strange*. *Strangeness* (amplification-hauntedness) is the distinctive ambience of the world during regression in the service of transcendence. As we shall see, enchantment is the distinctive ambience during regeneration in spirit and hallowed resplendence the distinctive ambience during transegoic integration.

Trance and Engulfment

So far we have noted the following changes that occur in the transition from the dark night of the senses to regression in the service of transcendence: (1) anxiety gives way to dread, and (2) aridity gives way to strangeness. To these changes we can now add that disconnected witnessing, dissociated consciousness, gives way to trance.

The ego going through the dark night of the senses is cut off from experience. It is unable to make contact and become involved. It is a disconnected witness. The ego undergoing regression in the service of transcendence in contrast is an *entranced* witness, a witness that is subject to being seized and held in thrall. Whereas the disconnected witness of the night of the senses is dissociatively isolated and therefore unable to achieve engagement, the entranced witness of regression in the service of transcendence is defenselessly open and therefore vulnerable to being captivated by influences acting upon it. The disconnected witness of the night of the senses is cut off from the world and therefore unable to get outside itself. In contrast, the entranced witness of regression in the service of transcendence is radically exposed and therefore unable to keep possession of itself.

I noted in chapter 7 that a form of trance is evident in the borderline condition. This point is made by Jerome Kroll (1988), who reports that borderlines frequently fall into states of empty abstraction. Such states, I suggested, are a consequence of the borderline's openness to the gravitational influence of the energy of the deep unconscious. The borderline, exposed to this influence, is sometimes caught in a tractional field. Inner dialogue stops and subjectivity becomes oppressively heavy, morbidly empty. The borderline finds states of this sort unbearable and frequently engages in wild and even self-destructive behavior to find relief from the abyssal gravity. The borderline is frequently driven to desperate measures to escape the grip of a power emanating from the dark underside of the soul.

Once regression in the service of transcendence begins, the ego no longer experiences the numinous power of the unconscious only in its expression as the power of the dark underside of the soul. For this power is now active within consciousness and, projected outwardly, eerily enlivens the world. The world is now charged with the numinous power that before was confined to psychic depths. This power therefore begins to take hold of the ego not only by drawing it inward toward a gravitational abyss but also by drawing it outward toward transfixing cathexis objects. The world pulsates with a power that both exaggerates and magnetizes things, that renders things both "supersurreal" and hypnotically attractive, both strange and entrancing. Trance, then, is a phenomenon that occurs when a weakened ego comes under the influence of awakened numinous power, which affects the ego both as an inner abyssal power and as an outer cathectic force.

The ego's hypnotic attraction to numinous power can lead to engulfment, which is the limit case of entrancement. The ego's susceptibility to being entranced by numinous power is also a susceptibility to being captivated and consumed by this power. Trance and engulfment indicate that numinous power is affecting the ego in an external (i.e., extraegoic) way; that is, by exercising an influence gravitationally or cathectically *upon* consciousness rather than infusively *within* consciousness. Trance indicates a binding of the ego by a gravitational or cathectic force; engulfment indicates a consequent absorption of the ego by such a force.

Engulfment, as a state of absorption, is a condition in which ego boundaries are eliminated and the ego merges with something beyond itself. This merger, however, is not a positive fusional experi-

ence. It is not a liberating union reflecting release from ego boundaries but rather a negative union reflecting a consuming assimilation
of the ego by an alien power. The disappearance of ego boundaries
that occurs in engulfment is a result of these boundaries collapsing
under external pressure rather than of them bursting from internal
pressure. Engulfment is an *implosive* incorporation rather than explosive dissolution of the ego.

The imploded character of absorbed states during regression in
the service of transcendence gives these states a heavy, inert, and vacant quality. The ego is held fast, subjected to an inexorable suction
or magnetic pull, and then absorbed in a negative, disconnected,
way. Absorbed states during regression in the service of transcendence therefore are dense and destitute rather than expansive and
creative. They are states of oppressive numbness rather than heightened aliveness.[3] States of heightened aliveness do occur during regression in the service of transcendence, but they are uncharacteristic
of the period. Highly energized infusive states such as intoxication,
transport, and ecstasy are especially rare. States of this sort, which
frequently appear in dramatic fashion during the period of initial
awakening, virtually disappear during regression in the service of
transcendence. As we shall see, highly charged infusive states reappear and belong most distinctively to the period of regeneration
in spirit.

Autonomous Fantasy and Hallucination

Like the other potentials of the nonegoic core of the psyche, the autosymbolic process is stirred into activity once the ego is reopened to
the nonegoic core. This process begins forging images that give embodiment to the ego's deepest desires and fears. The ego's deepest
desires at this point are those deriving from the derepression of
forbidden instinctual urges; and the ego's deepest fears are those relating to prospects of forsakenness, engulfment, and insanity. Accordingly, the autosymbolic process produces images that present
these desires and fears in dramatic form. The images painted by Hi-
eronymus Bosch can be considered extreme but also powerful examples of such fantasy production.

In spawning images of this sort, the autosymbolic process can
be a curse upon the soul. People who experience such images are
strongly resistant to acknowledging them as their own and typically
attribute them to evil influences acting upon them. In most religious
traditions, such images have been considered the work of demons.

This interpretation is all the more suggested in that these images can assume the magnitude of full-fledged hallucinations. In some instances persons undergoing regression in the service of transcendence are confronted with images (and voices) that seem entirely real, with apparitions of malevolent beings threatening harm or suggesting wickedness. Autonomous fantasy may only rarely manifest itself in this fully realistic way. Nevertheless, given the vulnerable openness and negatively weighted ambivalence characteristic of regression in the service of transcendence, hallucinations of the sort described can be considered symptomatic if not typical of the period.

"Resurrection" of the Body and Derepression of the Instincts

Primal repression, as we know, is a psycho*physical* structure that blocks the free flow of energy in the body. The lifting of primal repression therefore leads not only to an energization of experience generally but also to an energization of somatic experience in particular. Spiritual awakening is at the same time a bodily awakening.

Given the negative weighting of the ego's ambivalence during regression in the service of transcendence, the awakening of the body is perceived with suspicion and sometimes alarm. Strange new sensations and bodily responses emerge. A person, for example, may begin to experience "tingly" sensations or fluidic energy currents in the body or twinges and tics or involuntary muscle contractions and relaxations (e.g., the anal sphincter, visceral muscles, the diaphragm). These bizarre experiences indicate that the body is undergoing a process of derepression and "resurrection." The "tingly" sensations indicate the recharging of bodily tissue (especially erotogenic tissue); the fluidic currents indicate that energy has begun again to circulate in the body; the twinges and tics indicate the dissolution of somatic blockages or armors or the stimulation of new nerve centers; and the muscle contractions and relaxations, if they occur, indicate that a process of convulsive derepression and reopening is in progress. Needless to say, these unusual sensations and bodily responses are disconcerting and can be misperceived as symptoms of a pathological process.

In cases of more gradual awakening, the "resurrection" of the body is much more subtle and can unfold almost invisibly. In these cases, a person may recognize in retrospect that a profound transformation has taken place but have no recollection of discrete, or at least dramatic, changes having occurred. In cases of sudden and violent awakening on the other hand, the "resurrection" of the body is a process that can be conspicuously evident and extremely disconcerting to the person undergoing it. For in such cases a person might experience not only the phenomena just mentioned but also some of the (other) spontaneous "purifications" described in the literature of *hatha* yoga, for example, (1) snapping and popping sensations; (2) impulsion to assume strange bodily postures (*asanas* and *bandhas*); (3) fluctuations in the breath, involving both panting and cessation (*pranayama*); (4) violent convulsive contractions; (5) spontaneous orgasmic experiences; (6) a wide variety of bizarre involuntary movements (gestures, grimaces, hopping, dancing); and (7) spontaneous vocalizations (guttural sounds, roaring, humming). Phenomena such as these would have to be considered rare except in the case of people who have practiced *hatha* yoga (or the *kundalini* yoga of the Tantric tradition). Nevertheless, these phenomena, precisely in their strangeness and severity, present a powerful picture of how a sudden infusion of new life might affect a body that had long been repressed and energically dormant.

The "resurrection" of the body is at the same time a "resurrection" of the most bodily of the instincts: sexuality. The derepression of the body involves a release of energy from its genital organization. Psychic energy, which had been accessible primarily if not exclusively by means of sexual-genital arousal, is now permanently activated and begins being released from the sexual system without sexual-genital stimuli or stimulations. At first, this release is intermittent and has the distinct character of a sexual discharge, a discharge that, as just noted, can even produce spontaneous orgasmic experiences. In time, however, as the release of energy becomes more constant and the flow of energy reaches more of the body, the connection with the sexual system recedes into the background and what began, apparently, as an awakening of sexuality becomes an awakening of somatic experience generally: polymorphous sensuality. As more of the body is energized, the sexual system ceases defining the character of the awakening process and begins serving only as the point of release of an energy that is not itself specifically sexual in nature. In noting this gradual desexualization, however, the original point needs to be re-emphasized; namely, that, in the beginning, bodily awakening—at least when it occurs suddenly and powerfully—typically *does* have a distinctly sexual complexion or at least aspect. During regression in the service of transcendence, the awakening of the body typically is centered in an arousal of sexuality. Sexual feelings can arise spontaneously and in a manner that seems out of control.

The awakening of sexuality can be especially distressing to people whose moral training has had an antisexual bias. This is all the more true when antisexuality is rationalized in religious terms, as it usually is. For then sexuality and spirituality become irreconcilably opposed; any movement toward one is conceived as a movement away from the other. People of religious background for this reason can be devastated when, upon entering regression in the service of transcendence, they are importuned by sexual feelings and fantasies. This phenomenon is another example of John of the Cross's inverse law of spiritual development: An awakening of spirit can seem like the very opposite of a spiritual process. It can seem like an awakening of forbidden, even demoniacal, instinctuality.

We discussed John of the Cross's acknowledgment of these experiences in the last chapter. Many other striking examples can be found. Two such examples are, from the West, St. Catherine of Siena (1347–1380) and, from the East, Swami Muktananda (recently deceased). Evelyn Underhill offers the following account of Catherine's experience: "These irruptions from the subliminal region often take the form of evil visions, or of voices making coarse or sinful suggestions to the self. Thus St. Catherine of Siena . . . was tormented by visions of fiends, who filled her cell and 'with obscene words and gestures invited her to lust' " (1961, p. 392). And Muktananda (1978) reports that during his *kundalini* awakening he was visited by an apparition of a naked woman who made lascivious overtures and tried to entice him to violate his vow of chastity. The lewd and lascivious nature of these sexual experiences indicates not only an awakening of sexuality but also a strong antisexual bias and resistance to this awakening.

Concomitant with the awakening of sexuality is the unleashing of aggressive impulses. This unleashing, I suggest, is not the loosing of an aggressive drive in the sense of an inherently hostile or destructive force. Many critics of Freud's theory of aggression have argued that hostile or destructive aggressiveness is not innate but rather is the result of the frustration of a deeper "thrust" or assertion of life. Adopting this view, I suggest that aggression is not itself an instinctual drive but rather is a consequence of the dualistic negation of the spontaneity of nonegoic potentials. Under the regime of primal repression, nonegoic potentials are able to express themselves, if at all, only in opposition to a strong countercathectic inhibition. They are forced, that is, to assume an antagonistic character that they otherwise would not have. During the period of dualism, this antagonistic character of nonegoic potentials, like nonegoic potentials themselves, is for the most part unconscious. However, when primal repression is lifted and regression in the service of transcendence begins, this antagonistic character becomes shockingly evident to the ego. The ego experiences a violent upsurge of the repressed. Nonegoic potentials are released from constraints and assert themselves aggressively upon an object world that is perceived as "other." The violence of this regressive unleasing extends to all nonegoic potentials, including sexuality, which can at this point be infected with sadomasochistic feelings and images.

Redemptive versus Pathological Regression: On Distinguishing the Dark Night of Spirit from Psychosis

The account of regression in the service of transcendence just completed may in some respects sound like an account of psychosis, schizophrenia in particular. In severe instances regression in the service of transcendence is a psychotomimetic process. We need, then, to consider how regression in the service of transcendence differs from regression pure and simple, how redemptive regression differs from pathological regression.

Psychiatrist John Nelson (1990) has written an important book in which he carefully distinguishes between the symptomatologies of major psychotic conditions and those of transpersonal conditions that appear similar to psychosis. Drawing on my notion of regression in the service of transcendence and his own extensive clinical experience, Nelson notes the following differences between regression in the service of transcendence (RIST) and schizophrenia.

1. *Differences of onset.* Schizophrenia typically begins in the teens or twenties, whereas RIST is not firmly tied to any specific age category and frequently occurs at midlife or later. Moreover, RIST typically has a more clearly marked starting point than schizophrenia and is frequently precipitated by stressful life events such as the breakup of a relationship, losing a job, or childbirth,[4] or by intense practices such as yoga or meditation. Whereas schizophrenia typically follows a more protracted degenerative course, RIST is a phenomenon with more defined temporal boundaries and, in some cases, more recognizable occasions or triggering causes.
2. *Differences in affect.* People undergoing RIST experience intense affect, whether negative or positive. Dramatic highs and lows of feeling, from terror to occasional manic releases, occur during RIST, even though, as observed earlier, dread is the baseline affect. Such intensity of affect is in sharp contrast to schizophrenia,

which, as Nelson says, is characterized by "gray bleakness" and affect that is "shallow or incongruent with what the person is saying" (p. 248).

3. *Differences in insight.* People undergoing RIST experience profound self-insights, as deeply ingrained tendencies and hidden desires and fears are exposed to view. Many of these insights are unwelcome revelations that cause people undergoing RIST to experience remorse or guilt. The schizophrenic, in contrast, Nelson notes, rarely experiences insights such as these. Rather than achieving self-knowledge, the schizophrenic tends to fabricate delusions, to conjure up aberrant meanings that lend a false coherence to a disintegrating and chaotic experience. Many of the schizophrenic's delusions are paranoid and trigger a retreat from inner exploration. The person undergoing RIST on the other hand, however frightened, perseveres, as Nelson says, in "the defenseless inner exploration that is a hallmark of RIST" (p. 249).

4. *Differences in cognition and reality testing.* RIST, unlike schizophrenia, does not seriously affect secondary process or formal operational cognition and corresponding reality testing skills. The person afflicted with schizophrenia loses the ability to sustain secondary process cognition and succumbs to the magical thinking of primary process or preoperational cognition. And, concomitant with this deterioration in cognition, a deterioration in reality testing skills also occurs: The person afflicted with schizophrenia is frequently unable to distinguish between fantasy and reality. The person undergoing RIST, in contrast, suffers no significant impairment to secondary process cognition, even though, for this person, the creative process may have begun producing powerful symbolic images and even apparitions. Accordingly, the person undergoing RIST continues to be able to distinguish effectively between fantasy and reality. The person experiencing RIST is indeed in a strange new world, but this world is *known* to be strange. The person experiencing RIST is fascinated by the emerging numinous-nonegoic dimensions of experience. Exploration of these dimensions, as just noted, is a distinguishing feature of RIST.

5. *Differences in narrative significance.* RIST is an archetypal journey that can involve such universal themes as cataclysm, the end of the world, descent into the underworld, battle with dark forces (supernatural beings, beasts), search for miraculous treasure, engulfment by a primitive power, and the quest for redemption. Persons experiencing RIST tend to feel as if they are involved in a

process of collective significance. Persons suffering schizophrenia, on the other hand, are caught in an experience that tends to follow a private delusional script, a script full of merely personal persecutions, conspiracies, self-denigrations, or self-glorifications. Whereas RIST is a dark adventure rich in symbolic meanings of significance for all, schizophrenia is a frightening disintegration that engenders aberrant meanings in a desperate attempt to give sense to an experience that no longer makes sense. I do not mean to suggest that archetypal themes are absent from schizophrenia or that persons experiencing RIST do not succumb to deranged thinking. The point is rather that, in general, RIST has a more archetypal and universal significance, whereas schizophrenia unfolds in a more private delusional manner.

These points of difference indicate that RIST, although resembling psychosis in many ways, is not schizophrenia. Nor is it bipolar psychosis, even though RIST, and the period of regeneration in spirit that follows it, is subject to wild fluctuations of affect, from grim imploded feelings of dread, engulfment, and doom to wildly exploding feelings of intoxication and ecstasy. RIST, although responsible for bizarre altered states of consciousness, is not a process that inflicts serious injury upon the ego. Ego functions are not impaired, and the ego is not forced to retreat into secret realms or driven to behave in "crazy" or self-destructive ways. RIST is a process that ruthlessly but *noninjuriously* exposes the ego to reactivated nonegoic potentials. Nakedly exposed to these potentials, the ego is overwhelmed (disempowered, entranced, awed, engulfed, dissolved), to be sure; but it is not irreparably harmed or destroyed. The ego undergoing RIST possesses sufficient strength and discernment to weather the "return of the repressed" and, ultimately, find the redemption that is the implicit *telos* of the dark night of spirit.

REGENERATION IN SPIRIT

Regression in the service of transcendence can lead to many dire experiences that leave the ego with a sense that it is lost or perhaps on the verge of annihilation. The ego endures these experiences and survives. After each such experience, however, the ego feels as if less of its old self remains. For these experiences gradually erode the ego's residual sense of independent existence. They confront the ego with its powerlessness before nonegoic influences and force the ego to see not only its dependence upon but also its relatedness to non-egoic life. This process of confronting and yielding to the nonegoic unfolds toward a turning point at which the ego realizes that non-egoic life is not an alien "other," as the ego had thought, but rather is an "other" that is also "self." At this point the ego realizes that the nonegoic core is not an abyss, as previously it had seemed, but rather is the ego's own ultimate source. In achieving this realization, the ego sees that its battle against nonegoic potentials cannot succeed and must come to a halt because this battle is literally self-defeating: It is a battle waged by the ego against a deeper part of itself. In arriving at this insight, then, the ego begins to experience nonegoic potentials in a new, positive light. The ego ceases experiencing nonegoic potentials only as ominous forces of a dark underworld and begins experiencing them as enlivening and transporting spontaneities arising from an inner creative source.

The emergence of the new perspective just described marks a reversal in the ego's ambivalence toward nonegoic life. This ambivalence shifts from a predominantly negative to a predominantly positive weighting. The ego continues to be unnerved and overawed by nonegoic potentials, and the ego still suffers regressive relapses in its relation to the nonegoic core of the psyche. Nevertheless, the ego's experience of nonegoic life now becomes more positive than negative. Accordingly, the experiences distinctive of regression in the service of transcendence begin now to give way to positive correlates: negative object relations give way to positive object relations, dread gives way to spiritual ardor (intoxication, ravishment), strangeness gives way to enchantment, trance to transport, engulfment to ecstasy, "resurrection" of the body to "reincarnation" of the ego, derepression of the instincts to integration of the instincts, and tormenting fantasies to guiding visions.

Reversal of Ambivalence and the Reawakening of the Positive Side of Early Childhood Object Relations

The reversal from negatively weighted to positively weighted ambivalence is reflected in a corresponding reversal from predominantly negative to predominantly positive relations with others. This latter reversal is evident in three chief ways: (1) in a shift from a sense of being vulnerable and exposed before others to a sense of needing to disclose oneself to others; (2) in a shift from cynicism about others as "bad objects" to a newfound faith in others as "good objects"; and (3) in a shift from the negative to the positive side of early childhood object relations, that is, in a shift from negative oedipal and preoedipal projections to positive oedipal and preoedipal projections.

The new perspective that allows the ego to see the nonegoic core in a positive light also motivates the ego to give expression to this core and thereby to allow this most intimate part of itself to be seen by others. The ego's new perspective thus changes what had seemed to be a weakness (exposure) into a strength (openness, transparency). The ego no longer feels defenselessly exposed to the gaze of other people, and what hitherto was a struggle against such exposure now becomes a struggle for deep and authentic self-disclosure. This fundamental shift in existential posture is of course at first tentative and halting. The ego continues to be afraid, both of its own depths and of being seen by others. The ego, however, grows in courage and eventually becomes able to embrace its whole self and to allow its whole self to be seen by others.

In being able to see itself in a new, positive light, the ego is also able to see others in a new, positive light. The ego of course still sees that others, or most others, possess dark depths hidden beneath the ego identities they present to the world. In seeing this, however, the ego is no longer cynical about others—although, as we shall see later, the ego is prone to experience "healthy" disappointments in a few select others. Rather than being cynical, the ego now understands that dark depths and inauthentic ego identities are inescapable realities for souls that, stunted by primal repression and primal alienation, are divided against themselves and others. The ego at this point is therefore no longer disillusioned of others and even begins to experience a new faith in others. For the ego now sees that people "know not what they do." Moreover, the ego now sees that behind the surface of ego identity and at the center of the repressed depths of the soul there lies a redeemable core, a higher self—a self of spontaneity and generosity, outgoingness and outreachingness—that needs to be elicited into activity and induced to grow.

The ego has just found this self in itself and now begins to see it in others. For the most part the ego sees this self in others only as a negated possibility of which others are at once unconscious and deeply afraid. But the ego also sees this self in a few others—many more than it had anticipated—as a half-born or fully actualized and integrated reality. And in general the ego at this point is disposed to view other people primarily in terms of this higher self. The ego is accepting of those who have repressed this self in themselves and who, consequently, are prone to strike out against this self in others, for the ego understands the fears behind these denials. And the ego rejoices in those in whom this self is emerging or has come to full bloom, for these people, the ego now understands, are examplars of our highest humanity.

If during regression in the service of transcendence, the ego tends to see only the worst in people; during regeneration in spirit, it tends, in equal but opposite fashion, to see only the best in people. It tends to discount shortcomings and exaggerate what is good in people. In focusing on the higher self, the ego is prone to idealize those in whom this self has emerged, to see them as perfect "good objects," as people who are more understanding and compassionate than they really are. In doing this, the ego experiences a shift from the negative to the positive side of early childhood object relations and begins to look up to a few select people as persons in whom positive oedipal and preoedipal qualities are perfectly realized. The ego sees these persons as being perfectly understanding and "forgiving" (positive oedipal qualities) and perfectly kind and compassionate (positive preoedipal qualities).

This tendency toward one-sided idealization renders the ego susceptible to devaluing those it has idealized, because these select "perfect" others inevitably reveal their "humanness." This swing from idealization to devaluation, however, is not extreme; it is no longer the all-or-nothing swing of preoedipal or borderline splitting. It is rather a swing that brings the ego closer to equilibrium: a new and higher object constancy. The person undergoing regeneration in spirit is prone to exaggerate the good it sees in others but is not devastated when people presumed to be perfect are seen to be flawed. To see imperfections in idealized others is at this point more a matter of achieving realistic insight than suffering disillusionment. It is a matter of learning that spiritually evolved and gifted people are highly fallible, that they are much less godlike and much more human than had been realized.

Intoxication, Tearful Rejoicing, and Ravishment

If dread is the distinctive affective expression of regression in the service of transcendence, states of spiritual excess such as intoxication, tearful rejoicing, and ravishment are the distinctive affective expressions of regeneration in spirit. Dread is not confined to regression in the service of transcendence; it continues into regeneration in spirit. And states of spiritual excess begin long before regeneration in spirit. They begin, typically, with the "rupture of planes" that triggers initial awakening; and they continue, albeit with decreasing frequency, during regression in the service of transcendence. If, however, dread and states of spiritual excess are not confined within definite developmental boundaries, they are nonetheless representative of specific developmental stages, regression in the service of transcendence and regeneration in spirit, respectively. Accordingly, the transition from regression to regeneration is a turning point after which dread becomes the exception rather than the rule and states of spiritual excess become the rule rather than the exception.

States of spiritual excess are of three main types: intoxication, tearful rejoicing, and ravishment. Contrary to experiences like dread, trance, and engulfment, these states indicate that numinous power is working primarily *within* the ego (i.e., infusively) rather than *upon* the ego from the outside (i.e., gravitationally or cathectically). Intoxication, tearful rejoicing, and ravishment indicate that numinous power is surging upwardly from the nonegoic sphere into the sphere of consciousness, affecting the ego immediately and internally. These states also indicate that numinous power is affecting the ego with an intensity that the ego is unable fully to accommodate. They are states of spiritual overfullness. They are not only intensely positive but violently positive states.

Spiritual intoxication, obviously, is a state of euphoria, of wildly effusive well-being. It is a condition that results from a sudden infusion of numinous energy into consciousness. This potent energy supercharges the egoic system, amplifying and accelerating the ego's experience to uncontrollable levels. The supercharging of the egoic system sometimes leads to phenomena such as dancing, shouting, and glossolalia; and it sometimes leads not only to intense effusion but also to heated, manic confusion. In general, states of spiritual intoxication involve both infusion and at least some degree of disconcertion. They affect the ego violently, throwing it, to some degree, into disarray.

Tearful rejoicing is similar to intoxication in reflecting a violent inflowing and outpouring of numinous energy. Tearful rejoicing, however, is in important respects the opposite of intoxication. For whereas intoxication is heated and manic in character, tearful rejoicing is "wet" and leads to states of calm. Intoxication is a form of *pneumatic* infusion; it inflates the ego, precipitating expansive and excited states of mind. Tearful rejoicing in contrast is a form of *aqueous* infusion; it bathes the ego in currents of energy, causing the ego to cry in gratitude and feel deeply at peace. Aqueous infusion, which, during regression in the service of transcendence, was experienced in an ominous way as flooding, is here experienced in a profoundly positive way as "waters of grace." The ego, bathed in these waters, experiences feelings of gratitude and reverence and is soothed to the core of its being. Intoxication and tearful rejoicing, as opposites, frequently alternate during regeneration in spirit, intoxication wildly energizing the soul and tearful rejoicing "putting out the flames" and returning the soul to a "moist" sobriety.

Ravishment also reflects a violent infusive movement of numinous power. The major way in which ravishment differs from intoxication and tearful rejoicing is that, whereas the latter two states involve intense outpourings of affect, ravishment involves a sense of being inwardly wounded, penetrated, or pierced. To be ravished by numinous power is to "violated" by it in a way that is experienced in an exquisitely painful-pleasurable way. The psychic opening through which numinous power enters consciousness is here still very much a wound, but it is now a wound not only of agony but also of delicious pleasure. The ego that is ravished is experiencing the pains of spiritual labor. It undergoes convulsions, contractions, and painful-pleasurable infusions that cause it to wince and swoon. In being ravished, the ego feels that it is being penetrated in an excruciating yet also delectable way.

St. John of the Cross and St. Teresa of Avila offer many accounts of such "fiery darts of love" or "wounds of love." For example, in *The Living Flame of Love*, John of the Cross says: "And then in this cauterization, when the soul is transpierced with that dart, the flame gushes forth fiercely and with a sudden ascent, like the fire in a furnace or an oven when someone uses a poker or bellows to stir and excite it. And being wounded by this fiery dart, the soul feels the wound with unsurpassable delight. Besides being fully stirred in great sweetness . . . , it is aware of the delicate wound . . . in the heart of the pierced soul" (1991b, p. 661). And in *The Interior Castle*, St. Teresa says: "It [the soul] feels that it is wounded in the most exquisite way, but it doesn't learn how or by whom it was wounded. It knows clearly that the wound is something precious, and it would never want to be cured" (1980, p. 367). In their various descriptions of the wound of love, St. John of the Cross and St. Teresa make it clear that this wound burns or bleeds in an excruciating and yet highly pleasing way. The soul experiences an unbearable pain that is at the same time an irresistible and transfiguring pleasure. This is ravishment.

In being states of excess, intoxication, tearful rejoicing, and ravishment are states in which the ego is overfull with or overcome by numinous energy. Intoxication is a state in which the ego is energically overcharged; tearful rejoicing is a state in which the ego is swept away by feelings of grateful joy; and ravishment is a state in which the ego is penetrated by a power that is "too much." All of these states indicate that the ego is not yet accustomed to numinous energy and is therefore susceptible to being disconcerted, impassioned, or wounded by the influx of this energy. These states, therefore, although dramatic and intensely pleasurable, are symptoms of spiritual immaturity. St. Teresa stresses this point in *The Interior Castle* (Seventh Mansions, chapter 3), where she states that the soul that has arrived at final union with the divine ceases experiencing dramatic affective fluctuations and begins experiencing the peace of spiritual wholeness.

As regeneration in spirit approaches the ideal of transegoic integration, then, states of intoxication, tearful rejoicing, and ravishment begin to subside. They do so not because the ego is any less empowered by numinous energy or any less inspired or enriched by nonegoic potentials, but rather because the ego, in becoming harmoniously integrated with these sources of transegoic life, ceases being overfilled with or overcome by them. Ravishment subsides, as we shall see, because it gradually loses its violence and is transmuted into bliss. And intoxication and tearful rejoicing subside because they gradually fuse into a single, stable experience: the experience of radiant serenity or beaming gratitude, the feeling of blessedness.

Enchantment

The transition from regression in the service of transcendence to regeneration in spirit is registered in a shift in the general atmosphere of the world: the world changes from being strange to being enchanted. The world loses its surreal cast and takes on a magical quality that, although still reflecting ambivalence on the part of the ego, reflects an ambivalence that now is more positively than negatively charged.

Both the strange world of regression in the service of transcendence and the enchanted world of regeneration in spirit are worlds that, pervaded by numinous power, are fascinating and mysterious. However, whereas the strange world is fascinating and mysterious in a haunted-dreadful way, the enchanted world is fascinating and mysterious in either an amazing-exhilarating way (involving intoxication) or an awesome-beatific way (involving tearful rejoicing). The enchanted world is full of magical possibilities rather than ominous forces. Like the strange world, the enchanted world is alive with power and is therefore superreal. And like the strange world, the power that animates the world is numinous and "other," full of mystery. Unlike the strange world, however, the enchanted world is no longer surreal. In being animated by numinous power, the enchanted world is not made eerie and menacing; it is transfigured by spirit rather than haunted by ghosts.

The enchanted world, though, is still a world that reflects ambivalence. It is still mysterious and "other," even if in a way that evokes exhilaration or wonderment rather than dread. The ego, therefore, is not at home in the enchanted world. The ego's ambivalence still shows forth in a shudder before the numinous. This shudder, it should be noted, is now much less frequently the shudder of dread, discussed earlier. It is rather a shudder in response to the marvel or majesty, the splendor or sublimity, the sacred intensity or spiritual grandeur of the world. It is either an irrepressible vocal shaking or trembling associated with amazement or a speechless shiver associated with reverent humility and gratitude. Although the ego is no longer seriously unnerved by the world, neither is it completely in harmony with it. The ego still faces an immense and incomprehensible power that captivates, intoxicates, overawes, ravishes, and dissolves the ego. The ego's ambivalence becomes increasingly positive and decreasingly negative as regeneration in spirit unfolds toward transegoic integration; nevertheless, some degree of negativity—a steadily diminishing degree—remains throughout the regenerative period. The enchanted world is increasingly resplendent and hallowed, decreasingly dark and haunted; nevertheless, some degree of darkness and hauntedness remains until the work of regeneration is finished.

Transport and Ecstasy

To this point we have seen that the transition from regression in the service of transcendence to regeneration in spirit is marked by the following changes: (1) negative childhood object relations give way to positive childhood object relations, (2) dread gives way to states of spiritual excess, and (3) strangeness gives way to enchantment. To these changes we can now add that trance and engulfment give way to transport and ecstasy.

Like spiritual intoxication, to which they are closely related, transport and ecstasy are forms of wild pneumatic infusion. With transport, the ego is internally volatilized and inflated by numinous power. It is inwardly energized in a way that causes its self-boundaries to expand dramatically. Ecstasy is the final result of transport, for as the ego's boundaries expand, they also become increasingly tenuous until they finally vaporize in a state of deindividuated dynamic boundlessness. This state of boundlessness instantiates the literal meaning of the term *ecstasy:* to stand outside oneself. Transport and ecstasy are typically accompanied by intoxication as affective component and intermixed with tearful rejoicing as affective complement. Transport and ecstasy, however, are conceptually distinct from these (and other) numinous feeling states in that they convey the specific effects that infusively active numinous power can have on the ego's self-boundaries.

Ecstasy can be described as a condition, or perhaps event, of explosive ego dissolution, as distinguished from the implosive ego absorption of engulfment. Engulfment, if we remember, is an absorbed state that is a culminating effect of numinous power acting gravitationally or cathectically upon the ego: the ego is entranced, captivated, and finally implosively consumed by numinous power. In contrast, ecstasy is an infused state that is a culminating effect of numinous power acting pneumatically within the ego: the ego is energized, inflated, and finally explosively dissolved by numinous power. Both ecstasy and engulfment are states without ego boundaries and therefore without subject-object or self-other divisions. However, whereas engulfment eliminates ego boundaries by compressing them to the collapsing point, ecstasy eliminates ego boundaries by inflating them to the bursting point. Both engulfment and ecstasy are egoless states. However, whereas engulfment is an egoless state that is condensed, inert, and vacant, ecstasy is an egoless state that is expansive, wildly active, and overflowing.

Although ecstasy is a "peak experience," it, like intoxication, tearful rejoicing, and ravishment, is symptomatic of spiritual immaturity. Ecstasy indicates that the ego is not fully adjusted to the infusive movement of spiritual energy, which acts upon the ego in a way that violently dissolves its boundaries. The ego swooning in ecstasy is an ego still undergoing the spiritual inbirthing process, an ego not yet fully integrated with the nonegoic core of the psyche and not yet fully attuned to the spiritual power that emanates from that core. We have already noted that St. Teresa of Avila held that all intense spiritual experiences of an episodic sort, including transports and ecstasies, wane as the ego approaches full spiritual union or integration. This view is generally acknowledged, albeit in widely varying idioms, in contemplative literature throughout the world. Ecstatic states are generally considered states of preliminary, unstable infusion. Progress in contemplation, then, leads to progressively more composed infused states, states that are not only expansively infused but also poisedly absorbed. As Mircea Eliade (1969) observed, such states of infused absorption are states of *enstasy* rather than ecstasy. I shall discuss mature contemplation or enstasy in chapter 11.

Vision

The images produced during regeneration in spirit, in keeping with the general character of the stage, are decreasingly negative and increasingly positive. They are decreasingly fantasies of a disturbing or despairing sort (e.g., fantasies of "forbidden" sexuality or aggression or of abandonment, perdition, or psychosis) and are increasingly fantasies of a miraculous or redemptive sort (e.g., fantasies of divine intercession, saintly saviors, angels, spiritual transformation, Edenic or celestial perfection, apotheosis). The negative fantasies produced during regression in the service of transcendence magnify the predominantly negative experiences of that period, exaggerating those experiences into images of unmitigated evil, disintegration, or damnation. Working in the same manner but in the opposite direction, the positive fantasies produced during regeneration in spirit magnify the predominantly positive experiences of this period, exaggerating these experiences into images of unqualified goodness, redemption, or salvation. Given the ego's continuing ambivalence during regeneration in spirit, distressing negative fantasies still occur. They occur, however, with decreasing frequency. During regeneration in spirit, the ego tends to be witness more to fantasies that are one-sidedly positive than to fantasies that are one-sidedly negative.

During regression in the service of transcendence, as noted earlier, the creative imagination sometimes produces fantasies sufficiently realistic to possess the status of apparitions. Imaginal production of this sort continues during regeneration in spirit. During regeneration in spirit, however, the apparitions produced are characteristically embodiments of magical events and angelic beings rather than, as was more usually the case during regression in the service of transcendence, catastrophic events and demoniacal beings. That is, apparitions that emerge during regeneration in spirit are more often inspiring visions than menacing hallucinations. Hallucinations are symptomatic of deep psychic injury, even if the injury is ultimately a pathology in the service of transcendence. Visions on the other hand are indicative of deep regenerative healing. Visions indicate that the ego's spiritual wound is in the process of being mended.

They indicate that this wound is in the process, not of being closed, but rather of being transformed into a channel of creativity, grace, and intimacy.

"Reincarnation" of the Ego and Integration of the Instincts

The transition from regression in the service of transcendence to regeneration in spirit changes the way in which the ego experiences the awakening of the body. Coinciding with the more general revaluation that marks this transition, the ego's experience of the body undergoes a reversal in polarity from negative to positive. The awakening sensations and alterations of the body begin at this point to be more inviting than frightening, and correspondingly the ego begins to relate to the body more as its own organic self than as an "object" or "thing" that is undergoing an alarming recrudescence. The ego, having resisted the "resurrection" of the body, begins at this point to yield to its own "reincarnation." The ego returns to polymorphously sensual life.

As an embedded somatic structure, primal repression–primal alienation consists of a multitude of constrictions and armors. These layers of rigidity, which make up the defensive basis of the mental-egoic system, are challenged by upwelling energy when the ego undergoes regression in the service of transcendence. Much of regression in the service of transcendence is occupied with the work of breaking through this system of barriers. The energy rising from the nonegoic core is arrested at a point of obstruction and accumulates there until the obstruction is dissolved. The energy then breaks free and ascends to the next point of obstruction, accumulating there until that obstruction is dissolved, and so on. The dissolution of somatic barriers in this fashion is frequently experienced as a discharge of tension and energy and as a corresponding sensitization of the body area that had been blocked. The person undergoing this process thus experiences a progressive opening and enlivening of the body, beginning, typically, in the lower abdominal area and moving upward through the torso and chest cavity to the shoulders, the back of the neck, and the ears.

The character of this process changes as it unfolds. In the beginning, as we learned earlier, it seems as if the body is returning from the dead. As the process moves further along its course, however—that is, as more of the body is unblocked and animated and as the ego becomes increasingly accustomed to the infusive movement of energy—it seems less and less as if the body is being "resurrected" and more and more as if the ego is being "reincarnated." The alien otherness of the process gradually disappears and the ego begins to feel more at home in the body. As the body is gradually awakened, the ego gradually returns to the body and polymorphously sensual life. The ego is not fully "reincarnated" until the work of regeneration in spirit is finished. Nevertheless, the ego progressively reenters the body and experiences it less and less as "object" and more and more as "self."

Concomitant with this shift from "resurrection" to "reincarnation" is a shift from a violent unleashing of the instincts to an appreciative acceptance of the instincts as functional and enriching dimensions of bodily life. Sexuality, for example, which is sometimes alarmingly accentuated during the body's original awakening, gradually recedes from the forefront of attention as the awakening process unfolds. The progressive unblocking and animation of the body by the energy released from the sexual system makes this energy, in the ego's experience, increasingly an energy of somatic experience generally and decreasingly an energy of sexual experience in particular. Sexuality continues to color experience in a wide variety of ways, but it loses much of its salience and imperative force. Sexuality becomes one mode of nonegoic experience among others, a mode that, true to the general character of regeneration in spirit, gradually loses its alien and threatening aspect and is gradually owned by the ego as an integral dimension of self. In this way the "reincarnation" of the ego is at the same time an acceptance by the ego of its inherent sexuality.

And it is an acceptance by the ego of nonegoic life generally, the spontaneous expressions of which begin now to be embraced by the ego as its own self-expressions. Instead of continuing to struggle against nonegoic potentials, the ego now begins to struggle against its resistance to these potentials. Correspondingly, these potentials, instead of asserting themselves violently against the ego and aggressively against the world, now begin to manifest themselves in ways that empower the ego and constructively engage the world. The "aggressive drive" in this way shows itself to be simply the uninhibited spontaneity of the nonegoic sources of life. It shows itself to be simply the will to life, which the ego now increasingly accepts as its own will.

CONCLUSION

Regression in the service of transcendence is a return to origins that brings the ego back into intimate contact with both the nonegoic core of the psyche and other people. This return to origins is a genuinely regressive process in that it involves, to some degree, a disempowerment of the ego, a rending of the egoic system, and a subordination of the ego to overpowering influences. If, however, regression in the service of transcendence is a genuinely regressive process, it is not for that reason a merely regressive process. Regression in the service of transcendence is not just a backward developmental movement. It is rather a return to origins that reopens the ego to depth-psychological resources and interpersonal possibilities that the ego had long ago denied and left behind. Accordingly, once the ego has weathered the regressive return to origins, it begins to tap into the resources and realize the possibilities to which it has been reopened, and it begins thereby to be regeneratively transformed. This transition from regression to regeneration is the upward turn of the developmental spiral that leads ultimately to transegoic integration.

The spiral path passes through dangerous terrain. Regression in the service of transcendence can abort into regression pure and simple. The downward movement of the spiral, to use Ken Wilber's (1982) term, can collapse into a simple U-turn to origins, a mere retrogression to the preegoic.[5] This danger inherent to the path of transcendence is real and not to be taken lightly. It is, however, as we shall see in the next chapter, a danger that may be greater for some people than for others. In this chapter I have described regression in the service of transcendence and regeneration in spirit in ideal-typical terms, assuming that regression in the service of transcendence is radical, regressing the ego all the way to its origins, and that regeneration in spirit is thoroughgoing, leading to complete egoic-nonegoic, self-other integration. The ideal-typical, however, is not the usual. More usually, regression in the service of transcendence is not as radical as I have described it nor regeneration in spirit as thoroughgoing. Moreover, some people are more favorably disposed or prepared for the spiral journey and therefore are not challenged as severely as others. These qualifications acknowledged, however, it remains true that the spiral journey is an adventure into numinous realms that puts the ego at significant risk. It is a journey without guarantee of safe passage.

10

Gender and Transcendence

This chapter returns to the topic of gender. Having explored the topic of gender development in early childhood in chapter 3, I shall in this chapter turn to the topic of gender and transcendence. To prepare for the discussion in this chapter, I shall begin by briefly summarizing the main conclusions of chapter 3.

The analysis in chapter 3 arrived at the following five conclusions:

1. *The fact that, historically, the primary preoedipal caregiver has been female and the primary oedipal authority male has had consequences that are significantly different for boys and girls.* Being opposite in gender to the preoedipal mother leads boys strongly to dissociate themselves from the mother and the nonegoic potentials and intimate relationship she represents. And being the same gender as the oedipal father leads boys directly to identify with the father and the ego functions and independence he represents. In contrast, being the same gender as the preoedipal mother leads girls to remain more open to the mother and the nonegoic potentials and intimate relationship she represents. And being opposite in gender to the oedipal father leads girls to relate more indirectly and ambiv-

alently to the father and the ego functions and independence he represents. In these ways, gender asymmetries during preoedipal and oedipal development lead to very real gender differences in later life. In particular, gender asymmetries in early childhood predispose men to be more one-sidedly committed to ego functions and independence and more closed to nonegoic potentials and intimate relationship than women. And these asymmetries predispose women to be more open to nonegoic potentials and intimate relationship and more conflictually related to ego functions and independence than men.

2. *Gender differences with respect to ego functions and independence (EFI) and nonegoic potentials and relationship (NPR) are narrow rather than wide.* The gender differences just described are narrow rather than wide in the sense that they are relative differences based on greater corresponding similarities. As indicated in figure 3.1 (p. 88), the primary such similarity is that both women and men are situated on the EFI side of the NPR-EFI axis. The experience of both women and men is based on primal repression and primal alienation and, correspondingly, on egoic-nonegoic and self-other dualism. Both women and men are primarily committed to ego functions and independence and to a significant extent closed to nonegoic potentials and intimate relationship. For the reasons stated under conclusion 1, this is more true of men than women. Nevertheless, it is true of both women and men. The fact that men are situated closer to the EFI endpoint of the NPR-EFI axis than women and that women are situated closer to the NPR endpoint of the axis than men does not imply that women are situated on the NPR side of the axis. The fact that person A is more dominantly right-handed than person B does not imply that person B is left-handed.

3. *Gender differences on the NPR-EFI axis, although narrow rather than wide, are nonetheless perceived as if they were wide rather than narrow.* Because women are situated farther from the EFI endpoint of the NPR-EFI axis than men, women tend to perceive men as representing the EFI endpoint of the axis; and because men are situated farther from the NPR endpoint of the NPR-EFI axis than women, men tend to perceive women as representing the NPR endpoint of the axis. These perceptions are exaggerated, because both genders have primary positions on the NPR-EFI axis that are between rather than at the endpoints of the axis. Women's perception of men is exaggerated in the EFI direction; women, for example, see men as being more logical, assertive, and self-possessed than they

really are. And men's perception of women is exaggerated in the NPR direction; men, for example, see women as being more feeling oriented, sensitive, and disposed to relationship than they really are. Women and men, that is, are prone to misperceive their narrow differences as if they were wide.

4. *The misperception of narrow differences as wide involves a greater misperception of women than of men.* Because, under dualism, both women and men are on the EFI side of the NPR-EFI axis, the projection of women to the NPR endpoint of the axis is more of a distortion than is the projection of men to the EFI endpoint of the axis. Women's misperception of men exaggerates their EFI predominance. In contrast, men's misperception of women fails altogether to recognize their EFI predominance and assigns them complete NPR one-sidedness instead.

5. *The misperception of narrow differences as wide accurately reflects gender roles in a patriarchal society.* Although women's and men's perceptions of each other do not accurately reflect their actual locations on the NPR-EFI axis, they do accurately reflect the *social organization* of the genders. Patriarchal society not only perceives but also treats the genders as if their differences were wide rather than narrow. Men are not only perceived but also expected to behave as if they embodied the EFI endpoint of the NPR-EFI axis; and women are not only perceived but also expected to behave as if they embodied the NPR endpoint of the axis. Men are considered masculine to the extent that they are logical, assertive, and self-possessed; women are considered feminine to the extent that they are feeling oriented, sensitive, and disposed to relationship.

These five points are the basis of important gender differences throughout the period of dualism. They also are the basis of differences in women's and men's spiritual development. In this chapter I shall apply these points to the stages of transcendence and attempt to show that in each of these stages women and men follow distinctively different paths. As in chapter 3, the hypotheses set forth in this chapter are meant to apply to the genders only as groups or collectives; no inferences can be drawn about the experiences of individual women or men.

EMPOWERMENT VERSUS WITHDRAWAL

The notion that the spiritual journey involves a "dying to the world" or dark night of the senses, a disempowerment of the ego leading to detachment and withdrawal, has met with criticism from some feminists. Demaris Wehr (1987), for example, criticizes Jung by arguing that a period of withdrawal or "annihilation" of the ego is more characteristic of and advantageous to men than women. She says:

> Men whose need for control and domination is reinforced by patriarchy, who have experienced the ego's "mastery," probably do need to recognize the illusory, dangerous, as well as finally disappointing, nature of ego control. . . . "Annihilation of the ego" may open the way to that recognition. For many women, however, Jung advocates by this process their "annihilating" something they may not even have. Or if they have it, it may be so wounded as to need building-up, not "annihilation." . . . [Jung's] term "annihilation" comes close to reinforcing the self-abnegation in which women already engage to their detriment. (pp. 101–102)

Lack of power and exclusion from the world of public life have been forced on women by patriarchy. For this reason, according to Wehr and many others, what women need is ego empowerment and EFI expression in the world rather than ego disempowerment ("annihilation") and withdrawal from the world. In this view, disempowerment and withdrawal would only increase the detrimental self-denial already expected of women.

The conclusions just summarized support this view, but with a qualification. They support the view by indicating that developmentally acquired narrow differences, socially magnified as wide differences, have been used to rationalize restrictions upon women's participation in public life. They support the view in that they indicate that women have been put at a double (developmental and social) disadvantage in EFI expression. Accordingly, assuming that ego empowerment and full EFI expression are realistically possible for women—as they now increasingly are—it follows, just as Wehr argues, that women are not well advised to renounce an ego they have not yet had a chance fully to express and therefore develop. On the contrary, it follows that women's interest lies in pursuing ego empowerment and full EFI expression as priorities of their developmental process. Exponents of liberal feminism have stressed this point for a long time.

If women's interest lies in pursuing full EFI expression, that does not mean that women should forgo or avoid the night of the senses. All it means is that, when conditions allow, women's interest lies in seeking full EFI expression prior to or on the way to this initial stage of ego transcendence. Conditions, of course, have not always favored EFI expression for women. Throughout most of history women's disadvantage in EFI expression has been an incontestable reality. Women have been confined to the private sphere of caregiving while men alone have been encouraged to enter the public sphere of EFI expression. These constraints upon their egos, however, have not kept women from proceeding to the stages of transcendence. Throughout most of history, that is, women have had no choice but to withdraw from the world and "annihilate" (i.e., disengage or detach from) their egos without first having had a chance fully to participate in the world and thereby fully to express and develop their egos. To the extent that, presently, ego empowerment prior to ego transcendence is possible for women, Wehr is right in advocating ego empowerment and full EFI expression as immediate developmental goals for women. Ego transcendence, however, is not only possible but also desirable even when, socially and politically, ego empowerment is not a realistic option. In the ensuing discussion I shall assume, true to the contemporary context, that full EFI expression is possible for women and is therefore a developmental priority for women who have deferred such expression by giving themselves to traditional roles.

A point sometimes made by critics of liberal feminism is that women, in pursuing empowerment in "man's world," achieve not only equality with men but also similarity to men. They achieve not only equality with men in EFI expression but also similarity to men in degree of EFI-over-NPR predominance. Catherine Keller (1986) has argued against this view, maintaining that women can pursue empowerment and EFI expression without at the same time sacrificing their relational (NPR) capacities. She says:

> Women . . . are far less likely to have eradicated the sense of connection to others, nature and self which men seek to regain in later life. Yet it would be ludicrous to infer—as the complementary logic of the scheme might imply—that therefore women should develop masculine, matricidal egos as our second-half chore of individuation. Of course such logic may seem a propos when women, having raised families or otherwise given themselves to purely relational tasks in their earlier life, go about developing professional skills or asserting newfound strengths—but why submit this process, itself delayed

only by patriarchal social order, to the metaphors of masculine matriphobia? Would not this only pit women, Athena-style, against our deep Self? (1986, p. 116)

Keller recognizes the risk of "masculinization," the risk of becoming Athena-style women in a man's world. She stresses, however, that this risk is only a risk and, therefore, that women who have given themselves to traditional roles *can* enter the public arena and develop EFI skills and strengths without becoming like men in doing so.

Keller makes an important point in stating that women can overcome their EFI disadvantages without thereby sacrificing their greater NPR capacities. This point made, however, it does not follow, as Keller suggests it does, that women can realistically expect to develop worldly strengths and *deepen* relational capacities at the same time. For under conditions of dualism, it is very difficult to move in both EFI and NPR directions at once. Moreover, at the present time, movement into the world is for many women inseparably bound up with a struggle against traditional gender roles and the (negatively defined) NPR capacities associated with those roles. At present, many women need to liberate themselves from patriarchally dictated modes of relating and caring as part of their movement toward worldly empowerment. Again, as Keller explains, this movement toward empowerment does not require women to *sacrifice* their greater NPR capacities. It does, however, sometimes require women to put these capacities on hold while they are freeing themselves from the patriarchal definition of women's role and attempting to establish themselves in the world. Frequently, it is only after women have accomplished the double task of liberation and empowerment that they can return to their NPR capacities and experience them in a new, revalued way, namely, as native strengths rather than as male-defined weaknesses of female personhood.

To state this point in a dramatic way, we can say that women sometimes need to catch up with men (EFI) in order later to reclaim their lead on men (NPR). Because men possess a narrow EFI advantage over women, an advantage that is exaggerated by social norms and practices, women sometimes need to assert themselves in the EFI direction as a first priority in their midlife transition. Women's interest lies in asserting themselves in this manner even if doing so requires them to put NPR capacities temporarily on hold. For once women have achieved full EFI expression and thereby fulfilled their ego needs, they are able to return to the NPR capacities they had put on hold. Moreover, because women possess a narrow NPR advantage over men, an advantage that is widened by their experience as wives and mothers, it follows that, in returning to NPR capacities, women reclaim a *lead* on men in NPR development. If men have an advantage over women in ego development, women have an advantage over men in ego transcendence. Correspondingly, if women have had to follow men's lead in ego development, men will have to follow women's lead in ego transcendence.

As women are catching up with men on the EFI side of the NPR-EFI axis, men are already beginning to move away from the EFI side of the axis toward the NPR side. Having already fulfilled themselves as egos in the world, men, at midlife, begin to experience disillusionment and begin the process of withdrawal from the world. At this point, men and women are headed in opposite directions. Women are empowering and asserting themselves in the world, frequently postponing further NPR development; men are suffering disempowerment and withdrawal from the world, moving toward an eventual encounter with deep NPR realms. Women are breaking free from domestic "captivity" and moving into the light of the world; men are leaving the world and entering the dark nights of the senses and spirit. Women are experiencing the satisfactions of ego fulfillment; men are undergoing ego disempowerment and the initial difficulties of ego transcendence. Women at this point, we can say, are attempting to achieve something men have already achieved and are leaving behind. By all appearances, this puts men ahead of women on the developmental path.

It does not take long, however, for these appearances to change. For once women have satisfied their ego needs, they too are susceptible to disillusionment, withdrawal, and eventual reencounter with deep NPR realms. Because women, like men, are committed to EFI-dominant dualism, they too are subject to the developmental processes that right dualistic imbalances and reopen the ego to what dualism represses. Moreover, in being subject to these processes, women, I suggest, have an advantage in tending to suffer them less severely and for a shorter period of time than men do. Because women are less EFI dominant and more NPR receptive than men, that is, because women possess a narrow NPR advantage over men, women's movement of withdrawal from the EFI world and return to NPR realms is a relatively easier and shorter transition than is men's. Accordingly, although women, under contemporary conditions, may begin the movement of transcendence later than men, they usually overtake men somewhere in the course of this movement. Men may begin the movement of transcendence sooner than women, but they begin this movement from a point that is farther from the goal. Men, I suggest, have a harder time and take a longer time in "dying" to worldly selfhood and returning to NPR sources than women do.

The formula that women need to catch up with men (EFI) in order later to reclaim their lead on men (NPR) admits of many exceptions. The major exception, as noted earlier, is that most women throughout history have had to proceed to the stages of ego transcendence without having had a chance to achieve full EFI expression. A second exception is that increasing numbers of women at the present time are achieving EFI expression right along with men and therefore have no "catching up" to do. Moreover, even women who have chosen traditional gender roles may have little "catching up" to do, because traditional female roles not only draw on NPR capacities but also require considerable EFI strengths and skills. And a third exception to our formula is that many men, stereotypes to the contrary notwithstanding, are gifted with extraordinary NPR capacities. These exceptions acknowledged, the formula as stated can, I believe, be accepted as a general rule governing contemporary circumstances. Given the conditions described at the beginning of the chapter, men have a narrow EFI advantage over women and women a narrow NPR advantage over men. Consequently, given that full EFI expression is now a realistic possibility for women, it is true, generally, that women need to catch up with men (EFI) in order later to reclaim their lead on men (NPR).

JUNG'S CONCEPTION OF THE ANIMA AND ANIMUS: A CRITIQUE

Jung was a pioneer in the study of gender, especially the study of the psychological and spiritual significance of "feminine" symbols and archetypes. Many women have felt an affinity for analytical psychology because of its sensitivity to "feminine" values. Jung was the first to see that the deep or collective unconscious is fundamentally female in its gender complexion: it is originally the realm of the Great Mother; it is mediated by the archetype of the anima (which, in contrast to the animus, is female in gender); and it is the seat of such "feminine" potentials as feeling and creative imagination. Also, Jung, in his theory of the anima, was aware of the leadership role that women—or at least the "feminine"[1]—play in the individuation process in the second half of life. The anima, according to Jung, is the inner feminine side of men that moves men toward wholeness and, as embodied in such female figures as Diotima, Sophia, and Beatrice, guides men on the spiritual path.

Nothwithstanding his pioneering work in the area of gender, Jung was a product of his time and subject to deeply ingrained sexist biases. A growing number of feminists (Goldenberg 1976; Lauter and Rupprecht 1985; Wehr 1987; Young-Eisendrath 1992) have sharply criticized the androcentric assumptions of Jung's concepts. Jung's theory of the anima and animus in particular has been subject to criticism and reformulation (Hillman 1985; Kast 1986; Young-Eisendrath and Wiedemann 1987; Whitmont 1987, 1991). In this section I shall enter this discussion by presenting a brief exposition and critique of the theory of the anima and animus. Then, in the next section, I shall propose a reconstruction of the theory based on the five points stated at the beginning of the chapter. I begin with a brief exposition.

1. *Anima and animus are contrasexual components of the psyche.* The anima is the feminine underside of men's psyche, the animus the masculine underside of women's psyche. Because men, according to Jung, possess as their primary qualities autonomy and rationality (designated Logos), the anima in men is the source of the opposite, feminine, qualities of relationship and feeling (designated Eros). Correspondingly, because women, according to Jung, possess as their primary qualities relationship and feeling (Eros), the animus in women is the source of the opposite, masculine, qualities of autonomy and rationality (Logos). The anima, then, is the Eros in men, and the animus is the Logos in women.

2. *Anima and animus are missing complements needed for psychic wholeness.* As contrasexual components of the psyche, the anima and animus are subordinate and relatively unexpressed possibilities of experience. Men's consciousness is one-sidedly Logos; their anima or Eros is for the most part unconscious. And women's consciousness is one-sidedly Eros; their animus or Logos is for the most part unconscious. Accordingly, if men and women are to move in the direction of psychic wholeness and balance, they need to integrate the anima and animus, respectively, as far as possible. The anima is the missing complement to men's autonomous and rational personality; the animus is the missing complement to women's relational and feeling-oriented personality.

3. *Anima and animus are archetypes.* The anima and animus are not social or personal constructs, although social and personal variables affect the way in which the anima and animus are expressed. Rather, the anima and animus are inherited archetypes of the col-

lective unconscious that, as such, are universal to human experience. Also, as archetypes, the anima and animus can never be fully known. Their basic motifs and patterns of manifestation can be known and integrated, but not the archetypes themselves as deep creative sources of human experience.

4. *Anima and animus are bivalent.* As archetypes of the collective unconscious, the anima and animus are both attractive and threatening to the ego and, correspondingly, both positive and negative in the ways they manifest themselves to the ego. The anima, for example, is split into younger maiden and seductress opposites and older muse and witch opposites. And the animus, for example, is split into younger prince and rogue opposites and older wise man and dark magician opposites.

5. *Anima and animus projection.* To the extent that the anima and animus remain unconscious, they are perceived only as they are projected onto members of the opposite sex. To the extent that the anima and animus become conscious, they are perceived as inner aspects of one's own deeper self, as contrasexual voices, images, and transformative impulses leading one beyond one's conscious position to a deeper relationship with the unconscious and to greater psychic wholeness.

6. *Anima and animus possession.* A man in whom the anima has just begun to stir is overwhelmed by immature Eros. He becomes susceptible to capricious intimacies and maudlin or moody emotions. Such a man is said to be anima possessed. A woman in whom the animus has just begun to stir is driven by immature Logos. She becomes susceptible to petty argumentativeness and petulant or defiant assertions of independence. Such a woman is said to be animus possessed.

7. *Midlife anima and animus guides.* At midlife, typically, the anima and animus begin to manifest within consciousness. At this point, men begin to open to their own Eros and women to their own Logos. In this midlife opening to the contrasexual side of the personality, men and women are susceptible not only to anima or animus possession but also to the influence of a special type of anima or animus figure; namely, to beings—mythical, imaginal, or actual—who serve as goads or guides to the process of contrasexual integration. These beings are psychopomps, guides to the unconscious. They typically are figures of supernormal power and wisdom who lure or lead the ego into the stages of ego transcendence.

As these points make clear, the anima and animus, for Jung, are completely parallel notions, the animus having exactly the same status and performing exactly the same function for women that the anima does for men. On the surface this parallelism seems entirely as it should be. However, under the surface this parallelism can be seen to be contaminated with sexism. As several critics of Jung have pointed out, Jung's theory of the animus is similar to Freud's theory of penis envy in that it is a theory about women that, rather than being based on the experience of women, is based on an inference from the experience of men. Moreover, like the theory of penis envy, it is a theory about women that has detrimental implications for women.

Jung's theory of the anima and animus was based on Jung's own experience of the anima. In a seminar delivered in 1925 Jung described how, in his writing, he found himself listening to an inner voice, a female voice that he came to understand as the voice of the anima. After describing his experience with this voice, Jung went on to say this: "I decided she [woman] could not possibly have an anima, because then there would be no check on the woman from within. Then I came to the idea that woman must have an animus, but it was not till much later that I was able to develop this further because the animus is much harder to catch at work" (1925, p. 46). This seminar statement reveals that Jung's theory of the animus, despite later claims to the contrary (Jung 1951, p. 14), was an afterthought based on an inference from Jung's own experience rather than a hypothesis based directly on the experience of women. Although Jung's inference may seem plausible, it is full of difficulties. I shall briefly discuss two of the most serious difficulties.

First, because a basic meaning of *anima* is soul (or psyche), the inference that women do not have an anima but have an animus instead seems to imply that women have no soul. The anima, according to the anima-animus theory, represents the soulful, affective and intuitive, depths of *men's* unconscious. Women, lacking an anima, it seems, lack such depths. To be sure, Jung holds that women's conscious position is one of feeling and intuition. (More on this in a moment.) However, women's unconscious depths, according to the anima-animus theory, are opposite in quality to their conscious position. Women do not have an anima = soul deep within themselves; instead, they have an animus. Their unconscious is undeveloped Logos rather than submerged Eros.

To my knowledge, the "women-have-no-soul" implication of the anima-animus theory is never explicitly stated by Jung. Jung's position is unclear and even contradictory. As James Hillman (1985) has stressed, Jung's usage of the term *anima* is flawed by an ambiguity that leads to inconsistency. Jung uses the term both as a specific term designating men's contrasexual side and as a general term designating the life principle (i.e., psyche or soul). The first of these senses obviously applies only to men; the second sense applies—or *should* apply—to both women and men. Jung, however, does not distinguish between these senses and therefore falls prey to speaking at times as if the soul or deep (archetypal-instinctual-affective-intuitive) unconscious belongs to men alone while otherwise assuming that it belongs to both men and women. The very soul that the anima-animus theory seems to take away from women Jung otherwise assumed to be present in women. Nevertheless, if Jung never explicitly stated, and perhaps never explicitly recognized, the "woman-have-no-soul" implication, he did come close to acknowledging it. A tacit acknowledgment is present in the 1925 seminar statement, which begins, "After this I began to work on the problem already ancient in the world, 'Has woman a soul?' I decided she could not possibly have an anima, because. . ." (pp. 45–46).

A second regrettable implication of Jung's anima-animus theory—or at least regrettable inference that Jung drew from the theory—is that women, in effect, are inferior men. Women are inferior men because women's development toward wholeness aims at something that men have already achieved in a natural and superior way: Logos. Logos is a woman's inferior side and therefore, according to Jung, something that can never be natural to her. Accordingly, when women begin to come under the guiding influence of the animus, the best they can achieve is an awkward approximation of "true" masculine behavior. Women are never in their proper element when expressing Logos, according to Jung. Jung makes this point unmistakably clear. He says:

> This step towards social independence [on the part of women] is a necessary response to economic and other factors. . . . Certainly the courage and capacity for self-sacrifice of such women is admirable, and only the blind could fail to see the good that has come out of all these efforts. But no one can get round the fact that by taking up a masculine profession, studying and working like a man, woman is doing something not wholly in accord with, if not directly injurious to, her feminine nature. She is doing something that would scarcely be possible for a man to do. . . . Could he, for instance, be a nurse-maid or run a kindergarten? (1927, pp. 117–118)

Because it is "unnatural" for women to express Logos, they are prone to do so only in immature or ineffective ways, for example, by being opinionated rather than truly thoughtful, stubborn rather than genuinely autonomous. Women are prone to mere animus possession rather than true Logos expression.

But cannot an equal but opposite conclusion be drawn about men? Are not men, by the same line of reasoning, inferior women? In the passage just cited Jung does pose the rhetorical question whether a man could be a nursemaid or run a kindergarten; and on other occasions he acknowledged anima possession in men. The suggestion of these observations, however, is not that men are inferior women; if anything, the suggestion is just the opposite. Although men would be "out of place" in the nursery or preschool and although men are susceptible to immature and maudlin emotionality, they are nonetheless heir, potentially, to the profound feelings and insights of the anima. Women, possessing an animus rather than an anima, are not heir to these feelings and insights. That is to say, men's unconscious Eros, which is wise and deep, is superior to women's conscious Eros, which, as Jung's statement about nursemaids reveals, is suited primarily for raising children. In Erich Neumann's (1963) terms, men's unconscious Eros is the *transformative* (i.e., dynamic-creative) feminine, which is superior to women's conscious Eros, which is the merely *elementary* (i.e., maternal) feminine. In sum, then, not only is women's unconscious Logos (the animus) inferior to men's conscious Logos, but men's unconscious Eros (the anima) is superior to women's conscious Eros. Not only are women, at best, inferior men; men, potentially, are superior women.

Anima figures who serve as spiritual guides to men might be considered counterexamples to the point just made. For are not they evidence for the view that women have an NPR advantage over men that, at a certain developmental juncture, puts women ahead of men on the path of transcendence? Jung's answer, it seems, is no. James Hillman, who has made a close study of Jung's views on this matter, draws the conclusion that, for Jung, anima women are more products of male imagination than they are women of real depth and wisdom. He says: "But what of 'anima women,' those women who play the anima for men and are called in analytical psychology 'anima types.' Jung says that such women can best play this anima part by being empty themselves. They therefore catch the projections of men, mirroring and mimicking them, so that a man's inner woman is lived out by an anima type" (1985, p. 55). The anima woman, for Jung, then, is not a person of substance and depth; she is rather a person whose mysterious emptiness elicits anima projections from men. The seeming wisdom of the anima guide is therefore not the wisdom of the anima figure herself. It is rather the unfolding wisdom of the male psyche. For Jung, then, men do not really follow women on the spiritual path. They follow their own anima projections.

The foregoing observations indicate that Jung's theory of the anima and animus suffers from a pervasive bias against women. For this reason some Jungians and former Jungians, led by Naomi Goldenberg (1976), have advocated doing away with the anima-animus theory altogether, or at least that part of it that deals with the animus. Most Jungians, however, have argued in favor of keeping the theory but revising it to avoid the implications we have discussed. This latter alternative is, I believe, the better choice, because the theory of the anima and animus is based on an important and fundamentally sound insight, namely, that both women and men possess inner repressed contrasexual potentials. Accordingly, in the next section I shall reformulate the theory of the anima and animus in terms of the five points summarized at the beginning of the chapter.

JUNG'S CONCEPTION OF THE ANIMA AND ANIMUS: A RECONSTRUCTION

Those who have reformulated Jung's theory of the anima and animus have in most cases followed one or another of two primary strategies, either (1) retaining the notion that the anima and animus are archetypes while rejecting the notion that they are gender specific (Hillman 1985; Kast 1986; Whitmont 1987, 1991; Hill 1992; Stevens 1992), or (2) retaining the notion that the anima and animus are gender specific while rejecting the notion that they are archetypes, holding instead that they are social constructs (Young-Eisendrath 1990, 1992). The reconstruction that I shall propose follows the first of these strategies. I shall defend the view that the anima and animus are indeed archetypes but are not gender specific, that they are universal meanings present in both women and men. I shall also defend the view, however, that, owing to the conditions described at the beginning of the chapter, the anima and animus express themselves in women and men in significantly different ways.

The anima and animus are archetypes, I suggest, because they refer to the two basic poles of the human psyche: the NPR pole (represented by the anima) and the EFI pole (represented by the animus). We carry within ourselves an archetypal understanding of the two poles of the psyche and the distinctive modes of experience rooted in them. Every culture recognizes the basic duality of NPR and EFI. In the East, this duality is perhaps best known in terms of the distinction between yin and yang; and in the West, it is perhaps best known in terms of the distinction between the Dionysian and the Apollonian. Distinctions between body and mind, feeling and thought, image and concept, intuition and logic, spontaneity and discipline, receptivity and activity, surrender and assertion, and interconnection and autonomy are all dimensions of the more basic NPR-EFI duality, which is a root archetypal duality of the soul.

Because neither the NPR nor the EFI pole of the psyche is gender specific, it follows that neither the anima nor the animus is gender specific. In the view I am recommending, then, the anima is not the archetype of the "feminine," and the animus is not the archetype of the "masculine." Granted, owing to its original connection with the preoedipal mother, the NPR pole of the psyche is deeply associated with the female gender; and owing to its initial connection with the oedipal father, the EFI pole is strongly associated with the male gender. Despite these associations, however, neither the NPR nor the EFI pole of the psyche is exclusive to either gender. Both poles are biopsychically inherited and belong to human beings generally. The psyches of both women and men have both NPR and EFI poles, and therefore both women and men have both an anima and an animus.

If the anima and animus are not gender specific, they nonetheless express themselves in women and men in significantly different ways. For while both women and men are primarily committed to the EFI side of the NPR-EFI axis, men alone directly define themselves in EFI terms. Men alone directly identify with the animus. Men strive toward EFI mastery as part of their ego identity and ego ideal. They both measure themselves against and strive toward an EFI ideal of completely logical, assertive, and self-possessed personhood. Moreover, in striving for this EFI ideal, men, as we know, at the same time adopt a negative stance toward NPR modes of experience. Men not only directly identify with the animus; they also strongly dissociate themselves from the anima, which is repressed and relegated to the unconscious, indeed to the deep or collective unconscious.[2]

Women, in contrast, although also primarily committed to the EFI side of the NPR-EFI axis, do not directly define themselves in EFI terms and therefore are not directly identified with the animus. Exceptions notwithstanding, women, as explained in chapter 3, identify with the oedipal father as EFI exemplar only indirectly, by identifying with the mother's role in relation to the father. The mother qua wife has a vicarious identity through the father while simultaneously adopting a posture of difference from, indeed oppositeness to, the father. Accordingly, in identifying with the mother's role in relation to the father, the girl is able to sever continuing symbiotic ties with the preoedipal mother (and NPR) and establish a primary commitment to the oedipal father (and EFI) by, paradoxically, stressing nonidentity, and even contrariety, with the father. Identifying with the mother's role in relation to the father allows the girl to establish herself as only narrowly different from, and therefore basically the same as, the father on the condition that this narrow difference–basic identity be perceived as a wide difference–complete nonidentity. Precisely this kind of commitment to the oedipal father is repeated in the traditional marriage ceremony, in which the father gives the bride to her husband. The woman, who had been indirectly identified with the father, now begins to live vicariously through the husband.

Women's indirect identity-as-difference means that women do not adopt the animus as part of their ego identity and ego ideal but rather relate to it as an unrecognized alter ego and alter ego ideal, that is, as a part of themselves that cannot be acknowledged to exist within themselves. Rather than adopting the animus, as men do, women repress the animus, at once relegating it to the unconscious and projecting it upon men.[3] Accordingly, instead of directly aspiring to an EFI ideal, as men do, women aspire to a relationship with a man or men who are perceived to embody this ideal. This repressed-projected relationship that women have with the animus corresponds to how the animus is understood in standard Jungian theory. For women, the animus is unacknowledged throughout the first half of life and is expressed only vicariously in the lives of the men with whom women are primarily related. Only at about midlife, typically, does this indirect animus expression come to an end. Only at midlife, typically, do women begin to withdraw animus projections and begin directly to own the animus. This statement of course holds only generally. Many individual women own the animus much earlier and themselves consciously pursue EFI goals. The women's movement of the last twenty-five years has made this increasingly true. Nevertheless, the traditional pattern is still deeply ingrained, and many women still repress and project, rather than own, the animus throughout the first half of life, if not throughout the whole of life.

Women's indirect identity-as-difference means not only that women are forced to disavow and project the animus but also that they are forced to adopt the anima. In being allowed to identify with the animus only by playing the role of its opposite, the anima, women are forced to assume an identity with which they are at odds. They are forced to assume an anima identity and ego ideal despite experiencing deep conflict with precisely the NPR capacities that the anima represents. Commitment to the oedipal father is a commitment to what the father stands for and a commitment against what the father stands against. It is a dualistic pro-EFI–anti-NPR commitment. This dualistic commitment, as already noted, is directly evident in men's animus identification, which is an identification involving not only aspiration to an EFI ideal but also denigration of NPR modes of experience. For women, the dualistic pro-EFI–anti-NPR stance has the consequence of riddling their identification with the anima with negativity and therefore with acute ambivalence. Women can indirectly identify with EFI only by accepting an NPR counteridentity, and this counteridentity is itself a negative self-identity, an identity that accepts its own inferiority and lack of value. Under dualism, women are forced to assume an anti-anima anima identity.

The anti-NPR element of both men's EFI-animus and women's NPR-anima identifications requires that distinctions be made between the archetypal animus and the dualistic animus and between the archetypal anima and the dualistic anima. Whereas the archetypal animus is the innate representation of the EFI pole of the psyche, the dualistic animus is the archetypal animus *inflated with surplus value and contaminated with negative, anti-NPR, value.* And whereas the archetypal anima is the innate representation of the NPR pole of the psyche, the dualistic anima is the archetypal anima *divested of value and contaminated with negative, anti-NPR, value.* With this distinction in mind, we can say that, under dualism, men are identified with the dualistic animus and women with the dualistic anima. For the reasons summarized at the beginning of the chapter, it is not the archetypal animus and anima, but rather the dualistic animus and anima, that govern the self-systems of men and women, respectively, from latency to at least midlife.

The skewed identifications just discussed help explain why women and men enter midlife with such different developmental agendas.[4] Women, to the extent that they have identified with the dualistic animus only vicariously, begin withdrawing animus projections and asserting their own animus needs and propensities. This owning of the animus is at the same time, usually, a struggle for liberation from the dualistic anima. Identification with the dualistic anima is a straitjacket that limits women not only to NPR roles but to subservient, inferior roles. Accordingly, to own the animus, women who have given themselves to traditional roles frequently need to disown—or at least distance themselves from—the dualistic anima. In some cases this disowning of the dualistic anima may seem like a disowning of the anima altogether, and so it may be for a while. Nevertheless, as discussed earlier, once a woman has owned the animus, has achieved full EFI empowerment, she is able to return to the anima and to NPR possibilities, now disburdened of dualistic devaluations and constraints. That is to say, she is able to return to the *archetypal* anima and in doing so to reclaim her NPR advantage over men.

Men's midlife agenda is different. Having lived the dualistic animus, men experience no need for animus empowerment. Instead, they begin to "die" to the animus and withdraw from the world in a way that leads in the direction of the archetypal anima. For men, at this point, the dualistic animus undergoes deanimation and the archetypal anima begins, darkly and distantly, to exert an influence. During the night of the senses, men are drawn away from the world of EFI expression (animus deanimation) and drawn, apprehensively and resistantly, toward as yet unseen NPR possibilities (influence of the anima). Because the influence of the anima during the night of the senses is still invisible, men at this stage are susceptible to indirect anima manifestations, that is, to anima projections, to women representing dark, wild, and mysterious depths. At the very point in time, then, when women are withdrawing animus projections and becoming disenchanted with (conventional) men, men are putting out anima projections and becoming enchanted with (unconventional) women. Clearly, this is a difficult period for male-female relationships, many of which have foundered on these developmental crosscurrents. Again, women and men are proceeding in opposite directions at this point, and male-female relationships are for this reason subject to special challenges.

GOD THE FATHER AND THE GREAT GODDESS

God the Father is the projected deification of the dualistic animus; the Great Goddess is the projected deification of the archetypal anima. Under conditions of dualism, God the Father is the ruling deity of the cosmos; the Great Goddess is exiled from the world. Just as the oedipal father, the primal patriarch, rules on earth, so God the Father rules in heaven. And just as the preoedipal mother, the Great Mother, is repressed and relegated to the unconscious, so the Great Goddess lies in wait in the underworld. The Great Goddess is an invisible possibility of experience throughout the period of dualism. She does not become manifest until dualism comes to an end. At that point, she begins to emerge in consciousness, at first only as a dark and alien force, then as the power of spiritual regeneration, and finally as the source and ground of the ego's existence.

God the Father, as a deification of the dualistic animus, plays the same double role as the oedipal father. He is both an EFI model and a stern judge who rewards those who keep his law and punishes those who violate it. During dualism, men relate to God the Father as the ideal animus figure, as a cosmic ego ideal. Men relate to God the Father both as a being whose perfection is to be emulated and whose justice is to be feared. During dualism, women also relate to God the Father as an ideal animus figure, although, for women, God the Father is a being whose ideality is approached more through relationship than direct emulation. Whereas men more typically seek to be righteous like God the Father, women more typically seek to yield and be faithful to God the Father. Whereas men more typically strive to live in the image of God the Father, women more typically strive to surrender to God the Father and identify with God the Father only indirectly and vicariously, through relationship, through obedient submission to God the Father. The differing ways women and men relate to the oedipal father and dualistic animus are reflected in the differing ways women and men relate to God the Father.

Because, at midlife, women and men tend to change the ways in which they relate to the dualistic animus, they tend as well to change the ways in which they relate to God the Father. For men, the midlife turn marks a withdrawal from God the Father as cosmic ego ideal. As men begin to die to their own animus, they begin to die as well to the Animus on High. Men experience a loss of motivation to live righteously in the image of God the Father. This loss of motivation inevitably seems to them like backsliding, like a gradual loss of justification and worthiness before God the Father. In chapter 8 we saw how feelings such as these are integral to the night of the senses as described by John of the Cross. Persons in the night of the senses lose energy and motivation. Suffering from indifference, they cease performing the acts that hitherto had justified them before God the Father. Accordingly, they begin to experience "guilt." The underlying "guilt" inherent to the mental ego here begins to manifest itself in distinctively religious guise.

For women, as we have seen, the midlife turn more typically involves an ownership of, rather than a withdrawal from, the animus. As men are in the process of withdrawing from the animus, women are in the process of withdrawing animus projections from men. Because God the Father is in certain respects just such a projection, the midlife turn for women can involve an unmasking of God the Father. This unmasking characteristically expresses itself in a loss of personal trust in God the Father and an emerging resistance to surrendering to God the Father. Or the unmasking of God the Father can express itself, as it did in the early days of the contemporary women's movement, in an explicit feminist critique of God the Father. In the early work of Mary Daly (1973), for example, God the Father is unmasked as a man's god rather than a woman's god. God the Father is seen as having been created in the image of man for the purpose of ideologically reinforcing the favored position of men. Women, then, in withdrawing animus projections and in struggling to free themselves from the dualistic anima, may need to separate themselves from God the Father. They may need to separate themselves from God the Father as part of the process of finding themselves as women.

The transition from the dark night of the senses to the dark night of spirit is another juncture at which a change in the relationship with God the Father occurs. If we remember, John of the Cross describes this juncture as one at which one feels completely abandoned by God the Father. One faces a dark abyss, to which, it seems, one is deservedly condemned owing to one's unworthiness. One feels lost and beyond redemption, as if utterly forsaken by God the Father. Whether one has fallen from grace by withdrawing from God the Father (more typically the case for men) or by more actively divorcing oneself from God the Father (more typically the case for women) really does not matter here, because the primary feeling is one of being beyond hope of redemption. At this terrible juncture, one senses that one is no longer protected from the dark forces of the underworld.

The dark forces of the underworld are, of course, the forces of the Great Goddess fearfully apprehended by an ego that has repressed them. The ego at this point is on the verge of regression in the service of transcendence. The repressed forces of the deep unconscious are about to return to consciousness. The ego understandably feels doomed. The prospects, however, are not as dire as they seem. As we know, regression in the service of transcendence is not a merely regressive process. There are no guarantees; the process can abort into regression pure and simple. In general, however, the descent into the abyss by a person who is ready for it is the first, regressive, phase of a regressive-regenerative process that eventually brings the person to a condition of higher wholeness. To be sure, this first phase seems like the very opposite of a redemptive transformation. The forces encountered seem alien and destructive. Persons undergoing regression in the service of transcendence feel more like they are being punished by God the Father than like they are being transformed by the Great Goddess. A redemptive transformation, however, *is* in its initial phase. A transition from God the Father to the Great Goddess has occurred.

The Great Goddess is the Great Mother at a higher level of manifestation. The Great Mother, if we remember, is a subhuman goddess, a being of superhuman power but incomplete personhood. Reflecting the undeveloped nature and rudimentary cognition of the young child, the Great Mother is a being lacking in fully formed mind, will, personal feelings, and awakened sexual and aggressive instinctuality. The Great Mother is a superhuman power that is also a merely prepersonal or merely natural force. To return to Neumann's distinction, she represents the merely elementary rather than transformative feminine. In her Good Mother aspect, the Great Mother is a prepersonal source of comfort, protection, and nurture; and in her Terrible Mother aspect, the Great Mother is a prepersonal source of engulfing darkness and fury.

The Great Goddess, in contrast, is a transpersonal being, a being with all the superhuman power of the Great Mother and with fully formed personhood as well. She represents the transformative feminine. In her Good Goddess aspect, the Great Goddess is a source not only of the nurturing dispensations of the Good Mother but also of inspiration, regeneration, personal love, and grace. And in her Terrible Goddess aspect, the Great Goddess is a source not only of the dark dispensations of the Terrible Mother but also of evil intentions, seductive-rapacious sexuality, and ruthless cruelty. The Good Goddess is the Good Mother personalized and spiritualized. The Terrible Goddess is the Terrible Mother personalized and demonized.

In being "abandoned" to the abyss and the dark forces astir therein, the ego entering regression in the service of transcendence falls under the influence of the Great Goddess in her Terrible Goddess aspect (e.g., Kali, Medusa, Hekate). This encounter with the Terrible Goddess, it must be stressed, is an encounter with the archetypal anima *from the vantage point of dualism*, that is, from the vantage point of the imminent derepression of the nonegoic core of the psyche. Repression involves a deep-seated fear of the repressed and, consequently, an exaggeratedly negative perception of the repressed. The exaggeratedly negative aspects of the Terrible Goddess, then, are a reflection of this dualistic perspective and cannot be said to pertain to "goddess," anima, or NPR realms per se.

In the ancient goddess religions, for instance, the dark side of the Great Goddess is typically not evil in the same way as the Terrible Goddess I have described (see George 1992). The dark goddess of ancient goddess religions, associated with the moon and the aged crone, is a goddess of the natural cycle of death and regeneration. The darkness of the dark goddess is indeed symbolic of death, but of death as connected with new life. This connection with new life is not, however, a part of the Terrible Goddess experienced by persons entering regression in the service of transcendence, who believe that all life and hope have been lost and that they are in the clutches of a power of unqualified evil and unrelenting destructiveness. The Terrible Goddess is cut off from her dark goddess roots and transmogrified by a dualistic consciousness that fears the deep unconscious.

Because women are not as one-sidedly pro-EFI–anti-NPR as men, they, I suggest, suffer fewer and less protracted difficulties during the nights of the senses and spirit than men. Because women are not as one-sidedly pro-EFI as men, they experience less difficulty in the night of the senses when the ego is disempowered and EFI expression is undermined from within. And because women are not as anti-NPR as men, they are less threatened in the night of spirit by derepressing nonegoic life. Specifically, women's NPR advantage over men implies that the Terrible Goddess, who emerges during the night of spirit is not as terrible for women as she is for men. Given their residual identity with the preoedipal mother and the NPR realms she originally represented, women find the Terrible Goddess less alien, and therefore less seemingly antithetical to self, than men do. Accordingly, women, although frightened of the deep unconscious as dark abyss, as a dangerous power, as the Terrible Goddess, are not as frightened as men. Women perceive the Terrible Goddess not only as a destructive power but also, however incomprehensibly, as a redemptive power. Women sense that the Terrible Goddess is not completely alien and other but is somehow a deeply buried part of themselves. This discernment can be present at the outset of regression in the service of transcendence, and it grows into a clear insight as time passes. Men, given their gender-opposition to the preoedipal mother and the NPR realms she originally represented, encounter more difficulties and take longer in coming to the realization that the Terrible Goddess is a disowned part of themselves.

But men, too, eventually come to this realization. For the nonegoic core of the psyche is a deeper and higher self for both men and women. Accordingly, both men and women eventually arrive at a point at which the Great Goddess begins to lose her Terrible Goddess qualities and begins to reveal another, altogether different side. She begins to reveal herself as the Good Goddess. This point marks the transition from regression in the service of transcendence to regeneration in spirit. At this point the Great Goddess gradually ceases manifesting herself as seething abysses, infernal fires, and negative anima figures (e.g., witches, harlots, epiphanies of the Terrible Goddess) who lure the vulnerable ego into abyssal-infernal realms. Instead, she begins manifesting herself as upwelling springs, rising suns, and positive anima figures (e.g., Diotima, Sofia, Beatrice, the Virgin Mary) who regenerate and inspire the ego and lead it toward the goal of integration. As the turn is made from regression in the service of transcendence to regeneration in spirit, the Great Goddess gradually ceases appearing as alien and evil. She begins being seen as a power of regeneration rather than destruction, as a spiritual reality that had to purge the ego radically to prepare it for a new birth on a higher plane.

For those whose religious thought is committed exclusively to a monotheism of God the Father, the regenerative process just described is conceived in terms of the healing and redemptive action of the spiritual power of God the Father. For John of the Cross, for example, as for Christians generally, the regenerative process is conceived as the work of the Holy Spirit. John, after having suffered a sense of eternal forsakenness, as if abandoned by God the Father, eventually began to experience the miraculous regenerative grace of the Holy Spirit, which he conceived as a power, or rather person, of one substance with God the Father. In this context, the archetypal anima is expressed in predominantly male images. God the Father assumes credit for the work of the Great Goddess. This appropriation is part of the fate of the Great Goddess in cultures based on a monotheism of God the Father. In such cultures, the Great Goddess is repressed and condemned, and her life-giving, regenerative, function is arrogated by a male deity.

We are in a period of history when the Great Goddess is returning to consciousness. The women's movement is the primary vehicle of her return. Women are in growing numbers leaving the dualistic-patriarchal religions of God the Father, seeing them as basically hostile to themselves as women. Increasingly, women are turning to forms of goddess religion as they seek to find a spirituality that will heal and fulfill them as human beings. Women, however, are not alone in turning in this direction. Men, too, are beginning to turn, if not to goddess religion, at least to religious expressions conceived in "feminine" terms. Jung was ahead of his time in this regard. We are only beginning to catch up with him in learning that our archetype of divinity involves not only a male-animus but also a female-anima dimension.

Conclusion

The transcendence of dualism is a movement *away* from EFI, the dualistic animus, and God the Father and *toward* NPR, the archetypal anima, and the Great Goddess. This direction of movement is most characteristic of the dark nights of the senses and spirit, the stages of withdrawal from the world and regression in the service of transcendence. Once these stages have completed the work of dismantling dualistic structures and returning the ego to its nonegoic sources, the movement from EFI to NPR, from dualistic animus to archetypal anima, from God the Father to the Great Goddess is complete and the process leading to psychic integration begins.

The process leading to integration, regeneration in spirit, is *nonegoic dominant*. It is a process that roots the ego in the nonegoic core of the psyche as the superior source of the ego's being. In being nonegoic dominant, however, regeneration in spirit is not dualistic. Unlike dualistic ego dominance, which is anti-nonegoic (anti-NPR, anti-anima) the nonegoic dominance of regeneration in spirit is not anti-egoic (not anti-EFI, not anti-animus). On the contrary, regeneration in spirit is pro-egoic. The ego, having been regressed to the nonegoic core, is here rooted in the nonegoic core and begins being supported and redemptively transformed by spiritual power. Regeneration in spirit involves a higher regrounding and restoration of the ego and therefore of EFI and the animus as well.

Although the paths to integration differ significantly for women and men, the goal of integration is substantially the same. If women sometimes need to catch up with men (EFI) in order later to reclaim their lead on men (NPR), the paths of both women and men eventually converge as they approach the ideal of integration. This ideal can be described in many ways. It is an egoic-nonegoic integration, a self-other integration, an EFI-NPR integration, an animus-anima integration, and, if religious images are invoked, a God-Goddess (or God/ess[5]) integration. In this multidimensional integration, no traces of dualism remain. The ego, EFI, and the animus are all revalued, but not in a way that devalues the nonegoic core, NPR, or the anima. And the nonegoic core, NPR, and the anima are all freely and spontaneously expressive, but not in a way that interferes with the activity of the ego. On the contrary, the ego is empowered and inspired by these nonegoic sources, in which it is now regrounded. The integrated psyche is, then, a nonegoically based bipolar unity of the ego and the nonegoic core, of EFI and NPR, and of the animus and the anima. This bipolar unity is the subject of the next chapter.

11

The Goal of Transcendence: Integration

The unfolding interaction between the ego and the nonegoic core of the psyche aims ultimately at the goal of integration.[1] Integration is the final and fulfilling stage of human development. Integration presupposes that ego development is complete, that dualism has been overcome, and that regeneration in spirit has finished its work. Integration, accordingly, is the *telos* of human development. It is the end or goal toward which development as we know it aims. It is the highest point of resolution, synthesis, and self-realization to which we aspire. Integration, however, is not only an end. It is also a new beginning. For in being the fulfilling stage of human development, integration is the basis for life lived in the fullness of its powers. In achieving integration, we finally become complete human beings.

Regrettably, integration is a developmental goal that is remote and only rarely achieved. Our lives follow a spiral course of departure and higher return: the ego departs from the nonegoic core during the stages of ego development and then makes an ascending (spiraling, integrating) return to the nonegoic core during the stages of ego transcendence. This pattern of departure and higher return means that most of us live our lives as wayfarers rather than as native dwellers. We therefore suffer from a restless yearning for "home" that is rarely fulfilled. Most of us never return all the way home. In a sense, most of us live our lives in the mode of searching for life without ever quite finding it. For most of us, life is an unfinished odyssey.

FEATURES OF INTEGRATED LIFE

The features of integrated life do not appear suddenly and only at the end of the ego's journey. Rather, they appear in progressively realized fashion as the ego moves through the stages of transcendence, and in particular the stage of regeneration in spirit. As regression in the service of transcendence gives way to regeneration in spirit, the features of integrated life begin to come into view as ideal possibilities already implicit in experience. Accordingly, in this section I shall describe the features of integrated life to the extent that they can be projectively elaborated by an ego that is "approaching home."

Transparency and I-Thou Intimacy

The dismantling of primal alienation during the stages of transcendence progressively opens the ego to others. During regression in the service of transcendence, this opening is experienced negatively as exposure. The ego is denuded of its defenses and exposed to the penetrating gaze of others. During regeneration in spirit, this opening is experienced positively as disclosure. The ego no longer feels a need to hide its interior life and is moved to reveal itself authentically to others. Finally, as regeneration in spirit approaches integration, the opening of the soul culminates in transparency. The ego is no longer impelled either to hide or reveal itself, because at this point no part of itself is left hidden to be revealed. The integrated ego is neither secretive nor confessional; there is no division between what is lived on the inside and what is expressed on the outside. The integrated ego relates to others unguardedly and from the deepest center of the psyche.

Transparency is sometimes described as a new naiveté. This characterization is correct in that to be transparent is to express oneself without tailoring the way one appears to others. As the popular saying so aptly puts it, "what you see is what you get." If, however, transparency involves naiveté in this sense, it does not involve naiveté in any of the other senses of the term. For integrated people, in their transparency, are in no way lacking in discrimination in matters of prudence or in sensitivity to the feelings of others, nor are they lacking in the *ability* to deceive. Integrated people are entirely capable of creating appearances that camouflage inner thoughts or feelings. In being capable of deception, however—and this is the essential point—integrated people are not *prone* to deception. They are not subject to mechanisms of defense and disguise. Rather, integrated people, in their transparency, are given to spontaneous self-expression. They live life from the inside out. No longer needing to defend or prove themselves in the world, they give uninhibited expression to their innermost selves.

The unguarded openness of integration leads to intimacy. For the dismantling of primal alienation leads not only to "being seen" but also to "being touched" by others. During regression in the service of transcendence, this "being touched" is experienced negatively as vulnerability. Others are perceived as "bad objects" who prey upon the ego's defenselessness, manipulating the ego for selfish or cruel purposes. During regeneration in spirit, "being touched" is experienced positively as receptivity. Others, or at least a few significant others, are perceived as "good objects" who influence the ego in healing and redemptive ways. Finally, as regeneration in spirit approaches integration, "being touched" culminates in a mutual intimacy of interconnection and coexperiencing. The ego is not only touched by others but also touches others; the ego is not only influenced and transformed by others but also influences and transforms others. This intimacy is a mutuality of *internal* relationship. The ego, divested of all coverings, opens the soul and engages in "unprotected," interflowing contact with others. Moreover, the ego opens the soul in this way not just to a few select others but to everyone. The ego no longer divides human relationships into private and public domains and therefore excludes no one from the sphere of intimacy.

As a form of internal relationship, transegoic or integrated intimacy is in one important respect similar to the preegoic symbiosis between infant and caregiver. Both of these forms of relationship are examples of fully open intersubjectivity. The primary difference between the two, however—and this is an immense difference—is that transegoic intimacy is an intersubjectivity based on individuation, whereas preegoic symbiosis is an intersubjectivity that exists prior to (the infant's) individuation. Transegoic intimacy, unlike preegoic symbiosis, is not a fusion of subjectivities. It presupposes a dissolution of dualism, to be sure, but it does not involve an erasure of difference. It is an internal relationship that preserves independence and responsibility. In this sense, transegoic intimacy is, to use Martin Buber's (1970) term, an *I-Thou* intimacy. It is an internal touching or bonding of fully individuated persons. It is an intimacy rather than identity.

The bonding of I-Thou intimacy, as Buber stresses, is a bonding of mutual affirmation. The integrated person spontaneously reaches out to others in a way that affirms them and invites them to open themselves to the experience of cosubjectivity. The transparent openness of the integrated person is thus an other-centered, affirmative openness. The affirmation conveyed by this openness is more than a respect for others as autonomous persons; it is an immediate caring for others based on a kinship in spirit. Other people are no longer "other" in the sense of self-other dualism. They are no longer perceived only as centers of autonomy with private lives and individual needs and rights; they are also, now, perceived as sisters and brothers in a shared life. The transcendence of private-public dualism is at the same time the transcendence of we-they dualism. Others are no longer "they." They are members of the larger family of humankind, members with whom integrated persons share in the same kinds of caring kinship relationships as they do with members of their immediate biological families. I-Thou intimacy is in this way the source of what feminists have called an *ethics of care*. Considerations of autonomy, rights, and justice still obtain in their proper jurisdictions. For integrated persons, however, the primary moral motive is no longer the ego-based commitment to universal moral principles or justice; it is rather the heart-based feeling of care. Integrated persons, in transcending the self-other, private-public, and we-they dualisms, lead the way from civil society to true community.

One other noteworthy fact about integrated relationships is that they are based on a new level of object constancy. During regression in the service of transcendence, as we have seen, the ego is disillusioned of others, who are seen as "bad objects," as people who, despite deceptions to the contrary, are selfish and uncaring. Just the reverse is true during regeneration in spirit, during which the ego experiences a new faith in the core self of others and begins to idealize as "good objects" those in whom this core self is seen to be active. If the ego is overly pessimistic about others during regression in the service of transcendence, it is overly optimistic during regeneration in spirit. Its relationships with others during these periods are subject to splitting and contrary evaluations without middle ground. They are lacking in objectivity and stability, that is, in object constancy.

This inconstancy is gradually overcome as regeneration moves toward integration, for the ego eventually learns that the "good objects" it has idealized are far from perfect. This discovery is disillusioning, but not in a way that leads to a split, contrary opposite, assessment. Rather, it is disillusioning only in the sense that it eliminates the ego's exaggeration of the potential or actual goodness of others. Others remain primarily "good," as potential or actual higher selves. However, in remaining primarily "good," they also are seen with increasing clarity as limited beings, as beings who, even when fully human, remain merely human. And what applies to others applies also to the ego itself. The ego, having soared aloft in ecstasy during regeneration in spirit, is brought back to earth. It is disillusioned of thoughts of a heavenly destiny and made to confront its own small stature in the ultimate scheme of things. The ego comes to recognize that spirituality, both in others and itself, accentuates rather than surpasses humanness. The achievement of transegoic object constancy is at the same time the achievement of a realistic appraisal of one's own self.

Blessedness and Bliss

The states of spiritual excess distinctive of regeneration in spirit (viz., intoxication, tearful rejoicing, and ravishment) gradually subside as regeneration unfolds toward integration. They do so not because numinous power withdraws from consciousness or because the activity of nonegoic potentials in any way abates. Rather, they subside because the egoic system becomes increasingly attuned to the nonegoic sphere and increasingly able to experience the influx of nonegoic life without being disconcerted or "injured." States of spiritual excess subside because nonegoic life, in empowering the ego, gradually ceases overpowering it in the process. Integration marks the point at which the ego is fully attuned to nonegoic life and therefore no longer thrown into disarray by the expression of nonegoic potentials. The integrated ego, existing in harmony with the nonegoic sphere, experiences states of spiritual fullness that are no longer states of spiritual excess.

Intoxication and tearful rejoicing, as noted in chapter 9, are opposites in many respects. Intoxication is a condition that is "hot" and overexcited. Tearful rejoicing in contrast, although also a state of wild infusion, is a condition that is "wet" and subduing in its effect. Opposed in these ways, intoxication and tearful rejoicing tend to alternate with and counteract each other. Tearful rejoicing counteracts the wild disconcertion of intoxication by applying water to the fire and thereby returning consciousness to a state of sobriety. In doing this, however, tearful rejoicing tends to lead to a counterextreme, frequently leaving consciousness not only sober but sodden, emotionally saturated and misty-eyed. This sodden state is in turn counteracted by the return of "hot" energy, which reanimates consciousness. This reanimation of consciousness, however, like the preceding subduing of consciousness, frequently goes to extreme, overenergizing consciousness once again, leading back to "heated" intoxication. Such oscillations between pneumatically overexcited and aqueously sodden states are characteristic of regeneration in spirit.

These oscillations, however, gradually become less extreme as regeneration approaches integration. They do so because pneumatic and aqueous infusions begin eventually to intermix and thereby to limit and transform each other rather than merely to alternate with each other. Tearful rejoicing begins to intermix with intoxication in a way that brings sobriety and clarity without loss of energy or exuberance; and intoxication begins to intermix with tearful rejoicing in a way that brings intensity and delight without loss of composure or deeply centered gratitude. This progressive interactive transformation of opposites leads toward a goal that completely synthesizes pneumatic and aqueous infusions in a unity that is both radiant and cool, dynamic and calm, exuberant and sober, beaming and grateful. This resultant state is a feeling of fresh, superabundant, thankful clarity. It is a feeling of serene passion or joyful sobriety that is humbly appreciative of the beauty and perfection of the world. This state is the feeling of blessedness.

As intoxication and tearful rejoicing are transformed into the feeling of blessedness, ravishment is transformed into the feeling of bliss. Bliss is similar to ravishment in being a delicious feeling arising in connection with the movement of an inner infusive current. Bliss differs from ravishment, however, in that it is not admixed with pain. Ravishment is the pleasurable-painful feeling that occurs when numinous power "bleeds" through an opening in the soul that is experienced as a wound. Bliss in contrast is the purely pleasurable feeling that occurs when numinous power passes caressingly through the very same opening now experienced as a channel of grace. Bliss is essentially the same feeling as blessedness, only shorn of the cognitive meaning implicit in blessedness. The feeling of blessedness involves cognitive apprehension, and appreciation, of the beauty and perfection of the world. Bliss in contrast is simply the affective core of blessedness without this cognitive significance. Bliss is blessedness merely felt, not meant. Bliss is the feeling of an exquisite inner current that flows through an intimate aperture of the soul as it moves into consciousness and bathes the ego in ripples of delicate delight.

Being the affective core of blessedness, bliss also combines the opposite qualities of pneumatic and aqueous infusion in a way that mutes their extremes. Bliss is a feeling that involves warmth without hotness and liquidlike flow without wetness. The infusive current of bliss is a liquid warmth that sets the ego coolly aglow; it is a delicious upwelling energy that at once brightens and refreshes, energizes and soothes the ego. Given this paradoxical conjunction of opposites, it is understandable that the chief symbol for bliss would be honey or nectar. Honey possesses almost all of the right qualities. It is a life-giving substance that flows slowly and smoothly and is both sweet in taste and radiant in color. Honey possesses so many of the right qualities that it is almost a complete symbol for bliss. The only quality that honey does not possess is cool refreshingness. However, a substance that does possess this quality, along with others essential to the experience of bliss, is milk—which as *mother's* milk is in any case already deeply associated with the experience of bliss. Honey by itself, in its warm viscosity, is soothing in a way that suggests sleepy contentment. Milk, in contrast, or at least cooled milk, is soothing in a way that suggests rejuvenated alertness. Milk, unlike honey, conveys the exuberant sobriety of bliss. The perfect symbol for bliss therefore would be a substance that combines the relevant features of both milk and honey. It would be a silvery-gold liquid that flows smoothly and is vitalizing, refreshing, and sweet. Such a substance would be like the ambrosia that is said to be the food of the gods.

Blessedness and bliss are the most basic and pervasive feeling states of integrated life. In saying this, I do not mean to suggest that integrated life is without an emotional downside. Integrated persons, like everyone else, experience negative emotions, for example, sadness, anger, and situational fear. These negative emotions, however, tend to be passing fluctuations. The more basic tone of integrated life is subtly and powerfully positive.

Hallowed Resplendence

The world changes its character during the stages of transcendence. During the night of the senses, the world becomes a dead, flat wasteland. During regression in the service of transcendence, the world returns to life, indeed superabundantly so, becoming superreal in its qualities and potencies. However, in returning to life in this way, the world also becomes surreal, that is, haunted, strange. During regeneration in spirit, the world continues being superreal but ceases being surreal; it ceases being haunted and becomes enchanted. It becomes magical and marvelous rather than strange. Finally, as regeneration in spirit nears integration, the world progressively loses its enchanted quality and becomes hallowed. The world remains superreal; the world of integrated experience is a resplendent world. The world, however, loses the last vestiges of mystery and foreignness and becomes utterly native ground. It becomes a hallowedly resplendent home.

Hallowed resplendence is the objective correlate of blessedness and bliss. As such, it shares essential features with these feelings, one of which is the synthesis of qualitative opposites. I have explained how bliss fuses the hot and the wet to produce a feeling that is radiant but not hot and liquid but not wet. Similarly, hallowed resplendence fuses the hot and the wet to produce a worldly atmosphere that is scintillating but not hot and that is saturated with the juices of life but not wet. Everything in a hallowedly resplendent world possesses a gleaming or lush quality. Everything possesses burnished radiance, translucent depth, succulence, or dewy freshness. Powerfully exemplifying these qualities, the sparkling jewel and the garden paradise have served as the two chief symbols of hallowed resplendence.

The sparkling jewel, especially the diamond, is an effective symbol of hallowed resplendence because it combines both brilliance and crystalline cool. It is a union of fire and ice. The diamond is utterly translucent and illumined; it has no dark recesses (as still exist in the enchanted world). At the same time, however, the diamond is cool to the touch, and its multifaceted brilliance, rather than being glaring or harsh, is pleasing to the eye. For these reasons, the diamond is widely considered a symbol of fully realized consciousness. It is so for example in Vajrayana Buddhism, in which realized consciousness is said to perceive the *Vajradhatu* or "Diamond Realm." About this realm, Roger Corless says: "This is the Tantric equivalent of the Realm of Indra's Net. We see everything as pure, sparkling, and free from sorrow, and as it were full of magic. Every moment is experienced as fresh, as it is when reality is seen as the openness of the scintillation of the dharmas. . ." (1989, pp. 259–260). The diamond, in its sparkling clarity, is a well-chosen symbol for what the Buddhists call *shunyata*, dynamic emptiness. Similarly, from a more Western prespective, the diamond—and glistening stones and metals generally—are frequently said to be the building materials of the heavenly city, which is envisaged with jewel-bedecked buildings and streets made of gold or rare gems.

The sparkling jewel synthesizes the hot and the wet in a way that focuses attention on the glistening radiance of hallowed resplendence. The garden paradise in contrast synthesizes the hot and the wet in a way that focuses attention on the lush freshness of hallowed resplendence. The garden paradise is a setting saturated with the juices of life. Everything in it is at once virgin and in full bloom. Everything in the garden is embellished with voluptuous, extravagant qualities, for example, exploding colors, delicate floral scents, velvety textures. Moreover, the garden paradise is an environment graced with a celestial climate, a climate that, lit up and warmed by an equatorial sun, is kept fresh and cool by tropical showers. The garden paradise is a world that synthesizes qualitative opposites in a way that accentuates the pristine superabundance of a hallowedly resplendent world.

The developmental course leading from regression in the service of transcendence to regeneration in spirit and, finally, integration is a course that leads out of a dark and haunted region, passes through an enchanted realm, and arrives finally at a glistening paradise. The ego at last escapes from the terrifying forest it had entered during regression in the service of transcendence. At first, during regeneration in spirit, it finds its way to an enchanted wood, and then, arriving at integration, it breaks into the open and discovers a hallowedly resplendent world. This hallowedly resplendent world is one in which nothing is overcast or alien. The sky is sparkling and the earth is both sacred and native ground. The ego, in stepping onto this ground, finally returns "home."

Mature Contemplation

The implosive absorptions (trances, engulfments) of regression in the service of transcendence and the explosive dissolutions (transports, ecstasies) of regeneration in spirit lead eventually to more poised and lucid contemplative states that combine absorption and infusion without being subject to the violence of implosion or explosion. I shall follow Mircea Eliade (1969) and use the term *enstasy* to describe these more mature contemplative states. Unlike implosive absorption, which is a dark, dense, and inert condition, enstasy is a state that is luminous, spacious, and pneumatically alive. And unlike ecstasy, which is a wildly expansive and intoxicated condition, enstasy is a state that is stable and discerning. Mature contemplation, like so many other features of integrated life, is a synthesis of opposites. It is a synthesis of fusion and infusion, absorption and expansion, composure and inspiration.

Most spiritual traditions divide contemplative practice into three stages, which I shall call controlled attention, poised awareness, and contemplation proper. For example, in the classical yoga of Patanjali (see Aranya 1983), these three stages are referred to as *dharana*, *dhyana*, and *samadhi*. *Dharana* or controlled attention is the practice of keeping the mind alertly focused on a specific object (idea, image). *Dharana* requires effort because it goes against the grain of the egoic mind, which tends either to restless wandering or torpor. *Dharana*, then, is the effortful practice of keeping alert attention tied to a particular object. The sustained practice of *dharana* leads eventually to *dhyana*, which is an intermediate meditative level at which the countervailing tendencies toward restlessness and torpor are overcome and the mind is able to give easily flowing continuous attention to the chosen object. *Dhyana* is focused awareness that is effortless and steady, that is poised upon the object. *Samadhi*, finally, is the culminating stage of practice in which the division between subject and object collapses and the subject merges with the object in a state of contemplative absorption. In early experiences of *samadhi*, absorption can be dense and imploded to some degree. The ego is sometimes more hypnotically "sucked" into the object than invitingly drawn into it. As *samadhi* matures, however, it become less dense and more infused and inspired. That is, it matures into enstasy.

A similar division of stages is present in the Roman Catholic contemplative tradition (see Royo and Aumann 1962). In this tradition meditation or discursive prayer corresponds to the stage of controlled attention. The meditator brings focused attention upon the theme of meditation, making efforts to return the mind to the theme when the mind wanders and to reawaken the mind when it becomes drowsy. Meditation or discursive prayer matures into what St. Teresa of Avila called the *prayer of recollection*.[2] Recollection, which typically dispenses with a thematic focus, is a state of alert, silent receptivity to the influx of spirit. Recollection is similar to *dhyana* in being a state of poised awareness that no longer struggles against distraction or drowsiness. Because, however, recollection is usually practiced without a focal object, it is more a state in which the subject is unmovingly gathered within itself than a state in which, like *dhyana*, the subject is unwaveringly attentive to an object. Finally, contemplation proper commences when the subject ceases being silently receptive and begins being moved by the influx of numinous power, which inwardly expands, enlivens, inspires, and dissolves the subject. Such infused contemplation is similar to *samadhi* in being a state in which the ego merges with experience. It differs from *samadhi*, however, in that, in less mature instances, it tends to be more expansive than absorbed, more inflated than composed, more infused than fused. If *samadhi* can at first be implosive to some degree, infused contemplation can at first be explosive to some degree. Like *samadhi*, however, infused contemplation converges upon enstasy as it matures. *Samadhi*, as noted, converges upon enstasy by becoming more infused and inspired; infused contemplation, in contrast, converges upon enstasy by becoming more stable and composed.

This threefold division is not an accident of historical parallelism. It reflects the evolving psychoenergetics of the contemplative process. *Dharana* and discursive prayer (as forms of controlled attention), *dhyana* and recollection (as forms of poised awareness), and *samadhi* and infused contemplation (as forms of contemplation proper) represent three distinct stages in the ego's tapping of numinous energy. *Dharana* and discursive prayer represent the initial stage of energy mobilization. As forms of sustained effortful attention, *dharana* and discursive prayer summon energy and channel it toward the object of attention. *Dhyana* and recollection, respectively, are the results of this mobilization process, for the mobilization of energy eventually creates a concentration of energy sufficiently strong either to stabilize the positioning of awareness upon the object (*dhyana*) or, if the object has been dropped, to stabilize awareness in the posture of receptive openness (recollection). *Dhyana* and recollection are halfway steps to contemplation proper, because they reflect that the ego has come under the influence of numinous energy—the very energy that the ego itself has summoned. This energy, as a tractive power, either draws the ego to an object (*dhyana*) or gathers the ego within itself in a posture of composed receptivity (recollection). In influencing the ego in these ways, numinous energy has a discernible but primarily "external" (cathectic or gravitational) effect upon the ego, which is still a separate, bounded subject, a subject that has not yet been drawn out of itself into absorption or inwardly inspirited and infused.

The continued practice of *dhyana* or recollection, however, leads to contemplation proper. For the continued mobilization of energy leads finally to absorption or infusion. In the case of *dhyana*, the continued flow of energy to the meditative object progressively amplifies the cathectic charge of the object until the ego, responding to the cathexis, is not just drawn toward the object but is actually drawn out of itself and into the object: absorption, *samadhi*. And in the case of objectless recollection, the inner concentration of energy leads to a point at which the ego, having been drawn into receptive stillness, begins to experience the upwelling movement of energy intimately within itself: contemplative infusion. The concentration of energy, either in an object or in the subject, leads eventually to either absorption in the object (*samadhi*) or infusion of the subject (infused contemplation).

Psychoenergetically, then, the contemplative process has the following three distinct phases:

1. *Mobilization.* The ego's controlled attention draws upon energy resources.
2. *Cathexis.* Mobilized energy accumulates in the form of a cathexis, either an object cathexis or a pure power cathexis (i.e., a highly charged but unfocused concentration of energy). The ego, responding to the cathexis, is stabilized and able without effort to give attention to the object or maintain a stance of unpositioned openness. This cathectically stabilized consciousness is poised awareness.
3. *Absorption-infusion.* The continued mobilization of energy creates a cathexis of sufficient magnitude to absorb or infuse the subject. Absorptions may at first be dense and hypnotic, and infusions may at first be inflated and chaotic. In time, however, these extremes gradually limit and transform each other, and a superior contemplative state is brought into being. Absorption and infusion gradually become one as contemplation evolves into enstasy. Enstasy is contemplation in the full sense of the term.

Contemplation has matured when the three stages of contemplative development just described become telescoped into sequential moments of the contemplative process.[3] To achieve enstasy, the maturely integrated ego begins with controlled attention. This controlled attention can be either focused on an object (as in *dharana* and discursive prayer) or it can be steadfast alertness with open rather than focused attention (as in Buddhist *vipassana* meditation). In mature contemplation, controlled attention of either of these sorts is no longer a disciplined practice or stage of contemplative development. It is rather a momentary access route to enstasy, or more immediately to poised awareness. By controlling attention, the ego mobilizes energy to form an object cathexis or a pure power cathexis. Responding to the cathexis, the ego is stabilized in its awareness, either as fixed upon an object or as unpositioned and open. Again, the achievement of such poised awareness is not at this point a disciplined practice or stage of contemplative development but rather a moment of transition to enstasy. Accordingly, such poised awareness shifts fluidly into infused absorption, with or without an object. In this way, the moments of the mature contemplative process recapitulate the stages of contemplative development.

Enstasy is a distinctive feature of integrated life. The integration of the ego and the nonegoic core is reflected in the ability to enter stable infused absorptions. Experiences of engulfment and transport are rare after regeneration passes into integration. In general, integration involves a mutually facilitating interplay of egoic and nonegoic spheres and of the ego and numinous energy in particular. The ego is no longer resistant to numinous energy, and numinous energy no longer, or at most only rarely, implodes or explodes the ego. The ego is able to draw upon numinous energy, and numinous energy responds by empowering rather than overpowering the ego. Contemplative experience continues to evolve after integration is initially achieved. Infused absorptions of greater power, depth, and luminosity emerge. These absorptions, however, are not achievements beyond enstasy; they are, rather, superior forms of enstasy, the essentials of which have already been "mastered" by the time regeneration ends and integrated life begins.[4]

Tertiary Cognition

The autosymbolic process triggers disturbing fantasies during regression in the service of transcendence. These productions of the creative imagination gradually lose their distressing character and begin supporting and guiding the ego once regression in the service of transcendence gives way to regeneration in spirit. Finally, when integration is achieved, the autosymbolic process ceases being a cognitive resource disconnected from the ego and becomes a cognitive resource responsive to the ego, a resource that cooperates in the ego's contemplative explorations.

The ego never gains the direct control over the autosymbolic process that it has over its own functions. The autosymbolic process is a nonegoic potential that, like all nonegoic potentials, is spontaneous in its activity. In its spontaneity, however, the autosymbolic process need not be disconnected from the ego. The autosymbolic process is disconnected from the ego only under the conditions of dualism. Primal repression is responsible for reducing the autosymbolic process to the primary process of the unconscious and leaving the ego with a fantasy life that is only a pale substitute for the creative imagination. Owing to primal repression, the autosymbolic process remains hidden from consciousness throughout the period of dualism. The products of the autosymbolic process begin to return to consciousness only during regression in the service of transcendence and regeneration in spirit. The *activity* of the autosymbolic process, however, remains disconnected from the ego even during these periods. For although the creative materials produced by the autosymbolic process during these periods are consciously experienced by the ego, these materials are presented to the ego in a way that is completely unexpected and out of the blue. This hidden activity of the autosymbolic process continues even as regression in the service of transcendence gives way to regeneration in spirit and, correspondingly, the products of the autosymbolic process cease threatening the ego and begin supporting it instead. Not until regeneration in spirit is well along the way to integration does it become apparent to the ego that the autosymbolic process is responsive to the ego's influence. Once this realization dawns, however, it is increasingly confirmed. The ego nearing integration learns not only that it can enter stable contemplative absorptions but also that it can access and guide the autosymbolic process.

The integrated ego accesses the autosymbolic process in the same way it enters contemplative enstasy. For in drawing upon the numinous energy that produces absorption and infusion, the ego simultaneously draws upon nonegoic potentials generally, including the autosymbolic process. Accordingly, when the ego focuses its attention upon an object (theme, idea) and thereby produces a cathectic absorption, it simultaneously sets the autosymbolic process to work, prompting it to produce images and insights that reveal the nature of the object in new ways. In Patanjali's terms, contemplative absorptions of this sort are called *savitarka* or *savichara samadhi*, that is, absorptions that have not only a focal object but also spontaneous ideation that intuitively illuminates the object. Again, the ego never gains direct control over the autosymbolic process; nevertheless, it does learn how to tap into its spontaneity.

Access to the autosymbolic process of the sort just described is the basis of a new species of cognition, which, in psychoanalytic terms, can be called the *tertiary process*. I borrow this term from Silvano Arieti (1976), who used it to designate creative cognition that draws upon, and in so doing goes beyond, both the primary and the secondary processes. *Tertiary process* is an apt descriptive expression for integrated cognition, because integrated cognition is a creative cognition that not only taps the autosymbolic process (hitherto the primary process) but also brings this process under the discipline of maturely developed operational cognition (the secondary process). Tertiary cognition combines the creative concreteness of the auto-symbolic process with the reality-tested conceptual schemes and logical skills of the secondary process, and it does so in a way that far surpasses the possibilities of either the autosymbolic process or the secondary process working alone.

The autosymbolic process works in concrete materials, primarily images but also voices and other subtle analogues of sensory experience. It uses the full range of materials present in dreams. In using these materials, the autosymbolic process forges mental pictures and creates mental scenes rich in unpacked meanings and therefore in potential insights. We are all well aware of the immense creativity of the autosymbolic process as it expresses itself in dreams. This creativity, however, is not confined to dreams. It is also at the disposal of the integrated ego when it engages in contemplative exploration. Moreover, for the integrated ego, this creativity is greatly empowered by the availability of the secondary process rather than, as is the case in dreams, seriously limited by dualistic disconnection from this process. Under dualism, the autosymbolic process works as the *pre*egoic primary process rather than the *trans*egoic tertiary process. It is an immensely creative source of cognitive material, but it is cut off from consciousness and the developed conceptual structures and logical powers of the conscious ego. The creative productions of the primary process, therefore, are lower-primitive symbols that embody meanings in obscure and frequently contradictory ways. They are symbols that are indeed laden with meaning, but with meaning that is enigmatic and shifting rather than transparent and coherently limned.

Tertiary cognition brings the secondary process into complementary interaction with the autosymbolic process in two principle ways. First, as just suggested, the secondary process interacts with the autosymbolic process by disciplining it, by bringing it into conformity with the epistemic standards of the secondary process. Under conditions of dualism the autosymbolic process is an instrument of the unconscious. As such, the autosymbolic process operates in a way that, although richly creative, is heedless of the class boundaries and logical relationships that govern the secondary process. The products of the primary process, consequently, are logically wild; they are subject to unlimited condensations and displacements, transformations according to which anything can metamorphose into virtually anything else. Because this wildness of the imagination is a consequence of the dualistic disconnection of egoic and nonegoic spheres, it cannot be surmounted until dualism is overcome and the autosymbolic process is brought under the discipline of the secondary process.

The imposition of secondary-process norms in no way diminishes the creativity of the autosymbolic process. The autosymbolic process continues to produce materials that embody meanings previously unknown to the ego and, frequently, meanings that challenge conceptions long accepted by the ego. Such meanings, however, are no longer logically wild; rather, they are subject to rigorous epistemic requirements and tests. New meanings are required to intermesh coherently with the established conceptual network and to stand up to reality testing. And meanings that challenge established conceptions are expected to replace or reorganize those conceptions in a way that advances both theory and practice. In this way the creations of the autosymbolic process are no longer spawned in an isolated, ungoverned domain (the unconscious) and are instead thoroughly integrated with the conceptually organized and empirically based world of conscious experience. No longer confined to the underworld of the unconscious, the autosymbolic process becomes in this way a creative instrument that can explore the entire cosmos of experience.

In addition to bringing the autosymbolic process into conformity with secondary-process norms, the tertiary process also renders the autosymbolic process responsive to secondary-process content, that is, to concepts and hypotheses derived from conscious exploration of the world. Accordingly, in tertiary cognition, the autosymbolic process is responsive not only to exigencies of the deep psyche but also to the learning and questioning of the ego. The secondary process, that is, not only disciplines the autosymbolic process; it *seeds* it as well. Any subject the ego chooses to ponder becomes a matter for enstatic-creative contemplation. Focused attention on any object of inquiry draws upon the total resources of the nonegoic core of the psyche. Such attention mobilizes energy, leading to infused absorption, as we saw earlier; and such attention engages the autosymbolic process as well. The focusing of attention is at the same time the harnessing of autosymbolic creativity. The autosymbolic process is stirred into activity to explore meanings and possibilities that, under dualistic conditions, would be completely beyond its range.

The autosymbolic process, in all its creativity, is by no means infallible. I have already noted that creative insights garnered from autosymbolic activity must be coherently connected with established conceptions (either by consistent inclusion or by coherent reorganization) and that such insights must additionally stand up to reality testing. Much of contemplative literature, especially Eastern contemplative literature, overestimates the power of contemplative insight. Patanjali, the primary representative of classical Indian yoga, for example, suggests that *samadhi* on an object of inquiry is sufficient utterly to lay bare its essence. And Buddhism holds that the practice of contemplative insight (*vipassana*) is sufficient to reveal the fundamental characteristics of reality.[5] If modern Western epistemology has perhaps overstated the role of empiricism, verification, and reality testing, classical Eastern epistemology has perhaps overstated the role of inner contemplative revelation. A greater balance is needed; empirical testing and contemplative exploration are complementary and equally necessary epistemic activities. Empiricism without contemplation is disconnected from creative insight; contemplation without empiricism is disconnected from reality.

The tertiary process is a form of cognition that, in bringing together the autosymbolic and secondary processes, brings together symbol and concept, creativity and logic, intuition and verification. Integration, in uniting nonegoic potentials and ego functions, unites the full range of human cognitive resources.

Spiritual Embodiment

Spiritual awakening, as we know, is also a bodily awakening. The opening of the ego to the nonegoic core of the psyche is at the same time an opening of the body to the energy that issues from the nonegoic core. This energy, in rising from the core and breaking through physical knots and blockages, gradually reanimates the body. At first it "resurrects" the body in an ominous and threatening way; then it "reincarnates" the ego, returning it to polymorphously sensual life. Finally, after the awakening process is complete and the ego is fully integrated with bodily life, the energy of the nonegoic core begins to express itself somatically as *embodied spiritual power*.

A distinctive aspect of integrated experience is the identity of eros and spirit. Dualism divides these two expressions of our dynamic nature against each other. Primal repression carries with it an implicit condemnation of eros as antispiritual and a corresponding separation of spirit from anything sensual or corporeal. This dualistic division of eros and spirit seems to be confirmed during regression in the service of transcendence when the derepression of the nonegoic sphere triggers a release of energy from the sexual system and a consequent stirring of sexual and aggressive impulses. We saw in chapter 9 that this experience can be especially traumatic for people who are committed to the spiritual path. For whenever such people open themselves to the uplifting influence of spirit they simultaneously expose themselves to the predations of "lower" instincts. Fortunately, these difficulties brought on by the stirring of instinctual impulses are gradually resolved during regeneration in spirit. For once the power emanating from the nonegoic core has had a chance to circulate more freely through the body, it undergoes a transformation in appearance: It gradually ceases appearing as an invasive instinctual power and gradually begins appearing, in its true character, as a native enlivening power, as the power of polymorphously sensual life. Observing this transformation, the ego finally realizes that what had seemed a dangerous eruption of instinctuality is in fact a salutary awakening of somatic life generally. The ego realizes that eros is innocent of the condemnation that had been brought against it. This realization marks the point at which the ego ceases resisting the "resurrection" of the body and begins yielding to its own "reincarnation" in the body.

The main point here, though, is that, in yielding to "reincarnation," the ego gradually comes to see not only that eros is innocent of being an adversary of spirit but also that eros is in fact spirit itself dwelling within the body. This insight is to be credited above all to Tantrism, long considered a scandal within Hindu and Buddhist spirituality.[6] According to Tantrism, sexuality and spirituality are intimately related, so intimately related that sexuality, if practiced in a rigorously ritualized way, can be a means to spiritual awakening. In the Tantric view, sexual ecstasy and spiritual ecstasy are more than analogous; they are *consanguineous:* the eros of sexual ecstasy is none other than the numinous power or spirit of spiritual ecstasy. In crediting Tantrism with this insight, I do not mean to suggest that spirituality can be reduced to sexuality. Sexuality and spirituality are *not* identical. Sexuality is based in a specific psychophysiological center and is a distinct experiential modality. Spirituality on the other hand belongs to embodied life generally and is expressed through all experiential modalities. This difference is crucial. Notwithstanding this difference, however, sexuality and spirituality are intimately related, I suggest, in that the very energy that under dualistic conditions expresses itself primarily as sexual energy is none other than repressed spiritual power. I shall explain the relation of sexual energy to spiritual power more fully in the next section.

The "scandalous" relationship between sexuality and spirituality is well understood by the integrated person. The integrated person understands that erotogenic and spiritual experience are expressions of the same sacred power, a power that, when awakened, is a palpable presence within the body. The integrated person realizes that the body is the native vehicle of spirituality and therefore that spirituality is at home in the body and in all of the body's expressions. The transition from the enchanted world of regeneration in spirit to the hallowedly resplendent world of integration marks the point at which the ego feels at home in the world. The realization that eros, once awakened, is none other than spirit marks the point at which the ego feels at home in the body.

THE MARRIAGE OF THE EGO AND THE DYNAMIC GROUND

Having explained some of the specific ways in which spiritual power expresses itself in integrated life, I shall in this section speak more generally about spiritual power and about the ego's unfolding relationship with it. In addressing these matters, I shall be rendering explicit a number of points that have been left implicit in this and earlier chapters.

Both yoga psychology (see Feuerstein 1989) and psychoanalysis divide psychic energy into two major types: active and potential. Active energy is the energy normally available for psychomental functions. It is the energy that circulates through the body-mind, empowering psychomental systems and processes and charging psychomental events and objects. Potential energy in contrast is a dormant power that plays no or only a very limited role in conscious life. According to yoga, these two types of energy are called *prana* (active) and *kundalini* (potential), and both types of energy are thought to be expressions of a more fundamental power called *shakti*. According to psychoanalysis, both active and potential energy are forms of libido. Active energy is libido that is allowed to circulate freely in the body-mind; potential energy is libido that, owing to repression, is rendered dormant within the sexual system at the beginning of the latency period and that, following puberty, is stimulated by sexual activity and expressed through genital-based orgasm. If psychoanalysis holds that potential energy is energy that has been rendered dormant and limited to a sexual organization, yoga holds that potential energy is energy that can be reactivated and liberated from its "lower" instinctual connections. Yoga believes that the *kundalini* energy can be aroused, either spontaneously or by means of psychospiritual practice, and that the arousal of *kundalini* sets in motion a transformative process leading to spiritual realization.

In our terms, the *kundalini* energy or dormant libido is numinous or spiritual power as negated by primal repression and reduced to latency within the sexual system. This process of repression and reduction to latency was discussed in chapter 4, where the Freudian hydraulic model of repression was criticized. As proposed in that chapter, primal repression is a countercathexis that not only contains psychic energy (or numinous power) but that, in doing so, also deactivates it, rendering it dormant. Primal repression, therefore, contrary to the implications of the hydraulic model, does not involve a high degree of inner psychic pressure. Rather than containing energy under great pressure, primal repression, in "capping" the sexual system, quiets energy at its source and point of release, thereby "putting it to sleep." This sleeping energy is the "serpent power," the *kundalini* energy said to slumber in a coiled position at the base of the spine. In alchemy, this energy is the "elixir" or "philosopher's stone" said to lie latent in prime matter. And in popular mythology, this energy is the "genie" said to be asleep in the magic lamp.

Psychic energy cannot of course be rendered completely dormant; some amount of energy must be active and circulating to fuel psychomental processes. If, then, primal repression "caps" and thereby subdues the fire that burns within the nonegoic core of the psyche, it does not extinguish this fire. To extend the metaphor, primal repression might be said to reduce the fire to a small flame by reducing the amount of oxygen available to the fire. This flame represents the active energy produced and released by the nonegoic core when the nonegoic core is subject to the countercathectic inhibition of primal repression. That is, the flame represents active libido or *prana* as expressed under the conditions of dualism. This restricted organization of psychic energy, I suggest, is the dynamic status quo that, introduced with the latency period, prevails for most people throughout most of their lives. The awakening of sexuality during puberty changes this status quo only by allowing occasional transformations of potential energy into actual energy in the limited form of sexual-orgasmic discharge. Sexual orgasm is a dramatic experience during dualism; it also, however, is a merely occasional experience that, as such, is an exception to the dynamic norm. The norm during dualism is for energy to be divided into active psychic energy circulating (nonorgasmically, nonecstatically) in the body-mind and potential energy lying in wait in the nonegoic core of the psyche.

In yoga psychology the distinction between active and potential energy is conceived not only as a distinction between *prana* and *kundalini* but also as a distinction between *ida* and *pingala* (subsidiary energy pathways) on the one hand and the *sushumna* (the primary energy pathway) on the other. When the great power *shakti* is asleep in the form of *kundalini*, the flow of energy is restricted to the subsidiary channels *ida* and *pingala*, which are said to wind around the central *sushumna* in an ascending helical pattern. With *shakti* asleep as *kundalini*, the central channel is closed by a "knot" (*granthi*) at the base of the spine. This knot is one of several principal barriers that occlude the *sushumna* and prohibit the movement of *shakti* through the *sushumna*. Other knots are said to be located at the navel and throat.[7] These knots, I suggest, are part of the infrastructure of primal repression. They are layers of ossified countercathexis that block the flow of energy in the primary channel and thereby reduce energy to a mostly dormant or potential state, allowing only so much energy to be active as can be "combusted" and released through the subsidiary channels.

In the vocabulary of yoga psychology, then, dualism as a mode of energy organization divides *shakti* into active *prana* energy moving through the subsidiary *ida* and *pingala* pathways and potential *kundalini* energy lying dormant beneath the *sushumna*, which is blocked by a hierarchy of "knots." Correspondingly, in psychoanalytic terminology, the dualistic organization of libido divides libido into active libido, which is available for psychomental functions, and latent libido, which, owing to primal repression, is limited to a primarily potential status within the sexual system. Both yoga psychology and psychoanalysis point to a fundamental underlying power that has both active and potential expressions, an active expression as "ordinary" psychic energy and a potential expression as an extraordinary power arising from the depths of the soul. Yoga psychology understands that this underlying power is not only a psychic power but also a spiritual power: *shakti*, personified as the goddess Shakti. Psychoanalysis, regrettably, understands this power only as nonspiritual libido, or eros. In this book I have been calling this underlying power *numinous power* (following Rudolf Otto) or, simply, *spiritual power.* Whichever term is used, however, the point is that this underlying power, owing to dualism, has two significantly different expressions. It expresses itself both as life-maintaining psychic energy and as a potential power that, upon awakening, is life-transforming spirit.

Because dualism is responsible for the division between active and potential energy and the corresponding division between (active) psychic energy and (potential) spiritual power, the elimination of dualism is at the same time an elimination of these divisions: all energy becomes active energy; all energy becomes spiritual power.

Accordingly, in the integrated body-mind, psychic energy and spiritual power are no longer separate or even distinguishable. Spiritual power, upon awakening, merges with psychic energy and the two become one, as, for example, would happen if a vast underground lake were to surface and merge with preexisting rivers and streams. The awakening of spiritual power, then, leads eventually to the realization that what was thought to be "mere" psychic energy is in truth spiritual power and what had seemed to be a completely new spiritual power rising from psychic depths is in truth psychic energy. Under integrated conditions, the power of the nonegoic core is completely active and no longer divided in its expressions. It is a single vital force that both fuels and awakens, energizes and regenerates, animates and sanctifies psychophysical life. In coming to understand this unity of our dynamic life, the integrated person learns that the body-mind is not only an energy system but also the "temple of spirit."

In an earlier book ([1988] 2d ed. in press) I introduced the expression *Dynamic Ground* to designate the source of spiritual power. Using this expression, integration can be described as a marriage of the ego and the Dynamic Ground. More precisely, perhaps, it can be described as a *re*marriage of the ego and the Dynamic Ground, because, if we remember, the infant prior to the emergence of rapprochement and oedipal ambivalences is intimately at one with the Dynamic Ground as the inner, depth-psychological, dimension of the primordial Great Mother. This original unity or marriage is of course sundered by primal repression. Dualism is a divorce of the ego from the Dynamic Ground. Primal repression reduces the power of the Ground to latency, or virtually so, allowing that power to express itself only in the limited form of psychic energy (active libido, *prana*). This dualistic separation of the ego from the power of the Dynamic Ground is a separation of the ego from spiritual power. The dualistic ego is therefore a "worldly" ego, an ego for which spiritual power remains an "otherworldly" possibility, an alienated transcendent potential. This divorce of the ego from the Dynamic Ground lasts throughout the dualistic period. Regression in the service of transcendence and regeneration in spirit are the stages during which the ego finally returns to and becomes reconciled with the Dynamic Ground. Regression in the service of transcendence is a period of confrontation during which the ego is stripped of its defenses and nakedly reexposed to the Dynamic Ground. Regeneration in spirit is a period of "courtship" during which the ego learns how, once again, to live with the Dynamic Ground. This "courtship" leads finally to integration, which is the remarriage of the ego and the Dynamic Ground. Integration is the sacred wedding, the *hieros gamos*, of the two poles of our being.

INTEGRATION AS GOAL AND NEW BEGINNING

Human development, aiming at integration as its *telos*, follows a course of departure and higher return. The ego must dualistically depart from the Dynamic Ground before it is able to return to the Ground on the higher plane of integration. The pattern of departure and higher return indicates that human development has two principal goals: effective ego functioning (departure) and psychospiritual wholeness (higher return). The former of these goals is accomplished first. The development of ego functions is the principal purpose of the first half of life. This purpose is accomplished, however, only on the basis of dualism; the ego is able to develop its functions only because primal repression safely insulates the ego from the power of the Dynamic Ground (and nonegoic potentials generally). The goal of wholeness is typically postponed until ego development is complete, that is, until the adult tasks of forging an ego identity and learning to live in intimate relationships with significant others have been accomplished. The deep-seated need for wholeness typically does not begin to assert itself until midlife or later. The spiral path of transcendence and reunion with the Dynamic Ground is the developmental course of the second half of life.

In arriving at the *telos* of integration, a new life begins for the ego. The ego begins living life in its fullness, without developmental needs or deficits. In arriving at integration, the ego is mature in its functions and rooted in the nonegoic core of the psyche. It is effectively engaged in the world and open to the deepest of inner resources. It is secure in its individuated existence and faithfully united with the power of the Ground as spirit. In all of these ways the ego, in arriving at integration, is at last fully established on native ground. The person who has completed the developmental journey of departure and higher return is finished with "becoming" and is ready simply, and fully, "to be."

If the integrated person is no longer driven by a developmental agenda, that does not mean that integration precludes higher developmental possibilities. Integration contains significant possibilities for growth. All of the aspects of integrated life discussed in this chapter are capable of being deepened and strengthened. Moreover, a few developmental possibilities lying within integrated life are of a special sort. These possibilities, realized by only a select few, are better understood as gifts of genius or of grace than as individual attainments in any sense of the term. The three principal such gifts are saintly compassion, creative genius, and mystical illumination. These gifts are implicit in integrated life in that they are extraordinary extensions of specific features of integrated life. Saintly compassion can be understood as an extension of I-Thou intimacy, creative genius as an extension of tertiary cognition, and mystical illumination as an extension of objectless contemplative enstasy.

Saintly compassion is a way of relating intimately with others that is distinguished by its irresistible love of others. In saintly compassion, spirit not only reaches out to others in a caring way; it expresses itself as a powerful outpouring of love driven by the needs of the world. Saintly compassion is a pure transpersonal love not limited by constraints of self-interest. It is a selfless love, not in the sense of being self-sacrificing, but rather in the sense of experiencing the sufferings and joys of others as one's own. Saintly love is based on I-Thou intimacy in being a form of open, caring affirmation of others. Saintly love, however, clearly goes beyond I-Thou intimacy in the scope and imperative force of its caring. Saintly love is a love that recognizes no limits and accepts no compromises. It is an irresistible love for all people, indeed for all life on planet earth. Regrettably, such love must be considered a rarity, even among integrated persons. Saintly compassion is a truly extraordinary phenomenon. As precious as it is rare, it is one of the highest expressions, or rather graces, of human life.

Creative genius is also an extraordinary phenomenon requiring exceptional gifts. The creative process requires an access to nonegoic resources usually denied the ego under dualistic conditions. This fact does not imply that integration is a necessary condition of creativity. Most creative people are probably not integrated, and in all likelihood only a small minority of integrated people are creative geniuses. What is required for significant creativity is openness to the spontaneity of the nonegoic sphere and the ability to give disciplined expression to the images, voices, and insights that emerge from this sphere. More specifically, creativity requires both openness to the autosymbolic process and sustained engagement of secondary-process or operational cognitive skills. That is, it requires the primary elements of tertiary cognition. What is distinctive of integrated people is that these elements are not only available to be drawn upon but also effectively unified as a higher cognitive process. This superior cognitive organization means that integrated people tend to be creative people, even if few are creative geniuses. It also means that people possessing exceptional creative gifts tend to be even more creative if they happen also to be integrated. Integration is the basis on which creative gifts are best able to flower into true creative genius.

Mystical illumination, like saintly compassion and creative genius, is an extremely rare and precious phenomenon. Although contemplative enstasy, even objectless enstasy, is a distinctive attainment of integrated life, mystical illumination is a form of contemplative enstasy that far exceeds the norm of integrated experience. Mystical illumination is an experience of prodigious magnitude. In mystical illumination, the ego is not only infusively absorbed in spiritual power; it is infusively absorbed in the Dynamic Ground itself. Mystical illumination is not grounded in a limited cathexis or localized concentration of numinous energy; it is grounded in the very source of numinous energy. It is an infusive absorption in spiritual power in its plenitude and effulgence. The nonegoic core of the psyche opens, exposing the ego to the full power of the Dynamic Ground. This Ground, which once was the fathomless center of a dark abyss, is now a plenipotent nucleus emitting supramundane radiance. It is the godhead behind god; it is *nirguna* Brahman; it is *THE SOURCE* absorption in which produces the deepest and grandest vision that we as mortals are sometimes graced to behold. Mystical illumination, along with saintly compassion and creative genius, is a jewel in the crown of fulfilled humanness.

CONCLUSION

We have traveled a long road in this book. Chapters 1 through 6 retraced the path from infancy to adulthood, from preegoic immersion in nonegoic life to fully developed egoic life built upon a dualistic foundation. Chapter 7 described some of the difficulties that lie in wait at the far end of the path of ego development. Chapters 8 through 10 explored the path of ego transcendence from its beginnings in the dark night of the senses to its penultimate stage, regeneration in spirit. Finally, this chapter has sketched the principal features of integrated life, which is the goal of the path of transcendence. For most people, chapters 1 through 7 cover familiar ground. Most people follow the course of ego development to its end. Few people, however, get very far beyond this point; unfortunately, the ground covered in chapters 8 through 11 is unfamiliar to most people. The path of transcendence leading to integration is "the road less traveled." This fact notwithstanding, the path of transcendence is a path that people in every generation rediscover and pursue, if not all the way to the end at least well beyond the boundaries of life as it usually is lived.

According to the map presented in this book, the path of transcendence begins when the ego, having traveled what it had thought was the main path of life, finds itself at an impasse. Unable to push forward as before, the ego experiences despair and believes that meaningful life has come to an end: the dark night of the senses. Fortunately, the ego is eventually led beyond this impasse and set in motion again. Now, however, the ego finds itself on a path that veers off the main course and leads into dramatically unfamiliar territory, the realm of the *numinosum*. At first this realm is magical and wondrous: the illuminative way, pseudonirvana. But soon the atmosphere changes and the ego begins to be pulled downward on a harrowing course leading to darkness and, it seems, doom: regression in the service of transcendence, the dark night of spirit. Once again the ego believes that all is lost. Once again, however, the ego is led out of an apparently hopeless situation. Rather than perishing in the abyss, the ego is returned to its sources and, taking root therein, begins being healed and spiritually transformed: regeneration in spirit. The descending path of regression thus swings upward on a course of regeneration, a course that gradually decreases its angle of ascent until it stabilizes in a higher trajectory: integration. The spiritual path, as we have seen, follows a spiral course. It is a road that, veering off from what had been the main path of life, circles back on itself to higher ground, the Dynamic Ground.

The symbol of the road or path (*marga, tao,* pilgrimage, odyssey) is a universal symbol signifying that human life is a journey of departure and higher return, a journey the first half of which moves out into the world and the second half of which returns to psychic depths in order to achieve higher, integrated, existence. No one knows for sure why the first half of this journey is completed by almost everyone and the second half by only a few. Perhaps the evolutionary prerequisites for the second half of the journey are not yet fully in place. The path of transcendence may be a path that is still "under construction." It may, that is, represent the future of the species, a future into which only a minority of individuals have ventured.

Notes

Introduction

1. This way of describing Jung's conception of the unconscious is useful and generally accurate but not completely correct, as I shall explain later.

2. Transpersonal psychology's bias against the ego and in favor of extraegoic possibilities derives from the influence of Eastern spirituality and in particular the influence of the Buddhist notion of *anatta* or no-self. Jack Engler (1986) and Mark Epstein (1988), both working from the perspective of Buddhist object relations theory, have tried to correct this bias against the ego. As Epstein says, "The enlightened ego abides, but in a form which sustains the realization of impersonality" (p. 68).

3. I introduced this notion in an earlier book ([1988] 2d ed. in press).

Chapter 1. The Sources of Experience in Infancy

1. Classical psychoanalysis consists of the original drive theory and structural theory (id-ego-superego) in contrast to psychoanalytic ego psychology, object relations theory, and self psychology.

2. Following Ken Wilber (1980a, 1980b), I shall frequently shorten *pre-egoic* and *transegoic* to *pre* and *trans*, respectively.

3. The importance of properly making the pre-trans distinction is stressed by Ken Wilber (1980b). Wilber maps the many ways in which pre can be mistaken for trans, or vice versa, and cautions against the unfortunate consequences that can ensue from such mistakes.

4. Margaret Mahler is the senior author of *The Psychological Birth of the Human Infant*, and the views set forth in the book are based on ideas that Mahler had introduced earlier. Accordingly, I shall follow established practice and cite this work as expressing Mahler's views.

5. More accurately, regression in the service of transcendence corresponds to the first phase of the hero's journey: the descent into the underworld.

6. Piaget (1951; Piaget and Inhelder 1971) held that mental images, growing out of sensorimotor cognition, have an active, motoric rather than exclusively perceptual basis. Specifically, he believed that mental images derive from internalized action schemes that the child has acquired through imitation and is able to reproduce in the absence of the stimuli from which the schemes were acquired.

7. Mahler believes that the infant does not become aware of stimuli associated with the outer reference point, the caregiver, until sometime in the second month, because, as noted earlier, she believes that the initial weeks of life are lived in an oblivious, self-encapsulated, autistic state.

8. I referred earlier to the studies reported by T. G. R. Bower (1982) and Renée Baillargeon (1987) indicating that an initial sense of object permanence may be achieved earlier than Piaget had realized, namely, at four or five months rather than at eight or nine months. Interestingly, four or five months is approximately the age at which, according to Margaret Mahler (Mahler, Pine, and Bergman 1975), the infant begins to differentiate itself from symbiotic dual-unity with the primary caregiver. At about four or five months, it seems, the caregiver begins to come into focus as an integrated, enduring object, even though, at this point, the infant has only the vaguest apprehension of this object and cannot retain this object in memory without the aid of sensory cues. Accordingly, four or five months is the age at which the infant first adopts a transitional object (e.g., a stuffed animal or soft blanket). The transitional object allows the infant to remember and hang on to the caregiver when the caregiver is absent.

9. Our understanding of the archetype of the Great Mother as the child's first object representation derives primarily from the pioneering work of Carl Jung (1912, 1938) and Erich Neumann (1954, 1963, 1973).

CHAPTER 2. EGO FORMATION AND THE ORIGINS OF DUALISM IN EARLY CHILDHOOD

1. See note 4 of chapter 1.

2. In the last chapter I referred to recent studies (Bower 1982; Baillargeon 1987) showing that an initial sense of object permanence can be detected much earlier than Piaget had thought, namely, at four or five months rather than at eight or nine months.

3. Folklore, fairy tales, and popular mythology are full of these split, larger-than-life Good and Terrible Mothers and of "babes in the woods" and "bad little boys and girls" who, as "good children" and "terrible children," correspond to them. The stories of Cinderella, Hansel and Gretel, and the Wizard of Oz provide ready examples.

4. Following Heinz Hartmann (1952, 1955), many psychoanalysts have accepted the view that neutralization of drive energies (viz., libido and aggressive energy) is a necessary condition of object constancy. Margaret Mahler (1966, 1968) accepts this view, stressing the role of the primary caregiver in facilitating neutralization. Otto Kernberg (1976) also accepts the neutralization hypothesis. I shall discuss Kernberg's view later.

5. Freud maintained as early as *The Interpretation of Dreams* (1900) that the secondary process of the system of consciousness cannot accommodate primary process materials and therefore that a repressive elimination of these materials from awareness occurs as soon as the system of consciousness emerges and is sufficiently formed. Freud (1911b) termed this original, infantile, form of repression *primal* repression. After the introduction of the tripartite structural model (1923), Freud explained primal repression in terms of the ego's emergence from the id. Instinctual impulses of the id, Freud explained (1926, 1933), overwhelm the fledgling ego, flooding it with anxiety. The immature ego is helpless to deal with these impulses in any way other than by repressing them, banishing them to the id. Freud (1926, p. 94) states that this initial and basic repression likely occurs before the end of the oedipal period. The resolution of oedipal conflicts and the emergence of the superego, however, reinforce the id-ego separation initiated by primal repression. See Brenner (1957) and Madison (1961) for accounts of Freud's concept of primal repression.

6. Klein's notion of the depressive position, it should be noted, although usually interpreted as corresponding to the achievement of object constancy, is dated by Klein much earlier than Mahler's stage of transition to object constancy. Klein telescopes preoedipal development into the initial months of life. Her account remains insightful, however; and many of her ideas can be retained if they are reinterpreted in accordance with a more realistic timetable of development. My interpretation of Klein is indebted to Hamilton (1988).

7. Johanna Tabin (1985) takes exception to this way of characterizing the difference between preoedipal and oedipal stages, arguing that the child already relates in gendered ways with both parents during the preoedipal period. Without disagreeing with Tabin's general point, I would stress that the significance of the child-father relationship changes dramatically as a consequence of the rapprochement crisis and the child's response to that crisis. I shall be arguing that the child's rapprochement struggles redefine the role of the father and that this redefinition of role makes the child, the mother, and the father not only participants in a gendered threesome but also, now, participants in the distinctive oedipal triangle.

8. The gender-neutral terminology of *primary caregiver* and *secondary caregiver* is difficult to use when discussing the Oedipus complex, which, historically, has been not just a triangular configuration formed by the child, a primary caregiver, and a secondary caregiver, but a configuration formed by the child, the mother, and the father. Accordingly, in this section I shall frequently speak of the mother in the place of the primary caregiver and of the father in the place of the secondary caregiver.

9. Henri Parens (1979) argues that two stages of ambivalence can be distinguished in early childhood, a stage of dyadic ambivalence falling within the preoedipal period and a stage of triadic ambivalence coinciding with the oedipal period. Agreeing with Parens, I am proposing that the latter of these types of ambivalence is a new expression of the former type, an expression in which the original preoedipal ambivalence finds a mirror-opposite counterpart in a third party.

10. The incorporation of the primitive ego ideal within the larger superego system has its earliest origins in preoedipal idealization of the parents (Hartmann and Loewenstein 1962; Lampl-de Groot 1962). The preoedipal child's loss of narcissistic perfection causes the child to see this perfection in the parents, who therefore become ideal figures, embodiments of the child's own wish-fulfillment fantasies. According to Lampl-de Groot, the incorporation of the ego ideal within the superego is finalized at the end of the Oedipus complex, because the narcissistic ideality of the parents is at this point fully fused with their ethical authority. This final incorporation of the ego ideal within the superego, as I have explained, is accomplished in and through the agency of the oedipal father, the commitment to whom is of an inherently double, emulation-capitulation, sort: commitment to the oedipal father as a model to which to aspire (narcissism, ego ideal) is inherently bound up with commitment to him as a sovereign power to obey (ethics, the superego). The ego ideal remains embedded in the superego system until adolescence, at which time, as I shall explain in chapter 5, the struggle for independence from paternal-parental authority disjoins the individualistic strivings of the ego ideal from the paternal-parental imperatives of the superego.

11. The superego of course contains elements deriving from both parents and, as such, is an agency of parental authority generally. It is, however, primarily an agency of *paternal*-parental authority by virtue of the choice of the father over the mother that, as we have seen, brings oedipal conflict to a close.

CHAPTER 3. EGO AND GENDER

1. The idea that the preoedipal mother is a spectral presence haunting the patriarchal world is borrowed from Madelon Sprengnether (1990).

2. In imitating the mother's relationship with the father, the girl is indeed identifying with the mother. This identification, however, is an identification with the mother in her role as partner of the oedipal father rather than in her original role as preoedipal mother.

3. It follows from this interpretation—and seems quite evident anyway—that the desire to have a baby with the father, if it occurs, is a result not of penis envy but of "mother envy."

4. This view is advocated in its strongest form by radical separatist feminists such as Mary Daly (1978, 1984) and Marilyn Frye (1983). The view is espoused in more moderate form by many feminists who focus on womanspirit, goddess religion, or witchcraft, (e.g., Starhawk [1979, 1982], Charlene Spretnak [1982], Carol Christ [1987]).

CHAPTER 4. EGO DEVELOPMENT AND DUALISM IN LATENCY

1. These muscle groups are targeted in *hatha* or *kundalini* yoga, which recommends anal and abdominal *bandhas* or "locks" (i.e., muscle contractions and relaxations) as practices that can remove deep psychophysiological obstructions such as those involved in primal repression. I shall discuss the dismantling of primal repression in chapter 9.

2. Harry Hunt (1989) reviews studies that suggest that spontaneous imagination and voluntary fantasy may even be located in different parts of the brain, spontaneous imagination in both hemispheres or in the right hemisphere and voluntary fantasy in the left hemisphere.

3. The postures of primal alienation and primal repression complement each other as sides of a single larger bodily stance. This stance is for the most part invisible as a deeply embedded and invariant infrastructure of the mental-egoic system. Nevertheless, this primal stance has been recognized by somatically oriented therapies. I have already mentioned that *hatha* and *kundalini* yoga are aware of the anal and abdominal constrictions at the basis

of primal repression and recommend the practice of anal and stomach locks (*bandhas*) to release these constrictions. These forms of yoga also recommend a chin lock, which involves a tightening of muscles in the face, throat, neck, and, by extension, shoulders and chest. The tightening and relaxing of these muscles, I suggest, work to dislodge the embedded posture of primal alienation. In addition to these locks, yoga recommends a large number of postures (*asanas*), most of which work to dismantle or dissolve specific blockages, rigidities, or tensions connected with the overall posture of primal repression and primal alienation. In the West, Wilhelm Reich has helped us understand the somatic bases of dualism and its attendant psychopathologies. His work on "orgastic potency" (1942) seems, in a somewhat idiosyncratic way, to be directed against the somatic bases of primal repression, and his work on body armor as the physical correlate of psychological defense (1972) seems to be focused on the somatic bases of primal alienation.

4. The merging of the ego ideal and superego has two main phases. See note 10 of chapter 2 for a discussion of these phases.

5. As we shall see in the next chapter, the beginning of adolescence is marked, among other ways, by a separation of the ego ideal from the superego and by a corresponding exploration of identity possibilities in ways unsanctioned by the superego. These developments disturb the halcyon synthesis of latency and trigger a recapitulation of the conflictual object relations of the rapprochement and oedipal periods.

6. In dysfunctional or disadvantaged families, these object representations are sometimes not formed, and latency begins with a deficient foundation. Without the "borrowed ego strength" provided by these representations, the latency child is afflicted with pathological insecurities and confusions.

7. The "transductive" thought of the preconceptual substage of the stage of preoperations (two to four years) is a possible exception, because, as I shall explain it, this stage is based to a significant extent on the spontaneity of the imagination operating as autosymbolic process. In my interpretation, the cognition of this stage is expressed through spontaneously produced images that concretely embody the meanings of concepts that the ego is beginning to learn but has not yet explicitly comprehended. The cognition of this stage, then, relies on the spontaneity of the imagination at least as much as on the activity of the ego, and it should therefore be considered a form of cognition that is at least as much nonegoic and receptive (in relation to the ego) as ego-initiated and active.

8. I do not mean to suggest that ego-initiated and ego-receptive cognition are inherently mutually exclusive. I observed in note 7 that Piaget's preconceptual substage of the stage of preoperations may involve both ego activity and imaginal spontaneity. And the same is true, much later in the

developmental cycle, in forms of postdualistic cognition, in which egoic (formal operational) and nonegoic (imaginal, autosymbolic, contemplative) modes of cognition become fruitfully interactive.

9. *Enstasy* is Mircea Eliade's (1969) term for the contemplative state. This term, in contrast to *ecstasy*, indicates that the ego is not only "outside itself" but also *absorbed in* some cognitive content or realm.

10. Just as ego-initiated and ego-receptive cognition are in principle compatible, so, too, are active (egoic) and spontaneous (nonegoic) volition. The sides of these polarities are antagonistic only under conditions of dualism.

CHAPTER 5. EGO DEVELOPMENT AND DUALISM IN ADOLESCENCE

1. This energically based narcissism of infused self-absorption is only one of the types of narcissism to which the adolescent is susceptible. The adolescent is also prone to a more Kohutian type of narcissism focused on selfobjects. As we shall see, insecurities inherent to adolescent selfhood render the adolescent exceedingly dependent upon the supportive mirroring of selective selfobjects.

2. Blos, particularly in his later work, discusses adolescent regression primarily from an object-relational perspective, focusing on the adolescent ego's regressive recapitulation of prelatency interactions with parents and parental imagoes. I shall consider this aspect of adolescent regression in the next section. In the present context the focus is restricted to the psychodynamic aspects of adolescent regression, especially as those aspects can be understood in terms of the challenge to primal repression that occurs during adolescence.

3. Although the oedipal father and preoedipal mother are once again laid to rest, they are by no means completely erased from the psychic record. As we shall see in chapter 9, they can reappear in new imaginal and archetypal forms (no longer focused specifically on the parents) if and when the mental-egoic system begins to give way at the end of dualism.

4. Curiously, Klein's own treatment of adolescence in "Love, Guilt and Reparation" (1964) does not stress love, guilt, and reparation toward parents. She describes adolescents as being almost completely negative toward their parents: "There are, of course, children who can keep love and admiration for the parents themselves even while they are going through these [adolescent] difficulties, but they are not very common" (p. 97). And she says that adolescents, while experiencing "hatred" for their parents (bad objects), invest all hope of love and admiration in such people as teachers (good objects). This perspective exaggerates the negative side of the teenager's

relationship with parents and underestimates the teenager's ambivalence toward (and therefore love, guilt, and felt need to make reparation to) parents. Klein's ideas about the infant's feelings of love, guilt, and need to make reparation apply perfectly to the adolescent; it is curious that she did not make this application herself.

5. Cowan (1978) and Broughton (1983) review relevant studies.

6. Following James Baldwin, John Broughton divides the emergence of dualism into two periods: immature dualism (ages twelve to eighteen) and Cartesian dualism (eighteen to twenty). In the first period, although mind and body are much more thoroughly distinguished from each other than they were during the latency period, they are still thought to interpenetrate in vague ways. During this period, the mind is thought of as a wholly inner and invisible faculty or agency; it is no longer (inconsistently) conflated with the brain. Nevertheless, the mind is still thought somehow to interpenetrate with the brain. As one of Broughton's interviewees said, "The mind is what goes on in the brain" (1978, p. 87). Mind and body are not yet conceived as completely incommensurable substances or domains of experience. This strict Cartesian separation does not occur, according to Broughton, until about the age of eighteen.

7. The roles of relativism and idealism in adolescence have been much discussed. The role of relativism in particular has been the focus of a good deal of attention in the work of both Lawrence Kohlberg and William Perry. Kohlberg (Kohlberg and Kramer 1969) originally interpreted adolescent relativism as a regressive phenomenon, a temporary relapse to preconventional hedonism and egocentrism prior to a return to postconventional (principled, universal) morality. Kohlberg (1973) later revised this view and interpreted adolescent relativism as a transitional stage between conventional and postconventional morality, a stage that loosens the identification with convention so that the adolescent can attain a universal perspective. Perry (1970, 1981) also interprets relativism as a transitional stage. Focusing on college students, Perry sees relativism as an interim period between conventional "either-it's-right-or it's-wrong" dualism and a more mature contextually based sense of individual commitment. For a comparison of Kohlberg's and Perry's views, see Gilligan and Murphy (1979), Murphy and Gilligan (1980), and Gilligan (1981).

Chapter 6. Ego Development and Dualism in Early Adulthood

1. See Spiegel 1958; Blos 1962, 1968; Adatto 1980.

2. This new sense of interest and belonging is, of course, still predicated on primal repression and primal alienation. It is therefore a sense of interest in and belonging to the *dualistic* world.

3. Marxists explain the public-private division in terms of class division: the public sphere is the domain in which laborers produce value (in use or exchange) for the ruling class; the private sphere is the domain in which the family reproduces laborers. Most feminists explain the public-private division in terms of male supremacy: the public sphere is the domain in which men forge identities and exercise worldly powers; the private sphere is the sphere to which men retreat for nurture and to which women are domestically confined. These explanations account for important aspects of the public-private division as it has evolved historically. They do not, however, account for the whole phenomenon. The public-private division is a consequence not only of social causes but also, as we have just seen, of the human psychological need to pair off in long-term cocommitted love partnerships. Such partnerships function in each instance as a nuclear "we" over against "they."

4. This fact is evident, as we shall see in chapters 9 and 10, in traditional conceptions of the principal male deity as a cosmic oedipal figure, a stern lawgiver and judge.

5. Riegel's paper radically revises the Piagetian scheme by attaching a higher dialectical level of thought to each of Piaget's four stages of cognitive development: sensorimotor, preoperational, concrete operational, and formal operational cognition. Moreover, Riegel holds that the Piagetian stages are really *types* of thought each of which (except formal operational cognition) is capable of being dialectically restructured without necessarily having to progress all the way through the Piagetian sequence of stages. Basseches's work stays more closely within the original Piagetian program by recommending dialectical thought only as a fifth, postformal, stage of cognitive development.

6. Similar to Richards and Commons's metasystematic interpretation of postformal thought, Herb Koplowitz (1984) has proposed a system-theory interpretation. System theory (Bertalanffy 1968) explains phenomena in terms of their systematic interrelations with other phenomena. Unlike the formal operational or linear-analytic perspective, which traces the external connections among entities or variables, system theory focuses on patterns of interconnectedness within unifying contexts. System theory is holistic, explaining the behavior of entities or the relations among variables in terms of their interdependencies within the larger fields in which the entities or variables are located. These larger fields are themselves, in turn, fields within even larger fields, and so on. Ultimately, according to system theory, there is a largest field, a universal field that, presumably, is the fundamental matrix of all understanding and explanation. Koplowitz points to David Bohm's (1980) field of "holomovement," which includes the "implicate order" underlying phenomenal experience, as an example of an attempt to conceive such a fundamental matrix. Because system theory presupposes a universal field in which all things participate, it can, according to Koplowitz, be considered a type of unitive or "mystical" thought.

CHAPTER 7. MIDLIFE TRANSVALUATION AND PATHOLOGIES OF THE SELF

1. I owe the basic idea (and the title) of this chapter to David M. Levin (1987). Levin has made an important contribution to our understanding of depression, narcissism, and schizophrenia, which he describes as epidemic pathologies of nihilism or of the modern self. This chapter is also indebted to the work of James F. Masterson (1981, 1985, 1987, 1988). Masterson presents an illuminating account of the narcissistic and borderline personality disorders, which he (1988) calls the "personality disorders of our age." I gratefully acknowledge the substantial influence that Levin and Masterson have had upon my thinking in this chapter.

2. This conclusion is of course only a half truth. The fact is, as explained in the last chapter, that the identity project has both positive and negative motivations and functions. The positive motivations (to establish being, to earn value) and the positive function (to develop worldly selfhood) prevail in the early and middle phases of project, during early adulthood. The negative motivations (to escape "nothingness," to deny "guilt") and the negative function (to maintain masks or facades) prevail at the very outset of the project, during the transition from adolescence to adulthood, and then again in the later phases of the project, during midlife transition. When the positive motivations and function prevail, the tendency is to conceive of the identity project in positive terms, as a means of authentic self-expression leading to fulfillment. When, however, the negative motivations and function prevail, the tendency is to conceive of the identity project in equal but opposite negative terms, as a means of inauthentic flight predicated on deception and existential cowardice. The identity project is fundamentally two-sided; for developmental reasons, however, only one of these sides tends to be evident at any given time.

3. I recommend psychiatrist John Nelson's (1990) excellent book *Healing the Split* for a lucid discussion of this difficult but important issue. I shall discuss some of Nelson's ideas in chapter 9.

4. Kohut (1984) places narcissistic personality disorders in a middle range of severity between the psychoses and the neuroses. As Joan Lang (1987) explains, Kohut's principal criterion in this placement is therapeutic rather than structural. Although narcissistic disorders have important structural affinities with the borderline condition, Kohut places the borderline condition on the side of the psychoses because, by his definition, the person suffering from borderline personality disorder lacks a sufficiently cohesive self to be responsive to psychotherapy. Accordingly, for Kohut, the narcissistic disorders are character pathologies that are more serious than the neuroses but not so serious as to be beyond therapeutic amelioration. The more usual object relations view is to group narcissistic and borderline disorders

together in contrast to the psychoses on the one hand and the neuroses on the other. Kernberg (1975, 1984), for example, holds that the narcissistic disorder is a form of borderline pathology, differing from the borderline disorder proper primarily by virtue of the narcissist possessing a much more integrated and stable (and grandiose) self-concept.

5. Many object relations theorists correlate pathological narcissism, the borderline condition, and the psychoses with specific periods of preoedipal development, explaining these disorders as failures on the part of the child to negotiate the distinctive interpersonal or object-relational challenges of these periods. Different theorists, in explaining such failures, stress different factors, some, like Kohut, emphasizing the role played by the caregivers, others emphasizing drive conflicts, and still others structural deficits. Nevertheless, most theorists agree that conditions of greater severity are correlated with earlier developmental periods. Given its relatively high degree of ego consolidation or self-cohesion, narcissistic disorder is for this reason usually placed near the end of preoedipal development, just prior to the achievement of object constancy. Some theorists (e.g., Masterson 1981, 1987), however, place it much earlier because of its similarities to the grandiose narcissism of the infant. For a representative table of correlations between psychopathologies and preoedipal stages, see Hamilton (1988, p. 125).

6. Interestingly, both Kohut (1977) and Kernberg (1975) acknowledge that midlife is a period particularly prone to narcissistic difficulties. Colarusso and Nemiroff (1981) argue that narcissism occurs normatively as a developmental liability of midlife.

7. In chapter 5 I explained that the adolescent is prone not only to a Kohutian form of narcissism like the one discussed here but also to an energically based narcissism of introspective self-absorption. These two forms of narcissism suggest a general division of narcissism into two major types: (1) infusive narcissism, in which ego cathexis or narcissistic infusion of subjective life leads to self-absorption and self-inflation, and (2) object-directed narcissism, in which feelings of deficiency or inadequacy ("nothingness" and "guilt") lead to narcissistically exaggerated behaviors and overdependence on selfobjects. In chapter 9 I shall describe examples of infusive narcissism that can occur in the transition to transegoic stages of development.

8. More recent treatments of the depersonalization-derealization phenomenon can be found in Jacobson (1959), Stewart (1964), Arlow (1966), Meyer (1968), Hillman (1985), and Nieli (1987).

9. As discussed in note 2, the truth is that the mental ego's worldly identity is neither an authentic self possessing both being and worth (as the mental ego believes prior to disillusionment) nor a merely inauthentic social mask (as the mental ego believes after disillusionment). Worldly identity is an important vehicle through which the mental ego shapes itself and actu-

alizes its potentialities in the world. If, prior to disillusionment, the mental ego tends to take its identity too seriously; after disillusionment, it does not take its identity seriously enough.

10. This passage and the passage by Laing quoted in the next paragraph are cited in Millon (1981, p. 281). Millon's chapter on the schizoid personality provides an excellent history and analysis of the disorder.

11. I do not know who is to be credited for the expression *stably unstable*, which so aptly describes the borderline personality.

12. Most object relations theorists (e.g., Mahler 1972; Masterson and Rinsley 1975; Masterson 1981, 1987; Rinsley 1982, 1989; Kernberg 1980a, 1980b) agree that the borderline condition derives from the rapprochement subphase of the separation-individuation process. Most agree that the acute ambivalence experienced by the child for the primary caregiver during the rapprochement crisis is a precursor of the unstable, ambivalent relationships that borderlines experience in later life. Agreeing on this general point, object relations theorists disagree on the principal factors (e.g., constitutional weaknesses, drive conflicts, inadequate parenting) that determine which children grow through the rapprochement crisis unscathed and which are affected in a way that predisposes them to borderline difficulties later in life.

13. Chemical substances, of course, can also be used as medications that desensitize consciousness and thereby alleviate the mental ego's pain by numbing, rather than overriding, it.

14. See Leichtman (1989) for a discussion of the history of conceptions of the borderline disorder as a diagnostic category.

Chapter 8. the First Stage of Transcendence: The Dark Night of the Senses

1. This awakening corresponds roughly to the beginning of what is called the *illuminative way* in the Roman Catholic mystical tradition.

2. I follow the order presented in the *Dark Night*. These criteria are also discussed in the *Ascent of Mount Carmel* (Book Two, chapter 13).

3. Fitzgerald (1984) discusses some of the ways in which the night of the senses manifests itself in personal and social life.

4. See *Ascent of Mount Carmel* (Book Two, chapter 13) for a general discussion of signs indicating when one should discontinue discursive meditation and give oneself to quiet repose. See also St. Teresa's *Interior Castle* (Fourth Mansions, chapter 3) and *Way of Perfection* (chapters 28–29) for a description of silent, nondiscursive prayer, which Teresa calls the *prayer of rec-*

ollection. Teresa at times speaks of recollection as a state achieved by the meditator (later termed *acquired recollection*) and at times speaks of it as a state produced by the Holy Spirit (later termed *infused recollection*). This vacillation is understandable, because recollection is a type of prayer that occurs in the transition from (ego-active) discursive meditation to (ego-passive) infused contemplation. In the prayer of recollection, the ego engages in "negative volition." It surrenders the tendency to be active so that it can be drawn into the presence of spiritual power.

5. An encounter with the deeper (collective, archetypal) shadow occurs during the dark night of spirit, when the ego is tormented by seemingly demoniacal forces.

Chapter 9. The Spiral Path of Transcendence: Awakening, Regression, Regeneration

1. I introduced this expression in an earlier book ([1988] 2d ed. in press).

2. The notion of a rupture of planes is borrowed from Mircea Eliade (1969).

3. Stanislav Grof's (1975, 1985) theory of perinatal matrices suggests that the imploded absorptions of regression in the service of transcendence can be compared to the intrauterine state of contractedness and pressure just prior to birth. In terms of the night sea journey or hero's journey, imploded absorbed states correspond to the point of the journey at which the sun or hero, having descended into the ocean or underworld, is swallowed by a beast dwelling in the deep.

4. Christina Grof (Grof and Grof 1990) reports that her own *kundalini* awakening, and the spiritual emergency that eventually resulted from it, was initially triggered by the intensities of childbirth.

5. Wilber opposes the very notion of regression in the service of transcendence. His criticism (1980b) of Jung states that any deep journey into the unconscious of the general sort described by Jung is really *only* a regressive return to origins. According to Wilber, regression is not a necessary or integral part of transcendence. If regression occurs, it does so as an exception to the developmental norm.

Chapter 10. Gender and Transcendence

1. Later in this section I shall explain that Jung's acknowledgment of the spiritual leadership of women really does not go very far, because, for

Jung, when men follow women (anima figures), they are really following their own projections rather than anything substantive in the women themselves.

2. Because the NPR pole of the psyche is the seat of the deep or collective unconscious and because the anima is the archetype of the NPR pole, the anima, under dualism, properly belongs to the deep or collective unconscious. In contrast, because the EFI pole of the psyche is the seat of conscious egoic experience and because the animus is the archetype of the EFI pole, the animus, if unconscious, is part of the personal unconscious. More on this in note 3.

3. The animus, as the archetype of the EFI pole of the psyche, belongs either to the embedded personal unconscious (men) or the repressed personal unconscious (women). The embedded versus repressed distinction is to be credited to Ken Wilber (1980a). The embedded unconscious consists of those elements of the personality with which we are identified but of which we are unaware, elements so integral to the way we are constituted as subjects that we are unable to stand apart from them and cognize them as objects for a subject. Elements of ego identity and the ego ideal are generally embedded in this sense during early adulthood. Accordingly, because the animus is adopted by men as part of their ego identity and ego ideal, it belongs to men's embedded unconscious, and to the personal (i.e., intraegoic) embedded unconscious in particular. For women, in contrast, the animus is typically repressed and therefore part of the repressed unconscious. It is not, however, part of the repressed deep or collective unconscious, because it is the archetype of conscious EFI experience rather than of unconscious NPR experience. The animus is intraegoic rather than nonegoic. It is therefore, for women, part of the repressed personal unconscious.

4. Again, the discussion presupposes the contemporary context in which full EFI expression is a real possibility for women.

5. This term was coined by Rosemary Radford Ruether (1983).

CHAPTER 11. THE GOAL OF TRANSCENDENCE: INTEGRATION

1. This chapter draws upon an account of integration presented in an earlier book, *The Ego and the Dynamic Ground* ([1988] 2d ed. in press). Much of what I say here was first formulated in chapter 9 of that book. The presentation that follows extends that formulation and restates it in terms of the theoretical framework developed in this book.

2. For references and comments, see chapter 8, note 4.

3. Patanjali uses the term *samyama* to designate such a sequential telescoping of *dharana*, *dhyana*, and *samadhi*. See Aranya (1983, pp. 253–254).

4. Mystical illumination is an exception to this statement. Mystical illumination is an infused absorption of such rarity and extraordinary magnitude that it must be considered unique. I shall discuss mystical illumination later.

5. According to Buddhism, the three fundamental characteristics of existence are suffering (i.e., the "unsatisfactoriness" of things), impermanence, and voidness of self. The practice of insight is said to reveal these characteristics in an immediate intuitive way.

6. The unity of eros (or libido) and spirit is also espoused in the early work of Ken Wilber (1979).

7. See Feuerstein (1989).

References

Adatto, Carl P. (1980). "Late Adolescence to Early Adulthood." In *The Course of Life: Psychoanalytic Contributions Toward Understanding Personality Development.* Vol. 2, *Latency, Adolescence and Youth,* ed. S. I. Greenspan and G. H. Pollock. Washington, D.C.: NIMH.

Adelson, Joseph, and Margery Doehrman. (1980). "The Psychodynamic Approach to Adolescence." In *Handbook of Adolescent Psychology,* ed. J. Adelson. New York: John Wiley and Sons.

Adler, Gerald. (1985). *Borderline Psychopathology and Its Treatment.* New York: Jason Aronson.

American Psychiatric Association. (1987). *Diagnostic and Statistical Manual of Mental Disorders.* 3d ed., rev. Washington, D.C.: American Psychiatric Association.

Aranya, Hariharananda. (1983). *Yoga Philosophy of Patanjali.* Albany: State University of New York Press.

Arieti, Silvano. (1967). *The Intrapsychic Self.* New York: Basic Books.

———. (1976). *Creativity: The Magic Synthesis.* New York: Basic Books.

Arlin, Patricia K. (1975). "Cognitive Development in Adulthood: A Fifth Stage?" *Developmental Psychology* 11:602–606.

———. (1977). "Piagetian Operations in Problem Finding." *Developmental Psychology* 13:297–298.

———. (1984). "Adolescent and Adult Thought: A Structural Interpretation." In *Beyond Formal Operations: Late Adolescent and Adult Cognitive Development*, ed. M. L. Commons, F. A. Richards, and C. Armon. New York: Praeger.

———. (1989). "Problem Solving and Problem Finding in Young Artists and Young Scientists." In *Adult Development*. Vol. 1, *Comparisons and Applications of Developmental Models*, ed. M. L. Commons, J. D. Sinnott, F. A. Richards, and C. Armon. New York: Praeger.

Arlow, Jacob A. (1966). "Depersonalization and Derealization." In *Psychoanalysis—A General Psychology: Essays in Honor or Heinz Hartmann*, ed. R. M. Loewenstein, L. M. Newman, M. Schur, and A. J. Solnit. New York: International Universities Press.

Baillargeon, Renée. (1987). "Object Permanence in $3\frac{1}{4}$ and $4\frac{1}{2}$-Month-Old Infants." *Developmental Psychology* 23:655–664.

Basseches, Michael. (1980). "Dialectical Schemata: A Framework for the Empirical Study of the Development of Dialectical Thinking." *Human Development* 23:400–421.

———. (1984a). *Dialectical Thinking and Adult Development*. Norwood, N.J.: Ablex.

———. (1984b). "Dialectical Thinking as a Metasystematic Form of Cognitive Organization." In *Beyond Formal Operations: Late Adolescent and Adult Cognitive Development*, ed. M. L. Commons, F. A. Richards, and C. Armon. New York: Praeger.

———. (1989). "Dialectical Thinking as an Organized Whole: Comments on Irwin and Kramer." In *Adult Development*. Vol. 1, *Comparisons and Applications of Developmental Models*, ed. M. L. Commons, J. D. Sinnott, F. A. Richards, and C. Armon. New York: Praeger.

Bertalanffy, Ludwig von. (1968). *General System Theory*. New York: Braziller.

Blasi, Augusto. (1988). "Identity and the Development of the Self." In *Self, Ego, and Identity: Integrative Approaches*, ed. D. K. Lapsley and F. C. Power. New York: Springer.

Blos, Peter. (1962). *On Adolescence: A Psychoanalytic Interpretation.* New York: The Free Press.

———. (1967). "The Second Individuation Process of Adolescence." In *The Adolescent Passage: Developmental Issues.* New York: International Universities Press, 1979.

———. (1968). "Character Formation in Adolescence." In *The Adolescent Passage: Developmental Issues.* New York: International Universities Press, 1979.

———. (1972). "The Function of the Ego Ideal in Adolescence." *Psychoanalytic Study of the Child* 27:93–97.

———. (1974). "The Genealogy of the Ego Ideal." In *The Adolescent Passage: Developmental Issues.* New York: International Universities Press, 1979.

———. (1976). "When and How Does Adolescence End?: Structural Criteria for Adolescent Closure." In *The Adolescent Passage: Developmental Issues.* New York: International Universities Press, 1979.

Bohm, David. (1980). *Wholeness and the Implicate Order.* London: Routledge and Kegan Paul.

Bollas, Christopher. (1987). *The Shadow of the Object: Psychoanalysis and the Unthought Known.* New York: Columbia University Press.

Bower, T. G. R. (1979). *Human Development.* San Francisco: W. H. Freeman.

———. (1982). *Development in Infancy.* 2d ed. San Francisco: W. H. Freeman.

———. (1989). *The Rational Infant: Learning in Infancy.* New York: W. H. Freeman.

Brandt, David. E. (1977). "Separation and Identity in Adolescence." *Contemporary Psychoanalysis* 13:507–518.

Brazelton, T. Berry, Barbara Koslowski, and Mary Main. (1974). "The Origins of Reciprocity: The Early Mother-Infant Interaction." In *The Effect of the Infant on Its Caregiver,* ed. M. Lewis and L. Rosenblum. New York: John Wiley and Sons.

Brenner, Charles. (1957). "The Nature and Development of the Concept of Repression in Freud's Writings." *Psychoanalytic Study of the Child* 12:19–46.

Broughton, John M. (1978). "Development of Concepts of Self, Mind, Reality, and Knowledge." In *New Directions for Child Development: Social Cognition*, ed. W. Damon. San Francisco: Jossey-Bass.

————. (1980). "Genetic Metaphysics: The Developmental Psychology of Mind-Body Concepts." In *Body and Mind: Past, Present, and Future*, ed. R. W. Rieber. New York: Academic Press.

————. (1982). "Genetic Logic and the Developmental Psychology of Philosophical Concepts." In *The Cognitive Developmental Psychology of James Mark Baldwin*, ed. J. M. Broughton and D. J. Freeman-Moir. Norwood, N.J.: Ablex.

————. (1983). "The Cognitive-Developmental Theory of Adolescent Self and Identity." In *Developmental Approaches to the Self*, ed. B. Lee and G. C. Noam. New York: Plenum Press.

————. (1984). "Not Beyond Formal Operations but Beyond Piaget." In *Beyond Formal Operations: Late Adolescent and Adult Cognitive Development*, ed. M. L. Commons, F. A. Richards, and C. Armon. New York: Praeger.

Bruner, Jerome. (1966). "On Cognitive Growth." In J. Bruner et al., *Studies in Cognitive Growth: A Collaboration at the Center for Cognitive Studies*. New York: John Wiley and Sons.

Buber, Martin. (1970). *I and Thou*. Trans. W. Kaufmann. New York: Charles Scribner's Sons.

Burland, J. Alexis. (1980). "Unresolved Rapprochement Conflict and the Infantile Neurosis." In *Rapprochement: The Critical Subphase of Separation-Individuation*, ed. R. F. Lax, S. Bach, and J. A. Burland. New York: Jason Aronson.

Campbell, Joseph. (1949). *The Hero with a Thousand Faces*. New York: Pantheon Books.

Camus, Albert. (1942). *The Stranger*. Trans. S. Gilbert. New York: Alfred A. Knopf.

Chodorow, Nancy. (1974). "Family Structure and Feminine Personality." In *Woman, Culture and Society*, ed. M. Rosaldo and L. Lamphere. Stanford, Calif.: Stanford University Press.

————. (1978). *The Reproduction of Mothering: Psychoanalysis and the Sociology of Gender*. Berkeley: University of California Press.

————. (1979). "Feminism and Difference: Gender, Relation, and Difference in Psychoanalytic Perspective." *Socialist Review* 46: 51–69.

Christ, Carol. (1987). *Laughter of Aphrodite: Reflections on a Journey to the Goddess.* San Francisco: Harper and Row.

Colarusso, Calvin A., and Robert A. Nemiroff. (1981). *Adult Development: A New Dimension in Psychodynamic Theory and Practice.* New York: Plenum Press.

Condon, William S., and Louis W. Sander. (1974). "Neonate Movement is Synchronized with Adult Speech: Interactional Participation and Language Acquisition." *Science* 183:99–101.

Cooley, Charles H. (1902). *Human Nature and the Social Order.* New York: Charles Scribner's Sons.

Corless, Roger J. (1989). *The Vision of Buddhism: The Space Under the Tree.* New York: Paragon House.

Cowan, Philip A. (1978). *Piaget with Feeling: Cognitive, Social, and Emotional Dimensions.* New York: Holt, Rinehart and Winston.

Daly, Mary. (1973). *Beyond God the Father: Toward a Philosophy of Women's Liberation.* Boston: Beacon Press.

————. (1978). *Gyn/Ecology: The Metaethics of Radical Feminism.* Boston: Beacon Press.

————. (1984). *Pure Lust: Elemental Feminist Philosophy.* Boston: Beacon Press.

Demany, Laurent, Beryl McKenzie, and Elaine Vurpillot. (1977). "Rhythm Perception in Early Infancy." *Nature* 266:718–719.

Dinnerstein, Dorothy. (1976). *The Mermaid and the Minotaur: Sexual Arrangements and Human Malaise.* New York: Harper and Row.

Dostoyevsky, Fyodor. (1960). *Notes from Underground.* Trans. C. Garnett. In *Notes from Underground, Poor People, The Friend of the Family: Three Short Novels by Fyodor Dostoyevsky.* New York: Dell.

Eliade, Mircea. (1969). *Yoga: Immortality and Freedom.* Princeton, N.J.: Princeton University Press.

Engler, Jack. (1986). "Therapeutic Aims in Psychotherapy and Meditation." In *Transformations of Consciousness: Conventional and Con-*

templative Perspectives on Development, ed. K. Wilber, J. Engler, and D. Brown. Boston: Shambhala.

Epstein, Mark. (1988). "The Deconstruction of the Self: Ego and 'Egolessness' in Buddhist Insight Meditation." *Journal of Transpersonal Psychology* 20:61–69.

Erikson, Erik H. (1950). "Growth and Crises of the Healthy Personality." In *Identity and the Life Cycle.* Published in *Psychological Issues,* Monograph 1, 1959.

———. (1956). "The Problem of Ego Identity." In *Identity and the Life Cycle.* Published in *Psychological Issues,* Monograph 1, 1959.

———. (1963). *Childhood and Society.* 2d ed. New York: W. W. Norton.

Esman, Aaron H. (1980). "Adolescent Psychopathology and the Rapprochement Phenomenon." *Adolescent Psychiatry* 8:320–331.

Fairbairn, W. R. D. (1940). "Schizoid Factors in the Personality." In *Psychoanalytic Studies of the Personality.* London: Tavistock Publications, 1952.

Fantz, Robert L. (1963). "Pattern Vision in Newborn Infants." *Science* 140:296–297.

Fantz, Robert L., and Sonia Nevis. (1967). "Pattern Preferences and Perceptual-Cognitive Development in Early Infancy." *Merrill-Palmer Quarterly* 13:77–108.

Feuerstein, Georg. (1989). *Yoga: The Technology of Ecstasy.* Los Angeles: Jeremy Tarcher.

Fitzgerald, Constance. (1984). "Impasse and Dark Night." In *Living the Apocalypse,* ed. T. H. Edwards. San Francisco: Harper and Row.

Flax, Jane. (1983). "Political Philosophy and the Patriarchal Unconscious: A Psychoanalytic Perspective on Epistemology and Metaphysics." In *Discovering Reality: Feminist Perspectives on Epistemology, Metaphysics, Methodology, and Philosophy of Science,* ed. S. Harding and M. Hintikka. Dordrecht: D. Reidel.

———. (1990). *Thinking Fragments: Psychoanalysis, Feminism, and Postmodernism in the Contemporary West.* Berkeley: University of California Press.

Fordham, Michael. (1980). "The Emergence of Child Analysis" *Journal of Analytical Psychology* 25:311–324.

————. (1981). "Neumann and Childhood." *Journal of Analytical Psychology* 26:99–122.

Fraiberg, Selma. (1969). "Libidinal Object Constancy and Mental Representation." *The Psychoanalytic Study of the Child* 24:9–47.

Frankl, Viktor E. (1962). *Man's Search for Meaning*. Rev. ed. Boston: Beacon Press.

————. (1969). *The Will to Meaning: Foundations and Applications of Logotherapy*. New York: New American Library.

Freud, Anna. (1946). *The Ego and the Mechanisms of Defense*. New York: International Universities Press.

————. (1958). "Adolescence." *The Psychoanalytic Study of the Child* 13:255–278.

Freud, Sigmund. (1900). *The Interpretation of Dreams*. In *The Standard Edition of the Complete Psychological Works of Sigmund Freud*. Vol. 4. London: Hogarth Press, 1953.

————. (1911a). "Formulations on the Two Principles of Mental Functioning." In *Standard Edition*. Vol. 12. London: Hogarth Press, 1958.

————. (1911b). "Psychoanalytic Notes on an Autobiographical Account of a Case of Paranoia (Dementia Paranoides)." In *Standard Edition*. Vol. 12. London: Hogarth Press, 1958.

————. (1914). "On Narcissism: An Introduction." In *Standard Edition*. Vol. 14. London: Hogarth Press, 1957.

————. (1923). *The Ego and the Id*. In *Standard Edition*. Vol. 19. London: Hogarth Press, 1961.

————. (1926). "Inhibitions, Symptoms and Anxiety." In *Standard Edition*. Vol. 20. London: Hogarth Press, 1959.

————. (1930). *Civilization and Its Discontents*. In *Standard Edition*. Vol. 21. London: Hogarth Press, 1961.

————. (1931). "Female Sexuality." In *Standard Edition*. Vol. 21. London: Hogarth Press, 1961.

————. (1933). *New Introductory Lectures on Psycho-Analysis*. In *Standard Edition*. Vol. 22. London: Hogarth Press, 1964.

Frobenius, Leo. (1904). *Das Zeitalter des Sonnengotes*. Berlin: G. Reimer.

Frye, Marilyn. (1983). *The Politics of Reality: Essays in Feminist Theory.* Trumansburg, N.Y.: Crossing Press.

George, Demetra. (1992). *Mysteries of the Dark Moon: The Healing Power of the Dark Goddess.* San Francisco: HarperCollins.

Gilligan, Carol. (1981). "Moral Development." In *The Modern American College: Responding to the New Realities of Diverse Students and a Changing Society,* ed. A. W. Chickering. San Francisco: Jossey-Bass.

Gilligan, Carol, and Lawrence Kohlberg. (1978). "From Adolescence to Adulthood: The Rediscovery of Reality in a Postconventional World." In *Topics in Cognitive Development.* Vol. 2, *Language and Operational Thought,* ed. B. Z. Presseisen, D. Goldstein, and M. H. Appel. New York: Plenum Press.

Gilligan, Carol, and John M. Murphy. (1979). "Development from Adolescence to Adulthood: The Philosopher and the Dilemma of Fact." In *New Directions for Child Development,* No. 5, *Intellectual Development Beyond Childhood,* ed. D. Kuhn. San Francisco: Jossey-Bass.

Goffman, Erving. (1959). *The Presentation of Self in Everyday Life.* Garden City, N.Y.: Doubleday Books.

Goldenberg, Naomi. (1976). "A Feminist Critique of Jung." *Signs* 2:443–449.

Goldstein, William. (1985). *An Introduction to Borderline Conditions.* Northvale, N.J.: Aronson.

Grof, Christina, and Stanislav Grof. (1990). *The Stormy Search for Self.* Los Angeles: Jeremy Tarcher.

Grof, Stanislav. (1975). *Realms of the Human Unconscious.* New York: Viking Press.

———. (1985). *Beyond the Brain: Birth, Death, and Transcendence in Psychotherapy.* Albany: State University of New York Press.

———. (1988). *The Adventure of Self-Discovery.* Albany: State University of New York Press.

Group for the Advancement of Psychiatry (Committee on Adolescence). (1968). *Normal Adolescence: Its Dynamics and Impact.* New York: Charles Scribner's Sons.

Guntrip, Harry. (1952a). "A Study of Fairbairn's Theory of Schizoid Reactions." *British Journal of Medical Psychology* 25:86–103.

———. (1952b). "The Schizoid Personality and the External World." In *Schizoid Phenomena, Object Relations, and the Self.* New York: International Universities Press, 1969.

———. (1961). "The Schizoid Problem, Regression and the Struggle to Preserve an Ego." In *Schizoid Phenomena, Object Relations, and the Self.* New York: International Universities Press, 1969.

———. (1969). "The Regressed Ego, The Lost Heart of the Self, and the Inability to Love." In *Schizoid Phenomena, Object Relations, and the Self.* New York: International Universities Press.

Haaf, Robert A., and Richard Q. Bell. (1967). "A Facial Dimension in Visual Discrimination by Human Infants." *Child Development* 38:893–899.

Hamilton, Gregory N. (1988). *Self and Others: Object Relations Theory in Practice.* Northvale, N.J.: Jason Aronson.

Hartmann, Heinz. (1939). *Ego Psychology and the Problem of Adaptation.* New York: International Universities Press, 1958.

———. (1952). "The Mutual Influences of the Ego and the Id." *Psychoanalytic Study of the Child* 7:9–30.

———. (1955). "Notes on the Theory of Sublimation." *Journal of the American Psychoanalytic Association* 10:9–29.

Hartmann, Heinz, Ernst Kris, and Rudolph M. Loewenstein. (1946). "Comments on the Formation of Psychic Structure." *Psychoanalytic Study of the Child* 2:11–38.

Hartmann, Heinz, and Rudolf M. Loewenstein. (1962). "Notes on the Superego." *Psychoanalytic Study of the Child* 17:42–81.

Hegel, G. W. F. (1967). *The Phenomenology of Spirit.* Trans. A. V. Miller. Oxford: Oxford University Press.

Heidegger, Martin. (1953). "The Question Concerning Technology." Trans. W. Lovitt. In *Martin Heidegger, Basic Writings,* ed. D. F. Krell. New York: Harper and Row, 1977.

———. (1962). *Being and Time.* Trans. J. Macquarrie and E. Robinson. London: SCM Press.

————. (1982). *Nietzsche*. Vol. 4, *Nihilism*. Trans. F. A. Capuzzi. San Francisco: Harper and Row.

Hill, Careth S. (1992). *Masculine and Feminine: The Natural Flow of Opposites in the Psyche*. Boston: Shambhala Publications.

Hillman, James. (1985). *Anima: An Anatomy of a Personified Notion*. Dallas: Spring Publications.

Hume, David. (1888). *A Treatise of Human Nature*. Oxford: Clarendon Press.

Hunt, Harry T. (1989). *The Multiplicity of Dreams: Memory, Imagination, and Consciousness*. New Haven, Conn.: Yale University Press.

Hutt, S. J., Corinne Hutt, H. G. Lenard, H. V. Bernuth, and W. J. Muntjewerff. (1968). "Auditory Responsivity in the Human Neonate." *Nature* 218:888–890.

Inhelder, Barbel, and Jean Piaget. (1958). *The Growth of Logical Thinking from Childhood to Adolescence*. Trans. A. Parsons and S. Milgram. New York: Basic Books.

Isaacs, Susan. (1943). "The Nature and Function of Phantasy." In *Developments in Psycho-Analysis*, ed. M. Klein, P. Heimann, S. Isaacs, and J. Riviere. London: Hogarth Press, 1958.

Jacobson, Edith. (1959). "Depersonalization." *Journal of the American Psychoanalytic Association* 7:581–610.

————. (1964). *The Self and the Object World*. New York: International Universities Press.

John of the Cross, Saint. (1991a). *The Dark Night*. In *The Collected Works of Saint John of the Cross*. Rev. ed. Trans. K. Kavanaugh and O. Rodriguez. Washington, D.C.: ICS Publications.

————. (1991b). *The Living Flame of Love*. In *The Collected Works of St. John of the Cross*. Rev. ed. Trans. K. Kavanaugh and O. Rodriguez. Washington, D.C.: ICS Publications.

Johnson, Miriam M. (1988). *Strong Mothers, Weak Wives: The Search for Gender Equality*. Berkeley: University of California Press.

Jones, Ernest. (1922). "Some Problems of Adolescence." In *Papers on Psycho-Analysis*, 5th ed. Baltimore: Williams and Wilkins, 1948.

Josselson, Ruthellen L. (1980). "Ego Development in Adolescence." In *Handbook of Adolescent Psychology*, ed. J. Adelson. New York: John Wiley and Sons.

————. (1988). "The Embedded Self: I and Thou Revisited." In *Self, Ego, and Identity: Integrative Approaches*, ed. D. K. Lapsley and F. C. Power. New York: Springer.

Jung, Carl G. (1912). *Symbols of Transformation*. 2d ed. In *The Collected Works of C. G. Jung*. Vol. 5. Princeton, N.J.: Princeton University Press, 1967. This is a translation of *Symbole der Wandlung*, published in 1952, which is an extensive revision of *Wandlungen und Symbole der Libido*, first published in 1912.

————. (1925). *Analytical Psychology: Notes of the Seminar Given in 1925*, ed. W. McGuire. Princeton, N.J.: Princeton University Press, 1989.

————. (1927). "Women in Europe." In *Collected Works*. Vol. 10. 2d ed. Princeton, N.J.: Princeton University Press, 1970.

————. (1928). "On Psychic Energy." In *Collected Works*, Vol. 8. 2d ed. Princeton, N.J.: Princeton University Press, 1969.

————. (1938). "Psychological Aspects of the Mother Archetype." In *Collected Works*. Vol. 9. 2d ed. Princeton, N.J.: Princeton University Press, 1968; originally published in German in 1938; revised 1954.

————. (1951). *Aion: Researches into the Phenomenology of the Self*. In *Collected Works*. Vol. 9. Part II. Princeton, N.J.: Princeton University Press, 1959.

————. (1953). *Two Essays on Analytical Psychology*. In *Collected Works*. Vol. 7. New York: Pantheon Books.

Kagan, Jerome. (1981). *The Second Year: The Emergence of Self-Awareness*. Cambridge, Mass.: Harvard University Press.

————. (1984). *The Nature of the Child*. New York: Basic Books.

————. (1989). *Unstable Ideas: Temperament, Cognition, and Self*. Cambridge, Mass.: Harvard University Press.

Kant, Immanuel. (1929). *The Critique of Pure Reason*. Trans. N. K. Smith. Toronto: Macmillan.

Kast, Verena. (1986). *The Nature of Loving: Patterns of Human Relationships*. Wilmette, Ill.: Chiron Publications.

Kaye, Kenneth. (1982). *The Mental and Social Life of Babies: How Parents Create Persons*. Chicago: University of Chicago Press.

Keller, Catherine. (1986). *From a Broken Web: Separation, Sexism, and Self.* Boston: Beacon Press.

Kernberg, Otto. (1975). *Borderline Conditions and Pathological Narcissism.* New York: Jason Aronson.

———. (1976). *Object-Relations Theory and Clinical Psychoanalysis.* New York: Jason Aronson.

———. (1980a). "The Development of Intrapsychic Structures in the Light of Borderline Personality Organization." In *The Course of Life: Psychoanalytic Contributions Toward Understanding Personality Development.* Vol. 3, *Adulthood and the Aging Process,* ed. S. I. Greenspan and G. H. Pollock. Washington, D.C.: NIMH.

———. (1980b). "Mahler's Developmental Theory: A Correlation." In *Internal World and External Reality: Object Relations Theory Applied.* Northvale, N.J.: Jason Aronson.

———. (1981). "Self, Ego, Affects, and Drives." *Journal of the American Psychoanalytic Association* 30:893–916.

———. (1984). *Severe Personality Disorders: Psychotherapeutic Strategies.* New Haven, Conn.: Yale University Press.

———. (1987). "The Dynamic Unconscious and the Self." In *Theories of the Unconscious and Theories of the Self,* ed. R. Stern. Hillsdale, N.J.: Analytic Press.

Kierkegaard, Soren. (1941). *Concluding Unscientific Postscript.* Trans. W. Lowrie. Princeton, N.J.: Princeton University Press.

———. (1945). *Stages on Life's Way.* Trans. W. Lowrie. Princeton, N.J.: Princeton University Press.

———. (1954a). *Fear and Trembling.* In *Fear and Trembling and Sickness unto Death.* Trans. W. Lowrie. Princeton, N.J.: Princeton University Press.

———. (1954b). *Sickness unto Death.* In *Fear and Trembling and Sickness unto Death.* Trans. W. Lowrie. Princeton, N.J.: Princeton University Press.

———. (1959). *Either/Or.* Trans. D. F. Swenson, L. M. Swenson, and W. Lowrie; revised by H. A. Johnson. Garden City, N.Y.: Doubleday.

Klein, Melanie. (1934). "A Contribution to the Psychogenesis of Manic-Depressive States." In *Contributions to Psycho-Analysis, 1921–1945.* London: Hogarth Press, 1948.

———. (1940). "Mourning and Its Relation to Manic-Depressive States." In *Contributions to Psycho-Analysis, 1921–1945*. London: Hogarth Press, 1948.

———. (1948). "On the Theory of Anxiety and Guilt." In *Envy and Gratitude and Other Works, 1946–1963*. New York: Delta Books, 1975.

———. (1952a). "Some Theoretical Conclusions Regarding the Emotional Life of the Infant." In *Envy and Gratitude and Other Works, 1946–1963*. New York: Delta Books, 1975.

———. (1952b). "The Mutual Influences in the Development of the Ego and the Id." In *Envy and Gratitude and Other Works, 1946–1963*. New York, Delta Books, 1975.

———. (1958). "On the Development of Mental Functioning." In *Envy and Gratitude and Other Works, 1946–1963*. New York: Delta Books, 1975.

———. (1959). "Our Adult World and Its Roots in Infancy." In *Envy and Gratitude and Other Works, 1946–1963*. New York: Delta Books, 1975.

———. (1964). "Love, Guilt and Reparation." In M. Klein and J. Riviere, *Love, Hate and Reparation*. New York: W. W. Norton.

Knight, Robert P. (1953). "Borderline States." *Bulletin of the Menninger Clinic* 17:1–12.

Kohlberg, Lawrence. (1969). "Stage Sequence. The Cognitive-Developmental Approach to Socialization." In *Handbook of Socialization Theory Research*, ed. D. A. Goslin. Chicago: Rand McNally.

———. (1973). "Continuities in Childhood and Adult Moral Development Revisited." In *Life-Span Developmental Psychology: Personality Socialization*, ed. P. B. Baltes and K. W. Schaie. New York: Academic Press.

———. (1976). "Moral Stages and Moralization: The Cognitive-Developmental Approach." In *Moral Development Behavior*, ed. T. Lickona. New York: Holt, Rinehart and Winston.

———. (1984). *Essays on Moral Development*. Vol. 2, *The Psychology of Moral Development*. San Francisco: Harper and Row.

————. (1987). "The Child as Philosopher." In L. Kohlberg et al., *Child Psychology and Childhood Education*. New York: Longman.

Kohlberg, Lawrence, and Carol Gilligan. (1972). "The Adolescent as Philosopher." In *Twelve to Sixteen: Early Adolescence*, ed. J. Kagan and R. Coles. New York: W. W. Norton.

Kohlberg, Lawrence, and R. Kramer. (1969). "Continuities and Discontinuities in Childhood and Adult Moral Development." *Human Development* 12:93–120.

Kohut, Heinz. (1971). *The Analysis of the Self: A Systematic Approach to the Psychoanalytic Treatment of Narcissistic Personality Disorders*. New York: International Universities Press.

————. (1977). *The Restoration of the Self*. Madison, Conn.: International Universities Press.

————. (1984). *How Does Analysis Cure?*, ed. A. Goldberg and P. Stepansky. Chicago: University of Chicago Press.

Koplowitz, Herb. (1984). "A General System Stage and a Unitary Stage." In *Beyond Formal Operations: Late Adolescent and Adult Cognitive Development*, ed. M. L. Commons, F. A. Richards, and C. Armon. New York: Praeger.

Kroger, Jane. (1985). "Separation-Individuation and Ego Identity Status in New Zealand University Students." *Journal of Youth and Adolescence* 14:133–147.

————. (1989). *Identity in Adolescence: The Balance Between Self and Other*. London: Routledge.

Kroll, Jerome. (1988). *The Challenge of the Borderline Patient: Competency in Diagnosis and Treatment*. New York: W. W. Norton.

Laing, Ronald. D. (1960). *The Divided Self*. New York: Pantheon Books.

Lampl-de Groot, Jeanne. (1960). "On Adolescence." *Psychoanalytic Study of the Child* 15:95–103.

————. (1962). "Ego Ideal and Superego." *Psychoanalytic Study of the Child* 17:94–106.

Lang, Joan. (1987). "Two Contrasting Frames of Reference for Understanding Borderline Patients: Kernberg and Kohut." In *The Borderline Patient: Emerging Concepts in Diagnosis, Psychodynamics, and Treatment*, ed. J. S. Grotstein, M. F. Solomon, and J. A. Lang. Hillsdale, N.J.: Analytic Press.

Lauter, Estella, and Carol S. Rupprecht, eds. (1985). *Feminist Archetypal Theory: Interdisciplinary Re-Visions of Jungian Thought*. Knoxville: University of Tennessee Press.

Leichtman, Martin. (1989). "Evolving Concepts of Borderline Personality Disorders." *Bulletin of the Menninger Clinic* 53:229–249.

Levin, David M. (1985). *The Body's Recollection of Being: Phenomenological Psychology and the Deconstruction of Nihilism*. London: Routledge and Kegan Paul.

———. (1987). "Clinical Stories: A Modern Self in the Fury of Being." In *Pathologies of the Modern Self: Postmodern Studies on Narcissism, Schizophrenia, and Depression*, ed. D. M. Levin. New York: New York University Press.

———. (1988). *The Opening of Vision: Nihilism and the Postmodern Situation*. London: Routledge.

———. (1989). *The Listening Self: Personal Growth, Social Change and the Closure of Metaphysics*. London: Routledge.

Lewis, Michael, and Jeanne Brooks-Gunn. (1979). *Social Cognition and the Acquisition of Self*. New York: Plenum Press.

Lichtenberg, Joseph D. (1981). "Implications for Psychoanalytic Theory of Research on the Neonate." *International Review of Psycho-Analysis* 8:35–52.

———. (1983). *Psychoanalysis and Infant Research*. Hillsdale, N.J.: Analytic Press.

———. (1987). "Infant Studies and Clinical Work with Adults." *Psychoanalytic Inquiry* 7:311–330.

McDevitt, John B., and Margaret Mahler. (1980). "Object Constancy, Individuality, and Internalization." In *Self and Object Constancy: Clinical and Theoretical Perspectives*, ed. R. F. Lax et al. New York: Guilford Press, 1986.

Maddi, Salvatore R. (1967). "The Existential Neurosis." *Journal of Abnormal Psychology* 72:311–325.

———. (1970). "The Search for Meaning." In *Nebraska Symposium on Motivation*, ed. W. Arnold and M. Page. Lincoln: University of Nebraska Press.

Madison, Peter. (1961). *Freud's Concept of Repression and Defense, Its Theoretical and Observational Language.* Minneapolis: University of Minnesota Press.

Mahler, Margaret. (1966). "Notes on the Development of Basic Moods: The Depressive Affect." In *Psychoanalysis—A General Psychology: Essays in Honor of Heinz Hartmann,* ed. R. M. Loewenstein, L. M. Newman, M. Schur, and A. J. Solnit. New York: International Universities Press.

———. (1968). *On Human Symbiosis and the Vicissitudes of Individuation.* Vol. 1, *Infantile Psychosis.* New York: International Universities Press.

———. (1972). "A Study of the Separation-Individuation Process and its Possible Application to Borderline Phenomena in the Psychoanalytic Situation." *Psychoanalytic Study of the Child* 26: 403–424.

Mahler, Margaret, and John B. McDevitt. (1982). "Thoughts on the Emergence of the Self, with Particular Emphasis on the Body Self." *Journal of the American Psychoanalytic Association* 30:827–848.

Mahler, Margaret, Fred Pine, and Anni Bergman. (1975). *The Psychological Birth of the Human Infant.* New York: Basic Books.

Mandler, Jean. (1990). "A New Perspective on Cognitive Development in Infancy." *American Scientist* 78:236–243.

Masterson, James F. (1981). *The Narcissistic and Borderline Disorders: An Integrated Developmental Approach.* New York: Brunner/Mazel.

———. (1985). *The Real Self: A Developmental, Self, and Object Relations Approach.* New York: Brunner/Mazel.

———. (1987). "Borderline and Narcissistic Disorders: An Integrated Developmental Object-Relations Approach." In *The Borderline Patient: Emerging Concepts in Diagnosis, Psychodynamics, and Treatment.* Vol 1, ed. J. S. Grotstein, M. F. Solomon, and J. A. Lang. Hillsdale, N.J.: Analytic Press.

———. (1988). *The Search for the Real Self: Unmasking the Personality Disorders of Our Age.* New York: The Free Press.

Masterson, James F., and Donald B. Rinsley. (1975). "The Borderline Syndrome: The Role of the Mother in the Genesis and Psychic

Structure of the Borderline Personality." *International Journal of Psychoanalysis* 56:163–177.

Mead, George H. (1934). *Mind, Self, and Society.* Chicago: University of Chicago Press.

Merleau-Ponty, Maurice. (1962). *Phenomenology of Perception.* Trans. C. Smith. London: Routledge and Kegan Paul.

Meyer, Joachim-Ernst, ed. (1968). *Depersonalisation.* Darmstadt: Wissenschaftliche Buchgesellschaft.

Millon, Theodore. (1981). *Disorders of Personality.* New York: John Wiley and Sons.

Muktananda (Swami). (1978). *Play of Consciousness.* South Fallsburg, N.Y.: SYDA Foundation.

Murphy, John M., and Carol Gilligan. (1980). "Moral Development in Late Adolescence and Adulthood: A Critique and Reconstruction of Kohlberg's Theory." *Human Development* 23: 77–104.

Nelson, John E. (1990). *Healing the Split: A New Understanding of the Crisis and Treatment of the Mentally Ill.* Los Angeles: Jeremy Tarcher.

Neumann, Erich. (1954). *The Origins and History of Consciousness.* Princeton, N.J.: Princeton University Press.

———. (1963). *The Great Mother.* 2d ed. Princeton, N.J.: Princeton University Press.

———. (1973). *The Child: Structure and Dynamics of the Nascent Personality.* New York: G. P. Putnam's Sons.

Nieli, Russell. (1987). *Wittgenstein: From Mysticism to Ordinary Language.* Albany: State University of New York Press.

Nietzsche, Friedrich. (1966). *Thus Spoke Zarathustra.* Trans. W. Kaufmann. New York: Viking Press.

———. (1968). *The Will to Power.* Trans. W. Kaufmann and R. J. Hollingdale. New York: Vintage Books.

Nunberg, Herman. (1955). *Principles of Psychoanalysis: Their Application for the Neuroses.* New York: International Universities Press.

Otto, Rudolf. (1958). *The Idea of the Holy.* New York: Oxford University Press.

Parens, Henri. (1979). "Developmental Considerations of Ambivalence: Part 2 of an Exploration of the Relations of Instinctual Drives and the Symbiosis-Separation-Individuation Process." *Psychoanalytic Study of the Child* 34:385–420.

Perry, William G., Jr. (1970). *Forms of Intellectual and Ethical Development in the College Years: A Scheme.* New York: Holt, Rinehart and Winston.

———. (1981). "Cognitive and Ethical Growth: The Making of Meaning." In *The Modern American College: Responding to the New Realities of Diverse Students and a Changing Society,* ed. A. W. Chickering. San Francisco: Jossey-Bass.

Piaget, Jean. (1951). *Play, Dreams and Imitation in Childhood.* Trans. C. Gattegno and F. M. Hodgson. New York: W. W. Norton.

———. (1954). *The Construction of Reality in the Child.* Trans. Margaret Cook. New York: Basic Books.

———. (1972). "Intellectual Evolution from Adolescence to Adulthood." *Human Development* 15:1–12.

Piaget, Jean, and Barbel Inhelder. (1971). *Mental Imagery in the Child: A Study of the Development of Imaginal Representation.* Trans. P. A. Chilton. New York: Basic Books.

Reich, Wilhelm. (1942). *The Function of the Orgasm.* Trans. R. P. Wolfe. New York: Farrar, Straus and Giroux.

———. (1972). *Character Analysis.* Trans. V. R. Carfagno. New York: Simon and Schuster.

Richards, Francis A., and Michael L. Commons. (1984). "Systematic, Metasystematic, and Cross-Paradigmatic Reasoning: A Case for Stages of Reasoning Beyond Formal Operations." In *Beyond Formal Operations: Late Adolescent and Adult Cognitive Development,* ed. M. L. Commons, F. A. Richards, and C. Armon. New York: Praeger.

Riegel, Klaus. (1973). "Dialectical Operations: The Final Period of Cognitive Development." *Human Development* 16:346–370.

Rinsley, Donald B. (1982). *Borderline and Other Self Disorders: A Developmental and Object-Relations Perspective.* New York: Jason Aronson.

————. (1989). *Developmental Pathogenesis and Treatment of Borderline and Narcissistic Personalities*. Northvale, N.J.: Jason Aronson.

Roland, Alan. (1988). *In Search of Self in India and Japan: Toward a Cross-Cultural Psychology*. Princeton, N.J.: Princeton University Press.

Rovee-Collier, Carolyn K., Margaret W. Sullivan, Mary Enright, Debra Lucas, and Jeffrey W. Fagan. (1980). "Reactivation of Infant Memory." *Science* 208:1159–1161.

Royo, Antonio, and Jordan Aumann. (1962). *The Theology of Christian Perfection*. Dubuque, Iowa: Priory Press.

Ruether, Rosemary R. (1983). *Sexism and God-Talk: Toward a Feminist Theology*. Boston: Beacon Press.

Sartre, Jean-Paul. (1949). *Nausea*. Norfolk, Conn.: New Directions.

————. (1956). *Being and Nothingness*. Trans. H. Barnes. New York: Philosophical Library.

————. (1957). *The Transcendence of the Ego*. Trans. F. Williams and R. Kirkpatrick. New York: Noonday Press.

Schaffer, H. R. (1984). *The Child's Entry into a Social World*. London: Academic Press.

Schilder, Paul. (1928). *Introduction to Psychoanalytic Psychiatry*. New York: Nervous and Mental Disease Publishing Co.

Schlenker, Barry R. (1986). "Self-Identification: Toward an Integration of the Private and Public Self." In *Public Self and Private Self*, ed. R. F. Baumeister. New York: Springer.

Schwartz-Salant, Nathan. (1989). *The Borderline Personality: Vision and Healing*. Wilmette, Ill.: Chiron Publications.

Segal, Hanna. (1964). *Introduction to the Work of Melanie Klein*. New York: Basic Books.

————. (1991). *Dream, Phantasy and Art*. London: Routledge.

Sherrod, Lonnie R. (1981). "Issues in Cognitive-Perceptual Development: The Special Case of Social Stimuli." In *Infant Social Cognition: Empirical and Theoretical Considerations*, ed. M. E. Lamb and L. R. Sherrod. Hillsdale, N.J.: Lawrence Erlbaum Associates.

Sinnott, Jan D. (1981). "The Theory of Relativity: A Metatheory for Development?" *Human Development* 24:293–311.

———. (1984). "Postformal Reasoning: The Relativistic Stage." In *Beyond Formal Operations: Late Adolescent and Adult Cognitive Development*, ed. M. L. Commons, F. A. Richards, and C. Armon. New York: Praeger.

———. (1989). "Life-Span Relativistic Postformal Thought: Methodology and Data from Everyday Problem-Solving Studies." In *Adult Development*. Vol. 1, *Comparisons and Applications of Developmental Models*, ed. M. L. Commons, J. D. Sinnott, F. A. Richards, and C. Armon. New York: Praeger.

Spiegel, Leo A. (1958). "Comments on the Psychoanalytic Psychology of Adolescence." *Psychoanalytic Study of the Child* 13:296–308.

Spitz, René. (1951). "The Psychogenic Diseases in Infancy: An Attempt at Their Etiologic Classification." *Psychoanalytic Study of the Child* 6:255–275.

———. (1965). *The First Year of Life*. In collaboration with W. G. Cobliner. New York: International Universities Press.

Sprengnether, Madelon. (1990). *The Spectral Mother: Freud, Feminism, and Psychoanalysis*. Ithaca, N.Y.: Cornell University Press.

Spretnak, Charlene, ed. (1982). *The Politics of Women's Spirituality: Essays on the Rise of Spiritual Power within the Feminist Movement*. Garden City, N.Y.: Anchor Press.

Staples, Herman D., and Erwin R. Smarr. (1980). "Bridge to Adulthood: Years from Eighteen to Twenty-three." In *The Course of Life: Psychoanalytic Contributions Toward Understanding Personality Development*. Vol. 2, *Latency, Adolescence and Youth*, ed. S. I. Greenspan and G. H. Pollock. Washington, DC: NIMH.

Starhawk. (1979). *The Spiral Dance: A Rebirth of the Ancient Religion of the Great Goddess*. New York: Harper and Row.

———. (1982). *Dreaming the Dark: Magic, Sex and Politics*. Boston: Beacon Press.

Stein, Murray. (1983). *In Midlife: A Jungian Perspective*. Dallas: Spring Publications.

Stein, Waltraut J. (1967). "The Sense of Becoming Psychotic." *Psychiatry* 30:262–275.

Stern, Adolph. (1938). "Psychoanalytic Investigation of and Therapy in the Border Line Group of Neuroses." *Psychoanalytic Quarterly* 7:467–489.

Stern, Daniel. (1974). "Mother and Infant at Play: The Dyadic Inter-action Involving Facial, Vocal, and Gaze Behaviors." In *The Effect of the Infant on Its Caregiver*, ed. M. Lewis and L. Rosenblum. New York: John Wiley and Sons.

————. (1985). *The Interpersonal World of the Infant*. New York: Basic Books.

Stevens, Caroline T. (1992). "What is the Animus and Why Do We Care?" In *Gender and Soul in Psychotherapy*, ed. N. Schwartz-Salant and M. Stein. Wilmette, Ill.: Chiron Publications.

Stewart Walter A. (reporter). (1964). Panel: "Depersonalization." *Journal of the American Psychoanalytic Association* 12:171–186.

Tabin, Johanna. (1985). *On the Way to Self*. New York: Columbia University Press.

Teresa of Avila, Saint. (1980). *The Interior Castle*. In *The Collected Works of St. Teresa of Avila*. Vol. 2. Trans. K. Kavanaugh and O. Rodriguez. Washington, D.C.: ICS Publications.

Trevarthen, Colwyn. (1977). "Descriptive Analyses of Infant Communicative Behaviour." In *Studies in Mother-Infant Interaction*, ed. H. R. Schaffer. London: Academic Press.

————. (1979). "Communication and Cooperation in Early Infancy: A Description of Primary Intersubjectivity." In *Before Speech: The Beginning of Interpersonal Communication*, ed. M. Bullowa. Cambridge: Cambridge University Press.

Tronick, Edward, and Lauren Adamson. (1980). *People as Babies: New Findings on Our Social Beginnings*. New York: Collier Books.

Underhill, Evelyn. (1961). *Mysticism*. New York: E. P. Dutton.

Washburn, Michael. (1990). "Two Patterns of Transcendence." *Journal of Humanistic Psychology* 30:84–112.

————. (in press). *The Ego and the Dynamic Ground: A Transpersonal Theory of Human Development*. 2d ed., rev. Albany: State University of New York Press. This edition is an extensive revision of the first edition, published in 1988.

Washburn, Michael, and Michael Stark. (1979). "Ego, Egocentricity, and Self-Transcendence: A Western Interpretation of Eastern Teaching." In *The Meeting of the Ways: Explorations in East/West Psychology*, ed. J. Welwood. New York: Schocken Books.

Wehr, Demaris S. (1987). *Jung and Feminism: Liberating Archetypes*. Boston: Beacon Press.

Welch, John. (1990). *When God Dies: An Introduction to John of the Cross*. New York: Paulist Press.

Whitbourne, Susan, and Comilda Weinstock. (1986). *Adult Development*. 2d ed. New York: Praeger.

Whitmont, Edward. (1987). *The Return of the Goddess*. New York: Crossroad Press.

———. (1991). *The Symbolic Quest*. 2d ed. Princeton, N.J.: Princeton University Press.

Wilber, Ken. (1977). *The Spectrum of Consciousness*. Wheaton, Ill.: Theosophical Publishing House.

———. (1979). "Are the Chakras Real?" In *Kundalini, Evolution and Enlightenment*, ed. J. White. New York: Doubleday/Anchor.

———. (1980a). *The Atman Project*. Wheaton, Ill.: Theosophical Publishing House.

———. (1980b). "The Pre/Trans Fallacy." *Revision* 3:51–71.

———. (1981). *Up from Eden: A Transpersonal View of Human Evolution*. Garden City, N.Y.: Doubleday/Anchor.

———. (1982). "Odyssey: A Personal Inquiry into Humanistic and Transpersonal Psychology." *Journal of Humanistic Psychology* 22: 57–90.

———. (1990). *Eye to Eye: The Quest for a New Paradigm*. Expanded edition. Boston: Shambhala.

Winnicott, D. W. (1963a). "From Dependence towards Independence in the Development of the Individual." In *The Maturational Processes and the Facilitating Environment*. New York: International Universities Press, 1965.

———. (1963b). "Psychiatric Disorder in Terms of Infantile Maturational Processes." In *The Maturational Processes and the Facilitating Environment*. New York: International Universities Press, 1965.

Yalom, Irvin D. (1980). *Existential Psychotherapy*. New York: Basic Books.

Young-Eisendrath, Polly. (1990). "Rethinking Feminism, the Animus, and the Feminine." In *To Be a Woman: The Birth of the Conscious Feminine*, ed. C. Zweig. Los Angeles: Jeremy Tarcher.

————. (1992). "Gender, Animus, and Related Topics." In *Gender and Soul in Psychotherapy,* ed. N. Schwartz-Salant and M. Stein. Wilmette, Ill.: Chiron Publications.

Young-Eisendrath, Polly, and Florence Wiedemann. (1987). *Female Authority: Empowering Women through Psychotherapy.* New York: Guilford Press.

Index

Abandonment anxiety. *See* anxiety
Abyss: experience of, during night of spirit, 231, 232, 233, 242, 289; experience of, during regression in the service of transcendence, 231, 232, 233, 242
Adelson, Joseph, 142
Adler, Gerald, 207
Adolescence, 123–155; affective experience during, 127–128; ambivalence toward parents, 134, 135, 136, 137; and dualism, 123–124; ego development during, 141–151; and ego ideal, 137–138, 152; identity crisis of, 134–135; and narcissism, 126, 151; and object constancy, 136; object relations during, 130–142; psychodynamics of, 124–130; and regression, 128–129, 140–141, 154–155; as separation-individuation process, 133–136; sexuality, awakening of, 125, 126–127; splitting during, 134, 135–136; and superego, 137–138, 152

Adulthood, 156–182; ego development during, 157, 164–174; and ego ideal, 165–167; and generativity, 163; object choice of, 161–162; and object constancy, 136, 141, 158, 161; object relations during, 161–164; psychodynamics of, 158–161; as second level of latency, 158–159; and superego, 165–167
Affective experience: of borderline, 211–213; during adolescence, 127–128; during latency, 103–104; during regeneration in spirit, 259–262; during regression in the service of transcendence, 245–247
Aggression: during adolescence, 126–127; during regression in the service of transcendence,